THE WORLD OF
THE COMPUTER

THE WORLD OF
THE COMPUTER

Edited by *John Diebold*

RANDOM HOUSE NEW YORK

Library of Congress Cataloging in Publication Data
Diebold, John, 1926-   comp.
The world of the computer.
1. Electronic data processing. 2. Electronic
digital computers. 3. Computers and civilization.
I. Title
QA76.D52   001.6'4   73-3994
ISBN 0-394-47150-4

Manufactured in the United States of America
Designed by Paula Wiener
First Edition

ACKNOWLEDGMENTS

"The Life of A Philosopher" from *Charles Babbage and His Calculating Engine*, edited by Philip and Emily Morrison, copyright © 1961, is reprinted by permission of Dover Publications, Inc.

"The Analytical Engine" is excerpted from *The Analytical Engine*, by Jeremy Bernstein, copyright © 1963, 1964 by Jeremy Bernstein. It is reprinted by permission of Random House, Inc. and Martin Secker & Warburg, Ltd. It appeared originally in *The New Yorker*.

"Preliminary Discussion of the Logical Design of an Electronic Computing Instrument" from *The Complete Works of John von Neumann*, by Arthur W. Burkes, Herman H. Goldstine, and John von Neumann, is reprinted by permission of Pergamon Press Ltd.

"The Long-Range Effect of the Computer" from *The Use of Computers in Business Organizations*, by Frederic G. Withington, copyright © 1966, is reprinted by permission of Addison-Wesley Publishing Company, Inc.

"Unions, Employers, and the Computer," by Abraham J. Siegel, is reprinted from *Technology Review*, Vol. 72, Number 2, edited at the Massachusetts Institute of Technology, copyright © 1969 by the Alumni Association of M.I.T.

"The Corporation: Will It be Managed by Machines?," by Herbert A. Simon, is reprinted from *Management and Corporation: 1985*, edited by Anshen and Bach, copyright © 1961 by McGraw Hill, Inc. It is used with permission of McGraw Hill Book Co.

"Computers in State Government," by Alvin Kaltman, is reprinted from *Technology Review*, Vol. 74, Number 4, edited at the Massachusetts Institute of Technology, copyright © 1972 by the Alumni Association of M.I.T.

"Arrival of the Sales-Counter Computer," by Ron Brown, first appeared in *New Scientist*, the international weekly review of science and technology, 128 Long Acre, London WC2, England.

"The Little Railroad That Could," by Charles G. Burck, is reprinted

from *Computers in Humanistic Research: Readings and Perspectives,* copyright © 1967 by Prentice-Hall, Inc., Englewood Cliffs, New Jersey, is reprinted by permission.

"Machines and Societies," by D. M. Mackay, from *Man and His Future,* edited by Gordon Wolstenhome (Boston: 1963), is reprinted by permission of Little, Brown and Company and the Biba Foundation, London.

"Must Automation Bring Unemployment?," from *The Economic Consequences of Automation,* by Paul Einzig, copyright © 1956, 1957 by Paul Einzig, is reprinted by permission of W. W. Norton & Co., Inc., and Curtis Brown, Ltd.

"The Challenge of Automation to Education for Human Values," by Margaret Mead, is reprinted by permission from *Automation, Education, and Human Values,* edited by William W. Brickman and Stanley Lehrer, copyright © 1966 by School & Society Books, Division of Society for the Advancement of Education, Inc.

"Technology, Life and Leisure," by Dennis Gabor, was originally published in *Instrument Practice.* It is reprinted by permission of United Trade Press, Ltd.

"The Hard Road to Soft Automation," by Tom Alexander, is reprinted from the July 1971 issue of *Fortune Magazine* by special permission; copyright © 1971 Time, Inc.

"Data Banks and Dossiers," by Carl Kaysen, is reprinted from *The Public Interest,* No. 7 (Spring 1967), pp. 52–60. Copyright © 1967 National Affairs, Inc. Reprinted by permission of *The Public Interest.*

"The Wisdom of Man and the Wisdom of God," by Kenneth E. Boulding, from *Human Values on the Spaceship Earth,* copyright © 1966, is reprinted by permission of the National Council of the Churches of Christ in the U.S.A.

"The Obsolescence of Man," by Arthur C. Clarke, from *Profiles of the Future,* revised edition, by Arthur C. Clarke, copyright © 1961 by H.M.H. Publishing Co., is reprinted by permission of Harper & Row, Publishers, Inc., and Victor Gollancz, Ltd.

"The Many Faces of Intelligence," by Donald G. Fink, from *Computers and the Human Mind: An Introduction to Artificial Intelligence,* by Donald G. Fink, copyright © 1966 by Educational Services Inc., is reprinted by permission of Doubleday & Co., Inc.

"Computing Machinery and Intelligence," by Allan M. Turing, from *Computers and Thought,* edited by E. A. Feigenlaum and Julian Feldman, is reprinted with the permission of Basil Blackwell Publisher.

"The Imitation of Man by Machine," by Ulric Neisser, originally appeared in *Science,* Vol. 139, pp. 193–197, January 18, 1963, copyright © 1963 by the American Association for the Advancement of Science. Reprinted by permission of the author and *Science* magazine.

"God & Golem, Inc." is excerpted from the book of the same title by Norbert Wiener, copyright © 1964 by the M.I.T. Press. It is reprinted by permission of the M.I.T. Press.

"The importance of machines and innovation resides in the impact they have on human beings—in their roles as agents for social change. They affect not only the means but also the ends of individual and societal actions. . . . Information is at the heart of society, and its use profoundly affects this and future generations. Individuals and institutions are being put under enormous pressures, and we must seek to identify the causes and the directions of these pressures. Then we can hope to alter our institutions to meet the needs of man in a time of rapid and fundamental change."

JOHN DIEBOLD

Contents

THE WORLD OF
THE COMPUTER

Introduction

The computer is entering its second quarter-century and its fourth generation. During its short lifetime it has radically altered not only how we do things, but also what we do. In an era of accelerating change it has been perhaps the most important single factor in fostering that change. It has lifted many burdens but it is widely feared. It influences our lives but remains a mystery for most people. It has opened wholly new opportunities but threatens the jobs of many. It has made possible fantastic achievements, such as landing men on the moon, but it seems to endanger our privacy and even our values. Its basic technology is clearly understood, but the fundamental questions about its role in today's and tomorrow's world have hardly been framed, let alone answered satisfactorily.

The computer, in short, is exerting a pervasive but largely unregulated and little understood influence in our lives. It was no coincidence that the celebrations of the twenty-fifth anniversary of the building of the first electronic computer were restricted almost entirely to the industry itself. Even if pressed, it is doubtful whether the man in the street could name anyone —scientist, technologist or entrepreneur—connected with the birth and explosive development of the computer industry. And the questions now being raised by consumer custodians, civil libertarians and similar groups about the disturbing potential of computers to change modern life for the worse rather than the better are all too often mere echoes of questions that were first raised by the computer experts two decades ago.

Why have the computer ingénues been so slow to catch up with the implications of the computer? Part of the reason is undoubtedly the sheer grandeur of the technology that underlies it. Until 1945, when the first electronic computer was built, man's calculating speed had remained constant for several thousand years. It was set by his ability to handle the abacus. Between 1945 and 1951 that speed was increased one hundred times. Over the next twenty years it increased a thousand times more. At present computers perform calculations within nanoseconds —billionths of a second. A nanosecond is the same proportion of one second as a single second is of thirty years. Yet even this astonishing speed is too slow for some of the complex problems that are being lined up for computers to solve. Pressed by such problems, the computer manufacturers are coming up against an interesting limitation: the shortest distance between any two points inside a computer. Traveling at a speed of 186,000 miles per second—the speed of light—electrical impulses progress less than a foot within a nanosecond. Thus, as computers are designed to operate more and more speedily, they must also be reduced in size to overcome this basic physical limitation, and "think small" is becoming one of the catch phrases of the modern computer industry.

That the complexities of the computer are beyond the ability of the man in the street to understand is not surprising. Unfortunately they have also proved beyond the range of many men connected with the application of the computer by business and industry itself. Company after company has tried to computerize its stock inventory, its accounts or its mailing lists, either on its own or with the assistance of a specialist computer firm, only to retire from the effort financially damaged and psychologically scarred after incompatibilities, poor programs and misunderstandings have made the task apparently impossible. Each time the net result is that another group of businessmen comes to believe that the efficiency of computerization is simply a myth. Recent years have also seen a loss of ardor among some of the previously bullish computer promoters. By the early 1970's so many computer manufacturers had either left the business or suffered recurring losses that some members of the financial community began to suggest that the computer had had its inning just like some wildly speculative stock that had risen quickly and fallen deeply. This attitude was summed up by the question —perfectly serious—of one Wall Street banker: "The computer has just about had it, hasn't it?"

This attitude, which is not untypical among the uninitiated, misses the entire point of the computer revolution. Computers are more—much more—than a series of electronic devices, sophisticated adding machines or examples of advanced technology. Rather, they represent a set of fundamental theoretical insights into information theory, which concerns communications of every type, combined with the technology that allows us to build machine systems for processing information.

The handling and communication of information is a central phenomenon of our society, and the fuel of computers is raw information, which, in a sense, is the driving force of modern society. With the advent of the computer we have, in a moment of history, the ability to build machine systems dealing with an effect that is intensely and deeply related to the very concept of human society. For the first time we can build machines whose operation concerns the processes that make us human, rather than peripheral factors such as the provision of power and transport.

For this reason computers represent the most significant invention of this century. Computerization is just as basic a concept as that of electricity, and in future years computer time will undoubtedly be regarded as a public utility in the same way that electricity is regarded today. When we seek historical analogies to the discovery and growth of the computer, we must look beyond superficially similar events such as the Industrial Revolution, and instead place the computer at the head of the line of progress in human communications—the line that started with the development of speech and continued through the inventions of writing, printing and radio.

The fundamental nature of the insights involved in the development of the computer has a little-recognized outcome which perfectly answers the pessimistic assertions that the computer's time has passed. This is that the concepts which have produced the type of computers we now know have also opened the door to an infinite number of other information devices. In other words, we have so far seen only a few manifestations of computing machines; many more are in the wings waiting to be discovered.

This said, we must be careful not to undervalue present achievements in the computer field. The proliferation of the computer industry from its small beginnings in the middle forties has been one of the most astonishing success stories of business history, despite the slowdown of the late sixties that caused so much of the pessimism among the uninitiated. Today, two and one-half percent of the U. S. gross national product is tied up with computers and the people who use them. The industry's rate of expansion is such that, even if it holds relatively constant in the next few years, the annual expenditures for computer related products and services will overtake that of the whole electric power industry in 1980.

Despite this growth, the general public is far from accepting the computer with the same equanimity as that with which it accepts the telephone or the electricity supply. The most obvious reason for this is that computers are not yet in visible positions in daily life. We cannot summon them at the flick of a switch or the fingering of a dial. When the public does see computers, or direct evidence of their use, it is in connection with the exotic, such as a flight to the moon or the refinement of the model of a complex biological molecule. When the computer enters our daily lives, its presence is hardly apparent—except when it makes a mistake. We may notice the computer style numbering on our checks and payroll slips, but we see nothing of the technology and insights behind those numbers. And when we are victim of some computerized error, we are certainly in no mood to appreciate that technology and insight. "While the high-speed computer is man's most powerful intellectual tool, most of its past uses have been designed either to improve efficiency, save costs or perform previously impossible tasks," states Dartmouth President John G. Kemeny. "Little effort has been extended thinking up new services to make life better. This may be one reason why the man in the street feels resentment towards computers."

There are, however, some signs that this suspicion is evaporating. These signs stem mainly from new developments in the technology of computers, one of the most important being the increasing ease of communication between man and machine.

In the early days of automation, giving an instruction to a computer was a difficult, tedious and arcane task delegated to a few programming specialists, who, however good their intentions, inevitably represented barriers between the user and the computer. Since then, man-machine communication has become much more relaxed, owing to the development of relatively simple computer languages which retain only a few of the formalisms of the original means of communication. Such innovations have allowed businessmen, scientists and other users to carry on conversations directly with their machines without the intervention of these modern middlemen. More recently still, computer experts have devised means of presenting computers with drawings and pictures, and of communicating directly with computers by voice rather than by typewriter terminal. In time, anyone who wishes to use a computer will be able to instruct it in English, German, Russian or any other tongue, and hear it enunciate its replies in the same vernacular.

Another vital factor in opening the use of computers to an increasing variety of people has been the dramatic decreases that have taken place in the cost of computer time. Back in the 1940's a minute on a computer cost hundreds of dollars. Now a public library in Monterey, California, offers two and a half minutes of time on a small computer for a mere quarter. The cornerstone of this dramatic decrease in price has been the development of the technique known as time-sharing.

In their early days, because of the high price of computer time, computers operated according to the method known as batch processing. A batch of job requests is put onto magnetic tape and fed to the computer, which performs the jobs serially, completing each one before turning to the next. This method is extremely economic and efficient if little interaction is needed between the user and the program—that is, if the program is self-sufficient. If, however, it is necessary for the user to talk to the program while it is still running—to feed in updated figures, for example, or simply to debug minor errors in the program which become obvious only when the program is running—batch processing becomes a cumbersome procedure. The user is faced with a delay of possibly hours before he can interact with his program. And operating a program in a dynamic fashion by feeding in continuous updated data from a process being monitored or controlled by the program (the technical description of this procedure is "operating in real time") is impossible with batch processing.

The concept of time-sharing was developed to overcome these shortcomings. The time-shared computer is divided into a central processing unit, which performs the actual calculations, and an intermediate computer whose job it is to communicate with both the central processor and the multitude of users, and coordinate the users' requests for time on the device. The basic tasks of the intermediate computer are to line up the requests for computer time in order of priority, to put the users' data in correct form to be fed to the central processor, and to perform all other necessary tasks on the data short of carrying out the actual calculations. The unit calls on the central processor only when actual computing time is required, and then demands only a few seconds, or fractions of a second, at a time. As a result, while the processor is working on a number of different calculations within any short interval of time, the time-sharing unit as a whole reacts so quickly to each individual user's requests that the user has the illusion of complete control of the device.

Among the computer experts, time-sharing has meant a vast multiplication of their ability to use the computer in their work, whether it is aircraft design or organic chemistry. Some heavy users of computers are now equipped with terminals in their homes or offices, which they use to communicate with time-shared computers via the telephone lines. Indeed, the telephone system is now carrying so many messages to and from computers that a new branch of the communications industry, devoted to carrying computerized messages over long distances, has sprung up to threaten the entrenched position of the Bell System.

These developments have obviously meant more to the computer industry than greater efficiency for frequent users of the computer. They have opened up the use of computers to completely new classes of people—students, doctors, librarians and even scholars in literature and the liberal arts. Although such applications are limited so far, they are increasing, especially among the young, and it can be confidently predicted that within the next decade a far larger proportion of leaders in industry and the professions will be thoroughly familiar with computers and ready to experiment with them.

The increasing number of new computer applications brings into sharp focus another fundamental point about computing. Because it represents a set of basic insights into human communications, it will obviously have far greater impact on society than one would expect of a mere machine. One need only mention the impact of the Model-T Ford—a machine intimately connected with man's mobility—which in a few short years changed many of society's mores, from the use of leisure time to dating habits, to guess at some of the possibilities opened up by the computer. And unlike the Model-T, the concept which underlies the computer is so basic that new manifestations of it will continue to emerge from the laboratories. Already the expansion of the computer in its first quarter-century has been an excellent example of positive feedback: each new application of the computer has brought up the possibility of yet more applications. In turn, these secondary applications have led to further uses. Certainly the scope of today's information systems would astound any scientist working on computers in the late forties. At that time much credence was given to the forecast that a dozen high-speed computers would be able to handle all the calculations required in the United States. Now the number of computers installed in this country is approaching one hundred thousand.

During the last few years, this proliferation has been too obvious to escape the notice of the spokesmen for an apathetic public, who have brought into the open many of the social difficulties and policy problems brought about by computerization. In the process, these spokesmen have struck a sympathetic chord among many members of the general public who have had harrying experiences with the machines. Few people by now have not experienced, at first hand or vicariously through an acquaintance, the frustrating process of repeatedly receiving incorrect bills or dunning letters from a computerized billing department and being unable to get their complaints past the computer. Yet such experiences represent merely the tip of the iceberg when it comes to the dark side of the computer. Potentially, no area of our lives is free from the impact of computerization, for better or worse; and if its growth is not regulated in some way, that impact is most likely to be for worse.

Certainly, the current questioning of computerization has its merits. But it is also true that these questions have already been considered by the computer experts. As far back as the late forties Norbert Wiener was talking about the advisability of consultations between scientists and unions to allow the former to explain the impact of automation to the latter. Since then, computer scientists have repeated the need for regulation of their industry, but until recently their pleas have fallen on deaf ears. Now that these cries have been taken up by outsiders, the arguments have unfortunately become rather garbled. Many of the computer's critics understand neither the scope nor the limitations of computerization, and thus the great debate on the role of automation in society is all too often carried out in an aura of misinformation.

One typical example of such misinformation is the conventional attitude toward automation. All too often it is regarded as a faster, more efficient form of mass production. The vision of an automated society conjured up by some of its critics is one in which workers at the mercy of inhuman machines are turning out vast quantities of standardized products for consumers who have no choice but to take them or leave them. It is a grim picture indeed, but one that is totally misleading. Far from producing products of dull uniformity, the truly automated process is flexible enough to provide special options and features on each and every one of its products. And the men who run the automatic factory are more likely to be highly skilled engineers pushing the buttons which program the computer to provide these options than semi-skilled mechanics in thrall to the machines.

In truth, these two issues are far from the black and white cases that computer critics would have one believe. There is no doubt that the onset of automation has affected a number of jobs, changing the character of many and eliminating a few entirely. But this does not mean that automation has directly caused unemployment. In most cases automation has merely coincided with other factors more clearly related to the job market. Thus, the enormous concern about unemployment resulting from computerization which occupied much attention in the late fifties, and which has surfaced sporadically since then whenever unemployment figures have been high, has actually been a classic case of "having one's eye on the wrong ball." The real causes for the unemployment were to be found elsewhere—in the economic situation and the relative weaknesses of the industries whose employees were losing their jobs.

Similarly, the current threat to our privacy is not a simple result of the development of large computerized data networks. Far from the prime villain, the computer was merely a catalyst in producing the threat. The acquisition of large amounts of ordered data on the populace first came about in the early sixties with the growth of major new social programs funded by the Federal Government. These programs made the collection of large amounts of sensitive data on large numbers of people socially and politically respectable. The computer networks merely made it easier for bureaucrats to collate the data. "If the computer had arrived in 1880," states Alan F. Westin, a legal scholar who is one of the nation's foremost authorities on the questions the proliferation of computers raise regarding privacy, "the possibility of consolidated data systems through computerization would have been seen as a clear departure from the liberal tradition in government record handling."

In other words, computers do present a problem in regard to privacy, but a problem not entirely of their own making. By their mere existence, computers have removed one of the public's latter-day bastions of protection against governmental snooping —the inefficiency of traditional bureaucratic methods of gathering information.

The lesson from these two examples is that no area of our lives is beyond the scope of computerization. We must be continually on our guard to prevent new uses of the computer from becoming abuses of our freedom or humanity. Thus, computer experts, government officials and businessmen are well advised to concern themselves with what new social issues and policy problems will arise as automation continues its growth. While it is difficult to predict specific advances, we can forecast the more general developments that the computer will bring into specific areas, ranging from international relations to our personal lives.

In the international sphere, computerization may well lead to the evolution of new trade patterns. The determinants of comparative advantage, the diversity of markets and supplies, and the disparity of economic developments are changing rapidly today. In part, these reflected the specialization concepts of the Industrial Revolution. As the integrated systems concepts of automation, as well as the integrated communications and systems capabilities of this new technology, begin to pervade the economic scene, these older systems of trade will change. Even today we see a harbinger of this change in the development of multinational corporations—integrated international corporations staffed and owned by nationals of different countries. And this development, combined with the impact of automation, will start to weaken the language barriers that divide so many nations, as businessmen, scientists and government officials increasingly come to understand and use the common mathematical language of computerization.

The computer will also bring about vast changes in our domestic political outlook, as did the Industrial Revolution two centuries ago. That revolution led to regimented child labor and then to child labor laws, and regulations on wages, hours and working conditions to protect the workers from the excesses of the new factory environment. Now automation will free them from the bondage of the machine. Quasi-political organizations such as labor unions evolved to meet the special needs of the factory worker; but now that our working force has moved from the factory to the office, and office jobs are themselves changing in response to automation, these institutions will have to change —or new ones evolve—to meet the particular needs of the new working force. Most likely, the emphasis of these organizations will change from the prevention of exploitation to the insurance of utilization. Full employment, which has been viewed to date as an economic necessity, will have to be regarded in psychological or cultural terms. A "featherbed" job that may meet the demand of full employment cannot produce any psychological satisfaction for the worker. And in the wider field of politics, computerization will alter our sense of priorities, and focus more strongly than ever on the balance between individual liberty and social responsibility.

The group of people most affected by computerization at present is undoubtedly the business community. Already new techniques using the computer's capabilities are appearing on the business scene. They include operations research, which involves the construction of mathematical models to solve business problems; simulation, which uses the computer to answer "what would happen if" questions by the businessman who must make a decision between a number of different strategies; and gaming theory, the concept of planning in strategically competitive markets. Important as they are individually, their real contribution to business will be in impelling an integrated, rather than a departmentalized, conception of the business enterprise of the future.

Businessmen already accept the advent of the computer, although many still harbor lingering resentments toward it, but to the man in the street, the computer remains an invisible and mysterious entity. Before long, however, the computer will have made itself as much a part of the furniture in the home as is the television set today, and computers really will be treated with the same familiarity as the electricity supply.

The basis for this attitude will be the home computer terminal, a device which will consist in essence of a computer keyboard, a television screen and a copying machine. Using this terminal, businessmen will be able to spend many of their working hours at home, communicating with their colleagues over electronic communication systems; doctors will be able, in many cases, to consult with their patients at a distance—indeed, a television link which allows doctors and psychiatrists to consult with and diagnose patients has already been developed by researchers at the Massachusetts General Hospital and Dartmouth College; lawyers will be able to summon up searches of relevant legal documents and suitable precedents for their current cases; and housewives will be able to order the week's groceries automatically, using a list of products and prices provided automatically on the television screen at the touch of a button. But most of all, this incursion of the computer into our homes will affect our leisure habits, just as strongly as did the advent of television.

In future years, of course, we can expect to have more leisure time. The growth of automation will inevitably reduce the working hours of all but a select few in the most creative and people-oriented professions (such as doctors, journalists and politicians), leaving a void in people's home lives which even television cannot be expected to fill completely. But the home computer will provide ample opportunities for leisure pursuits.

One area ripe for increased interest is that of information-gathering and reference. In terms of content, newspapers and magazines will change to allow for much greater interaction between readers and reporters than exists today. Instead of the static process of providing the reader with what editors believe he needs, the use of the computer will enable the reader to request specific material that he wants—a book review, a base-ball score, a financial analysis or a political backgrounder.

The arts are also ripe for change in the coming era of increased leisure time. Traditionally, art and music have depended for their existence on the patronage of the privileged. When increased leisure becomes commonplace and the average man has more discretionary energy as well as discretionary income, the arts will assume a very different place in our lives. Rather than being the playthings of the leisured few, they will be beholden to, and expected to reflect the tastes of, everybody. One might perhaps add the hope that this new excursion to the arts will improve public tastes.

One other field ripe for expansion when leisure becomes a way of life is education. The combination of computerized educational programs and the home computer terminal will allow lifelong education to become a reality for each and every member of the population. Professionals will be able to take refresher courses in their specialties in their own homes, while non-professionals will be able to turn their minds to any subject which takes their fancy—ranging from art appreciation to elementary calculus, and from pottery-making to basic Chinese.

Of course, the computerized world of tomorrow will face its own social problems. One of the major fields of controversy will undoubtedly concern the introduction of computers into such traditionally humanistic fields as medicine and education. We can expect the traditionalists in both professions—and other branches of the liberal arts now catching the attention of the computer experts—to fight tooth and nail against the slightest hint of computerization, claiming that it will destroy the essential humanity of their endeavors. But with the growing familiarity with computers among students, in high schools as well as colleges, it seems likely that the question is when, rather than if, computers will be introduced into these fields. And the major issues are likely to be the pace of such introduction and the way in which computerized medicine and education is controlled by the professional authorities. The end result will most likely be systems of medicine and education in which the strengths of both man and machine are utilized in complementary fashion.

Cooperation between man and machine at a more fundamental level is likely to be another critical issue in the future world of the computer. This is the actual combination of man and machine in one being—the cyborg. Vannevar Bush, the United States scientific coordinator during World War II, has forecast that one day man will be able to link his brain directly with computers, and relatively primitive man-machine combinations, in the form of artificial limbs responding to electrical signals from the brain in just the same way as the real limbs they replace, are already in use. This forthcoming ability of man to augment his brain power, together with the emerging possibility of controlling his body through genetic engineering, will mean that after millions of years of existence, Homo sapiens can finally free himself from the course of development dictated by natural evolution. This is an awesome power indeed, and accompanied by infinite dangers as well as infinite opportunities. In plotting our own course of evolution, we will have to develop, along with everything else, the fundamental qualities of humanity that cannot be duplicated by machines—wisdom, morality and nobility.

Intimately connected with cyborgs, of course, is cybernetics— the science of control and communication in machines and human beings. The construction of the first computer stimulated scientific efforts to discover the basis of human thought, and these investigations have since broadened into an inquiry into the nature of thought itself. The inquiries have focused on two major questions: what is the essentially human ingredient, if any, of human thought, and can computers think? The answers, when they emerge, will have cosmic significance.

What is most exciting—and most terrifying—is the possibility that machines may in time match, and even better, the mental abilities of men. Some of the more bullish predictions by the advocates of thinking computers—notably, that a computer would by now be chess champion of the world—have failed to come to fruition, but enough evidence of computer intelligence is emerging to make the idea that computers will outthink us at least credible. As one example, checker-playing computer programs have been devised which can learn from their mistakes and eventually defeat their human creators. Thus the possibility must be squarely faced that twenty-first-century man will no longer be in control of his own destiny. For better or worse he may have become the servant rather than the master of the computer.

Even if man can retain his control over his machines, the advent of the computer will have exerted a profound theological effect on his life, and specifically on his view of his place in the universe. In the Middle Ages men believed that they were the supreme creatures of the universe, the only children of the deity. Then came Copernicus and his theory that the earth was not the center of creation. Four centuries later Charles Darwin informed disbelieving theologians that man was descended from the apes, and the concept of man's supreme position slipped further away. Now radioastronomers are finding evidence of the organic molecules intimately associated with life in vast clouds of gas in space, and molecular biologists are beginning to conclude that the formation and development of living things is, under certain circumstances, a probability rather than a one-in-a-billion chance. Man's view of his place in creation is being eroded once again, and the computer, with its apparent ability to think like men—and perhaps outthink them—is eroding it even further. From being the center of the universe five hundred years ago, man faces the prospect of taking second place to computers on his own planet within the next century.

The purpose of this anthology is to survey the development of the computer from its earliest days to the present, and to anticipate some of the developments and controversies which will attend computerization in coming years. Many of the opinions are speculative and controversial, but the authors are agreed on one fact about the world of the computer: its development will take us beyond the civilization of an industrial society and will raise an entirely new set of social, economic and business problems. They will tax our ingenuity—and our humanity—to the utmost.

I

The Computer
Past and Present

Introduction
to Section I

In today's world a computer is no further away than our pay check, our monthly bank statement or our telephone bill. On the spectacular level, computers guide orbiting spacecraft and steer radiotelescopes; at a more mundane level they perform the tasks of numerous inventory and payroll clerks. Indeed, although few people ever find the need to come face to face with one, computers are as much part of our daily lives as television. And just like television, computers are basically phenomena of the second half of the twentieth century. The foundations of today's computer industry, however, were laid in the late thirties and forties, with the development of the bulky, clumsy and—in retrospect —incredibly slow and simple instruments like the ENIAC and UNIVAC, which now take pride of place in the science museums. This section traces the history of these enterprises, up to the time the first commercial computer was unveiled.

Despite its apparent novelty, the computer is well rooted in ancient history. According to some theories, the ruins at Stonehenge—a roughly circular array of massive stones on England's stark Salisbury Plain—were part of an ancient computer designed by Druid priests to foretell solar eclipses. However, the first example of a digital computer was probably an instrument which is still in common use today—the abacus. Consisting merely of sets of beads strung on wires, the abacus is a portable computer whose capacity to solve problems is limited only by its size. In the hands of a skilled operator, it can produce astonishingly fast calculations; in one classic contest soon after

World War II, a Japanese abacus operator consistently solved mathematical problems faster than a U. S. Army private using the most up-to-date electric desk calculator then available.

The abacus is a simple example of a digital type of computer. It is a device which actually counts digits. The next calculator of significance on the scene was an analogue device—the slide rule. Instead of counting numbers directly, the slide rule measures lengths, which are proportional, or analogous, to numbers. The slide rule was invented in 1622, perhaps 4,000 years after the abacus, by the English mathematician William Oughtred. Its limitation, which is common to all analogue devices, is the precision with which the lengths involved in its calculations can be judged, in this case, by the human eye. In today's analogue computers, the limitation is the precision with which the electronic signals which represent numbers can be measured. Indeed, the difference between the abacus and the slide rule points up the basic difference between digital and analogue computers which is still relevant to computing today. Digital computers are, despite the example of the Japanese abacus operator, relatively slow when compared with analogue devices, and are also more difficult to program; analogue devices are much less accurate. The disadvantages of digital devices are gradually being overcome, however, and in the interim computer users can also turn to hybrid computers, made up of both analogue and digital computers with suitable interconnections, which retain the merits, but not the deficiencies, of both systems.

After the slide rule, the next step toward the modern computer came in 1642, with the invention of an adding machine by Blaise Pascal, the brilliant French philosopher and mathematician. Within thirty years Gottfried William von Leibnitz, the equally brilliant German mathematician, had drawn up plans for a more ambitious machine that could multiply as well as add. In 1694 that machine was working, although not very reliably, on calculating tables of logarithms, which had themselves only been introduced a century earlier.

Even at that time the emergence of the machines was cause for suspicion among some prominent thinkers. Among the critics was Dean Jonathan Swift, who wrote this satirical account in *Gulliver's Travels:*

The first Professor I saw was in a very large Room, with Forty Pupils about him. After Salutation, observing me to look earnestly upon a Frame, which took up the greatest part of both the Length and Breadth of the Room; he said, perhaps I might wonder to see him employed in a Project for improving speculative knowledge by practical and mechanical Operations. But the World would soon be sensible of its Usefulness; and he flattered himself that a more noble exalted Thought never sprang in any other Man's Head. Every one knew how laborious the usual Method is of attaining to Arts and Sciences; whereas by his Contrivance, the most ignorant Person at a reasonable Charge, and with a little bodily Labour, may write books in Philosophy, Poetry, Politicks, Law, Mathamaticks, and Theology, without the least Assistance from Genius or Study. He then led me to the Frame, about the Sides whereof all his Pupils stood in Ranks. It was a Twenty Foot Square, placed in the Middle of the Room. The Superfices was composed of several Bits of Wood, about the Bigness of a Dye, by some larger than others. They were all linked together by slender Wires. These Bits of Wood were covered on every Square with Papers pasted on them; and on these Papers were written all the Words of their Language in the several Moods, Tenses, and Declensions, but without any Order. The Professor then desired me to observe, for he was going to set his Engine to work. The Pupils at his Command took each the hold of an Iron Handle, whereof there were Forty fixed around the Edges of the Frame; and giving them a sudden Turn, the whole Disposition of the Words was entirely changed. He then commanded Six and Thirty of the Lads to read the several lines softly as they appeared on the Frame; and where they found three or four Words together that might make Part of a Sentence, they dictated to the four remaining Boys who were Scribes. This work was repeated three or four Times, and at every Turn the Engine was so contrived, that the Words shifted into New Places, as the square Bits of Wood moved upside down.

Six hours a-Day the young Students were employed in this Labour; and the Professor showed me several Volumes in large Folio already collected, of broken Sentences, which he intended to piece together, and out of those rich Materials to give the World a compleat Body of Arts and Sciences.

The next major step came from a somewhat unlikely source —the weaving industry. One of the problems of the industry around the turn of the nineteenth century was that of controlling large numbers of flying needles, to create specific patterns in the material. A Frenchman, Joseph Jacquard, hit upon a solution that became in time the basis of computer input—the use of punched cards. By punching holes in a card at the points where he wanted the needles actuated, Jacquard obtained accurate and cheap control over the weaving process. Almost a century later a Dr. Herman Hollerith used similar cards to count Americans in the 1890 census. Spurred by this success, Hollerith turned his mind to commercial applications of the method, and after a series of mergers with Hollerith's firm had produced a corporation known as International Business Machines, the cards were referred to as IBM cards.

Jacquard's invention had already set the scene for the most extraordinary chapter of all in the development of the computer —the design of "the analytical engine" by English engineer and mathematician Charles Babbage. Around the end of the Napoleonic Wars, Babbage conceived the idea of a machine which would calculate precisely and accurately the tables of logarithms, sines, cosines and other mathematical functions, which Babbage had found to be full of errors. The machine—called the difference engine because it was based on the differences between the squares of numbers—consisted of hundreds of gears, shafts, ratchets and counters, took four years to build and weighed two tons.

When completed, it successfully calculated the mathematical tables to an accuracy of six decimal places, but Babbage, like many modern technologists, was not content to stop there. In 1833 he conceived the idea of the analytical engine, a device which, unlike the difference engine, would be able to perform any arithmetical calculation, and would be able to link such calculations together to solve, at least in theory, any arithmetic problem presented to it. The first chapter of this section contains Babbage's own account of the machine which, unfortunately, proved far too advanced for the technology of the time. By the time Babbage died, in 1871, the machine was still incomplete, having consumed a large governmental grant and much of the mathematician's own personal fortune.

Modern work on the computer actually got under way more

than fifty years later, with the invention of a somewhat different machine—a large-scale calculator known as the differential analyzer. This was invented by a group at the Massachusetts Institute of Technology headed by Dr. Vannevar Bush. At the time Bush was a young engineer working at the limits of electronic technology; later he was to become the United States' leading spokesman for science policy.

Bush's differential analyzer was designed to solve the differential equations that lie at the heart of virtually every problem in physics and engineering and is, unlike Babbage's instrument, an analogue machine. Analogue computers represent the quantities involved in their calculations by electrical signals directly proportional to those quantities; digital machines—including Babbage's analytical engine and most modern computers—break down the quantities into digits, or "bits," of information. Analogue machines are generally faster in operation, while the digital computers can tackle more complicated problems; today the two concepts are often combined in so-called "hybrid computers."

Bush's machine, in fact, was limited even in analogue terms, since it could only solve ordinary differential equations, in which a single quantity was unknown; the more complicated—and more common—problems involving more than one unknown were beyond its grasp. Nevertheless, the differential analyzer was the first concrete step toward today's computer industry.

It was not until the 1940's that any serious extension of Charles Babbage's work was undertaken. Once the commitment was made, however, the results began to come in quick succession. As Jeremy Bernstein's account shows, new understanding of computer theory was rapidly followed by construction of the Harvard Mark 1 electronic calculator and the production of ENIAC—the world's first electronic computer. Accompanying Bernstein's account are two of the fundamental documents of the computer age—a U. S. Army report on what a computer is and does, written in 1944, and the patent application for ENIAC, filed in 1946.

Despite numerous developments in computer technology since those heady days, the profile of the digital computer has remained much the same. Every computer consists of four basic parts: an input terminal, an information store, a processor, and an output terminal. The computer operator informs the machine of his wishes by writing a program—a set of concise instructions written in such a way that the machine will interpret them correctly —and inserting them in the input terminal via punched cards, paper or magnetic tape, or other suitable means. The first action of the computer is to store the incoming data and information in its memory, which may consist of magnetic discs, magnetic tapes or tiny iron rings strung on wire grids. Thus stored, the information is instantly available to the processor, the part of the computer that actually carries out the calculations. Finally, the answer, or a request for more information, appears at the output terminal, in typed, graphic or spoken form.

Once the basic principles of the digital computer had been established, the experts turned their attention to its likely applications and social consequences, and came up with a series of forecasts that seem remarkably perceptive even in the light of today's knowledge. One of the first applications foreseen for the new computer, described here in an article by the editor of this volume, was that of the automatic factory, in which the machine would displace human workers from some of their most tedious and dehumanizing tasks. The likely social consequences of such a development, such as mass unemployment and excessive leisure time, were shockingly apparent then, and it appeared quite possible that the concept might become a *fait accompli* before such consequences could be adequately considered.

Fortunately, perhaps, that has not happened. Development of the automatic factory has been so slow that the selfsame problems that exercised the experts in the early fifties are still before us. As Charles Silberman, a noted commentator on the industrial scene, wrote in the late sixties, "two years of field research and economic and statistical analysis make it clear that automation has made substantially less headway in the United States economy than the literature on the subject suggests. Fifteen years after the concepts of 'feedback' and 'closed-loop control' became widespread, and ten years after computers starting coming into common use, no fully automated process exists for any major product in any industry in the United States." Plainly, then, the experts and legislators have a little breathing time in which to consider the vital questions of the computer's impact that are detailed in the remaining sections of this book.

The Life of a Philosopher

Charles Babbage

Three hundred years ago, when even highly educated men could hardly manage more than their two-times table, the need for calculating machines was self-evident. "It is unworthy of excellent men to lose hours like slaves in the labor of calculation which could safely be relegated to anyone if machines were used," wrote the German mathematician Leibnitz. Yet beyond the slide rule, which was invented in 1622, no calculating machine existed, even in concept, until Victorian times. Then, however, came the remarkable scientific "vision" of the "analytical engine," a precursor of today's computers, designed by Charles Babbage, a mathematician who could have served as the model for any fictional mad inventor. It was he who wrote to Alfred, Lord Tennyson complaining that one stanza from his Lordship's "otherwise beautiful poem" "The Vision of Sin" was inaccurate: instead of "every moment dies a man/ every moment one is born," chided Babbage, the verse should have read "every moment dies a man/every moment 1 1/16 is born." Yet whatever his critical abilities, Babbage did understand the principle of calculating machines. The device he designed with the purpose of calculating logarithmic tables contained all the elements of modern digital computers, including punch-card programming and memory storage. That Babbage could not build his analytical engine was the fault of the limited technology of the day, rather than of any deficiencies in design. What follows is Babbage's own account of his extraordinary invention.

The earliest idea that I can trace in my own mind of calculating arithmetical Tables by machinery arose in this manner: —

One evening I was sitting in the rooms of the Analytical Society, at Cambridge, my head leaning forward on the Table in a kind of dreamy mood, with a Table of logarithms lying open before me. Another member, coming into the room, and seeing me half asleep, called out, "Well, Babbage, what are you dreaming about?" to which I replied, "I am thinking that all these Tables (pointing to the logarithms) might be calculated by machinery."

I am indebted to my friend, the Rev. Dr. Robinson, the Master of the Temple, for this anecdote. The event must have happened either in 1812 or 1813.

About 1819 I was occupied with devising means for accurately dividing astronomical instruments, and had arrived at a plan which I thought was likely to succeed perfectly. I had also at that time been speculating about making machinery to compute arithmetical Tables.

One morning I called upon the late Dr. Wollaston, to consult him about my plan for dividing instruments. On talking over the matter, it turned out that my system was exactly that which had been described by the Duke de Chaulnes, in the Memoirs of the French Academy of Sciences, about fifty or sixty years before. I then mentioned my other idea of computing Tables by machinery, which Dr. Wollaston thought a more promising subject.

I considered that a machine to execute the mere isolated operations of arithmetic, would be comparatively of little value, unless it were very easily set to do its work, and unless it executed not only accurately, but with great rapidity, whatever it was required to do.

On the other hand, the method of differences supplied a general principle by which *all* Tables might be computed through limited intervals, by one uniform process. Again, the method of differences required the use of mechanism for Addition only. In order, however, to insure accuracy in the printed Tables, it was necessary that the machine which computed Tables should also set them up in type, or else supply a mould in which stereotyped plates of those Tables could be cast.

I now began to sketch out arrangements for accomplishing

the several partial processes which were required. The arithmetical part must consist of two distinct processes—the power of adding one digit to another, and also of carrying the tens to the next digit, if it should be necessary.

The first idea was, naturally, to add each digit successively. This, however, would occupy much time if the numbers added together consisted of many places of figures.

The next step was to add all the digits of the two numbers each to each at the same instant, but reserving a certain mechanical memorandum, wherever a carriage became due. These carriages were then to be executed successively.

Having made various drawings, I now began to make models of some portions of the machine, to see how they would act. Each number was to be expressed upon wheels placed upon an axis; there being one wheel for each figure in the number operated upon.

The circular arrangement of the axes of the Difference Engine round large central wheels led to the most extended prospects. The whole of arithmetic now appeared within the grasp of mechanism. A vague glimpse even of an Analytical Engine at length opened out, and I pursued with enthusiasm the shadowy vision. The drawings and the experiments were of the most costly kind. Draftsmen of the highest order were necessary to economize the labour of my own head; whilst skilled workmen were required to execute the experimental machinery to which I was obliged constantly to have recourse.

In order to carry out my pursuits successfully, I had purchased a house with above a quarter of an acre of ground in a very quiet locality. My coach-house was now converted into a forge and a foundry, whilst my stables were transformed into a workshop. I built other extensive workshops myself, and had a fire-proof building for my drawings and draftsmen. Having myself worked with a variety of tools, and having studied the art of constructing each of them, I at length laid it down as a principle—that, except in rare cases, I would never do anything myself if I could afford to hire another person who could do it for me.

The complicated relations which then arose amongst the various parts of the machinery would have baffled the most tenacious memory. I overcame that difficulty by improving and extending a language of signs, the Mechanical Notation, which in 1826 I had explained in a paper printed in the "Phil. Trans." By such means I succeeded in mastering trains of investigation so vast in extent that no length of years ever allotted to one individual could otherwise have enabled me to control. By the aid of the Mechanical Notation, the Analytical Engine became a reality: for it became susceptible of demonstration.

The most important part of the Analytical Engine was undoubtedly the mechanical method of carrying the tens. On this I laboured incessantly, each succeeding improvement advancing me a step or two. The difficulty did not consist so much in the more or less complexity of the contrivance as in the reduction of the *time* required to effect the carriage. Twenty or thirty different plans and modifications had been drawn. At last I came to the conclusion that I had exhausted the principle of successive carriage. I concluded also that nothing but teaching the Engine to foresee and then to act upon that foresight could ever lead me to the object I desired, namely, to make the whole of any unlimited number of carriages in one unit of time. One morning, after I had spent many hours in the drawing-office in endeavouring to improve the system of successive carriages, I mentioned these views to my chief assistant, and added that I should retire to my library, and endeavour to work out the new principle. He gently expressed a doubt whether the plan was *possible,* to which I replied that, not being able to prove its impossibility, I should follow out a slight glimmering of light which I thought I perceived.

After about three hours' examination, I returned to the drawing-office with much more definite ideas upon the subject. I had discovered a principle that proved the possibility, and I had contrived [a] mechanism which, I thought, would accomplish my object.

I now commenced the explanation of my views, which I soon found were but little understood by my assistant; nor was this surprising, since in the course of my own attempt at explanation, I found several defects in my plan, and was also led by his questions to perceive others. All these I removed one after another, and ultimately terminated at a late hour my morning's work with the conviction that *anticipating* carriage was not only within my power, but that I had devised one mechanism at least by which it might be accomplished.

The Analytical Engine consists of two parts:

1. The store in which all the variables to be operated upon, as well as those quantities which have arisen from the result of other operations, are placed.

2. The mill into which the quantities about to be operated upon are always brought.

Every formula which the Analytical Engine can be required to compute consists of certain algebraical operations to be performed upon given letters, and of certain other modifications depending on the numerical value assigned to those letters.

There are therefore two sets of cards, the first to direct the nature of the operations to be performed—these are called operation cards: the other to direct the particular variables on which those cards are required to operate—these latter are called variable cards. Now the symbol of each variable or constant, is placed at the top of a column capable of containing any required number of digits.

Under this arrangement, when any formula is required to be computed, a set of operation cards must be strung together, which contain the series of operations in the order in which they occur. Another set of cards must then be strung together, to call in the variables into the mill, the order in which they are required to be acted upon. Each operation card will require three other cards, two to represent the variables and constants and their numerical values upon which the previous operation card is to act, and one to indicate the variable on which the arithmetical result of this operation is to be placed.

But each variable has below it, on the same axis, a certain number of figure-wheels marked on their edges with the ten digits: upon these any number the machine is capable of holding can be placed. Whenever variables are ordered into the mill, these figures will be brought in, and the operation indicated by the preceding card will be performed upon them. The result of this operation will then be replaced in the store.

The Analytical Engine is therefore a machine of the most general nature. Whatever formula it is required to develop, the law of its development must be communicated to it by two sets of cards. When these have been placed, the engine is special for that particular formula. The numerical value of its constants must then be put on the columns of wheels below them, and on setting the Engine in motion it will calculate and print the numerical results of that formula.

Every set of cards made for any formula will at any future time recalculate that formula with whatever constants may be required.

Thus the Analytical Engine will possess a library of its own. Every set of cards once made will at any future time reproduce the calculations for which it was first arranged. The numerical value of its constants may then be inserted.

The Tables to be used must, of course, be computed and punched on cards by the machine, in which case they would undoubtedly be correct. I then added that when the machine wanted a tabular number, say the logarithm of a given number, that it would ring a bell and then stop itself. On this, the attendant would look at a certain part of the machine, and find that it wanted the logarithm of a given number, say of 2303. The attendant would then go to the drawer containing the pasteboard cards representing its table of logarithms. From amongst these he would take the required logarithm card, and place it in the machine. Upon this the engine would first ascertain whether the assistant had or had not given him the correct logarithm of the number; if so, it would use it and continue its work. But if the engine found the attendant had given him a wrong logarithm, it would then ring a louder bell, and stop itself. On the attendant again examining the engine, he would observe the words, "Wrong tabular number," and then discover that he really had given the wrong logarithm, and of course he would have to replace it by the right one.

Any number which the Analytical Engine is capable of using or of producing can, if required, be expressed by a card with certain holes in it; thus

Number				Table						
2	3	0	3	3	6	2	2	9	3	9
●	●	○	●	●	●	●	●	●	●	●
●	●	○	●	●	●	●	●	●	●	●
○	●	○	●	●	●	○	○	●	●	●
○	○	○	○	○	●	○	○	●	○	●
○	○	○	○	○	●	○	○	●	○	●
○	○	○	○	○	●	○	○	●	○	●
○	○	○	○	○	○	○	○	●	○	●
○	○	○	○	○	○	○	○	●	○	●
○	○	○	○	○	○	○	○	●	○	●

The above card contains eleven vertical rows for holes, each row having nine or any less number of holes. In this example the tabular number is 3 6 2 2 9 3 9, whilst its number in the order of the table is 2 3 0 3. In fact, the former number is the logarithm of the latter.

The Analytical Engine will contain,

1. Apparatus for printing on paper, one, or, if required, two copies of its results.
2. Means for producing a stereotype mould of the tables or results it computes.
3. Mechanism for punching on blank pasteboard cards or metal plates the numerical results of any of its computations.

Of course the Engine will compute all the Tables which it may itself be required to use. These cards will therefore be entirely free from error. Now when the Engine requires a tabular number, it will stop, ring a bell, and ask for such number. In the case we have assumed, it asks for the logarithm of 2 3 0 3.

When the attendant has placed a tabular card in the Engine, the first step taken by it will be to verify the *number* of the card given it by subtracting its number from 2 3 0 3, the number whose logarithm it asked for. If the remainder is zero, then the engine is certain that the logarithm must be the right one, since it was computed and punched by itself.

Thus the Analytical Engine first computes and punches on cards its own tabular numbers. These are brought to it by its attendant when demanded. But the Engine itself takes care that the *right* card is brought to it by verifying the *number* of that card by the number of the card which it demanded. The Engine will always reject a wrong card by continually ringing a loud bell and stopping itself until supplied with the precise intellectual food it demands.

It will be an interesting question, which time only can solve, to know whether such tables of cards will ever be required for the Engine. Tables are used for saving the time of continually computing individual numbers. But the computations to be made by the Engine are so rapid that it seems most probable that it will make shorter work by computing directly from proper formulæ than by having recourse even to its own Tables.

The Analytical Engine I propose will have the power of expressing every number it uses to fifty places of figures. It will multiply any two such numbers together, and then, if required, will divide the product of one hundred figures by a number of fifty places of figures.

Supposing the velocity of the moving parts of the Engine to be not greater than forty feet per minute, I have no doubt that:

Sixty additions or subtractions may be completed and printed in one minute.

One multiplication of two numbers, each of fifty figures, in one minute.

One divsion of a number having 100 places of figures by another of 50 in one minute.

In the various sets of drawings of the modifications of the mechanical structure of the Analytical Engines, already numbering upwards of thirty, two great principles were embodied to an unlimited extent:

1. The entire control over *arithmetical* operations, however large, and whatever might be the number of their digits.

2. The entire control over the *combinations* of algebraic symbols, however lengthened those processes may be required. The possibility of fulfilling these two conditions might reasonably be doubted by the most accomplished mathematician as well as by the most ingenious mechanician.

The difficulties which naturally occur to those capable of examining the question, as far as they relate to arithmetic, are:

(*a*) The number of digits in *each constant* inserted in the Engine must be without limit.

(*b*) The number of constants to be inserted in the Engine must also be without limit.

(*c*) The number of operations necessary for arithmetic is only four, but these four may be repeated an *unlimited* number of times.

(*d*) These operations may occur in any order, or follow an *unlimited* number of laws.

The following conditions relate to the algebraic portion of the Analytical Engine:

(*e*) The number of *literal* constants must be *unlimited*.

(*f*) The number of *variables* must be *without limit*.

(*g*) The combinations of the algebraic signs must be *unlimited*.

(*h*) The number of *functions* to be employed must be *without limit*.

This enumeration includes eight conditions, each of which is absolutely *unlimited* as to the number of its combinations.

Now it is obvious that no *finite* machine can include infinity. It is also certain that no question *necessarily* involving infinity can ever be converted into any other in which the idea of infinity under some shape or other does not enter.

It is impossible to construct machinery occupying unlimited space; but it is possible to construct finite machinery, and to use it through unlimited time. It is this substitution of the *infinity of time* for the *infinity of space* which I have made use of, to limit the size of the engine and yet to retain its unlimited power.

The Analytical Engine

Jeremy Bernstein

Babbage's work lay neglected for more than three quarters of a century until the needs of the Second World War sparked the U.S. scientific community to press on with development of an updated analytical engine. Then, however, the research produced rapid dividends, culminating in the unveiling of the first true electronic computer in 1946. In this account Jeremy Bernstein, a physicist equally at home in the pages of scientific journals and popular magazines—he is an associate professor at New York University and a regular contributor to *The New Yorker*—recalls those early years of the computer age. He recounts the often haphazard trail of lost memoranda and chance meetings that finally led to an invention that could have emerged at any time in the fifteen years before it finally made the scientific scene. Here, for the first time, we come across the familiar acronyms of today's electronic technology—ENIAC, UNIVAC and, even more important, IBM.

The modern era of mechanical computation began about 1925, at the Massachusetts Institute of Technology, when Dr. Vannevar Bush and some associates made a large-scale analogue calculator. It had electric motors, but otherwise it was entirely mechanical. The quantities being computed were represented by the number of degrees through which certain gears had rotated, and this meant that the accuracy of the computations was limited by the precision with which the angles could be measured. In 1935, the M.I.T. group began designing a second model, which introduced, along with other improvements, an electrical method for measuring the angles. This model was completed in 1942, but the fact was kept secret until the end of the war, because the Bush machines were extensively used for the computation of artillery firing tables. (A rumor was deliberately circulated that it had been impossible to finish the new model.) Computing the tables involved solving "ordinary" differential equations—equations with just one variable—and the machines were reasonably fast, by human standards; solving a typical equation, which might have taken a human computer a week, took the machines about half an hour. However, as is true of all analogue calculators, there were intrinsic limitations to their flexibility. Most problems in physics and engineering involve the solution of partial differential equations—equations with many variables—something entirely beyond the capacity of the Bush calculators.

In 1937, Howard Aiken, who is a professor of information technology at the University of Miami, in Florida, and president of Howard Aiken Industries, Inc., with headquarters in New York, began work at Harvard on his Ph.D. thesis in physics. The theoretical aspects of the thesis involved the solution of so-called nonlinear ordinary differential equations, which could be done only by means of numerical approximation, and the computations needed to reach these approximate solutions proved to be extremely long. Aiken began considering possible methods of doing the computations on machines, and he soon invented a machine that would evaluate simple polynomials. After a year or two, during which he invented variations on this machine that would solve more complex kinds of problems, it occurred to him that all these machines were, in their logical organization, essentially identical, and he started thinking about the construction of a single general-purpose machine, capable of dealing with any of the problems. He was able to get support for his project from the International Business Machines Corporation, and in 1939 work on the machine—the Automatic Sequence Controlled Calculator, Mark I, as it became known— was begun at I.B.M. in a collaboration between Aiken and four I.B.M. engineers named J. W. Bryce, C. D. Lake, B. M. Durfee, and F. E. Hamilton. The Mark I was completed in 1944, and was put into operation at Harvard. About three years after Professor Aiken began working on computers, he discovered Babbage. He was startled to find that he and Babbage had been preoccupied by the same problems. As Professor Aiken put it recently, "If Babbage had lived seventy-five years later, I would have been out of a job." In fact, the operating manual of the Mark I begins with a quotation from Babbage's book: "If, unwarned by my example, any man shall succeed in constructing an engine embodying in itself the whole of the executive department of mathematical analysis . . . I have no fear of leaving my reputation in his charge, for he alone will be able fully to appreciate the nature of my efforts and the value of my results." When Professor Aiken first came across these lines, he felt that Babbage was addressing him personally from the past.

The Mark I was designed to perform computations by following automatically—that is, without manual intervention on the part of the machine operator—a sequence of instructions that had been prepared for it by a programmer. The instructions were fed into it on a punched paper tape, and the numbers on which the instructions were to operate were stored in registers. One might wish to give the machine an instruction like this: "Take a number out of Register 32, put the number into Register 64, and then read the next line on the coding tape." This instruction would appear in the form of the sequence of numbers 32647, in which the 7 was the code for instructing the machine to read the next line, while 32 and 64 referred to the "addresses" —the particular registers—in which the numbers had been stored. Computations were broken down into small steps, and each step had to be expressed in terms of the primitive instructions that the machine could follow. As machine computations generally involve an enormous number of steps, the programmer had to go about writing down meticulously a very long sequence of such instructions—a tedious business.

The Mark I was electro-mechanical; the basic operations were performed by mechanical parts that were controlled electrically. Typical of these was the ordinary telephone relay—a device in which a metal bar attached to a spring can be raised by the pulling action of an electromagnet. When the magnet is turned off, the bar falls, completing a circuit. Such relays were used not only in the Mark I but also in some interesting smaller computing devices that were under development at about the same time at Bell Telephone Laboratories, under the direction of Dr. George R. Stibitz, a mathematician there. The Mark I used about three thousand of the relays. Like most mechanical devices, and unlike the basic electronic devices of today, they were relatively large and slow. Each relay was about an inch long, and could be opened or closed in about a hundredth of a second. It took some four and a half seconds for the Mark I to multiply two twenty-three-digit numbers—the largest numbers it could handle. What with its relays and other mechanical parts, the Mark I's calculating was audible. As a student at Harvard, I used to drop in now and then and have a look at it. It was situated in a red brick structure just behind the physics building, and when it was working, one could go in and listen to the gentle clicking of the relays, which sounded like a roomful of ladies knitting.

It would not be completely unreasonable to say that by the time the Mark I machine went into operation, it was almost obsolete. (This is not meant as a reflection on the machine; it operated for more than fifteen years and turned out quantities of mathematical tables that are still being used.) However, about a year earlier, at the Moore School of Electrical Engineering of the University of Pennsylvania, Dr. J. Presper Eckert, an electrical engineer, and Dr. John Mauchly, a physicist, had begun work on the ENIAC—the Electronic Numerical Integrator and Calculator. This was the first electronic computer, for instead of relays and other semi-mechanical devices Eckert and Mauchly used vacuum tubes. The current in a tube is composed of flowing electrons, and changing the tube's state involves stopping or starting the flow. These electrons have a tiny mass as compared to the mass of the iron bar that has to be moved when a telephone relay is switched. In a vacuum tube, very strong electrical forces are brought to bear on the electrons, giving them very high accelerations in extremely short times, and the state of the tube can be changed in about a millionth of a second. By the time the first model of the ENIAC was ready for operation, early in 1946, it was by far the most complex electronic device in the world.

A large factor in the decision to build the ENIAC was military pressure. In 1943, the Moore School and the Aberdeen Proving Ground, in Maryland, were conducting a joint project involving the computation of artillery firing tables for the Army. The Moore School contingent, which used a Bush analogue computer and employed a hundred girls to do hand computations as a necessary adjunct to the machine operations, was under the command of a young first lieutenant in the Army Ordnance Corps named Herman H. Goldstine, who had been an assistant professor of mathematics at the University of Michigan before the war. When I went to see Dr. Goldstine, who is director of mathematical research at the I.B.M. Thomas J. Watson Research Center, in Yorktown Heights, he told me that the results produced by the hundred girls and the machine were not very satisfactory—that indeed, by the time Eckert and Mauchly began work on the ENIAC the situation had become "desperate." Back in the summer of 1942, Mauchly had written an informal report on the possibilities of making an electronic computer. In the course of things, the report got lost. Early in 1943, Mauchly and Eckert reconstructed it from a secretary's shorthand notes, and Eckert added an appendix containing some explicit suggestions as to how Mauchly's ideas might be embodied in electronic hardware. Dr. Goldstine, who was serving as liaison officer between the Moore School group and Army Ordnance, decided to try to get the backing of Army Ordnance for the project. On April 9, 1943, there was a meeting—attended by, among other people, Colonel Leslie E. Simon, then director of the Ballistic Research Laboratory at Aberdeen, and Professor Oswald Veblen, of the Institute for Advanced Study, at Princeton, who was one of this country's most distinguished mathematicians— at which the potentialities of the ENIAC were discussed. After hearing about the machine, Veblen stood up and said, "Simon, back that thing!" The Army backed it.

Strangely, there was nothing in the completed ENIAC that could not have been put together at least a decade before the war, if anyone had had the incentive to do it. Early in 1962, Harold Bergstein, who was then editor of a magazine called

Datamation, interviewed Eckert and Mauchly. Part of the interview, as published, went this way:

BERGSTEIN: Since the ENIAC was a direct result of your efforts and government money during World War Two, when would you speculate that the [electronic] digital computer might have been invented (a) if there had been no war, and (b) if there were no Eckert and Mauchly to invent it?

ECKERT: I think you certainly would have had computers about the same time. There are a lot of things which cannot linger long without being born. Actually, calculus was invented simultaneously by two different individuals. It's been the history of invention over and over again that when things are kind of ready for invention, then somebody does it.

What puzzles me most is that there wasn't anything in the ENIAC in the way of components that wasn't available 10 and possibly 15 years before. . . . The ENIAC could have been invented 10 or 15 years earlier and the real question is, why wasn't it done sooner?

MAUCHLY: In part, the demand wasn't there. The demand, of course, is a curious thing. People may need something without knowing that they need it.

In the summer of 1944, the late Professor John von Neumann, who was then a consultant to the group engaged on the atomic-bomb project at Los Alamos, started working in the field of electronic computing; his job at Los Alamos was to find techniques for performing the immensely involved numerical computations that were necessary in the design of nuclear weapons. By any standard, von Neumann was one of the most creative and versatile scientists of the twentieth century. He began his career as a chemical engineer, and though he turned to pure mathematics and theoretical physics, he retained a profound feeling for engineering practicalities. Indeed, his contributions to computing machines ranged from articulating the general logical theory of their design to working out the details of the construction of specific circuit elements. Von Neumann was born in Budapest, and after receiving his Doctor's degree, in 1926, he was a *Privatdozent* first in Berlin and then in Hamburg. He came to the United States in 1930 and spent three years at Princeton University. Then, in 1933, he became one of the first permanent members of the Institute for Advanced Study (Einstein was another of the original members), and he remained there until the summer of 1955, when he was appointed to the Atomic Energy Commission. A great deal of von Neumann's work in mathematics was inspired by problems that arose in the mathematical formulation of physics. He was able to take apparently unrelated concepts in theoretical physics and organize them into beautifully compact logical structures. Furthermore, he was one of the formulators of the "theory of games." This is the mathematical study of the strategy for winning very complex games. Such games can serve as models for economic or military strategy. A book that von Neumann wrote with the economist Oskar Morgenstern, *Theory of Games and Economic Behavior*, is a fundamental contribution to the field of operational research. Von Neumann had a phenomenal capacity for doing mental computations of all kinds. His thought processes were extremely fast, and often he would see through to the end of someone's argument almost before the speaker had got out the first few sentences. Recently, one of von Neumann's colleagues said in affectionate explanation of von Neumann's power, "You see, Johnny wasn't human. But after living with humans for so long he learned how to do a remarkable imitation of one."

During the summer of 1944, Goldstine ran into von Neumann in a railroad station near the Aberdeen Proving Ground. Von Neumann was also serving as a consultant for Aberdeen, and he and Goldstine knew each other slightly. Goldstine told von Neumann that the Moore School group appeared to be well on its way to building an electronic computer that would be about a thousand times as fast as any of the existing electro-mechanical ones. Von Neumann immediately became much excited about the idea. As Goldstine has put it, "Once Johnny saw what we were up to, he jumped into electronic computers with both feet." Von Neumann's enthusiasm for the prospect of electronic computers can be fully appreciated only if one attempts to visualize the degree of complexity of the sort of calculations that were necessary in nuclear weapons design. In a fascinating description of von Neumann's life and work which appeared in the May 1958 issue of the *Bulletin of the American Mathematical Society*, Dr. Stanislaw Ulam of Los Alamos, a close friend, and a collaborator of von Neumann's on weapons-design work, wrote:

"After one discussion in which we outlined the course of such a calculation von Neumann turned to me and said, 'Probably in its execution we shall have to perform more elementary arithmetical steps than the total in all the computations performed by the human race heretofore.' We noticed, however, that the total number of multiplications made by the school children of the world in course of a few years sensibly exceeded that of our problem."

Von Neumann began an active collaboration with the Moore School group. At this time there were a good many exchanges of ideas among the members of the group, and it is almost impossible to give a completely coherent account of who invented what. In any event, certain aspects of the work culminated in a series of reports written by von Neumann and Goldstine, with the help in the first report of Arthur W. Burks, who is a member of the Philosophy Department of the University of Michigan. That first report, entitled "Preliminary Discussion of the Logical Design of an Electronic Computing Instrument," appeared on June 28, 1946. Curiously, although it has turned out to be one of the basic papers in the electronic-computing field, it was until recently published only in the form of a U.S. Army Ordnance Department report.

In 1945, some time before the ENIAC went into operation, the Moore School group began working on the design and construction of a stored-program computer, to be called the EDVAC, or Electronic Discrete Variable Automatic Computer. It was completed in 1950 at the Aberdeen Proving Ground—and was still in operation there as late as 1962—but not by the original group, which had split up after the war, von Neumann returning to Princeton along with Goldstine, while Eckert and Mauchly began designing machines commercially. (The first stored-program computer actually completed was the EDSAC—for Electronic Delay Storage Automatic Calculator—built at the mathematical laboratory of the University of Cambridge. It went into operation in May, 1949.) UNIVAC I—for Universal Automatic

Computer—the first commercial stored-program computer, was built for Sperry-Rand by Eckert and Mauchly, and upon its completion, in 1951, was delivered to the Bureau of the Census. (In October, 1963, UNIVAC I was officially retired to the Smithsonian Institution after more than seventy-three thousand hours of operational use.) At Princeton, von Neumann supervised the construction of an experimental computer that embodied his ideas on machine organization. It went into operation in 1952. Paul Armer, of the Rand Corporation, in Santa Monica, wrote in a recent issue of *Datamation*: "The machine (variously known as the I.A.S., or Princeton, or von Neumann machine) was constructed and copied (never exactly), and the copies were copied. One version of it, built at Rand, was affectionately entitled JOHNNIAC (over von Neumann's objections). Most of the copies are still in operation, although the [original] I.A.S. machine now has its place in history at the Smithsonian."

Preliminary Discussion of the Logical Design of an Electronic Computing Instrument

Arthur W. Burkes, Herman H. Goldstine, John von Neumann

As we saw in the previous article, one of the most important landmarks in the early years of computer technology was a two-part report by three experts who had originally come together in the inauspicious surroundings of the U.S. Army's Aberdeen Proving Ground in Maryland. The men were Arthur Burkes, a member of the Philosophy Department at the University of Michigan; Herman Goldstine, an Army Ordnance Officer who had been in civilian life an Assistant Professor of Mathematics at the same university; and John von Neumann of Princeton's Institute for Advanced Study, surely one of the most accomplished of all mathematical geniuses. Although highly technical, this report, issued as an Army Ordnance Department Report in 1946, sums up succinctly what a computer is and what it does.

Part One

This report is intended as the first of two papers dealing with some aspects of the overall logical considerations arising in connection with electronic computing machines. An attempt is made to give in this, the first half of the report, a general picture of the type of instrument now under consideration and in the second half a study of how actual mathematical problems can be coded, i.e. prepared in the language the machine can understand. . . .

1.0 Principal component of the machine.

1.1 Inasmuch as the completed device will be a general-purpose computing machine it should contain certain main organs relating to arithmetic, memory-storage, control and connection with the human operator. It is intended that the machine be fully automatic in character, i.e., independent of the human operator after the computation starts. A fuller discussion of the implications of this remark will be given in section 3 below.

1.2 It is evident that the machine must be capable of storing in some manner not only the digital information needed in a given computation such as boundary values, tables of functions (such as the equation of state of a fluid) and also the intermediate results of the computation (which may be wanted for varying lengths of time), but also the instructions which govern the actual routine to be performed on the numerical data. In a special-purpose machine these instructions are an integral part of the device and constitute a part of its design structure. For an all-purpose machine it must be possible to instruct the device to carry out any whatever computation can be formulated in numerical terms. Hence there must be some organ capable of storing these program orders. There must, moreover, be a unit which can understand these instructions and order their execution.

1.3 Conceptually we have discussed above two different forms of memory: storage of numbers and storage of orders. If, however, the orders to the machine are reduced to a numerical code and if the machine can in some fashion distinguish a number from an order, the memory organ can be used to store both numbers and orders.

1.4 If the memory for orders is merely a storage organ there must exist an organ which can automatically execute the orders stored in the memory. We shall call this organ the *Control*.

1.5 Inasmuch as the device is to be a computing machine there must be an arithmetic organ in it which can perform certain of the elementary arithmetic operations. There will be, therefore, a unit capable of adding, subtracting, multiplying and dividing. It will be seen that it can also perform additional operations that occur quite frequently.

The operations that the machine will view as elementary are clearly those which are wired into the machine. To illustrate, the operation of multiplication could be eliminated from the device as an elementary process if one were willing to view it as a properly ordered series of additions. Similar remarks apply to division. In general, the inner economy of the arithmetic unit is determined by a compromise between the desire for speed of operation—a non-elementary operation will generally take a long time to perform since it is constituted of a series of orders given by the Control—and the desire for simplicity, or cheapness, of the machine.

1.6 Lastly there must exist devices, the input and output organ, whereby the human operator and the machine can communicate with each other. This organ will be seen to constitute a secondary form of automatic memory.

2.0 First remarks on the memory.

2.1 It is clear that the size of the memory is a critical consideration in the design of a satisfactory general-purpose computing machine. We proceed to discuss what quantities the memory should store for various types of computations.

2.2 In the solution of partial differential equations the storage requirements are likely to be quite extensive. In general, one must remember not only the initial and boundary conditions and any arbitrary functions that enter the problem but also an extensive number of intermediate results.

a) For equations of parabolic or hyperbolic type in two independent variables the integration process is essentially a double induction: to find the values of the dependent variables at time $t + \Delta t$ one integrates with respect to x from one boundary to the other by utilizing the data at time t as if they were coefficients which contribute to defining the problem of this integration.

Not only must the memory have sufficient room to store these intermediate data but there must be provisions whereby these data can later be removed, i.e., at the end of the (t + $\triangle$t) cycle, and replaced by the corresponding data for the (t + 2$\triangle$t) cycle. This process of removing data from the memory and of replacing them with new information must, of course, be done quite automatically under the direction of the Control.

b) For total differential equations the memory requirements are clearly similar to, but smaller than, those discussed in a) above.

c) Problems that are solved by iterative procedures such as systems of linear equations or elliptic partial differential equations, treated by relaxation techniques, may be expected to require quite extensive memory capacity. The memory requirement for such problems is apparently much greater than for those problems in a) above in which one needs only to store information corresponding to the instantaneous value of one variable (t in a) above), while now entire solutions (covering all values of all variables) must be stored. This apparent discrepancy in magnitudes can, however, be somewhat overcome by the use of techniques which permit the use of much coarser integration meshes in this case, than in the cases under a).

2.3 It is reasonable at this time to build a machine that can conveniently handle problems several orders of magnitude more complex than are now handled by existing machines, electronic or electro-mechanical. We consequently plan on a fully automatic electronic storage facility of about 4,000 numbers of 40 binary digits each. This corresponds to a precision of $2^{-40} \sim .9 \cdot 10^{-12}$, i.e., of about 12 decimals. We believe that this memory capacity exceeds the capacities required for most problems that one deals with at present by a factor of about 10. The precision is also safely higher than what is required for the great majority of present day problems. In addition, we propose we have a subsidiary memory, which is also automatic, of much larger capacity on some medium such as magnetic wire or tape.

3.0 First remarks on the control and code.

3.1 It is easy to see by formal-logical methods, that there exist codes that are in abstracto adequate to control and cause the execution of any sequence of operations which are individually available in the machine and which are, in their entirety, conceivable by the problem planner. The really decisive considerations from the present point of view, in selecting a code, are more of a practical nature: simplicity of the equipment demanded by the code, and the clarity of its application to the actually important problems together with the speed of its handling of those problems. It would take us much too far afield to discuss these questions at all generally or from first principles. We will therefore restrict ourselves to analyzing only the type of code which we now envisage for our machine.

3.2 There must certainly be instructions for performing the fundamental arithmetic operations. The specifications for these orders will not be completely given until the arithmetic unit is described in a little more detail.

3.3 It must be possible to transfer data from the memory to the arithmetic organ and back again. In transferring information from the arithmetic organ back into the memory there are two types we must distinguish: transfers of numbers as such and transfers of numbers which are parts of orders. The first case is quite obvious and needs no further explication. The second case is more subtle and serves to illustrate the generality and simplicity of the system. Consider, by way of illustration, the problems of interpolation in the system. Let us suppose that we have formulated the necessary instructions for performing an interpolation of order n in a sequence of data. The exact location in the memory of the (n + 1) quantities that bracket the desired functional value is, of course, a function of the argument. This argument probably is found as the result of a computation in the machine. We thus need an order which can substitute a number into a given order—in the case of interpolation the location of the argument or the group of arguments that is nearest in our table to the desired value. By means of such an order the results of a computation can be introduced into the instructions governing that or a different computation. This makes it possible for a sequence of instructions to be used with different sets of numbers located in different parts of the memory.

To summarize, transfers into the memory will be of two sorts: *total substitutions*, whereby the quantity previously stored is cleared out and replaced by a new number. *Partial substitutions* in which that part of an order containing a *memory location-number*—we assume the various positions in the memory are enumerated serially by memory location-numbers—is replaced by a new memory location-number.

3.4 It is clear that one must be able to get numbers from any part of the memory at any time. The treatment in the case of orders can, however, be more methodical since one can at least partially arrange the control instructions in a linear sequence. Consequently the Control will be so constructed that it will normally proceed from place n in the memory to place (n + 1) for its next instruction.

3.5 The utility of an automatic computer lies in the possibility of using a given sequence of instructions repeatedly, the number of times it is iterated being either preassigned or dependent upon the results of the computation. When the iteration is completed a different sequence of orders is to be followed, so we must, in most cases, give two parallel trains of orders preceded by an instruction as to which routine is to be followed. This choice can be made to depend upon the sign of a number (zero being reckoned as plus for machine purposes). Consequently we introduce an order (*the conditional transfer order*) which will, depending on the sign of a given number, cause the proper one of two routines to be executed.

Frequently two parallel trains of orders terminate in a common routine. It is desirable, therefore, to order the control in either case to proceed to the beginning point of the common routine. This *unconditional transfer* can be achieved either by the artificial use of a conditional transfer or by the introduction of an explicit order for such a transfer.

3.6 Finally we need orders which will integrate the input-output devices with the machine.

3.7 We proceed now to a more detailed discussion of the machine. Inasmuch as our experience has shown that the moment one chooses a given component as the elementary memory unit one has also more or less determined upon much of the balance of the machine, we start by a consideration of the memory organ. In attempting an exposition of a highly integrated device like a computing machine we do not find it possible, however, to give an exhaustive discussion of each organ before completing its description. It is only in the final block diagrams that anything approaching a complete unit can be achieved.

4.0 The memory organ.

4.1 Ideally one would desire an indefinitely large memory capacity such that any particular aggregate of 40 binary digits, or *word*, would be immediately available—i.e., in a time which is somewhat or considerably shorter than the operation time of a fast electronic multiplier. This may be assumed to be practical at the level of about 100 microseconds. Hence the availability time for a word in the memory should be 5 to 50 microseconds. It is equally desirable that words may be replaced with new words at about the same rate. It does not seem possible physically to achieve such a capacity. We are therefore forced to recognize the possibility of constructing a hierarchy of memories, each of which has greater capacity than the preceding but which is less quickly accessible.

The most common forms of storage in electrical circuits are the flip-flop or trigger circuit, the gas tube and the electromechanical relay. To achieve a memory of n words would, of course, require about 40 n such elements, exclusive of the switching elements. *We saw earlier that a fast memory of several thousand words is not at all unreasonable for an all-purpose instrument. Hence, about 10^5 flip-flops or analogous elements would be required! This would, of course, be entirely impractical.*

We must therefore seek out some more fundamental method of storing electrical information than has been suggested above. One criterion for such a storage medium is that the individual storage organs, which accommodate only one binary digit each, should not be macroscopic components, but rather microscopic elements of some suitable organ. They would then, of course, not be identified and switched to by the usual macroscopic wire connections, but by some functional procedure in manipulating that organ.

One device which displays this property to a marked degree is the iconoscope tube. In its conventional form it possesses a linear resolution of about one part in 500. This would correspond to a (two-dimensional) memory capacity of 500 × 500 = 2.5 · 10^5. One is accordingly led to consider the possibility of storing electrical charges on a dielectric plate inside a cathode-ray tube. Effectively such a tube is nothing more than a myriad of electrical capacitors which can be connected into the circuit by means of an electron beam.

Actually the above mentioned high resolution and concomitant memory capacity are only realistic under the conditions of television-image storage, which are much less exigent in respect to the reliability of individual markings than what one can accept in the storage for a computer. In this latter case resolutions of one part in 20 to 100, i.e. memory capacities of 400 to 10,000 would seem to be more reasonable in terms of equipment built essentially along familiar lines.

At the present time the Princeton Laboratories of the Radio Corporation of America are engaged in the development of a storage tube, the *Selectron,* of the type we have mentioned above. This tube is also planned to have a non-amplitude-sensitive switching system whereby the electron beam can be directed to a given spot on the plate within a quite small fraction of a millisecond. Inasmuch as the storage tube is the key component of the machine envisaged in this report we are extremely fortunate in having secured the cooperation of the RCA group in this as well as in various other developments.

An alternate form of rapid memory organ is the feedback delay line described in various reports on the EDVAC. (This is an electronic computing machine being developed for the Ordnance Department, U.S. Army, by the University of Pennsylvania, Moore School of Electrical Engineering.) Inasmuch as that device has been so clearly reported in those papers we give no further discussion. There are still other physical and chemical properties of matter in the presence of electrons or photons that might be considered but since none is yet beyond the early discussion stage we shall not make further mention of them.

4.2 We shall accordingly assume throughout the balance of this report that the Selectron is the modus for storage of words at electronic speeds. As now planned this tube will have a capacity of $2^{12} = 4,096$, or approximately 4,000 binary digits.

To achieve a total electronic storage of about 4,000 words we propose to use 40 Selectrons, thereby achieving a memory of 2^{12} words of 40 binary digits. (Cf. again 2.3.)

4.3 There are two possible means for storage a particular word in the Selectron Memory—or in fact in either a delay line memory or in a storage tube with amplitude-sensitive deflection. One method is to store the entire word in a given tube and then to get the word out by picking out its respective digits in a serial fashion. The other method is to store in corresponding places in each of the 40 tubes one digit of the word. To get a word from the memory in this scheme requires, then, one switching mechanism to which all 40 tubes are connected in parallel. Such a switching scheme seems to us to be simpler than the technique needed in the serial system and is, of course, 40 times faster. We accordingly adopt the parallel procedure and thus are led to consider a so-called *parallel machine,* as contrasted with the serial principles being considered for the EDVAC. (In the EDVAC the peculiar characteristics of the acoustic delay line, as well as various other considerations, seem to justify a serial procedure. For more details cf, the reports referred to in 4.1.) The essential difference between these two systems lies in the method of performing an addition; in a parallel machine all corresponding pairs of digits are added simultaneously, whereas in a serial one these pairs are added serially in time.

4.4 To summarize, we assume that the fast electronic memory consists of 40 Selectrons which are switched in parallel by a common switching arrangement. The inputs of the switch are controlled by the Control.

4.5 Inasmuch as a great many highly important classes of problems require a far greater total memory than 2^{12} words, we now consider the next stage in our storage hierarchy. Although the solution of partial differential equations frequently involves the manipulation of many thousands of words, these data are generally required only in blocks which are well within the 2^{12} capacity of the electronic memory. Our second form of storage must therefore be a medium which feeds these blocks of words to the electronic memory. It should be controlled by the Control of the computer and is thus an integral part of the system, not requiring human intervention.

There are evidently two distinct problems raised above. One can choose a given medium for storage such as teletype tapes, magnetic wire or tapes, movie film or similar media. There still remains the problem of automatic integration of this storage medium with the machine. This integration is achieved logically by introducing appropriate orders into the code which can instruct the machine to read or write on the medium, or to move it by a given amount or to a place with given characteristics. We discuss this question a little more fully in 6.8.

Let us return now to the question of what properties the secondary storage medium should have. It clearly should be able to store information for periods of time long enough so that only a few percent of the total computing time is spent in re-registering information that is "fading" off. It is certainly desirable, although not imperative, that information can be erased and replaced by new data. The medium should be such that it can be controlled, i.e., moved forward and backward, automatically. This consideration makes certain media, such as punched cards, undesirable. While cards can, of course, be printed or read by appropriate orders from some machine, they are not well adapted to problems in which the output data are fed directly back into the machine, and are required in a sequence which is non-monotone with respect to the order of the cards. The medium should be capable of remembering very large numbers of data at a much smaller price than electronic devices. It must be fast enough so that, even when it has to be used frequently in a problem, a large percentage of the total solution time is not spent in getting data into and out of this medium and achieving the desired positioning on it. If this condition is not reasonably well met, the advantages of the high electronic speeds of the machine will be largely lost.

Both light- or electron-sensitive film and magnetic wires or tapes, whose motions are controlled by servo-mechanisms integrated with the Control, would seem to fulfill our needs reasonably well. We have tentatively decided to use magnetic wires since we have achieved reliable performance with them at pulse rates of the order of 25,000 per second and beyond.

4.6 Lastly our memory hierarchy requires a vast quantity of dead storage, i.e., storage not integrated with the machine. This storage requirement may be satisfied by a library of wires that can be introduced into the machine when desired and at that time become automatically controlled. Thus our dead storage really is nothing but an extension of our secondary storage medium. It differs from the latter only in its availability to the machine.

4.7 We impose one additional requirement on our secondary memory. It must be possible for a human to put words onto the wire or other substance used and to read the words put on by the machine. In this manner the human can control the machine's functions. It is now clear that the secondary storage medium is really nothing other than a part of our input-output system.

4.8 There is another highly important part of the input-output which we merely mention at this time, namely, some mechanism for viewing graphically the results of a given computation. This can, of course, be achieved by a Selectron-like tube which causes its screen to fluoresce when data are put on it by an electron beam.

4.9 For definiteness in the subsequent discussions we assume that associated with the output of each Selectron is a flip-flop. This assemblage of 40 flip-flops we term the *Selectron Register*.

5.0 The arithmetic organ.

5.1 In this chapter we discuss the features we now consider desirable for the arithmetic part of our machine. We give our tentative conclusions as to which of the arithmetic operations should be built into the machine and which should be programmed. Finally, a schematic of the arithmetic unit is described.

5.2 In a discussion of the arithmetical organs of a computing machine one is naturally led to a consideration of the number system to be adopted. In spite of the long-standing tradition of building digital machines in the decimal system, we feel strongly in favor of the binary system for our device. Our fundamental unit of memory is naturally adapted to the binary system since we do not attempt to measure gradations of charge at a particular point in the Selectron but are content to distinguish two states. The flip-flop again is truly a binary device. On magnetic wires or tapes and in acoustic delay line memories one is also content to recognize the presence or absence of a pulse or (if a carrier frequency is used) of a pulse train, or of the sign of a pulse. (We will not discuss here the ternary possibilities of a positive or negative or no pulse system and their relationship to questions of reliability and checking, nor the very interesting possibilites of carrier frequency modulation.) Hence if one contemplates using a decimal system with either the Iconoscope or delay line memory one is forced into a binary coding of the decimal system—each decimal digit being represented by at least a tetrad of binary digits. Thus an accuracy of ten decimal digits requires at least 40 binary digits. In a true binary representation of numbers, however, about 33 digits suffice to achieve a precision of 10^{10}. The use of the binary system is therefore somewhat more economical of equipment than is the decimal.

The main virtue of the binary system as against the decimal is, however, the greater simplicity and speed with which the elementary operations can be performed. To illustrate, consider multiplication by repeated addition. In binary multiplication the product of a particular digit of the multiplier by the multiplicand is either the multiplicand or null according as the multiplier digit is 1 or 0. In the decimal system, however, this product has ten possible values between null and nine times the multiplicand, inclusive. Of course, a decimal number has only $\log_{10}2 \sim .3$ times as many digits as a binary number of the same accuracy, but even so multiplication in the decimal system is considerably larger than in the binary system. One can accelerate decimal multiplication by complicating the circuits, but this fact is irrelevant to the point just made since binary multiplication can likewise be accelerated by adding to the equipment. Similar remarks may be made about the other operations.

An additional point that deserves emphasis is this: an important part of the machine is not arithmetical, but logical in nature. Now logics, being a yes-no system, is fundamentally binary. Therefore a binary arrangement of the arithmetical organs contributes very significantly towards producing a more homogenous machine, which can be better integrated and is more efficient.

The one disadvantage of the binary system from the human

point of view is the conversion problem. Since, however, it is completely known how to convert numbers from one base to another and since this conversion can be effected solely by the use of the usual arithmetic processes there is no reason why the computer itself cannot carry out this conversion. It might be argued that this is a time consuming operation. This, however, is not the case. Indeed a general-purpose computer used as a scientific research tool, is called upon to do a very great number of multiplications upon a relatively small amount of input data, and hence the time consumed in the decimal to binary conversion is only a trivial percent of the total computing time. A similar remark is applicable to the output data.

In the preceding discussion we have tacitly assumed the desirability of introducing and withdrawing data in the decimal system. We feel, however, that the base 10 may not even be a permanent feature in a scientific instrument and consequently will probably attempt to train ourselves to use numbers base 2 or 8 or 16. The reason for the bases 8 or 16 is this: since 8 and 16 are powers of 2 the conversion to binary is trivial; since both are about of the size of 10, they violate many of our habits less badly than base 2.

5.3 Several of the digital computers being built or planned in this country and England are to contain a so-called "floating decimal point." This is a mechanism for expressing each word as a characteristic and a mantissa—e.g., 123. 45 would be carried in the machine as (0.12345, 03), where the 3 is the exponent of 10 associated with the number. There appear to be two major purposes in a "floating" decimal point system both of which arise from the fact that the number of digits in a word is a constant, fixed by design considerations for each particular machine. The first of these purposes is to retain in a sum or product as many significant digits as possible and the second of these is to free the human operator from the burden of estimating and inserting into a problem "scale factors"—multiplicative constants which serve to keep numbers within the limits of the machine.

There is, of course, no denying the fact that human time is consumed in arranging for the introduction of suitable scale factors. We only argue that the time so consumed is a very small percentage of the total time we will spend in preparing an interesting problem for our machine. The first advantage of the floating point is, we feel, somewhat illusory. In order to have such a floating point one must waste memory capacity which could otherwise be used for carrying more digits per word. It would therefore seem to us not at all whether the modest advantages of a floating binary point offset the loss of memory capacity and the increased complexity of the arithmetic and control circuits.

There are certainly some problems within the scope of our device which really require more than 2^{-40} precision. To handle such problems we wish to plan in terms of words whose lengths are some fixed integral multiple of 40 and program the machine in such a manner as to give the corresponding aggregates of 40 digit words the proper treatment. We must then consider an addition or multiplication as a complex operation programmed from a number of primitive additions or multiplications. There would seem to be considerable extra difficulties in the way of such a procedure in an instrument with a floating binary point.

The reader may remark upon our alternate spells of radicalism and conservatism in deciding upon various possible features for our mechanism. We hope, however, that he will agree on closer inspection, that we are guided by a consistent and sound principle in judging the merits of any idea. We wish to incorporate into the machine—in the form of circuits—only such logical concepts as are either necessary to have a complete system or highly convenient because of the frequency with which they occur and the influence they exert in the relevant mathematical situations.

5.4 On the basis of this criterion we definitely wish to build into the machine circuits which will enable it to form the binary sum of two 40 digit numbers. We make this decision not because addition is a logically basic notion but rather because it would slow the mechanism as well as the operator down enormously if each addition were programmed out of the more simple operations of "and," "or," and "not." The same is true for the subtraction. Similarly, we reject the desire to form products by programming them out of additions, the detailed motivation being very much the same as in the case of addition and subtraction. The cases for division and square-rooting are much less clear.

It is well known that the reciprocal of a number a can be formed to any desired accuracy by iterative schemes. One such scheme consists of improving an estimate X by forming $X' = 2X - aX^2$. Thus the new error $1 - aX'$ is $(1 - aX)^2$ which is the square of the error in the preceding estimate. We notice that in the formation of X^1, there are two bonafide multiplications—we do not consider multiplication by 2 as a true product since we will have a facility for shifting right or left in one or two pulse times. If then we somehow could guess $1/a$ to a precision of 2^{-5}, 6 multiplications—3 iterations—would suffice to give a final result good to 2^{-40}. Accordingly a small table of 2^4 entries could be used to get the initial estimate of $1/a$. In this way a reciprocal $1/a$ could be formed in 6 multiplication times, and hence a quotient b/a in 7 multiplication times. Accordingly we see that the question of building a divider is really a function of how fast it can be made to operate compared to the iterative method sketched above: in order to justify its existence, a divider must perform a division in a good deal less than 7 multiplication times. We have however conceived a divider which is much faster than these 7 multiplication times and therefore feel justified in building it, especially since the amount of equipment needed above the requirements of the multiplier is not important.

It is, of course, also possible to handle square roots by iterative techniques. In fact, if X is our estimate of $a^{1/2}$, then $X' = \frac{1}{2}(X + a/X)$ is a better estimate. We see that this scheme involves one division per iteration. As will be seen below in our more detailed examination of the arithmetic organ we do not include a square-rooter in our plans because such a device would involve more equipment than we feel is desirable in a first model.

5.5 The first part of our arithmetic organ requires little discussion at this point. It should be a parallel storage organ which can receive a number and add it to the one already in it, which is also able to clear its contents and which can transmit what it contains. We will call such an organ an *Accumulator*. It is quite conventional in principle in past and present computing machines of the most varied types (e.g.: desk multipliers, standard IBM counters, more modern relay machines, the ENIAC). There are, of course, numerous ways to build such a binary accumulator. We distinguish two broad types of such devices: static and dynamic or pulse-type accumulators. It is first necessary to make a few remarks concerning the arithmetic of binary addition. In a parallel accumulator, the first step in an addition is to add each digit of the addend to the corresponding digit of the augend. The second step is to perform the carries, and this must be done in sequence since a carry may produce a carry. In the worst case, 39 carries will occur. Clearly it is inefficient to allow 39 times as much time for the second step (performing the carries) as for the first step (adding the digits). Hence either the carries must be accelerated, or use must be made of the average number of carries or both . . .

5.7 . . . It is convenient to discuss at this point our treatment of negative numbers, and in order to do that right, it is desirable to make some observations about the treatment of numbers in general.

Our numbers are 40 digit aggregates, the left-most digit being the sign digit, and the other digits genuine binary digits, with positional values $2^{-1}, 2^{-2}, . . ., 2^{-39}$ (going from left to right). Our accumulator will, however, treat the sign digit, too, as a binary digit with the positional value 2^0—at least when it functions as an adder. For numbers between 0 and 1 this is clearly all right: the left-most digit will then be 0, and if 0 at this place is taken to represent a + sign, then the number is correctly expressed with its sign and 39 binary digits.

Let us now consider one or more unrestricted 40 binary digit numbers. The Accumulator will add them, with the digit-adding and the carrying mechanisms functioning normally and identically in all 40 positions. There is one reservation, however: if a carry originates in the left-most position, then it has nowhere to go from there (there being no further positions to the left), it is "lost." This means, of course, that the addend and the augend, both numbers between 0 and 2, produced a sum exceeding 2, and the accumulator, being unable to express a digit with a positional value 2^1, which would now be necessary, omitted 2, i.e. the sum was formed correctly, excepting a possible error 2. If several such additions are performed in succession, then the ultimate error may be any integer multiple of 2, i.e. the accumulator is an adder which allows errors that are integer multiples of 2—it is an adder *modulo 2*.)

It should be noted that our convention of placing the binary point immediately to the right of the left-most digit has nothing to do with the structure of the adder. In order to make this point clearer we proceed to discuss the possibilities of positioning the binary point in somewhat more detail.

We begin by enumerating the 40 digits of our numbers (words) from left to right. In doing this we use an index $h = 1$, ., 40. Now we might have placed the binary point just as well between digits j and $j+1$, $j=0, 1, . , 40$. Note, that $j=0$ corresponds to the position at the extreme left (there is no digit $h=j=0$); $j=40$ corresponds to the position at the extreme right (there is no position $h= j+1 = 41$); and $j=1$ corresponds to our above choice. Whatever our choice of j, it does not affect the correctness of the Accumulator's addition. (This is equally true for subtraction, but not for multiplication and division. Indeed, we have merely multiplied all numbers by 2^{j1} (as against our previous convention), and such a "change of scale" has no effect on addition (and subtraction). However, now the accumulator is an adder which allows errors that are integer multiples of 2^j— it is an adder *modulo 2^j*. We mention this because it is occasionally convenient to think in terms of a convention which places the binary point at the right end of the digital aggregate. Then $j=40$, our numbers are integers, and the accumulator is an adder *modulo 2^{40}*. We must emphasize, however, that all of this, i.e. all attributions of values to j, are purely convention—i.e. it is solely the mathematicians interpretation of the functioning of the machine—and not a physical feature of the machine. This convention will necessitate measures that have to be made effective by actual physical features of the machine—i.e. the convention will become a physical and engineering reality—only when we come to the organs of multiplication.

. . . Since x and y are 39 digit binaries, their exact product xy is a 78 digit binary (we disregard the sign digit throughout). However, A will only hold 39 of these. These are clearly the left 39 digits of xy. The right 39 digits of xy are dropped from

A one by one in the course of the 39 steps, or to be more specific, of the 39 right shifts. We will see later that these right 39 digits of xy should and will also be conserved. The left 39 digits, which remain in A, should also be rounded off, but we will not discuss this matter here.

To complete the general picture of our multiplication technique we must consider how we sense the respective digits of our multiplier. There are two schemes which come to one's mind in this connection. One is to have a gate tube associated with each flip-flop of AR in such a fashion that this gate is open if a digit is 1 and closed if it is null. We would then need a 39 stage counter to act as a switch which would successfully stimulate these gate tubes to react. A more efficient scheme is to build into AR a shifter circuit which enables AR to be shifted one stage to the right each time A is shifted and to sense the value of the digit in the right-most flip-flop of AR. The shifter itself requires one gate tube per stage. We need in addition a counter to count out the 39 steps of the multiplication, but this can be achieved by a six stage binary counter. Thus the latter is more economical of tubes and has one additional virtue from our point of view which we discuss in the next paragraph.

The choice of 40 digits to a word (including the sign) is probably adequate for most computational problems but situations certainly might arise when we desire higher precision, i.e. words of greater length. A trivial illustration of this would be the computation of π to more places than are now known (about 700 decimals, i.e. about 2,300 binaries). More important instances are the solutions of N linear equations in N variables for large values of N. The extra precision becomes probably necessary when N exceeds a limit somewhere between 20 and 40. A justification of this estimate has to be based on a detailed theory of numerical matrix inversion which will be given in a subsequent report. It is therefore desirable to be able to handle numbers of 39k digits and sign by means of program instructions. One way to achieve this end is to use k words to represent a 39k digit number with sign. (In this way 39 digits in each 40 digit word are used, but all sign digits, excepting the first one, are apparently wasted.) It is, of course, necessary in this case to instruct the machine to perform the elementary operations of arithmetic in a manner that conforms with this interpretation of k-word complexes as single numbers. In order to be able to treat numbers in this manner, it is desirable to keep not 39 digits in a product, but 78. To accomplish this end (conserving 78 product digits) we connect, via our shifter circuit, the right-most digit of A with the left-most non-sign digit of AR. Thus, when in the process of multiplication a shift is ordered, the last digit of A is transferred into the place in AR made vacant when the multiplier was shifted.

5.9 To conclude our discussion of the multiplication of positive numbers, we note this:

As described thus far, the multiplier forms the 78 digit product, xy, for a 39 digit multiplier x and a 39 digit multiplicand y. We assumed $x \geq O$, $y \leq O$ and therefore had $xy \geq O$, and we will depart from these assumptions only in 5.10. In addition to these, however, we also assumed $x < 1$, $y < 1$, i.e. that x, y have their binary points both immediately right of the sign digit, which implied the same for xy. One might question the necessity of these additional assumptions.

Prima facie they may seem mere conventions, which affect only the mathematician's interpretation of the functioning of the machine, and not a physical feature of the machine. Indeed: if x had its binary point between digits j and $j+1$ from the left and y between k and $k+1$, then our above method of multiplication would still give the correct result xy, provided that the position of the binary point in xy is appropriately assigned. Specifically: let the binary point of xy be between digits χ and $\chi + 1$. x has the binary point between digits j and $j+1$, and its sign digit is 0, hence its range is $0 \leq x < 2^{j-1}$. Similarly y has the range $0 \leq y < 2^{k-1}$, and xy has the range $0 \leq y < 2^{1-1}$. Now the ranges of x and y imply that the range of xy is necessarily $0 \leq xy < 2^{j-1} 2^{k-1} = 2^{j+k-2}$. Hence $\chi = j+k-1$. Thus it might seem that our actual positioning of the binary point—immediately right of the sign digit, i.e. $j=k=1$—is still a mere convention.

It is therefore important to realize that this is not so: the choices of j and k actually correspond to very real, physical, engineering decisions. The reason for this is as follows: it is desirable to base the running of the machine on a sole, consistent mathematical interpretation. It is therefore desirable that all arithmetical operations be performed with an identically conceived positioning of the binary point in A. Applying this principle to x and y gives $j = k$. Hence the position of the binary point for xy is given by $j+k-1 = 2j-1$. If this is to be the same as for x, and y, then $2j-1 = j$, i.e. $j = 1$ ensues—that is our above positioning of the binary point immediately right of the sign digit.

There is one possible escape: To place into A not the left 39 digits of xy (not counting the sign digit 0), but the digits j to $j+38$ from the left. Indeed, in this way the position of the binary point of xy will be $(2j-1) - (j-1) = j$, the same as for x and y.

This procedure means that we drop the left j-1 and right 40-j digits of xy and hold the middle 39 in A. Note, that positioning of the binary point means that $x < 2^{j-1}$, $y < 2^{j-1}$ and xy can only be used if $xy < 2^{j-1}$. Now the assumptions secure only $xy < 2^{j-2}$. Hence xy must be 2^{j-1} times smaller than it might be. This is just the thing which would be secured by the vanishing of the left j-1 digits that we had to drop from A as shown above.

If we wanted to use such a procedure, with those dropped left j-1 digits really existing, i.e. with $j \neq 1$, then we would have to make physical arrangements for their conservation elsewhere. Also the general mathematical planning for the machine would be definitely complicated, due to the physical fact that A now holds a rather arbitrarily picked middle stretch of 39 digits from among the 78 digits of xy. Alternatively, we might fail to make such arrangements, but this would necessitate to see to it in the mathematical planning of each problem, that all products turn out to be 2^{j-1} times smaller than their a priori maxima. Such an observance is not at all impossible, indeed similar things are unavoidable for the other operations. (E.g. with a factor 2 in addition [of positives] or subtraction [of opposite sign quantities]. However, it involves a loss of significant digits, and the choice $j=1$ makes it unnecessary in multiplication.)

We will therefore make our choice $j=1$, i.e. the positioning of the binary point immediately right of the sign digit, binding for all that follows. . . .

Part Two

5.11 ... In discussing the multiplicative organs of our machine
we must return to a consideration of the types of accumulators.
The static accumulator operates as an adder by simultaneously
applying static voltages to its two inputs—one for each of the
two numbers being added. When steady-state operation is
reached the total sum is formed complete with all carries. For
such an accumulator the above discussion is substantially complete, except that it should be remarked that such a circuit
requires at most 39 rise times to complete a carry. Actually it is
possible that the duration of these successive rises is proportional to a lower power of 39 than the first one.

Each stage of a dynamic accumulator consists of a binary
counter for registering the digit and a flip-flop for temporary
storage of the carry. The counter receives a pulse if a 1 is to be
added in at that place; if this causes the counter to go from 1 to
0, a carry has occurred and hence the carry flip-flop will be set.
It then remains to perform the carries. Each flip-flop has associated with it a gate, the output of which is connected to the
next binary counter to the left. The carry is begun by pulsing all
carry gates. Now a carry may produce a carry, so that the process needs to be repeated until all carry flip-flops register 0. This
can be detected by means of a circuit involving a sensing tube
connected to each carry flip-flop. An alternative scheme is to
connect a gate tube to each binary counter which will detect
whether an incoming carry pulse would produce a carry and
will, under this circumstance, pass the incoming carry pulse
directly to the next stage. This circuit would require at most 39
rise times for the completion of the carry.

At the present time the development of a static accumulator
is being concluded. From preliminary tests it seems that it will
add two numbers in about 5μ and will shift right or left in
about 1μ.

We return now to the multiplication operation. In a static
accumulator we order simultaneously an addition of the multiplicand with sign deleted or the sign of the multiplicand and a
complete carry and then a shift for each of the 39 steps. In a
dynamic accumulator of the second kind just described we order

in succession an addition of the multiplicand with sign deleted or the sign of the multiplicand, a complete carry, and a shift for each of the 39 steps. In a dynamic accumulator of the first kind we can avoid losing the time required for completing the carry (in this case an average of 5 pulse times) at each of the 39 steps. We order an addition by the multiplicand with sign deleted or the sign of the multiplicand, then order one pulsing of the carry gates, and finally shift the contents of both the digit counters and the carry flip-flops. This process is repeated 39 times. A simple arithmetical analysis which may be carried out in a later report, shows that at each one of these intermediate stages a single carry is adequate, and that a complete set of carries is needed at the end only. We then carry out the complement corrections, still without ever ordering a complete set of carry operations. When all these corrections are completed and after round off, described below, we then order the complete carry mentioned above . . .

. . . 5.13 We might mention at this time a complication which arises when a floating binary point is introduced into the machine. The operation of addition which usually takes at most 1/10 of a multiplication time becomes much longer in a machine with floating binary since one must perform shifts and round-offs as well as additions. It would seem reasonable in this case to place the time of an addition at about ⅓ to ½ of a multiplication. At this rate it is clear that the number of additions in a problem is as important a factor in the total solution time as are the number of multiplications.

5.14 We conclude our discussion of the arithmetic unit with a description of our method for handling the division operation. Before proceeding let us consider the so-called *restoring* and *non-restoring* methods of division. In order to be able to make certain comparisons, we will do this for a general base m = 2, 3 . . . .

Assume for the moment that divisor and dividend are both positive. The ordinary process of division consists of subtracting from the partial remainder (at the very beginning of the process this is, of course, the dividend) the divisor, repeating this until the former becomes smaller than the latter. For any fixed positional value in the quotient in a well-conducted division this need be done at most m-1 times: If, after precisely k = 0, 1, . . . , m-1 repetitions of this step, the partial remainder has indeed become less than the divisor, then the digit k is put in the quotient (at the position under consideration), the partial remainder is shifted one place to the left, and the whole process is repeated for the next position, etc., etc. Note that the above comparison of sizes is only needed at k = 0, 1, . . . , m-2, i.e. before step 1 and after steps 1, . . . , m-2. If the value k = m-1, i.e. the point after step m-1, is at all reached in a well-conducted division, then it may be taken for granted without any test, that the partial remainder has become smaller than the divisor, and the operations on the position under consideration can therefore be concluded. (In the binary system, m = 2, there is thus only one step, and only one comparison of sizes before this step.) In this way this scheme, known as the *restoring* scheme, requires a maximum of m-1 comparisons and utilizes the digits 0, 1, . . . , m-1 in each place in the quotient. The difficulty of this scheme for machine purposes is that usually the only economical method for comparing two numbers as to size is to subtract one from the other. If the partial remainder r_n were less than the dividend d, one would then have to add d back into $r_n - d$ in order to restore the remainder. Thus at every stage an unnecessary operation would be performed. A more symmetrical scheme is obtained by *not restoring*. In this method (from here on we need not assume the positivity of divisor and dividend) one compares the signs of r_n and d, if they are of the same sign, the dividend is repeatedly subtracted from the remainder until the signs become opposite; if they are opposite, the dividend is repeatedly added to the remainder until the signs again become like. In this scheme the digits that may occur in a given place in the quotient are evidently ± 1, ± 2 . . . , $\pm (m-1)$, the positive digits corresponding to subtractions and the negative ones to addition of the dividend to the remainder.

Thus we have 2(m-1) digits instead of the usual m digits. In the decimal system this would mean 18 digits instead of 10. This is a redundant notation. The standard form of the quotient must therefore be restored by subtracting from the aggregate of its positive digits the aggregate of its negative digits. This requires carry facilities in the place where the quotient is stored.

We propose to store the quotient in the Accumulator Register AR, which has no carry facilities. Hence we could not use this scheme if we were to operate in the decimal system.

The same objection applies to any base m for which the digital representation in question is redundant —i.e. when $2(m\text{-}1) >$ m. Now $2(m\text{-}1) >$ m whenever $m > 2$, but $2(m\text{-}1) = m$ for $m = 2$. Hence, with the use of a register which we have so far contemplated, this division scheme is certainly excluded from the start unless the binary system is used.

Let us now investigate the situation in the binary system. We inquire if it is possible to obtain a quasi-quotient by using the non-restoring scheme and by using the digits 1, 0 instead of 1, -1. Or rather we have to ask this question: Does the quasi-quotient bear a simple relationship to the true quotient?

Let us momentarily assume this question can be answered affirmatively and describe the division procedure. We store the divisor initially in the *Accumulator* A, the dividend in the *Selectron Register SR,* and wish to form the quotient in AR. We now either add or subtract the contents of SR into A, according to whether the signs in A and SR are opposite or the same, and insert correspondingly a 0 or 1 in the right-hand place of AR. We then shift both A and AR one place left, with electronic shifters that are parts of these two aggregates.

Multiplication required an ability to shift right in both A and AR. We have now found that division similarly requires an ability to shift left in both A and AR. Hence both organs must be able to shift both ways electronically. Since these abilities have to be present for the implicit needs of multiplication and division, it is just as well to make use of them explicitly in the form of explicit orders. It will, however, turn out to be convenient to arrange some details in the shifts, when they occur explicitly under the control of those orders, differently from when they occur implicitly under the control of a multiplication or a division.

The process described above will have to be repeated as many times as the number of quotient digits that we consider appropriate to produce in this way. This is likely to be 39 or 40.

6.0 The control

6.1 It has already been stated that the computer will contain an organ, called the Control, which can automatically execute the orders stored in the Selectrons. Actually, for a reason stated in 6.3, the orders for this computer are less than half as long as a forty binary digit number, and hence the orders are stored in the Selectron memory in pairs.

Let us consider the routine that the Control performs in directing a computation. The Control must know the location in the Selectron memory of the pair of orders to be executed. It must direct the Selectrons to transmit this pair of orders to the Selectron Register and then to itself. It must then direct the execution of the operation specified in the first of the two orders. Among these orders we can immediately describe two major types: an order of the first type begins by causing the transfer of the number, which is stored at a specified memory location, from the Selectrons to the Selectron Register. Next, it causes the arithmetical unit to perform some arithmetical operations on this number (usually in conjunction with another number which is already in the arithmetical unit), and to retain the resulting number in the arithmetical unit. The second type order causes the transfer of the number, which is held in the arithmetical unit, into the Selectron Register, and from there to a specified memory location in the Selectrons. (It may also be that this latter operation will permit a direct transfer from the arithmetical unit into the Selectrons.) An additional type of orders consists of the transfer orders of 3.5. Further orders control the inputs and the outputs of the machine. The process described at the beginning of this paragraph must then be repeated with the second order of the order pair. The entire routine is repeated until the end of the problem.

6.2 It is clear from what has just been stated that the Control must have a means of switching to a specified location in the Selectron memory, for withdrawing both numbers for the computation and pairs of orders. Since the Selectron memory (as tentatively planned) will hold $2^{12} = 4096$ forty-digit words (a word is either a number or a pair of orders), a twelve-digit binary number suffices to identify a memory location. Hence a switching mechanism is required which will, on receiving a twelve-digit binary number, select the corresponding memory location.

The type of circuit we propose to use for this purpose is known as a decoding or many-one function table. It has been developed in various forms independently by J. Rajchman and P. Crawford. It consists of n flip-flops which register an n digit binary number. It also has a maximum of 2^n output wires. The flip-flops activate a matrix in which the interconnections between input and output wires are made in such a way that one and and only one of 2^n output wires is selected (i.e. has a positive voltage applied to it). These interconnections may be established by means of resistors or by means of non-linear elements (such as diodes or rectifiers); all these various methods are under investigation. The Selectron is so designed that four such function table switches are required, each with a three digit entry and eight (2^3) outputs. Four sets of eight wires each are brought out of the Selectron for switching purposes, and a particular location is selected by making one wire positive with respect to the remainder. Since all forty Selectrons are switched in parallel, these four sets of wires may be connected directly to the four function table outputs.

6.3 Since most computer operations involve at least one number located in the Selectron memory, it is reasonable to adopt a code in which twelve binary digits of every order are assigned to the specification of a Selectron location. In those orders which do not require a number to be taken out of or into the Selectrons these digit positions will not be used.

Though it has not been definitely decided how many operations will be built into the computer (i.e. how many different orders the Control must be able to understand), it will be seen presently that there will probably be more than 2^5 but certainly less than 2^6. For this reason it is feasible to assign 6 binary digits for the order code. It thus turns out that each order must contain eighteen binary digits, the first twelve identifying a memory location and the remaining six specifying an operation. It can now be explained why orders are stored in the memory in pairs. Since the same memory organ is to be used in this computer for both orders and numbers, it is efficient to make the length of each about equivalent. But numbers of eighteen binary digits would not be sufficiently accurate for problems which this machine will solve. Rather, an accuracy of at least 10^{-10} or 2^{-33} is required. Hence it is preferable to make the numbers long enough to accommodate two orders.

Our numbers will actually have 40 binary digits each. This allows 20 binary digits for each order, i.e. the 12 digits that specify a memory location, and 8 more digits specifying the nature of the operation (instead of the minimum of 6 referred to above). It is convenient to group these binary digits into *tetrads,* groups of 4 binary digits. Hence a whole word consists of 10 tetrads, a half word or order of 5 tetrads, and of these 3 specify a memory location and the remaining 2 specify the nature of the operation. Outside the machine each tetrad can be expressed by a base 16 digit. (The base 16 digits are best designated by symbols of the 10 decimal digits 0 to 9, and 6 additional symbols, e.g. the letters a to f.) These 16 characters should appear in the typing for and the printing from the machine.

The specification of the nature of the operation that is involved in an order occurs in binary form, so that another many-one or decoding function is required to decode the order. This function table will have six input flip-flops (the two remaining digits of the order are not needed). Since there will not be 64 different orders, not all 64 outputs need be provided. However, it is perhaps worthwhile to connect the outputs corresponding to unused order possibilities to a checking circuit which will give an indication whenever a code word unintelligible to the control is received in the input flip-flops.

The function table just described energizes a different output wire for each different code operation. As will be shown later, many of the steps involved in executing different orders overlap. (For example, addition, multiplication, division, and going from the Selectrons to the register all include transferring a number from the Selectrons to the Selectron Register.) For this reason it is perhaps desirable to have an additional set of control wires, each of which is activated by any particular combination of different code digits. These may be obtained by taking the output wires of the many-one function table and using them to operate tubes which will in turn operate a one-many (or coding) function table. Such a function table consists of a matrix, as before, but in this case only one of the input wires is activated at any one time, while various sets of one or more of the output wires are activated. This particular table may be referred to as the recoding function table.

RECODING FUNCTION TABLE

SYMBOLIZATION

Complete	Abbre-viated	
1. $S(x) \rightarrow Ac^+$	x	Clear Accumulator and add number located at position x in the Selectrons into it.
2. $S(x) \rightarrow Ac$	x_	Clear Accumulator and subtract number located at position x in the Selectrons into it.
3. $S(x) \rightarrow AcM$	x M	Clear Accumulator and add absolute value of number located at position x in the Selectrons into it.
4. $S(x) \rightarrow Ac M$	x _M	Clear Accumulator and subtract absolute value of number located at position x in the Selectrons into it.
5. $S(x) \rightarrow Ah^+$	x h	Add number located at position x in the Selectrons into the Accumulator.
6. $S(x) \rightarrow Ah$	x h_	Subtract number located at position x in the Selectrons into the Accumulator.
7. $S(x) \rightarrow AhM$	x hM	Add absolute value of number located at position x in the Selectrons into the Accumulator.
8. $S(x) \rightarrow Ah M$	x _hM	Subtract absolute value of number located at position x in the Selectrons into the Accumulator.
9. $S(x) \rightarrow R$	x R	Clear Register* and add number located at position x in the Selectrons into it.
10. $R \rightarrow A$	A	Clear Accumulator and shift number held in Register into it.
11. $S(x) XR \rightarrow A$	x X	Clear Accumulator and multiply the number located at position x in the Selectrons by the number in the Register, placing the left-hand 39 digits of the answer in the Accumulator and the right-hand 39 digits of the answer in the Register.

12. A÷S(x) → R	x ÷	Clear Register and divide the number in the Accumulator by the number located in position x of the Selectrons, leaving the remainder in the Accumulator and placing the quotient in the Register.
13. Cu → S(x)	x C	Shift the Control to the left-hand order of the order pair located at position x in the Selectrons.
14. Cu' → S(x)	x C'	Shift the Control to the right-hand order of the order pair located at position x in the Selectrons.
15. Cc → S(x)	x Cc	If the number in the Accumulator is ≥ 0, shift the Control as in Cu → S(x).
16. Cc' → S(x)	x Cc'	If the number in the Accumulator is ≥ 0, shift the Control as in Cu' → S(x).
17. At → S(x)	x S	Transfer the number in the Accumulator to position x in the Selectrons.
18. Ap → S(x)	x Sp	Replace the left-hand 12 digits of the left-hand order located at position x in the Selectrons by the left-hand 12 digits in the Accumulator.
19. Ap' → S(x)	x Sp'	Replace the left-hand 12 digits of the right-hand order located at position x in the Selectrons by the left-hand 12 digits in the Accumulator.
20. L	L	Multiply the number in the Accumulator by 2, leaving it there.
21. R	R	Divide the number in the Accumulator by 2, leaving it there.

* Register means Arithmetic Register.

The twelve flip-flops operating the four function tables used in selecting a Selectron position, and the six flip-flops operating the function table used for decoding the order, are referred to as the *Function Table Register,* FR.

6.4 Let us consider next the process of transferring a pair of orders from the Selectrons to the Control. These orders first go into SR. The order which is to be used next may be transferred directly into FR. The second order of the pair must be removed from SR (since SR may be used when the first order is executed), but can not as yet be placed in FR. Hence a temporary storage is provided for it. The storage means is called the *Control Register,* CR, and consists of 20 (or possibly 18) flip-flops, capable of receiving a number from SR and transmitting a number to FR.

As already stated (6.1), the Control must know the location of the pair of orders it is to get from the Selectron memory. Normally this location will be the one following the location of the two orders just executed. That is, until it receives an order to do otherwise, the Control will take its orders from the Selectrons in sequence. Hence the order location may be remembered in a twelve stage binary counter (one capable of counting 2^{12}) to which one unit is added whenever a pair of orders is executed. This counter is called the *Control Counter,* CC.

The details of the process of obtaining a pair of orders from the Selectron are thus as follows. The contents of CC are copied into FR, the proper Selectron location is selected, and the contents of the Selectrons are transferred to SR. FR is then cleared, and the contents of SR are transferred to it and CR. CC is advanced by one unit so the Control will be prepared to select the next pair of orders from the memory. (There is, however, an exception from this last rule for the so-called transfer orders. This may feed CC in a different manner, cf. the next paragraph below.) First the order in FR is executed and then the order in CR is transferred to FR and executed. It should be noted that all these operations are directed by the Control itself, not only the operations specified in the Control words sent to FR but also the automatic operations required to get the correct orders there.

Since the method by means of which the Control takes order pairs in sequence from the memory has been described, it only remains to consider how the Control shifts itself from one sequence of control orders to another in accordance with the operations described in 3.5. The execution of these operations is relatively simple. An order calling for one of these operations contains the twelve digit specification of the position to which the Control is to be switched, and these digits will appear in the left-hand twelve flip-flops of FR. All that is required to shift the

Control is to transfer the contents of these flip-flops to CC. When the Control goes to the Selectrons for the next pair of orders it will then go to the location specified by the number so transferred. In the case of the unconditional transfer, the transfer is made automatically; in the case of the conditional transfer it is made only if the sign counter of the Accumulator registers zero.

6.5 In this report we will discuss only the general method by means of which the Control will execute specific orders, leaving the details until later. It has already been explained (5.5) that when a circuit is to be designed to accomplish a particular elementary operation (such as addition), a choice must be made between a static type and a dynamic type circuit. When the design of the Control is considered, this same choice arises. The function of the Control is to direct a sequence of operations which take place in the various circuits of the computer (including the circuits of the Control itself). Consider what is involved in directing an operation. The Control must signal for the operation to begin, it must supply whatever signals are required to specify that particular operation, and it must in some way know when the operation has been completed so that it may start the succeeding operation. Hence the control circuits must be capable of timing the operation. It should be noted that timing is required whether the circuit performing the operation is static or dynamic. In the case of a static type circuit the Control must supply static control signals for a period of time sufficient to allow the output voltages to reach the steady-state condition. In the case of a dynamic type circuit the Control must send various pulses at proper intervals to this circuit.

If all circuits of a computer are static in character, the control timing circuits may likewise be static, and no pulses are needed in the system. However, though some of the circuits of the computer we are planning will be static, they will probably not all be so, and hence pulses as well as static signals must be supplied by the Control to the rest of the computer. There are many advantages in deriving these pulses from a central source, called the *clock*. The timing may then be done either by means of counters counting clock pulses or by means of electrical delay lines (an RC circuit is here regarded as a simple delay line).

Since the timing of the entire computer is governed by a single pulse source, the computer circuits will be said to operate as a synchronized system.

The clock plays an important role both in detecting and in localizing the errors made by the computer. One method of checking which is under consideration is that of having two identical computers which operate in parallel and automatically compare each other's results. Both machines would be controlled by the same clock, so they would operate in absolute synchronism. It is not necessary to compare every flip-flop of one machine with the corresponding flip-flop of the other. Since all numbers and control words pass through either the Selectron Register or the Accumulator soon before or soon after they are used, it suffices to check the flip-flops of the Selectron Register and the flip-flops of the Accumulator which hold the number registered there; in fact, it seems possible to check the Accumulator only. The checking circuit would stop the clock whenever a difference appeared, or stop the machine in a more direct manner if an asynchronous system is used. Every flip-flop of each computer will be located at a convenient place. In fact, all neons will be located on one panel, the corresponding neons of the two machines being placed in parallel rows so that one can tell at a glance (after the machine has been stopped) where the discrepancies are.

The merits of any checking system must be weighed against its cost. Building two machines may appear to be expensive, but since most of the cost of a scientific computer lies in development rather than production, this consideration is not so important as it might seem. Experience may show that for most problems the two machines need not be operated in parallel. Indeed, in most cases purely mathematical, external checks are possible: smoothness of the results, behavior of differences of various types, validity of suitable identities, redundant calculations, etc. All of these methods are usually adequate to disclose the presence or absence of error in toto, their drawback is only that they may not allow the detailed diagnosing and locating of errors at all or with ease. When a problem is run for the first time, so that it requires special care, or when an error is known to be present, and has to be located—only then will it be necessary as a rule, to use both machines in parallel. Thus, they can be used as separate machines most of the time. The essential feature of such a method of checking lies in the fact that it checks the computation at every point (and hence detects transient errors as well as steady-state ones) and stops the machine when the error occurs so that the process of localizing the fault is greatly simplified. These advantages are only partially gained by duplicating the arithmetic part of the computer, or by following one operation with the complement operation (multiplication by division, etc.), since this fails to check either the memory or the Control (which is the most complicated, though not the largest, part of the machine).

The method of localizing errors, either with or without a duplicate machine, needs further discussion. It is planned to design all circuits (including those of the Control) of the computer so that if the clock is stopped between pulses the computer will retain all its information in flip-flops so that the computation may proceed unaltered when the clock is started again. This principle has already demonstrated its usefulness in the ENIAC. This makes it possible for the machine to compute with the clock operating at any speed below a certain maximum, as long as the clock gives out pulses of constant shape regardless of the spacing between pulses. In particular, the spacing between pulses may be made indefinitely large. The clock will be provided with a mode of operation in which it will emit a single pulse whenever instructed to do so by the operator. By means of this, the operator can cause the machine to go through an operation step by step, checking the results by means of the indicating-lamps connected to the flip-flops. It will be noted that this design principle does not exclude the use of delay lines to obtain delays as long as these are only used to time the constituent operations of a single step, and have no part in determining the machine's operating repetition rate. Timing coincidences by means of delay lines is excluded since this requires a constant pulse rate.

6.6 The orders which the Control understands may be divided into two groups: those that specify operations which are performed within the computer and those that specify operations involved in getting data into and out of the computer. At the present time the internal operations are more completely planned than the input and output operations, and hence they will be discussed more in detail than the latter. The internal operations which have been tentatively adopted are listed in Table I. It has already been pointed out that not all of these operations are logically basic, but that many can be programmed by means of others. In the case of some of these operations the reasons for building them into the Control have already been given. In this section we will give reasons for building the other operations into the Control and will explain in the case of each operation what the Control must do in order to execute it.

6.6.7 One basic question which must be decided before a computer is built is whether the machine is to have a so-called floating binary (or decimal) point. While a floating binary point is undoubtedly very convenient in coding problems, building it into the computer adds greatly to its complexity and hence a choice in this matter should receive very careful attention. However, it should first be noted that the alternatives ordinarily considered (building a machine with a floating binary point vs. doing all computation with a fixed binary point) are not exhaustive and hence that the arguments generally advanced for the floating binary point are only of limited validity. Such arguments overlook the fact that the choice with respect to any particular operation (except for certain basic ones) is not between building it into the computer and not using it at all, but rather between building it into the computer and programming it out of operations built into the computer.

Building a floating binary point into the computer will not only complicate the Control but will also increase the length of a number and hence increase the size of the memory and the arithmetic unit. Every number is effectively increased in size, even though the floating binary point is not needed in many instances. Furthermore, there is considerable redundancy in a floating binary point type of notation, for each number carries with it a scale factor, while generally speaking a single scale factor will suffice for a possibly extensive set of numbers. By means of the operations already described in the report a floating binary point can be programmed. While additional memory capacity is needed for this, it is probably less than that required by a built-in floating binary point since a different scale factor does not need to be remembered for each number.

To program a floating binary point involves detecting where the first zero occurs in a number in A. Since A has shifting facilities this can best be done by means of them. In terms of the operations previously described this would require taking the given number out of A and performing a suitable arithmetical operation on it: for a (multiple) right shift a multiplication, for a (multiple) left shift either one division, or as many doublings (i.e. additions) as the shift has stages. However, these operations are inconvenient and time-consuming, so we propose to introduce two operations (L and R) in order that this (i.e. the single left and right shift) can be accomplished directly. These operations make use of facilities already present in A and hence add very little equipment to the computer. It should be noted that in many instances a single use of L and possibly of R will suffice in programming a floating binary point. . .

6.8 In this section we will consider what must be added to the Control so that it can direct the mechanisms for getting data into and out of the computer and also describe the mechanisms themselves. Three different kinds of input-output mechanisms are planned.

First: Several magnetic wire storage units operated by servomechanisms controlled by the computer.

Second: Some viewing tubes for graphical portrayal of results.

Third: A typewriter for feeding data directly into the computer, not to be confused with the equipment used for preparing and printing from magnetic wires. As presently planned the latter will consist of modified Teletypewriter equipment.

6.8.1 Since there already exists a way of transferring numbers between the Selectrons and A, therefore A may be used for transferring numbers from and to a wire. The latter transfer will be done serially and will make use of the shifting facilities of A. Using A for this purpose eliminates the possibility of computing and reading from or writing on the wires simultaneously. However, simultaneous operation of the computer and the input-output organ requires additional temporary storage and introduces a synchronizing problem, and hence it is not being considered for the first model.

Since, at the beginning of the problem, the computer is empty, facilities must be built into the Control for reading a set of numbers from a wire when the operator presses a manual switch. As each number is read from a wire into A, the Control must transfer it to its proper location in the Selectrons. The CC may be used to count off these positions in sequence, since it is capable of transmitting its contents to FR. A detection circuit on CC will stop the process when the specified number of numbers has been placed in the memory, and the Control will then be shifted to the orders located in the first position of the Selectron memory.

It has already been stated that the entire memory facilities of the wires should be available to the computer without human intervention. This means that the Control must be able to select the proper set of numbers from those going by. Hence additional orders are required for the code. Here, as before, we are faced with two alternatives. We can make the control capable of executing an order of the form: take numbers from positions p to $p + s$ on wire No. k and place them in Selectron locations v to $v + s$. Or we can make the Control capable of executing some less complicated operations which, together with the already given control orders, are sufficient for programming the transfer operation of the first alternative. Since the latter scheme is simpler we adopt it tentatively.

The computer must have some way of finding a particular number on a wire. One method of arranging for this is to have each number carry with it its own location designation. A method more economical of wire memory capacity is to use the Selectron memory facilities to remember the position of each wire. For example, the computer would hold the number t_1 specifying which number on the wire is in position to be read. If the Control is instructed to read the number at position p_1 on this wire, it will compare p_1 with t_1; and if they differ, cause the wire to move in the proper direction. As each number on the wire passes by, one unit is added or subtracted to t_1 and the comparison repeated. When $p_1 = t_1$ numbers will be transferred from the wire to the Accumulator and then to the proper location in the memory. Then both t_1 and p_1 will be increased by 1, and the transfer from the wire to Accumulator to memory repeated. This will be iterated, until $t_1 + s$ and $p_1 + s$ are reached, at which time the Control will direct the wire to stop.

Under this system the Control must be able to execute the following orders with regard to each wire: start the wire forward, start the wire in reverse, stop the wire, transfer from wire to A, and transfer from A to wire. In addition, the wire must signal the Control as each digit is read and when the end of a number has been reached. Conversely, when recording is done the Control must have a means of timing the signals sent from A to the wire, and of counting off the digits. The 2^6 counter used for multiplication and division may be used for the latter purpose, but other timing circuits will be required for the former.

If the method of checking by means of two computers operating simultaneously is adopted, and each machine is built so that it can operate independently of the other, then each will have a separate input-output mechanism. The process of making wires for the computer must then be duplicated, and in this way the work of the person making a wire can be checked. Since the wire servomechanisms cannot be synchronized by the central clock, a problem of synchronizing the two computers when the wires are being used arises. It is probably not practical to synchronize the wire feeds to within a given digit, but this is unnecessary since the numbers coming into the two organs A need not be checked as the individual digits arrive, but only prior to being deposited in the Selectron memory.

6.8.2 Since the computer operates in the binary system, some means of decimal-binary and binary-decimal conversions is highly desirable. Various alternative ways of handling this problem have been considered. In general we recognize two broad classes of solutions to this problem.

First: The conversion problems can be regarded as simple arithmetic processes and programmed as *sub-routines* out of the orders already incorporated in the machine. The conversion time of a word—about 5 milliseconds—is comparable to the reading or withdrawing time for a word—about 2 milliseconds— and is trivial as compared to the solution time for problems to be handled by the computer. It should be noted that the treatment proposed there presupposes only that the decimal data presented to or received from the computer are in tetrads, each tetrad being the binary coding of a decimal digit—the information (precision) represented by a decimal digit being actually equivalent to that represented by 3.3 binary digits. The coding of decimal digits into tetrads of binary digits and the printing of decimal digits from such tetrads can be accomplished quite simply and automatically by slightly modified Teletype equipment.

Second: The conversion problems can be regarded as unique problems and handled by separate conversion equipment incorporated either in the computer proper or associated with the mechanisms for preparing and printing from magnetic wires. Such convertors are really nothing other than special purpose digital computers. They would seem to be justified only for those computers which are primarily intended for solving problems in which the computation time is small compared to the input-output time, to which class our computer does not belong.

6.8.3 It is possible to use various types of cathode ray tubes, and in particular Selectrons for the viewing tubes, in which case programming the viewing operation is quite simple. The viewing Selectrons can be swtched by the same function tables that switch the memory Selectrons. By means of the substitution operation Ap → S (x) and Ap' → S (x), six-digit numbers specifying the abscissa and ordinate of the point (six binary digits represent a precision of one part in $2^6 = 64$, i.e. of about 1.5% which seems reasonable in such a component) can be substituted in this order, which will specify that a particular one of the viewing Selectrons is to be activated.

6.8.4 As was mentioned above, the mechanisms used for preparing and printing from wire for the first model, at least, will be modified Teletype equipment. We are quite fortunate in having secured the full cooperation of the Ordnance Development Division of the National Bureau of Standards in making these modifications and in designing and building some associated equipment.

By means of this modified Teletype equipment an operator first prepares a checked paper tape and then directs the equipment to transfer the information from the paper tape to the magnetic wire. Similarly a magnetic wire can transfer its contents to a paper tape which can be used to operate a Teletypewriter. (Studies are being undertaken to design equipment that will eliminate the necessity for using paper tapes.)

The statement of a new problem on a wire involves data unique to that problem interspersed with data found on previously prepared paper tapes or magnetic wires. The equipment discussed in the previous paragraph makes it possible for the operator to combine conveniently these data onto a single magnetic wire ready for insertion into the computer.

It is frequently very convenient to introduce data into a computation without producing a new wire. Hence it is planned to build one simple typewriter as an integral part of the computer. By means of this typewriter the operator can stop the computation, type in a memory location (which will go to the FR), type in a number (which will go to A and then be placed in the first mentioned location), and start the computation again.

6.8.5 There is one further order that the Control needs to execute. There should be some means by which the computer can signal to the operator when a computation has been concluded, or when the computation has reached a previously determined point. Hence an order is needed which will tell the computer to stop and to flash a light or ring a bell.

Electronic Numerical Integrator and Computer (U.S. Patent)

John Presper Eckert, Jr., and John W. Mauchly

Here is another landmark technical document: the patent application for the first electronic computer, filed on June 26, 1947. At that time the device, known as the ENIAC, for Electronic Numerical Integrator and Calculator, was easily the world's most complex electronic instrument. Its inventors were an electrical engineer, J. Presper Eckert, Jr., and a physicist, John W. Mauchly, both of the University of Pennsylvania, who later moved on to greater triumphs with the invention of the UNIVAC machine, the first commercial computer with a stored program. The ENIAC patent application—filing number 3,120,606 —was assigned to the Sperry Rand Corporation, which also sponsored the UNIVAC.

3,120,606
ELECTRONIC NUMERICAL INTEGRATOR
AND COMPUTER
John Presper Eckert, Jr., and John W. Mauchly, Philadelphia,
Pa., assignors, by mesne assignments, to Sperry Rand Corporation,
a corporation of Delaware
Filed June 26, 1947, Ser. No. 757,158
148 Claims. (Cl. 235—160)

This invention relates to methods and apparatus for performing computations involving arithmetical operations, at extremely high speeds, and with minimum use of mechanical elements, as generally so termed, and more particularly, relates to the art of electrical computing machines, with particular reference to a machine utilizing electronically produced pulses (i.e., sharp voltage changes not greater than five microseconds in duration) to represent digits and numbers, and using such pulses for control and programming operations, thus obviating the need for mechanically moving parts for these purposes. The present invention also relates to the method of using such pulses for computational purposes.

In the progress of development of computing machines from the time of the use of pebbles or grains, and the application of the abacus, to the extensive mechanical or partly mechanical and partly electrical machines of the present day, the aim has been to remove from the mind of man as much as possible of the responsibility of remembering numbers, remembering the necessary computations to be performed, remembering and writing the results of parts of computations, and how and when to use such results of such parts in complete equations, as well as to effect the necessary operations more rapidly and without physical labor.

The art and technique of aids to computation and calculation have been the subject of extensive development, extending through simple adding machines to present day complex computing machines, which include electric devices, in part in answer to the need and demand for greater speed and the elimination of moving mechanisms whose inertia sets a definite limit to the practicable speed of operation.

With the advent of everyday use of elaborate calculations, speed has become paramount to such a high degree that there is no machine on the market today capable of satisfying the full demand of modern computational methods. The most advanced machines have greatly reduced the time required for arriving at solutions to problems which might have required months or days by older procedures. This advance, however, is not adequate for many problems encountered in modern scientific work and the present invention is intended to reduce to seconds such lengthy computations.

In automatic machines the manner of controlling the storing in memory devices of the necessary numerical components and the "programming" of the pickup of these numbers and their transfer to particular operating units, as well as the special programming of peculiar internal arithmetic operations in the units, has involved a problem of foremost importance which it is here sought to advance. In such machines it is convenient to designate as "memories" those parts or elements which are so constituted as to predetermine and cause definite effects from signals transmitted to the system. External memories may consist of switches and coupling between units, arbitrarily made in accordance with the planned use of the apparatus for the solution of a given problem, and of means such as tapes or punched cards and reading machines by which numerical data (numbers pulses) and program instructions (characteristic control pulse signals) are introduced into the apparatus. Functions of the machine by which numbers are stored and control pulse signals stored for subsequent transmission or collection from storage, as well as any automatically generated or guided to particular units, may be termed internal memories.

It is an especial aim to reduce the requirement of external memories in such machines, and to provide for the replacement thereof by internal memories, so that approach to more fully automatic operation is attained by the mere insertion of data in pulse form and the automatic generation within the machine of the necessary further data, including control pulses.

A machine has been constructed at the University of Pennsylvania which embodies our invention. This machine, hereinafter referred to as ENIAC (from the initials of its name, "Electronic Numerical Integrator and Computer") is the first general purpose automatic electronic digital computing machine known to us. Its speed considerably exceeds that of any non-electronic machine, and its accuracy is in general superior to that of any non-digital machine (such as a differential analyzer).

The ENIAC is extremely flexible, and is not fundamentally restricted to any given class of problems. However, there are problems for which its speed is limited by the input and output devices, so that it is impossible to derive the full benefit of its high computing speed in such cases. The ENIAC carries out its entire computing schedule automatically, but the sequence which it is to follow must be set up manually beforehand. The primary intended use of the ENIAC is to compute large families of solutions all based on the same program of operations, in which case the time spent in manual set-up is relatively unimportant.

Automation—The Advent of the Automatic Factory

John Diebold

Soon after the invention of the digital computer, it became clear to some that the machine had applications far beyond the narrow scientific spheres in which it was then used, and that such new applications would inevitably have wide-ranging implications for society. In this contribution, written in 1952, the editor of this book looks first at the opportunity for applying computers to industry, then examines the state of the art and, finally, reflects on the social implications of the computer. Here is a first glimpse at the problems of automation—notably, its impact on employment and leisure time—which were to gain increasing importance in subsequent years, and which will be considered at greater length in later selections.

It is my thesis that a much higher degree of industrial automation is both desirable and technologically possible. The achievement of such a level of automation does not require the postulation of basic technological innovations, for the limiting factor is not technology but the difficulty which men experience in thinking fruitfully in the terms required. But although technology will not form the ultimate limit to the development of automatic machinery, the desires of consumers will put an effective limit to the economic functions which machines will perform. The fears of some that machines will become all pervasive—fears which are today couched in the same terms as the broadsheets and pamphlets of the Luddites—will prove to be even less valid than were those fears expressed at the beginning of the steam age.

A computing machine is a device which handles a number of variables, manipulating them in a predetermined and variable manner, and producing answers, or output, logical according to the rules built into the machine. Computing machines are classified as either digital or analog. A digital device, as the name implies, is one which performs mathematical operations with numbers expressed in the form of digits which can assume only discrete values. The results yielded by such a device are expressed in digits. The precision of such a machine is determined by the number of digits which can be handled. An analog computer is one in which numbers are converted for purposes of calculation into physically measurable quantities such as lengths, voltages, or angles of displacement. Computed results are obtained by the interaction of moving parts or electrical signals. The precision of results, as contrasted with a digital device, depends upon the precision with which the machine is fabricated, the skill with which it is operated, and the precision with which the answer can be read.

At the present time neither of these types of computers has come into wide industrial use. Analog computers will be used to an increasing extent in the control of machine tools, in the operation of certain processes, etc. But for overall factory control, for the programming of production, and for the coordination of the fabricating and materials handling machines of an automatic production line, it is the digital computer to which we must turn.

Digital computers provide the accuracy which is needed for the overall control of an automatic factory, and they serve as a check to the possibility of a cumulative error which might occur if analog computers were used. A digital computer is actually slower in operation than an analog machine; however, slow in this business is no hindrance industrially. Early in our study Professor Howard Aiken, Director of the Harvard Computation Laboratory, laughingly told us, "The units one uses in the computer business are micro-seconds and mega-bucks." And it is the need for micro-seconds in the very complicated mathematical work for which these machines were first built, that produces the cost in mega-bucks. The greatest cost of computers—and the magnitude at present is two to three million dollars for a full scale machine—is the cost of making them react in microseconds. For industrial process control, even for control of a large plant, reactions in a tenth of a second could be fully adequate. In addition, the cost of computers at present is very much a function of the custom building. An order for a small number of similar machines could substantially lower this cost, since a great number of repetitive circuits are used in each machine, thus leading to mass production of the circuits, even though the total number of complete machines demanded was small. Added to this is the fact that present computers are used for solving a great variety of mathematical problems, thus they must be fully flexible. A machine designed specifically for use in an industrial plant can be much simpler, and less flexible, consequently much cheaper.

But how, specifically, can a computer be used industrially? One example is the coordination of a number of production and assembly lines. The great number of variables now handled by the production planning and expediting people could be easily and automatically handled by a computer. The great headache in developing such a system is of course the problem of taping, or building in the "memory" necessary for the machine to act in the manner desired, and the development of input taping, so that changes in production rate, etc. make sense to the machine. It is very difficult to talk about these machines without going further into the details of their construction. For those not desiring to do this it is enough to know that a computer makes logical choices between a series of two alternatives, going from one to the next. The machine can be applied to any task requiring logic. The chief problem in applying them industrially is the problem of determining all the many alternatives to a particular set of conditions—alternatives which human operators carry about in their heads, and which do not occur to one until the task of drawing up a computer schedule is faced.

Today, four large scale digital computing systems using electromechanical relays as primary elements in the arithmetic, storage, transfer, and input-output units are in operation. These four large scale digital computing systems are Harvard Mark I, Harvard Mark II, the Bell Telephone Laboratory's Relay Computing Systems, and the IBM Pluggable Sequence Relay Calculator.

Harvard Mark I—Howard Aiken of Harvard University, T. J. Watson of IBM, and three others developed this machine, starting in 1939. The relays, counters, cam contacts, typewriters, card feeds and card punches employed in this calculator are all standard parts of the tabulating machinery manufactured by IBM.

The external outline of Mark I consists of a 51 foot panel, 8 feet in height, and 6 feet in depth. Along the 51 foot panel are mounted: (1) the sequence control which directs the programming with punched tape, (2) three interpolators which are tape fed units for selecting data required in the interpolation process, (3) functional counters for controlling the interpolation of functions, as well as controlling the printing mechanism, (4) a multiplying-dividing unit for 23 digit accuracy, (5) 72 storage counters for the intermediate storage of results up to 23 digits capacity, and (6) a storage unit with a capacity of 60 23-digit numbers which can be introduced to the machine by manually setting dial switches. The mechanical drive for this computer is a four-horsepower electric motor. The total assembly weighs approximately five tons.

The machine operations are controlled by orders introduced on a coded 24-hole punched tape which consists of three columns of eight holes each. This input tape also controls the time required for the tape to add two numbers, since it is that time which is required for the tape to move one step forward. The control tape can be advanced at the rate of about 200 units per minute.

Mark I can perform arithmetic operations on numbers up to 23 digits in length. Addition and subtraction are performed with a set of 72 electromechanical adding-storage registers which can store 23-digit numbers and can combine numbers which are generated by the machine in the course of its operation.

The 72 registers used in the arithmetic operations provide intermediate storage. Numbers are transferred from one part of the machine to another by timed electrical pulses of 50 volts amplitude on a single transfer bus. It is not therefore possible to transfer simultaneously more than one number.

Harvard Mark II—This calculator was designed by Harvard University for the Naval Proving Ground at Dahlgren, Maryland.

Mark II uses electromechanical relays for the internal storage of numbers, for the transfer of numbers, for performing basic arithmetical operations, and for sequence control of these processes. This machine handles ten-digit decimal numbers. The addition of two ten-digit figures consumes 125 milliseconds, while the multiplication of two ten-digit figures requires 250 milliseconds. About 100 ten-digit numbers can be stored in the machine. Additional internal or intermediate storage may be supplied by punching data on tapes for introduction to the machine at a later time. The machine registers its results on punched tape.

This calculator has twelve input mechanisms for introducing commands and numbers to the machine. All of these input mechanisms employ a punched paper tape. Commands are introduced to the machine on one group of four input tapes. Another group of four input tapes introduces numbers to the machine in any prearranged order. The remaining group of four input tapes is used for suppling the calculator with coded tables of mathematical functions. Eight hundred functional values can be introduced on these punched tapes.

Results are recorded through the use of four page printers, or can be punched in paper tape for future use, if needed.

Six algebraic and transcendental functions are stored permanently within the machine. These functions are the reciprocal, the reciprocal square root, the logarithm, the exponential, the cosine, and the arc tangent. These functions can be calculated for any problem to eight or nine significant figures during a time period of five to twelve seconds.

Bell Telephone Laboratory's Relay Computing Systems—The Bell Laboratory began to design its computing system in 1938, using the apparatus and circuit design techniques used generally in the dial telephones. Six types of computers, designated Models I to VI have been built. Models V and VI are in the large scale computing machine class.

The input mechanism of Model V is similar to that of other digital machines. It introduces both numbers and orders to the machine on a perforated paper tape. About two seconds are required for the machine to read and transfer in a seven-digit number of average length. Addition can be carried out in 0.3 second, multiplication in about 1.0 second. Input speed of the numbers is therefore slightly lower than the unit time of operations for the machine.

The essential difference between Bell's system and the other electromechanical calculators is the biquinary number system which it employs as contrasted to the binary system generally used.

The machine can store thirty seven-digit decimal numbers. A unit of sixty-two relays, required to store one seven-digit number, is called a register. The BTL machine has forty-four such registers, thirty for storage, and fourteen for performing other operations.

BTL's recently developed machine, Model VI, has been constructed in similar fashion to Model V. Its chief feature distinguishing it from Model V is that the input and output mechanisms are attached to the machine through remote control.

IBM Pluggable Sequence Relay Calculator—This relay calculator operates on numbers read from punched cards, undertakes a sequence of operations activated by relay networks, and punches the results of these calculations on cards. The machine has a total of thirty-six storage and computing registers. The normal capacity of the machine is six-digit decimal numbers, although higher capacity than this can be obtained with sequence operation. In comparison with the standard IBM calculating punch, this calculator has a very high operating speed. It is approximately ten times faster on all operations than the calculating punch.

Electronic Computing Systems in Operation

In order that more complicated physical and mathematical problems may be solved in an economical time interval, the operating time for automatic computing systems must be decreased wherever possible. By using electronic vacuum tubes for switching, storage, and arithmetic functions, a saving of time on these functions is effected over devices using electromechanical relays. It is probable that for some time to come, input and output mechanisms using data punched on cards, paper tape, registered as dots on film, or as marks on a magnetic medium will be employed along with the vacuum tubes in the most advanced large scale digital computers.

The Displacement of Workers

There will be a great difference in the reaction of the interested parties, namely workers, unions, and the community, depending upon whether an entirely new plant is built for the automatic process or whether an old plant is remodeled for this purpose. The new plant will cause no direct labor displacement and is, therefore, much less likely to cause any trouble. Changing over a plant currently in operation, however, will bring about labor displacement which will be felt by everyone in the plant and the community. Since this second example presents a problem for society, we will confine our discussion to it.

Union attitude toward changing to completely automatic processes may include some obstructionism, but it is likely to be one of acceptance provided the union membership shares in the benefits of the change. To do this the unions will strive to keep more than the required number of people on the job by shortening the work day and/or demanding higher take-home pay for those people retained on the job. Such demands will decrease the savings gained from installing a completely automatic system and will probably tend to slow down the speed with which they are introduced. How much the unions can do against this and other technological changes depends largely upon their bargaining strength.

Moreover, we believe that the manner in which automatization is introduced will strongly temper one way or another the immediate reaction of the workers, the union, and the community. If carelessly managed, the union and the community at large will strongly object to it. The immediate furor will probably die down after a year or two, but what happens during this transition period may cause the demands for and the enactment of legislation and the imposition of controls which may leave lasting harmful effects—that is, if the introduction is not handled intelligently.

Every worker in a plant which is to be automatized will not be able to keep his job. Will other employment be available to these workers? We expect that the increased productivity from automatization and other technical developments will cause increased demands for all types of goods and services which will open new jobs just as it has in the past. The recent increase in the service and trade industry groupings are encouraging. We feel that the effects of completely automatic production will not be substantially different from those of technological developments in the past. That is, although severe temporary dislocations may occur, they can be worked out within a relatively short period through newly added employment opportunities elsewhere. Although the population and the proportion of older people will be increasing, we do not think that the automatic factory will aggravate this potentially serious problem.

Adaptation of Workers to a New Kind of Work Situation

Automatization will no longer allow workers to handle their work but will confine them to "button-pushing" and routine maintenance jobs around the factory. We feel that this work is no more and, perhaps, less degrading than doing the work manually. Is it not better to regiment machines than men?

It is true that this type of job may be very boring for some people and, therefore, very undesirable. Nevertheless, some people are well-suited for this kind of work. To discover who these people are will require a careful personnel screening. In attempting to get the best-adapted people to work in the automatic production lines, companies may run into trouble with union seniority rules.

The Problem of Leisure Time

The introduction of automatization could lead to more leisure time for those working in the affected companies since union pressure will probably demand shorter shifts in order to provide more jobs for the work to be done. In addition, organized labor is continuously driving for shorter hours on its own—a movement completely independent of the results of automatization.

What will people do with this additional leisure time? We must recognize that many workers would now prefer a 30-hour or less week provided that they could earn enough in that time to provide them with enough money to buy the things they want and need. For this reason, we believe that many of the problems which numerous people impute to the existence of additional leisure time do not exist.

Leisure time can be initially utilized by doing odd jobs around the home. Besides these tasks, there are countless other things that people can do with their time. It will give them the opportunity to spend more time with their families. Some may just want to enjoy themselves in sports, travel, or other types of recreation. Many people have hobbies upon which unlimited time could be spent. Still others may want to devote their free time to the pursuit of culture, whether it be through additional formalized education or informal activity of their own.

The existence of this leisure time gives a great opportunity to engage in many worthwhile projects which the fast pace of our industrial civilization has been passing by. Billions of man-hours could be well spent on such projects as soil conservation, reforestation, purifying our polluted water resources, and numerous reclamation projects which will replenish our rapidly consumed natural resources. To get the average man interested in these projects will require an enlightened leadership. We feel that this leadership must be generated by the government since it is such an immense undertaking.

We conclude, therefore, that people will not encounter any substantial trouble in utilizing leisure time. There are always things to do; in fact, we often complain that we never have nearly enough time to do what we would like to do. Moreover, an enlightened leadership can help to channel some of the leisure time into worthwile projects long neglected which will increase our overall well-being. Rather than confronting us as a problem, the utilization of leisure time will serve as a challenge for leading a more useful life.

II

Computers in Use

Introduction
to Section II

Some years ago a study of an insurance company by the U. S. Bureau of Labor Statistics provided an interesting insight into business attitudes toward automation. The company was installing computers, and as a result, laying off a large proportion of its office staff. But the main opponents to the introduction of the machines were not the staff whose jobs were directly threatened; the most vociferous complaints came from the firm's vice-presidents, who feared that the loss of human employees under their supervision would reduce their own importance, even though the amount of work for which each vice-president would be responsible would be increased by the introduction of the machines.

Although it tells us more about human nature than about machines, this anecdote does illustrate one point very basic to the introduction of automation into any business or profession: computers affect an organization from top to bottom. In the light of this fact, the often suspicious attitudes of many professions to the introduction of automation into their field became easily understandable. The computer is not only a threat, but an inhuman type of threat. Opponents of automation fear not only for their jobs, but also for their organization's whole existence. Yet despite these attitudes, computers have made their way into many fields of human endeavor, from the scientific laboratory to the tax office, and from the classroom to the subway car.

One trap often encountered by critics of automation is its misidentification with mass production. Certainly the two have much in common, but a truly automated process is inherently more flexible than a typical production line. Automation does not mean standardization, nor does it imply the thralldom of hundreds of skilled workers—or teachers, or surgeons, for that matter—to the machines. In fact, it does the reverse; by taking on the tasks most tedious for human workers, it gives them the chance to apply their unique skills to their own—and their organization's—best advantage.

From the viewpoint of business management, this factor is one of the computer's greatest assets. By dealing with all the tedious clerical tasks that take up a large proportion of a manager's time, the computer allows the executive to concentrate on his primary task—that of actually managing. However, as the contributions by Frederic Withington and Abraham Siegel illustrate, the computer has presented business management with a number of short-term problems. Many managers, trained in the traditional business-school techniques, are finding themselves involved in power struggles with computer experts, and a few computer-equipped companies are coming up against computer-equipped unions at the bargaining table. These problems, however, are merely teething troubles in comparison with the long-term prospects alluded to by Herbert Simon; among the manager's nightmares for the future is the prospect of coping with takeover threats from the computers themselves.

For the present-day computers that offer no takeover threat, the key task in any type of management enterprise is data-collection. By gathering all the salient facts and figures, the computer provides the executive with all the objective knowledge he needs to make his own human decision. For this reason, state and local governments have been attracted to automation, and have already made a few timid sallies into the field. As Alvin Kaltman reports, many of the pioneering efforts in this direction have been poorly designed and managed; but automation still offers great promise in making the governmental legislative process more efficient, and thus saving the taxpayers' money.

Money-saving of another form is the object of advocates of the cashless society—a state of affairs that will become possible only with great help from automation. As Ron Brown describes in his article "The Arrival of the Sales Counter Computer," a number of steps must be taken to change our cash system from the present state, in which computers are largely used by individual banks and financiers, to a nationwide scheme that can provide instant transfer of funds at the push of a button.

Perhaps the field in which there is least argument about the entry of the computer is urban transport. Throughout the sixties it was plain that mass-transit systems across the United States were in serious decay, and that the individual traveler was getting less service for his money. The onset of automation rapidly changed all that. Although the automated transport systems were beset by a number of starting problems, they were clearly superior to their human-controlled predecessors. Thus, Charles G. Burck relates the tale of a commuter railroad whose passengers and management both benefited greatly from the application of automation, and Siegfried Breuning takes a look at the likely prospects of automated automobiles.

Transportation is, of course, hardly a field that requires emotional or spiritual contact between human beings. Education is an entirely different matter and is, in fact, one of the most active battlegrounds for conflicts between automation and its critics. The basic argument of the critics is that when applied to essentially human enterprises, the computer will have a kind of Midas effect, staining everything and everyone it touches with inhuman, inflexible, machinelike attitudes. Thus, the opponents of educational automation argue that increasing use of computers will force teachers to become mere machine-minders, and make children into miniature zombies, learning by rote at a pace selected by the machine. Even putting aside all arguments about the virtues of current methods of education, the advocates of education automation feel that they have a strong case in opposition to those charges. Buckminster Fuller and Charles Silberman point out, for example, that machines will actually allow students more freedom than they have nowadays to pursue their studies at their own pace, while teachers will have all the time they need to teach children in the one-to-one situation that is most conducive to education. And in a companion article, Maya Pines describes a fascinating example of computerized education in action.

The reaction of the medical profession to impending automation has in many ways been just as frenzied as that of the educational establishment and for much the same reasons. No doctor wishes his or her patient to feel that he is at the mercy of a machine for his treatment and diagnosis. Thus, development of medical automation has been very gradual, and as Octo Barnett and his colleagues report, the field has yet to be put under the searching microscope of thorough cost analysis. Nevertheless, in some situations machines can assist the doctor or team of doctors in a way that no human can, and Michael Crichton provides an example of medical treatment at the very forefront of the automation revolution. And this type of cooperation between man and machine is likely to develop in a more personal fashion; D. S. Halacy describes the possible development of the cyborg—the combination of an individual man and an individual machine that combines the basic strengths of both.

Finally, the computer is making its mark in the academic world. Not surprisingly, it has found multitudinous applications in the scientific laboratory since its invention, one area of which is described by Anthony Oettinger. But the computer is also moving into fields regarded previously as immune from the influence of any non-human. Carl Overage recounts the development of a computerized science library that should, in future years, serve as the model for the public library down the street, and Stephen Parrish writes about the ultimate assault by the computer on the ivory tower—its infiltration into the esoteric atmosphere of the humanities.

The Long-Range Effect of the Computer

Frederic G. Withington

The introduction of automation plainly demands a totally new philosophy for running the corporation—a philosophy which will inevitably have profound effects on corporate structure. In this article a staff member of Arthur D. Little, Inc., the management consultants, outlines the profile of the "computerized organization of the future," and of the new professionals who will be needed to staff it.

Effect on Management

There has been much speculation about the role of top management in the computerized organization of the future. There are many points of view, some of them predicting quite sensational changes in the nature of the management function. In trying to perceive the facts, we shall consider both the nature of the computer's utility to management, and the actual changes that have occurred in some computer-using organizations.

It is relatively easy to identify the top management responsibilities that will *not* be changed by the computer. The individual organization's identity and objectives will not be directly affected by the existence of computers in it; therefore, the men in top positions will still hold full responsibility for the accomplishments of the firm, and for its successes or failures in meeting stated objectives. Nor are measurements of performance likely to change: corporate growth and financial performance will, as

100

far as one can see, always be the key criteria for top management. Thus the basic motivations of top management are unlikely to change.

It is also self-evident that allocation of resources to programs and investments designed to produce future returns must continue to be based at least partly on intuition and good judgment. A computer can summarize and relate facts much more rapidly and in more detail than has ever been possible before, but it does not create any new facts. Management's forward planning involves an attempt to read the future, to estimate the unknown, and to chart a course which produces maximum return with minimum risks. There will be important changes in the nature of forward planning, because the computer will enable management to simulate the outcomes of many alternative sets of conditions, a function now performed mainly by "best estimate" and "feel." However, the unknowns will still be unknowns, and in the last analysis management will still have to rely largely on judgment and intuition.

When it comes to directing operations on a day-to-day basis, there promises to be greater change. More facts have always been available about the present situation of an organization and its environment than about the future situation. The problem has been that the facts could not be assembled quickly enough to be useful, and even if they were, management would not have either the means or the time to relate them and consider their significance in time to influence day-to-day operational decisions. This problem has been virtually removed by the advent of the computerized information system. It is possible, at least in theory, to construct data-gathering systems and mathematical models which will enable the computer to work with top management in producing much more explicit and optimized operational decisions than have ever been possible before. It seems likely, then, that the process of operational decision making will become much less intuitive and much more precise, since management will have many more "hard facts" on which to base decisions—and all this, at a speed that will make it possible to simulate and evaluate the effects of a wide range of alternative actions, before the time for action has passed.

It would seem, then, that the computer will make the job of

operational management much simpler. Yet, the computer must be provided with rules and models which relate facts to one another and to the decisions the manager must make. The computer is purely quantitative; it cannot accept varying probabilities unless it has been told precisely how to do so, and it can never have a "feel" for the relative significance of different facts. In a sense, then, management faces a harder job than before. Instead of sitting back and relying on experience and judgment (because of an absence of information), management will be forced to look at quantitative relationships between the organization and its environment in a degree of detail that has never been required previously. Systems analysts, operations research specialists, and consultants may help, but management must work alongside them, because experience and knowledge of the business are just as important as knowledge of mathematical techniques.

It is already clear that the younger candidates for management, and recent graduates of business schools, are thinking in terms of quantitative relationships, models, and statistical information far more than their predecessors ever did. Eventually, it will become second nature to managers to think in those terms. In the meantime, managers not used to such thinking will have a difficult adjustment to make. It is true, of course, that once the basic relationships between causes and effects have been developed they are unlikely to change radically or rapidly; therefore, once the work of constructing models and relationships has been done for an organization it does not have to be redone. The model has to be improved, modified, and tailored to changing conditions, but this is a much easier job than the initial construction of the model. Nevertheless, change from qualitative to quantitative management will require a period of transition, followed by a period of settling down into new ways of doing things. The next generation of managers, used to being supported by computer systems working out relationships between data on the basis of steadily evolving models, may look back to the present and wonder how today's organizations could possibly have been managed. It may seem to them that the job must have been incredibly difficult, because of the lack of data and knowledge of its significance. This thought may be consoling, but it does not alter the fact that the transition period, in which managers are learning to think quantitatively rather than intuitively, and in which the decision rules and models are being established for the first time, will be a difficult one.

Another aspect of computer use that will affect management is the computer's ability to shorten the planning period. Until now, information about new conditions has had to "percolate" slowly up the organizational ladder; it had to be summarized, assessed, and understood at each level before action was taken. As a result, it has been accepted as inevitable, in many organizations, that a year or two must elapse before any really major changes to meet new conditions can be planned and implemented. The use of computerized systems promises to reduce information "percolation" time dramatically. Organizations will have systems that can capture data at the point of occurrence, transmit and process them at once, compare their significance to existing data according to prestored rules, at computer speeds, and present results simultaneously to management at all levels of the organization. Obviously, in such a system the information flow time almost disappears. Some commentators have therefore concluded that planning cycles will become so short that the organization and its products will be able to change virtually overnight.

However, one must realize that information-processing time is not the only determinant of the length of the planning cycle. Often it is necessary to collect information over a period of time, in order to demonstrate that changes in conditions are permanent, rather than simply temporary or accidental. Moreover, it often takes time to evaluate the optimum action to be taken—should it be organizational change, pricing change, or the development of new products? Therefore, although the computerized organization of the future will have a significantly faster reaction time than the organization of today, the planning cycle will not by any means disappear.

To summarize, it appears that the overall management responsibility for developing plans and providing direction for the business organization is not going to be dramatically changed by the advent of the computer. Day-to-day operational decision making is, however, likely to change greatly, as lower-level management becomes quantitative rather than intuitive. It seems probable that in this respect a painful and difficult transition must be undergone by most businesses, but once the transition has been made, lower-level management may not only be more effective than it is now, but may also seem easier.

Effect on the Organization's Structure

In order to make optimum use of a computer-based information system, the basic structure of the organization must change.

Almost every authority who has studied this question agrees that such change is likely, for the use of the computer encourages centralization of decision making, and this, of course, implies change in the organizational structure itself. Centralization is encouraged in two ways. First, before the computer was available, centralized decision making was not feasible simply because there were too many data for centralized management to consider. Therefore, it was left to decentralized management to handle the relatively limited bodies of data connected with individual, limited operations. With the aid of a computer, centralized management can give adequate consideration to all relevant data and, in doing so, can produce better decisions than were possible under the previous, fragmented system.

Second, the full power of a computer system is realized only when the system is provided with a comprehensive data base describing the environment of and conditions within the organization. Each operating department of an organization could, theoretically, develop its own data collection system to provide its own data base. But as these systems grow, they will become closer and closer duplicates of one another, and since such systems are expensive, it is not sensible to operate duplicates. It is therefore universally concluded that comprehensive data collection systems should be developed centrally.

Central system development inevitably implies a degree of loss of control by operating departments. This is not so apparent when the system is first designed; it will be "sold" to the operating departments as a remote service function irrelevant to questions of control. But with the key data for operating decisions now "at the fingertips" of central management for the first time, human nature dictates that central management will start to make the operating decisions, even if it had no such intention at the start.

Another force for change in organizational structures is related to the changed reaction time inherent in the use of computer-based planning systems, as discussed in the last section. It would be senseless to have a highly effective and integrated information system informing top management of significant events as they occur, but to have operating departments still "percolating" information through their old chains of command. If this were the case, top management would know of events occurring in the organization days or weeks before the managers of the departments in which the events occur. By implication, new information systems designed to decrease top management reaction time will also bring changes in the structures of the operating departments, so that they too can utilize the systems.

It is generally concluded, then, that a functionally structured organization that wishes to make use of a companywide data-processing system will change in the process. It would be very helpful if the nature of this change could be predicted, so that management could lay plans for an orderly evolution of the organization into whatever the new form will be. Unfortunately, predictions of this kind are not possible, because the "computerized organization of the future" does not yet exist. In fact, as we have said, it is only recently that organizations have begun to appreciate the potential of the computer tool; it is unlikely that any of them will show its full effects for a generation or more, if only because it takes time to change the habits of large numbers of people. All we can do, therefore, is to observe changes that have occurred in the organizations furthest advanced in using the new tools, and to extrapolate from their example to that of more typical organizations.

The Department of Defense

Of all organizations in the United States, the one closest to the computerized organization of the future may be the United States Department of Defense. This organization has had to act swiftly in meeting new challenges and responsibilities. In less than thirty years the reaction times required of the Department of Defense have changed from weeks to minutes. At the same time the number of factors to consider in each reaction has increased enormously. The forces available for deployment in a given situation were formerly those in the immediate area affected; now, both friendly and hostile forces all over the world may be involved. The most important decisions (e.g., use of nuclear weapons) must be reserved for the Secretary of Defense or the President; there is no alternative. Somehow, the Department of Defense must see that "top management" is fully informed of developing situations anywhere on earth, and is presented with evaluations of alternative actions in minutes or hours at most; it must then convert broad action decisions into detailed operational orders, and communicate these orders to all commanders involved, wherever they may be. To meet these needs, the Department of Defense has necessarily made the maximum possible use of all modern communications and data-processing tools, regardless of cost. In fact, many of the technological developments in the field have been brought about through research financed by the Department for its own needs. It is reasonable to hypothesize, then, that the Department of Defense is the most advanced organization in the country (or the world) in the use of data communications and data-processing tools, and that it can provide an instructive example of how the use of them affects the structure of an organization.

At the beginning of World War II there was no Department of Defense as such. There were separate War and Navy Departments, each with a civilian secretary, and the secretaries were members of the Cabinet reporting to the President. Functionally, the structure was split along service lines; the Army (War Department) was responsible for events occurring on land and the Navy for events at sea. Each service was assigned certain responsibilities in various parts of the world by relatively broad instructions from the President, transmitted through the Cabinet. The orders would be passed down the chain of command, becoming increasingly detailed, until they were received by the commanders who were to carry them out. There was relatively little attempt to direct the carrying out of the orders from

Washington; communications to distant points were limited to a relatively low volume of radio and telegraphic messages, used to give broad instructions and report summaries of activities. At times it was necessary for Army and Navy commanders to cooperate in joint operations, but such relationships would be established on a temporary basis within the operational area involved, to last only for the duration of the operation.

This organization worked well enough at the time; however, as we entered the era of the thermonuclear rocket and the cold war, it became clear that a tactical move in, say, some small country in Asia could have worldwide political significance and might require alerting or using forces anywhere, as dictated by top-level diplomatic and military decisions. But to do this, provisions would have to be made for the following:

communication of substantial volumes of data from the tactical zone to Washington in a matter of minutes;

immediate evaluation of the information received and consideration of possible courses of action, on the basis of data describing the state of the forces of the United States, its allies, and its potential enemies;

transmission, also in minutes, of detailed commands back to the tactical zone, to major commands in all parts of the world, and to widely dispersed strategic weapons bases.

Obviously, the old organization, with its chains of command and its assumption that local commanders will handle local operations independently of one another, was no longer satisfactory. The armed forces were therefore reorganized and combined into the modern Department of Defense in a series of steps, the major one of which was the reorganization act of 1947.

The Army and Navy still exist as separate services, each with its secretary; the Air Force has been added as a third service. All three report, along with the departmentwide Defense Supply Agency, to the Secretary of Defense (a new position), and he in turn reports to the President. The Secretary of Defense is supported by a number of assistant secretaries and other staff members. So far, the organization does not look radically different from the previous one. However, the lower echelons of command show an entirely new structure. There are eight commands, organized on geographic and functional lines rather than on service lines. Each command contains appropriately detailed elements of Army, Navy, and Air Force resources. The only criterion in determining the mix of forces in a given command is an evaluation of what is required to carry out the mission of that command, and the officer in charge may be a member of any one of the services. (There is a tendency for the command to be headed by an officer from the service providing the predominant force within the command. For example, the Commander in Chief of the Pacific has so far always been a Naval officer because the majority of the Pacific forces are Navy forces. This is not implicit in the organization, however, and there are many examples in other commands of successive commanding officers coming from different services.)

These functional and geographic commands report, along with several supporting agencies, to the Joint Chiefs of Staff, a group that consists of the military head of each of the services, plus a chairman who is a senior military officer appointed from any of the services. (Customarily, the position of chairman has rotated among the services.) The Joint Chiefs of Staff report directly to the Secretary of Defense and thence to the President.

The Army, Navy, and Air Force no longer direct any military operations. They exist for the purposes of providing, supporting, and administering forces assigned to the geographic and functional commands. From their ranks are drawn the eight geographic-functional commanders and their staffs, and, of course, the personnel of the Joint Chiefs of Staff. All operational responsibilities belong to the heads of the commands, reporting directly to the Joint Chiefs of Staff and then to the Secretary of Defense.

In a time of crisis the Secretary of Defense (perhaps also the President) will be physically located in the command center of the Joint Chiefs of Staff, or at least in close communication with it. Thus there are effectively only two levels in the command structure: the operational commander on the spot, and "top management." This makes quick reactions possible, but it also means that great quantities of operational information flow directly to top management. To deal with this, the defense organization is supported by an immense complex of communications and data-processing equipment designed to facilitate command control. Masses of data can be transmitted within minutes between any part of the world and the Joint Chiefs of Staff facilities in Washington. Computerized command and control systems exist for every command (and for many elements of the commands) as well as for the Joint Chiefs, and these systems are able to digest, evaluate, and display information with the full capability of the latest and most powerful computer systems.

Thus the Department of Defense is now an organization with a sharp division between operational and support functions. The operational portion is as streamlined as possible; it has an extremely short chain of command facilitated by modern communications and data-processing equipment. In the streamlining process, every possible support and staff function has been removed from the operational area. The service branches, set off to one side, are responsible for recruiting and training personnel, for assigning them to the individual commands, for designing and providing weapons and equipment of all kinds, and for supply, logistics and support of every item of equipment and personnel. Thus, for example, a Navy ship operating within any of the commands anywhere in the world is continually being supported by the Department of the Navy. However, when the time comes to direct that ship on an operational mission the streamlined and highly automated operational organization issues the orders.

Extrapolation to civilian organizations

Will the eventual changes in industrial organizations be at all similar to those that have taken place in the Department of Defense? Perhaps. It is true that the Department of Defense is hundreds of times bigger and more complex than most businesses, and has responsibility of global scope; it is also true that the objectives of the Department of Defense are quite different from those of business organizations. However, the basic forces causing change in the Department of Defense are not dissimilar to those which affect business organizations. For competitive reasons there is a need to increase reaction time by using modern communications and data reduction methods. There is also a desire to optimize operational decision making, again with the aid of the computer. And pressure is always present to accomplish the organization's missions with a minimum expenditure. Most of the functions that must be performed in a business organization have their counterparts in the Department of Defense, too. Products must be designed, manufactured, distributed, and serviced. Personnel must be hired, trained, motivated, evaluated, and promoted. All these similiarities between business organizations and the Department of Defense make it seem at least possible that some parallel evolution may take place.

Let us consider what might happen to the organization of a typical manufacturing company if it were to evolve in a manner similar to that of the Department of Defense. Imagine that there are four major departments: Engineering, Manufacturing, Marketing, and Accounting. The Manufacturing Department includes a planning division and the management of these plants. The Marketing Department also has a planning division, and a sales division organized along regional lines. Some degree of internal structure may be assumed in Engineering or Accounting, also. The departments report to a top management group which is assisted by a central staff.

Let us now suppose that this organization spends many years developing applications for computers and communications systems. Mathematical models of the organization's activities are developed and decision rules are established so that data about the company's condition and environment can be directly reflected in operating decisions. The organization learns to optimize the day-to-day operating decisions, to shorten the planning cycle, and to take quick and specific actions in response to events occurring in its environment. In the process, the organization allows its structure to change freely.

The following structure might emerge: Most of the old operating departments still exist—Engineering, Manufacturing (under which the three plants are still included), and Marketing. However, the Accounting Department has disappeared. The planning divisions that existed within Manufacturing, Marketing, and perhaps other departments have also disappeared, for now the purpose of these departments is simply to support and administer their respective functions within the organization. The Engineering Division develops products, tests them, and prepares them for manufacture. It also sees to the staff of engineers and technicians employed in product development, and administers the program of personnel recruiting and training for field service operations. The Manufacturing Department is still responsible for the operation of its three plants—for efficiency and economy in manufacturing, and for training and administration of production workers. However, it no longer establishes production schedules for the plants as it once did. Similarly, the Marketing Department is still responsible for obtaining, training, and administering sales personnel, as well as for market research, sales support, and knowledge of the competitive situation. However, the setting of sales quotas, assignment of sales territories, handling of customers' orders and other "tactical decisions" are no longer within its jurisdiction.

In addition, a new Planning Department has been created. This department is needed because plans can no longer be developed for one part of the organization independently of the other parts. Plans are not made by or for the functional departments, as before; they are now developed for the organization as a whole. The operations control group (see below) determines the requirements for plans, and furnishes the data and capability of its computerized systems to help the Planning Department. In the old organization, no single group could comprehend or utilize all the data relating to all the functions of the organization. This meant that the organization accepted less-than-perfect plans, based on separate units of data rather than a unified body of data. With the support of the computer system, its models, and its files of data, it becomes possible for planning to be done centrally with better results.

The operational functions of the Accounting Department (keeping track of individual financial transactions and accounts) have been wholly taken over by the computer system, and broad responsibility for financial planning has been taken over by the Planning Division. The organization still needs a treasurer, auditors, and controllers of funds; these are now to be found either as part of the management group or within a new entity, the operations control group.

The operations control group is the heart of the new organizational structure. It reports directly to top management and works closely with it; in fact, top management may choose to become part of the group and work with the computer system in directing detailed operations. The parallel with the Department of Defense is evident, in that the operations control group is responsible for all decisions, from daily operating schedules for the plants to decisions about investments in new plants. It works directly with all the company's operating forces or "agents." An agent is any coherent, single-purpose unit that can be assigned specific missions and can respond to specific instructions. This may be a salesman, a buyer, an advertising agency, a lawyer, etc. Or it may be the manager of a sizable operation. Thus the manager of each of the three production plants is an agent of the operations control group, for he receives his operating schedule and production quotas from it.

Each agent is linked by rapid communications media to an "operations control center," where messages to and from all agents are processed by the central computer, and integrated with one another and with the files of the central computer. A very large quantity of data flows in and out of the operations center, because thousands of routine messages about sales, shipments, billings, and the like are received and generated in the course of the working day. Probably the great majority of these will be handled automatically by the computer without being brought to the attention of the personnel in charge of the operations center. The personnel, however, can obtain from the computer the record of any given transaction at any time. Moreover, the computer will automatically give them reports such as summaries of the day's operations. It is programmed to recognize many kinds of exceptional transactions and to automatically bring them to the attention of operations management; the principle of "management by exception" is practiced very extensively. Whenever instructions are to be given to salesmen, plant managers, or other agents, the computer may be asked to develop an optimum set of instructions based on its decision rules and mathematical models. After review and approval or modification by operations management, the instructions are automatically transmitted to the agents.

The advantages of such an organization are clear. The operations center gathers information from a multitude of sources and is in a position to act with great rapidity. If a salesman obtains a large order, for example, it should be possible in a matter of hours to develop new production schedules, and issue instructions to plant managers and to buyers of raw materials. The operating decisions will also be more efficient. In the old organization such short-notice production changes and raw materials orders were probably wasteful and unnecessarily expensive. In the new organization schedules revised on short notice are as efficient as the original schedules, thanks to the computer's models and speed of operation. It should also be possible to react very rapidly to competitive circumstances. If one of the salesmen in the field discovers and reports that a competitor has a new product on the market, operations management and top management will be informed within minutes. Management, using the computer to assist in assessing the consequences of various courses of action, can plan its countermove and convert the decision into a mass of detailed orders for agents in a matter of hours. The orders can then be disseminated automatically to the agents, and the countermove has been made. The whole organization, in a word, has changed direction overnight—something heretofore impossible.

The example just presented involved a manufacturing organization in a competitive market, where production schedules and even products might change rapidly. Not all organizations operate under such conditions—public utilities, banks, and insurance companies, for example, are unlikely to feel the same pressures to the same degree. Therefore they may never have to change so drastically.

In any event, an organization like that described in our example will not be a reality for some time to come—not even the Department of Defense is so advanced. Between our hypothetical company and present-day organizations there lies a vast amount of work in the development of data-gathering systems, decision rules, mathematical models, and the like.

As we have said, this hypothetical organization structure is based on observations of the evolution of the Department of Defense, and of changes that have occurred in the most advanced computer-using industrial organizations. There is no guarantee that this hypothesis is correct. It is presented for the information and consideration of management. It is perhaps most useful as an example of the kind of broad-scale organizational thinking which managements of business organizations should entertain, as their ability to employ the power of computer and communications systems increases.

Effect on Personnel

It has been noted by some commentators that an organization such as the one just described is rather like the small one-man business of yesterday, with the "boss" giving orders directly to the personnel and controlling every detail of the operation. Such organizations are highly efficient (assuming that the "boss" is capable), but they also have some drawbacks, especially in the areas of personnel motivation and development. There appears to be a danger that individual creativity and initiative in the organization's employees will be stifled because of reliance on the computer system. Once decision rules have been established which optimize the elementary decisions of the organization, there will be a natural tendency to rely totally on these decisions —to assume that the superior wisdom of those who established the rules, and the superior capability of the computer system in administering them, leaves no room for judgment or interpretation on the part of the agent on the spot.

To put it another way, the use of computers in explicit decision making may eventually have a "depersonalizing" effect on the decision process. When one person tells another what to do, the personal relationship between the two may encourage the subordinate to discuss the order with his superior—to contribute his own knowledge and perhaps to obtain a desirable modification to the order. The subordinate knows his superior's place in the organization, his degree of knowledge or experience with a given matter, and so on. In a computerized organization the individuals receive impersonal instructions from the system; since most employees are likely to feel that "you can't beat the system," they may see no obvious alternative to slavish obedience. It may be expected that most employees will proceed to do exactly what the system tells them, and thereby relieve themselves of all responsibility for the desirability or accuracy of the instructions.

This is obviously undesirable. There will never be a decision-making system so perfect that it will give exactly the right answers all the time. There will always be situations, particularly in dealing with human customers, and human agents of other organizations, where there is no substitute for the impression gained of the situation on the spot, or for the tact and diplomacy of the agent dealing with the customer. It should always be possible for the organization's agents to modify or even overrule the instructions given them by the operations organization. However, this could not be allowed to become general or chaos would result. Apparently an uneasy compromise between the extremes of slavish obedience and general disobedience must exist. It will necessarily be an unhappy one subject to at least occasional error. Certainly, it means that system designers must always provide means for agents to confer with the human managers of the operations organization, so that a degree of "personality" can be preserved.

Most organizations operate in a world of people, and must retain the capability to modify the machine's "optimum" decisions because of human idiosyncrasies and other intangible factors. It follows that there will be no reduction in the numbers of people employed by organizations for purposes of customer contact, negotiations with other firms, or supervision of human-operated production and distribution facilities. Some commentators, allowing their imagination free rein, have hypothetized situations in which computer systems "representing" organizations communicate directly with one another, arranging purchases, shipments, and accounting transactions between the organizations. In fact, however, such interconnections appear to be extremely unlikely; at the heart of business relationships lies the principle that individuals should negotiate with one another for preferential treatment in terms of price, delivery, or product quality. A world without bargaining between human agents of organizations would be almost inconceivable.

The likelihood that human agents will be retained is borne out by experience with advanced information retrieval systems. Most designers of such systems focus their attention on the mechanism for obtaining complete and accurate responses to a questioner's inquiries. They assume that the machine's output, delivered to the questioner, will meet his needs if it includes the correct answers. However, experience with such systems shows that human agents play an indispensable role. Only a human agent can help the questioner formulate his question in the most suitable form for machine processing, and explain to the questioner the limitations of the files which are searched, the probability that he will find more information in other files, the meaning and content of the format in which the machine has printed the information, and so forth. Even in relatively simple systems where it might be assumed that the machine could work directly with the customer, it has turned out not to be so. One may assume with some confidence, then, that whatever the computerized organization will look like in the future, it will have at least as many personnel as it does today to represent it in its relationships with the rest of the world.

The agent in the computerized organization of the future will have an increasing responsibility, compared to his counterpart in today's organization. In the traditional, vertically structured organization one's supervisor is always near at hand for consultation when one is in doubt; in the computerized organization the agent reports only to the operations control group. He is therefore more on his own, either to accept more responsibility for representing the company or to rely entirely on the decisions of the machine.

Production and distribution workers are not directly affected by the change to the new organizational structure. Schedulers, inventory and accounting clerks, and other supporting personnel will have been largely replaced, it is true. However, the requirement for direct production and distribution workers will be changed only insofar as their tools may be automated, and this is a consideration separate from changes in the organization's structure.

The new type of organization will face very difficult problems in personnel training and development. For one thing, it will need a sizable number of high-level, highly trained staff specialists to maintain, operate, and improve the systems and files of the operations control group. Similar specialists will also be required for the Planning Division, to work on new models and new systems, and to use the current ones in developing optimum operating plans. These staff people have as their basic resource skills of the intellect. This stands in contrast to the kind of skill and wisdom that is derived from experience and that is so vital in top management positions, as well as in many of the organization's agents. In other words, the staff specialists are useful to the organization for what they know and for what they can conceptualize, rather than for what they can carry out. They are, therefore, a different breed from most of the organization's employees and must somehow be hired, given experience in the organization, and motivated in such a way that they "pull together" with the rest of the organization. This problem already exists with systems analysts and operations research specialists, but there are so few of them in today's organization that the problem is minor. Presumably, relatively few of the company's agents will be suited by education or experience for this professional staff, and at the same time few members of the professional staff will themselves be suitable for top management. Thus the staff positions probably will have to be filled directly from outside the company, and there must be a separate promotion and management structure for the staff employee within the Planning Division and the operational organization, quite independent of the personnel and management structure of the parent organization. This situation is fraught with danger, because the Planning Division can easily become internally motivated, responding only poorly to the needs of the organization supporting it. In fact, the Department of Defense has had this very difficulty with some of the professional groups set up to support it.

Another problem comes from the gap between the agent in the field and the manager in the operations control group. With only two basic levels of managing personnel, how will the agent in the field suddenly jump across the gap and become one of those who manages the company, who creates the decision rules for the agents of the future to carry out, and who must, in order to be part of the central operating staff, have a complete grasp of all the company's operations? Each agent performs only one task; surely there will not be time to rotate candidates for promotion through all the significant positions in the organization; therefore, this important question is not easily answered.

The conventional organization, with its many levels of vertical structure, enables individuals to gradually acquire broader experience as they move up the management ladder. Of course, the vertically structured functional departments of the organization still exist in our computerized organization, albeit without operational authority. We may refer again to the Department of Defense, where it is the responsibility of the individual services to recruit, train, and develop personnel for all management levels in the operating side of the organization. Presumably this approach can be used in the business organization of the future. In some way the manufacturing, marketing, and other vestigial functional departments must find a way to expose the company's agents within their jurisdiction to successively broader responsibilities and training courses, which will fit them for management positions in operations control. This will not be simple, because the intermediate management jobs which were used in the traditional organization to fit individuals for top management will no longer exist; some substitute must be found. Perhaps more formal management training will be the answer.

It is possible that all the speculations entertained in this chapter are wrong. The computerized organization of the future may be something entirely different from the one discussed here. But there is little doubt that the organization of the future will be different from the organization of today. Proof of this statement is provided by the already abundant examples of organizations that are changing their structures to accommodate and make use of the powers of the computer. The important thing, perhaps, is simply that management be aware that full use of the new tool will require major accommodations on the part of the organization. Thus the ground will be prepared for an orderly evolution.

The transition from the functionally oriented, qualitatively managed organization of today to the integrated, quantitatively managed organization of tomorrow is going to be immensely difficult and painful. Not only is a tremendous amount of theoretical and conceptual work required, but also the personnel at every level must be retrained and must reorient their thinking. In the meantime, programs for the use of computers must proceed in sensible stages which can be carried out by existing organizations, with their present personnel and present levels of experience. At each stage, management must be realistic and hard-headed, yet it must not lose sight of the fact that each development cycle is simply one step along a road whose end may be only dimly perceived. Frederick R. Kappel, Chairman of American Telephone and Telegraph Company, was right when he said of computers: ". . . of all the tools mankind has ever had, this is the one that most peremptorily requires us all to use our heads."

Unions, Employers, and the Computer

Abraham J. Siegel

In the field of industrial relations, computers are no longer the exclusive province of the businessman. Labor unions are increasingly turning to computers for data and models that will assist them in their negotiations with management, and in their day-to-day organizational tasks. In this contribution a Massachusetts Institute of Technology professor of industrial relations who is a recognized authority on collective bargaining describes just how the machines affect the relationship between labor and management.

In the past five years, companies and unions have moved dramatically from storing information in "mammoth filing systems" to using computers as the base for management information facilities, which help plan strategy and make basic decisions. One result of this change is that unions are making use of computers in their bargainings with company management.

Neither of the parties to the bargaining process has developed essentially new or secret data; what computers do is to facilitate accurate, simplified arrangements of data, revealing patterns as they develop and supplying details as needed. The effect of the computer on bargaining is best seen by starting at an early stage in the evolution of company/union relationships, where no bargaining occurs, and working forward.

Computers Behind the Lines

The major company use of computers, of course, is for personnel administration. Employee records—basic personal data, skill inventories, compensation records, and so on—must be kept whether or not unions bargain with the company. Trade unions have sought assistance from the computer in a variety of organizing efforts; for example, efforts to "sign up" the still unorganized branches of partially organized conglomerate or multiplant companies.

The computer helps in the preparation of profiles of the work force composition, of union election histories, and of company records of unfair labor practices. The A.F.L.-C.I.O. Industrial Union Department has data banks on all of these matters. For example, the results of more than 50,000 elections conducted under the National Labor Relations Board in the past eight years are available to union organizers. In addition, individual unions may obtain records of their successes and failures, discover where they are being challenged by other unions, and so on. Records of unfair labor practices are available, categorized by company, union and region. These data will help an organizer identify towns, companies and individual plants which may be ripe for unionization drives. By recognizing patterns in anti-union campaigns, he may be able to build more effective counter-campaigns.

Lists of companies whose employees have recently voted a union "out" in decertification elections provide the organizer with targets where a base of former trade union members and sympathizers exists. Organizers now find it easier to compare conditions in union plants with those in their target plants. In short, these data can help an organizer spot more effectively which regions to organize, what companies resist most effectively, what union campaign methods work most efficiently, and which members of the target work force are the best potential allies.

Trade unions have also used information data banks in lobbying for changes in working conditions. For example, Woodrow L. Ginsburg, who until recently served as Research Director for the A.F.L.-C.I.O.'s Industrial Union Department, describes how computer analysis helped make an effective case for minimum wages for the sawing and logging industry.

Finally, we should mention here a point alluded to both by Ginsburg and by Wilbur Daniels (International Ladies' Garment Workers' Union)—the help that unions now get in coping with the "runaway shop" problem. By correlating names of officers of old and new establishments (obtained from county records and corporation papers, newspapers, and so on) unions can more easily spot companies which, by relocation, seek to evade organization.

All this we can call the "organizing" stage. Next comes the stage of resisted or unconsummated bargaining. Ginsburg cites examples of unions that were able to build strong cases for backwages claims against companies which, over a period of years, had refused to bargain despite the fact that the union was lawfully recognized as the bargaining agent. One such case employed a computer-based analysis of average wage increases received by the workers in the company which had failed to bargain, contrasted with those received in comparable companies in the industry.

Bargaining with the Machine

In the third stage of relations between company and union, collective bargaining is a "going concern." Here the computer may contribute either (1) in preparations for the negotiation of agreements, (2) during negotiation, (3) in the administration of the agreement; or (4) may be used jointly by management and union in the collective bargaining process.

Preparations for the negotiation of agreements can include contract analysis, study of company economic profiles, coding and costing of anticipated or proposed demands, and the development of mathematical models to predict work force needs (to help analyze the impact of probable demands on a variety of company dimensions).

In its national survey of key contracts, the Industrial Union Department has put 22 key contract provisions of 208 major contracts (151 manufacturing companies, 57 nonmanufacturing companies), covering 3½ million workers employed in over 4,000 facilities, into its computer system—which is kept continuously updated. This information enables unions to put price tags (from the company viewpoint) on complex union demands. Comparisons of contract benefits of one company with those of its major competitors in the industry or with other comparable firms can have significant bargaining results.

The I.U.D. also coordinates the activities of 77 corporate or industry-wide committees to help unions cope with new problems posed by widely diversified corporations that cut across the jurisdictions of many of them. Various unions dealing with the same corporation seek to hammer out together the basic demands they will make of it. As an aid toward this objective, the I.U.D. has gathered economic profiles of about 200 major companies, providing detailed records of finances, product lines, plant locations, mergers and acquisitions, key officers, relationships with other companies, records of which divisions of a company are profitable and which are not, and so on.

It is not necessary to elaborate on how computers can help unions and companies to estimate the costs of proposed demands. Neither is it necessary to say much about the development of mathematical models—as yet, a relatively infrequent use of information technology both by unions and by companies, though the likelihood is that such modeling will increasingly become recognized as a useful tool for both the parties.

It is clear that the linking of specific files—National Labor

Relations Board election results, unfair practice charges, contract analyses, corporate economic profiles—provides the unions with a broad view of the industrial relations picture of the firms with which they deal. It is clear also that if companies can anticipate the impact of probable demands they are better able to frame alternatives (which may indeed be more favorable to both parties). Such preparations for negotiations, and the administration of agreements afterwards, at present make far more use of electronic data processing than does the process of negotiation itself. Such is the finding of a survey by William G. Caples, former Vice-President for Industrial Relations of the Inland Steel Company and now President of Kenyon College.

Checking the Results

The postnegotiation stages involve substantial use of computer technology. For example, the late Charles M. Mason, a Vice-President of United Air Lines, described the aid rendered by computers in the indexing and reporting of grievances—a function especially important in his company, since grievances arise and are handled at so many locations. Such analysis can also help to check union claims that people are disturbed about one or another particular clause in a contract. The grievance index will give the frequency of employees' complaints with respect to any particular contract provision. Similarly, "arbitration analysis" can help in spotting divergent interpretations of specific contract provisions.

Wilbur Daniels has discussed the Ladies' Garment Workers' concern with the enforcement and policing of contracts in an industry where the opportunity for contract violations are many. The sources of the enforcement problem, in this instance, clearly lie in the industry's structure. Many small employers, a high turnover (20 to 30 per cent), a predominantly female labor force with complex piecework incentives, and increasing geographical dispersion: all lead to elusive, inadequate, or inaccurate records. The computer-aided union can now check on whether earnings provisions are being put into practice by auditing payrolls provided on tape. It can police the payment of minimum guarantees. The computer is especially helpful in discerning whether or not a particular group is "making out." The union can easily check contributions to benefit funds by matching contributions to payrolls and company sales. Daniels makes the interesting point that the role of the business agent is still vital in contract enforcement but notes that the computer not only helps the union representative but prods him toward more effective enforcement. Daniels suggests that some of the union's business agents may feel that Big Brother may be watching not only the employer but them also. Daniels feels that the trade union must educate the agent to the uses and potential of "that thing at 1710 Broadway" before such fears fully disappear.

Mason further described computer-aided techniques which go beyond grievance analysis, to help estimate the effectiveness of specific programs—for example, of policies relating to salaries or to turnover reduction. (This field of work is related to the more general one of the cost-benefit analysis of company policies, already familiar to the student of modern management techniques, and in any case, going far beyond the scope of this article.)

In using this technology for the administration of an agreement, Mason stressed, one must build and reinforce people's confidence in the total information system. He did not feel that this necessarily involved (as has been suggested) the use of a "neutral computer," but rather that the trust of the company's employees will be won through ongoing exposure to the accuracy and fairness of the system. Accuracy and fairness must be a basic operating principle, if we seek to avoid situations like the Renault experience where workers (uninformed about the basics of the management's information system) struck because they protested the use of computers in the selection of people for lay-offs. People, he felt, should have the right to discuss what they feel are errors in the system at any time and should be involved from the beginning in the installation of computer applications for such implementing procedures.

Flying people, Mason pointed out, are generally "machine- and change-oriented" and never have objected to the new technology *per se*. They have been concerned only with how the technology affects working conditions. He suggested implicitly that this can be transferable as an operating principle to other situations, although perhaps with some greater measure of effort.

Exploring the Possible

It seems to be widely considered that, where bargaining parties agree to a joint study group, it would be useful to have computer-assisted "fact-generation." However, it is first necessary to agree on what data are relevant to the issues being bargained. In fact, there are few cases of bargaining parties sharing analyses.

Mason suggested that joint use and joint queries by trade union and management may not prevail simply because they may not be advisable in the light of basic strategy in bargaining: "Many times," he said, "you want to know an answer but you don't want the other party to know you are even interested in the question. You discard more than you adopt, but you have to educate yourself with respect to the options without publicity or without sharing these views at too early a point in the bargaining process."

This is perhaps the most important new element introduced into the bargaining situation by the computer—the extension of the realm of the possible which man may explore in mulling over substantive proposals or reactions to substantive demands.

At present it seems clear that the uses of computers and computer technology in collective bargaining are in their infancy. But they are also at the cutting edge, and prospects for the steady expansion of electronic data processing in most aspects of collective bargaining are excellent. On the union side, it is evident that the Industrial Union Department has been the major spearhead in the application of information systems to decision making and strategy in bargaining. Many individual unions, of course, use computers for straightforward housekeeping chores, but at present it is not likely that more than a dozen large ones have developed their own computer-based information systems for bargaining. (Among the unions which have developed such uses are the Machinists, the Automobile Workers, the Communications Workers, the Laborers, the Maritime

Union, the Newspaper Guild, the Federation of State, County, and Municipal Employees, the Steel Workers, and the Ladies' Garment Workers.) Many more unions, of course, have availed themselves of the services of the Industrial Union Department.

On management's side too, computer-based data processing has yet to be used by the majority of companies for strategic decision making in collective bargaining. (Caples found that 46 per cent of the companies responding to his survey have begun using computers for *preparation* for collective bargaining, which as we have seen is an early stage of evolution.)

Why So Slow?

In sum, the use of computers in bargaining and other behavioral areas has lagged behind their use in the physical sciences; and within the employment relations area, collective bargaining tends to lag behind general personnel administration. Why?

Caples and others identify the following basic reasons. First, the data available to the trade union or the company in machine-readable form are often less than adequate. Time is not always available for programming, and in any case, hand methods are often adequate. There have been frequent difficulties with hardware, software, modelling and gaming situations; and trade union leaders, often unfamiliar with and hence fearful of the new technology and language, have too often been reluctant to move ahead.

Caples stresses a second basic consideration. Personnel administration involves counting and identifying people, recording and analyzing their actions, and the collecting and paying of money, all of which lend themselves readily to numerical and logical treatment. Collective bargaining problems, on the other hand, are more loosely structured. Says Caples: "The use of computers presupposes considerable advance understanding of the problem scope, availability of accurate input, reliable factoral weighting and logical resolution of problems; somehow these elements still are rarities in the bargaining process."

However, in Caples's survey two-thirds of the respondents indicated that they intend to develop or improve the use of computers in bargaining, and a substantial proportion indicate that definite plans for such applications are already on hand. Caples himself expresses "cautious optimism," and sees developments as occurring primarily in the preparation for negotiations and in the interpretation and administration of contracts. In the actual bargaining process, he says, discussion turns on the assumptions—not easily quantified—that underlie the particular sets of facts presented to support a bargaining position or objective.

It is clear that unions and companies both need more efficient ways of maintaining and retrieving information about employees and of consolidating the masses of raw data which each now possesses. Vast amounts of information are also required from both parties by the Government. (The Labor-Management Reporting and Disclosure Act and the Pension Fund Disclosure Act are but two illustrations of this increased call for consolidated data.) In addition, increased information is needed for collective bargaining over more complex issues, such as health-and-welfare and retirement fund management.

Technological progress in hardware and software will tend to diminish some of the impediments referred to earlier. Parties also react to each other: The use of electronic data processing by a company in connection with bargaining will tend to spur its exploration by a union, and vice versa.

The Corporation: Will It Be Managed by Machines?

Herbert A. Simon

For most businessmen, the critical problems in dealing with computers concern the short-range effects of automation. The advent of automation has destroyed many a minor empire built up within a company by years of careful personnel selection, and has put numerous conventionally trained businessmen in competition with computer "whiz-kids" for the control of corporations. Given such considerations, few observers have had the foresight to look ahead to the day in which management may be automated. One of the few is Herbert Simon of Carnegie-Mellon University, a highly respected authority in the field of artificial intelligence. Here he assesses the probable capabilities of computers in the year 1985.

My work on this paper has been somewhat impeded, in recent days, by a fascinating spectacle just outside my office window. Men and machines have been constructing the foundations of a small building. After some preliminary skirmishing by men equipped with surveying instruments and sledges for driving pegs, most of the work has been done by various species of mechanical elephant and their mahouts. Two kinds of elephants dug out the earth (one with its forelegs, the other with its trunk) and loaded it in trucks (pack elephants, I suppose). Then, after an interlude during which another group of men

128

carefully fitted some boards into place as forms, a new kind of elephant appeared, its belly full of concrete which it disgorged into the forms. It was assisted by two men with wheelbarrows—plain old-fashioned man-handled wheelbarrows—and two or three other men who fussily tamped the poured concrete with metal rods. Twice during this whole period a shovel appeared—on one occasion it was used by a man to remove dirt that had been dropped on a sidewalk; on another occasion it was used to clean a trough down which the concrete slid.

Here, before me, was a sample of automated, or semi-automated, production. What did it show about the nature of present and future relations of man with machine in the production of goods and services? And what lessons that could be learned from the automation of manufacturing and construction could be transferred to the problems of managerial automation? I concluded that there were two good reasons for beginning my analysis with a careful look at factory and office automation. First, the business organization in 1985 will be a highly automated man-machine system, and the nature of management will surely be conditioned by the character of the system being managed. Second, perhaps there are greater similarities than appear at first blush among the several areas of potential automation—blue-collar, clerical and managerial. Perhaps the automated executive of the future has a great deal in common with the automated worker or clerk whom we can already observe in many situations today.

First, however, we must establish a framework and a point of view. Our task is to forecast the changes that will take place over the next generation in the job of the manager. It is fair to ask: Which manager? Not everyone nor every job will be affected in the same way; indeed, most persons who will be affected are not even managers at the present time. Moreover, we must distinguish the gross effects of a technological change, occurring at the point of impact of that change, from the net effects, the whole series of secondary ripples spreading from that point of initial impact.

Many of the initial effects are transitory—important enough to those directly involved at the time and place of change, but of no lasting significance to the society. Other effects are neither apparent nor anticipated when the initial change takes place but flow from it over a period of years through the succession of reactions it produces. Examples of both transient and indirect effects of change come to mind readily enough—e.g., the unemployment of blacksmiths and the appearance of suburbia, respectively, as effects of the automobile.

Since our task is to look ahead, I shall say little about the transient effects of the change in the job of the manager. I do not mean to discount the importance of these effects to the people they touch. In our time we are highly conscious of the transient effects, particularly the harmful ones, the displacements of skill and status. We say less of the benefit to those who acquire the new skills or of the exhilaration that many derive from erecting new structures.

Of course, the social management of change does not consist simply in balancing beneficial transient effects against harmful ones. The simplest moral reasoning leads to a general rule for the introduction of change: The general society which stands to benefit from the change should pay the major costs of introducing it and should compensate generously those who would otherwise be harmed by it. A discussion of the transient effects of change would have to center on ways of applying that rule. But that is not the problem we have to deal with here.

Our task is to forecast the long-run effects of change. First of all, we must predict what is likely to happen to the job of the individual manager, and to the activity of management in the individual organization. Changes in these patterns will have secondary effects on the occupational profile in the economy as a whole. Our task is to picture the society after it has made all these secondary adjustments and settled down to its new equilibrium.

Let me now indicate the general plan I shall follow in my analysis. In the first section, "Predicting Long-run Equilibrium," I shall identify the key factors—the causes and the conditions of change—that will mold the analysis. Then I shall show how a well-known tool of economic analysis—the doctrine of comparative advantage—permits us to draw valid inferences from these causes and conditions. In the second section, "The New Technology of Information Processing," I shall describe the technological innovations that have appeared and are about to appear in the areas of production and data processing, and I shall use this material to draw a picture of the business organization in 1985, with particular attention to the automation of blue-collar and clerical work. In the third section, "The Automation of Management," I shall consider more specifically the role of the manager in the future business organization. In the final section, "The Broader Significance of Automation," I shall try to identify some of the important implications of these developments for our society and for ourselves as members of it.

Predicting Long-run Equilibrium

To predict long-run equilibrium, one must identify two major aspects of the total situation: (1) the variables that will change autonomously and inexorably—the "first causes," and (2) the constant, unchanging "givens" in the situation, to which the other variables must adjust themselves. These are the hammer and the anvil that beat out the shape of the future. The accuracy of our predictions will depend less upon forecasting exactly the course of change than upon assessing correctly which factors are the unmoved movers and which the equally unmoved invariants. My entire forecast rests on my identification of this hammer and this anvil.

The Causes of Change

The growth in human knowledge is the primary factor that will give the system its direction—in particular, that will fix the boundaries of the technologically feasible. The growth in real capital is the major secondary factor in change—within the realm of what is technologically feasible, it will determine what is economical.

The crucial area of expansion of knowledge is not hard to predict, for the basic innovations—or at least a large part of them—have already occurred and we are now rapidly exploiting them. The new knowledge consists in a fundamental understanding of the processes of thinking and learning or, to use a more neutral term, of complex information processing. We can now write programs for electronic computers that enable these devices to think and learn. This knowledge is having, and will have, practical impacts in two directions: (1) because we can now simulate in considerable detail an important and increasing part of the processes of the human mind, we have available a technique of tremendous power for psychological research; (2) because we can now write complex information-processing programs for computers, we are acquiring the technical capacity to replace humans with computers in a rapidly widening range of thinking and deciding tasks.

Closely allied to the development of complex information-processing techniques for general purpose computers is the rapid advance in the technique of automating all sorts of production and clerical tasks. Putting these two lines of development together, I am led to the following general predictions: Within the very near future we shall have the *technical* capability of substituting machines for any and all human functions in organizations. Within the same period, we shall have acquired an extensive and empirically tested theory of human cognitive processes and their interaction with human emotions, attitudes and values.

To predict that we will have these technical capabilities says nothing of how we shall use them. Before we can forecast that, we must discuss the important invariants in the social system.

The Invariants

The changes that our new technical capability will bring about will be governed, particularly in the production sphere, by two major fixed factors in the society. Both of these have to do with the use of human resources for production.

1. Apart from transient effects of automation, the human resources of the society will be substantially fully employed. Full employment does not necessarily mean a forty-hour week, for the allocation of productive capacity between additional goods and services and additional leisure may continue to change as it has in the past. Full employment means that the opportunity to work will be available to virtually all adults in

the society and that, through wages or other allocative devices, the product of the economy will be distributed widely among families.

2. The distribution of intelligence and ability in the society will be much as it is now, although a substantially larger percentage of adults (perhaps half or more) will have completed college educations.

These assumptions—of capability of automation, accompanied by full employment and constancy in the quality of the human resources—provide us with a basis for characterizing the change. We cannot talk about the technological unemployment it may create, for we have assumed that such unemployment is a transient phenomenon—that there will be none in the long run. But the pattern of occupations, the profile showing the relative distribution of employed persons among occupations, may be greatly changed. It is the change in this profile that will measure the organizational impact of the technological change.

The change in the occupational profile depends on a well-known economic principle, the doctrine of comparative advantage. It may seem paradoxical to think that we can increase the productivity of mechanized techniques in all processes without displacing men somewhere. Won't a point be reached where men are less productive than machines in *all* processes, hence economically unemployable?

The paradox is dissolved by supplying a missing term. Whether man or machines will be employed in a particular process depends not simply on their relative productivity in physical terms but on their cost as well. And cost depends on price. Hence—so goes the traditional argument of economics—as technology changes and machines become more productive, the prices of labor and capital will so adjust themselves as to clear the market of both. As much of each will be employed as offers itself at the market price, and the market price will be proportional to the marginal productivity of that factor. By the operation of the marketplace, manpower will flow to those processes in which its productivity is comparatively high relative to the productivity of machines; it will leave those processes in which its productivity is comparatively low. The comparison is not with the productivities of the past, but among the productivities in different processes with the currently available technology.

I apologize for dwelling at length on a point that is clearly enough stated in the *Wealth of Nations*. My excuse is that contemporary discussion of technological change and automation still very often falls into error through not applying the doctrine of comparative advantage correctly and consistently.

We conclude that human employment will become smaller relative to the total labor force in those kinds of occupations and activities in which automatic devices have the greatest comparative advantage over humans; human employment will become relatively greater in those occupations and activities in which automatic devices have the least comparative advantage.

Thus, if computers are a thousand times faster than bookkeepers in doing arithmetic, but only one hundred times faster than stenographers in taking dictation, we shall expect the number of bookkeepers per thousand employees to decrease but the number of stenographers to increase. Similarly, if computers are a hundred times faster than executives in making investment decisions, but only ten times faster in handling employee grievances (the quality of the decisions being held constant), then computers will be employed in making investment decisions, while executives will be employed in handling grievances.

The New Technology of Information Processing

The automation of manufacturing processes is a natural continuation and extension of the Industrial Revolution. We have seen a steady increase in the amount of machinery employed per worker. In the earlier phases of mechanization, the primary function of machinery was to replace human energy with mechanical energy. To some extent in all phases, and to a growing extent in recent developments, another goal has been to substitute mechanical for human sensing and controlling activities. Those who distinguish the newer automation from the older mechanization stress our growing ability to replace with machines simple human perceiving, choosing and manipulating processes.

The Nearly Automatic Factory and Office

The genuinely automatic factory—the workerless factory that can produce output and perhaps also, within limits, maintain and repair itself—will be technically feasible long before too many years have elapsed. From very unsystematic observation of changes going on in factories today, one might surmise that the typical factory of 1985 will not, however, be fully automatic. More likely the typical factory will have reached, say, the level of automaticity that has been attained in 1960 by the most modern oil refineries or power generating stations.

The same kinds of technical developments that lead toward the automatic factory are bringing about an even more rapid revolution—and perhaps eventually a more complete one—in large-scale clerical operations. The very abstract nature of symbol manipulation facilitates the design of equipment to do it, and the further automation of clerical work is impeded by fewer technical barriers than the further automation of factory production. We can conjecture that by 1985 the departments of a company concerned with major clerical functions—accounting, processing of customers' orders, inventory and production control, purchasing and the like—will have reached an even higher level of automation than most factories.

Both the factory and the office, then, are rapidly becoming complex man-machine systems with a very large amount of production equipment, in the case of the factory, and computing equipment, in the case of the office, per employee. The clerical department and the factory will come more and more to resemble each other. The one will present the picture of a small group of employees operating (I am tempted to use the more accurate phrase "collaborating with") a large computing system; the other, the picture of a similar small group of employees operating a large production system. The interrelation of man with machine will become quite as important a design problem for such systems as the interrelation of man with man.

Now we must not commit the error I warned against in discussing the doctrine of comparative advantage. When we foresee fewer employees in factory and office, we mean fewer per unit of output and fewer per unit of capital equipment. It does not follow that there will be fewer in total. To predict the occupational profile that will result, we must look more closely at the prospective rates of automation in different occupations.

Before we turn to this task, however, it is worth reporting a couple of the lessons that are currently being learned in factory and clerical automation:

(1) Automation does not mean "dehumanizing" work. On the contrary, in most actual instances of recent automation jobs were made, on the whole, more pleasant and interesting, as judged by the employees themselves, than they had been before. In particular, automation may move more and more in the direction of eliminating the machine-paced assembly-line task and the repetitive clerical task. It appears generally to reduce the work-pushing, man-driving and expediting aspects of first-line supervision.

(2) Contemporary automation does not generally change to an important extent the profile of skill levels among the employees. It perhaps calls, on the average, for some upgrading of skills in the labor force, but conflicting trends are observable at different stages in automation.

The Occupational Profile

To predict the occupational distribution of the employed population in 1985, we would have to go down the list of occupations and assess, for each, the potentialities of automation. Even if we could do this, our inferences would not be quite direct. For we also have to take into account (1) income elasticity of demand—the fact that as productivity rises, the demands for some goods and services will rise more rapidly than the demands for others; (2) price elasticity of demand—the fact that the most rapidly automated activities will also show the greatest price reductions, so that the net reduction in employment in these activities will be substantially less than the gross reduction at a constant level of production.

As a fanciful example, let us consider the number of persons engaged in the practice of psychiatry. It is reasonable to assume that the demand for psychiatric services, at constant prices, will increase more than proportionately with an increase in income.

Hence, the income effect of the general increase in a society's productivity will be to increase the proportion of psychiatrists in the employed population. Now, let us suppose that a specific technological development permits the automation of psychiatry itself, so that one psychiatrist can do the work formerly done by ten. It is not at all clear whether a 90 per cent reduction in price of psychiatric services would increase the demand for those services by a factor of more or less than ten. But if the demand increased by a factor of more than ten, the proportion of persons employed in psychiatry would actually increase.

Thus prediction of the occupational profile depends on estimates of the income and price elasticity of demand for particular goods and services as well as estimates of relative rates of increase in productivity. This is not the only difficulty the forecaster faces. He must also be extremely cautious in his assumptions as to what is, and what is not, likely to be automated. In particular, automation is not the only way to reduce the cost of a process—a more effective way is to eliminate it. An expert in automation would tell you that the garbage collector's job is an extremely difficult one to automate (at any reasonable cost) in a straightforward way. It has, of course, simply been eliminated in many communities by grinding the garbage and transporting it in liquid through the sewerage system. Such Columbus-egg solutions of the production problem are not at all rare, and will be an important part of automation.

Another Approach to Prediction

With all these reservations and qualifications is any prediction possible? I think it is, but I think it requires us to go back to some fundamentals. The ordinary classification of occupations is basically an "end-use" classification—it indicates what social function is performed by each occupation. To understand automation, we must begin our classification of human activities at the other end—what basic capacities does the human organism bring to tasks, capacities that are used in different proportions for different tasks?

Viewed as a resource in production, a man is a pair of eyes and ears, a brain, a pair of hands, a pair of legs and some muscles for applying force. Automation proceeds in two ways: (1) by providing mechanized means for performing some of the functions formerly performed by a man, and (2) by eliminating some of these functions. Moreover, the mechanized means that replace the man can be of a general-purpose character (like the man) or highly specialized.

The steam engine and the electric motor are relatively general-purpose substitutes for muscles. A butter-wrapping machine is a special-purpose substitute for a pair of hands which eliminates some eye-brain activities the human butter wrapper would require. A feedback system for controlling the temperature of a chemical process is a special-purpose substitute for eyes, brain and hands. A digital computer employed in preparing a payroll is a relatively general-purpose substitute for eyes, brain and hands. A modern multitool milling machine is a special-purpose device that eliminates many of the positioning (eye-brain-hand) processes that were formerly required in a sequence of machining operations.

The earlier history of mechanization was characterized by: (1) rapid substitution of mechanical energy for muscles; (2) partial and spotty introduction of special-purpose devices that performed simple, repetitive eye-brain-hand sequences; (3) elimination, by mechanizing transport and by coordinating sequences of operations on a special-purpose basis, of many human eye-brain-hand sequences that had previously been required.

Thus, man's comparative advantage in energy production has been greatly reduced in most situations—to the point where he is no longer a significant source of power in our economy. He has been supplanted also in performing many relatively simple and repetitive eye-brain-hand sequences. He has retained his greatest comparative advantage in (1) the use of his brain as a flexible general-purpose problem-solving device, (2) the flexible use of his sensory organs and hands, and (3) the use of his legs, on rough terrain as well as smooth, to make this general-purpose sensing-thinking-manipulating system available wherever it is needed.

This picture of man's functions in a man-machine system was vividly illustrated by the construction work going on outside my window. Most of the energy for earth digging was being supplied by the mechanical elephants, but each depended on its mahout for eyes and (if you don't object to my fancy) for eye-trunk coordination. The fact that the elephant was operating in rough, natural terrain made automation of the mahout a difficult, although by no means insoluble, technical problem. It would almost certainly not now be economical. But other men—the men with wheelbarrows particularly—were performing even more manual and primitive tasks. Again, the delivery of the concrete to the forms could have been much more fully automated but at a high cost. The men provided a flexible, if not very powerful, means for delivering small quantities of concrete to a number of different points over uneven terrain.

Flexibility and general-purpose applicability is the key to most spheres where the human has a comparative advantage over the machine. This raises two questions:

(1) What are the prospects for matching human flexibility in automatic devices?

(2) What are the prospects for matching humans in particular activities by reducing the need for flexibility?

The second question is a familiar one throughout the history of mechanization; the first alternative is more novel.

Flexibility in Automata

We must consider separately the sensory organs, the manipulatory organs, the locomotive organs and the central nervous system. Duplicating the problem-solving and information-handling capabilities of the brain is not far off; it would be surprising if it were not accomplished within the next decade. But these capabilities are so much involved in management activity that we shall have to discuss them at length in a later section.

We are much further from replacing the eyes, the hands and the legs. From an economic as well as a technological standpoint, I would hazard the guess that automation of a flexible central nervous system will be feasible long before automation of a comparably flexible sensory, manipulative or locomotive system. I shall state later my reasons for thinking this.

If these conjectures are correct, we may expect (other things being equal) automation of thinking and symbol-manipulating functions to proceed more rapidly than the automation of the more complex eye-brain-hand sequences. But before we grasp this conclusion too firmly, we need to remove one assumption.

Environmental Control a Substitute for Flexibility

If we want an organism or mechanism to behave effectively in a complex and changing environment, we can design into it adaptive mechanisms that allow it to respond flexibly to the demands the environment places on it. Alternatively, we can try to simplify and stabilize the environment. We can adapt organism to environment or environment to organism.

Both processes have been significant in biological evolution. The development of the multicellular organism may be interpreted as simplifying and stabilizing the environment of the internal cells by insulating them from the complex and variable external environment in which the entire organism exists. This is the significance of homeostasis in evolution—that in a very real sense it adapts the environment to the organism (or the elementary parts of the organism) and hence avoids the necessity of complicating the individual parts of the organism.

Homeostatic control of the environment (the environment, that is, of the individual worker or the individual machine) has played a tremendous role in the history of mechanization and in the history of occupational specialization as well. Let me cite some examples that show how all-pervasive this principle is:

(1) The smooth road provides a constant environment for the vehicle—eliminating the advantages of flexible legs.

(2) The first step in every major manufacturing sequence (steel, textiles, wood products) reduces a highly variable natural substance (metallic ore, fiber, trees) to a far more homogeneous and constant material (pig iron, thread, boards or pulp). All subsequent manufacturing processes are thus insulated from the variability of the natural material. The application of the principle of interchangeable parts performs precisely the same function for subsequent manufacturing steps.

(3) By means of transfer machines work in process in modern automated lines is presented to successive machine tools in

proper position to be grasped and worked, eliminating the sensory and manipulative functions of workers who formerly loaded such tools by hand.

We see that mechanization has more often proceeded by eliminating the need for human flexibility—replacing rough terrain with a smooth environment—than by imitating it. Now homeostatic control of the environment tends to be a cumulative process. When we have mechanized one part of a manufacturing sequence, the regularity and predictiveness secured from this mechanization generally facilitates the mechanization of the next stage.

Let us apply this idea to the newly mechanized data-processing area. One of the functions that machines perform badly at present, humans rather well, is reading printed text. Because of the variability of such text, it would seem that the human eye is likely to retain for some time a distinct comparative advantage in handling it. But the wider the use of machines in data processing, the more pains we will take to prepare the source data in a form that can be read easily by a machine. Thus, if scientific journals are to be read mostly by machines, and only small segments of their scanning presented to the human researchers, we shall not bother to translate manuscripts into linotype molds, molds into slugs, and slugs into patterns of ink on paper. We shall, in time, use the typewriter to prepare computer input— punched tape or cards, for example, and simply by-pass the printed volume.

Now these considerations do not alter our earlier conclusion that humans are likely to retain their comparative advantage in activities that require sensory, manipulative and motor flexibility (and, to a much lesser extent, problem-solving flexibility). They show, however, that we must be careful not to assume that the particular activities that now call for this flexibility will continue to do so. The stabilization of the environments for productive activity will reduce or eliminate the need for flexible response at many points in the productive process, continuing a trend that is as old as multicellular life. In particular, in the light of what has been said of the feasibility of automating problem solving, we should not make the simple assumption that the higher-status occupations, and those requiring most education, are going to be the least automated. There are perhaps as good prospects technically and economically for automating completely the job of a physician, a corporate vice-president or a college teacher, as for automating the job of the man who operates a piece of earth-moving equipment.

Man as Man's Environment

In most work situations, an important part of man's environment is man. This is, moreover, an exceedingly "rough" part of his environment. Interacting with his fellow man calls on his greatest flexibility both in sensory activity and response. He must read the nuances of expressions, postures, intonations; he must take into account in numerous ways the individuality of the person opposite him.

What do we mean by *automating* those activities in organizations that consist in responding to other men? I hardly know how to frame the question, much less to answer it. It is often asserted—even by people who are quite sophisticated on the general subject of automation—that personal services cannot be automated, that a machine cannot acquire a bedside manner or produce the positive effect that is produced by a courteous sales clerk.

Let me, at least for purposes of argument, accept that proposition. (It leaves me uneasy, for I am aware of how many people in our own culture have affective relations with such mechanisms as automobiles, rolling mills—and computers.) Accepting it does not settle the question of how much of man's environment in the highly automatized factory or office will be man. For much of the interpersonal activity called for in organizations results from the fact that the basic blue-collar and clerical work is done by humans, who need supervision and direction. Another large chunk of interpersonal activity is the buying and selling activity—the work of the salesman and the buyer.

As far as supervisory work is concerned, we might suppose that it would decrease in the same proportion as the total number of employees; hence that automation would not affect the occupational profile in this respect at least. This may be true in first approximation, but it needs qualification. The amounts and types of supervision required by a work force depend on many things, including the extent to which the work pace is determined by the men or by machines and the extent to which the work is prescheduled. Supervision of a machine-paced operation is a very different matter from supervision of an operation where the foreman is required to see that the workers maintain a normal pace—with or without incentive schemes. Similarly, a highly scheduled shop leaves room for much less expediting activity than one where scheduling is less formal and complete.

As a generalization, I would predict that work-pushing and expediting will make up a much smaller part of the supervisory job at lower and middle levels in highly automated operations than they generally do at present. Whether these activities will be replaced, in the total occupational profile, by other managerial activities we shall have to consider a little later.

What about the salesman? I have little basis for conjecture on this point. If we think that buying decisions are not going to be made much more objectively than they have in the past, then we might conclude the automation of the salesman's role will proceed less rapidly than the automation of many other jobs. If so, selling will account for a larger fraction of total employment.

Summary: Blue-Collar and Clerical Automation

We can now summarize what we have said about the prospects of the automatic factory and office and about the general characteristics of the organization that the executive of 1985 will manage. Clearly, it will be an organization with a much higher ratio of machines to men than is characteristic of organizations today. The men in the system can be expected to play three kinds of roles:

(1) There will be a few vestigial workmen—probably a smaller part of the total labor force than today—who will be part of in-line production, primarily doing tasks requiring relatively flexible eye-brain-hand coordination (a few wheelbarrow pushers and a few mahouts).

(2) There will be a substantial number of men whose task is to keep the system operating by preventive and remedial

maintenance. Machines will play an increasing role, of course, in maintenance functions, but machine powers will not likely develop as rapidly relatively to those of men in this area as in in-line activities. Moreover, the total amount of maintenance work—to be shared by men and machines—will increase. For the middle run, at least, I would expect this group to make up an increasing fraction of the total work force.

(3) There will be a substantial number of men at professional levels, responsible for the design of product, for the design of the productive process and for general management. We have still not faced the question of how far automation will go in these areas, and hence we cannot say very firmly whether such occupations will be a larger or smaller part of the whole. Anticipating our later analysis, I will conjecture that they will constitute about the same part as they do now of total factory and office employment.

A second important characteristic of future production and data-processing organizations is that some of the kinds of interpersonal relations—in supervising and expediting—that at present are very stressful for most persons engaged in them will be substantially reduced in importance.

Finally, in the entire occupied population, a larger fraction of members than at present will be engaged in occupations where personal service involving face-to-face human interaction is an important part of the job. I am confident in stating this conclusion; far less confident in conjecturing what these occupations will be, for the reasons already set forth.

In some respects—especially in terms of what work means to those engaged in it—this picture of the automated world of the future does not look drastically different from the world of the present. Under the general assumptions we made—rapid automation, but under full employment and with a stable skill profile—it will be a happier or more relaxed place than it is now; perhaps more of us will be salesmen. As far as man's productive life is concerned, these do not appear to be earth-shaking changes. Moreover, our conclusions do not depend very sensitively on the exact degree of automation we predict: A little more or a little less would not change the occupational picture much.

The Automation of Management

I have several times sidestepped the question of how far and how fast we could expect management activities to be automated. I have said something about supervision, but little about the large miscellany of management activities involving decision making, problem solving and just plain "thinking."

In what follows I shall use the terms "decision making" and "problem solving" in a broad sense to refer interchangeably to this whole range of activities. Decision making in this sense involves much more than the final choice among possible courses of action. It involves, first of all, detaching the occasions for decision—the problems that have to be dealt with—and directing the organization's attention to them. It involves, second, developing possible problem solutions—courses of action— among which the final choice can be made. Discovering and defining problems, elaborating courses of action and making final choices are all stages in the decision-making process. When the term decision making is used, we generally think of the third stage, but the first two account for many more man hours of effort in organizations than the third. Much more management effort is allocated to attention-directing functions and to the investigation, fact gathering, design and problem solving involved in developing courses of action than to the process of selection. Decision making, defined in this broad way, constitutes the bulk of managerial activity.

The problems that managers at various levels in organizations face can be classified according to how well structured, how routine, how cut and dried they are when they arise. On the one end of the continuum are highly programmed decisions: routine procurement of office supplies or pricing standard products; on the other end of the continuum are unprogrammed decisions: basic, once-for-all decisions to make a new product line, or strategies for labor negotiations on a new contract or major styling decisions. Between these two extremes lie decisions with every possible mixture of programmed and nonprogrammed, well-structured and ill-structured, routine and nonroutine elements.

There is undoubtedly a rough, but far from perfect, correlation between a manager's organization level and the extent to which his decisions are programmed. We would expect the decisions that the president and vice-president face to be less programmed, on the average, than those faced by the factory department head or the factory manager.

We are now in the early stages of a technological revolution of the decision-making process. That revolution has two aspects, one considerably further advanced than the other. The first aspect, concerned largely with decisions close to the programmed end of the continuum, is the province of the new field called *operations research* or *management science.* The second aspect, concerned with unprogrammed as well as programmed decisions, is the province of a set of techniques that are coming to be known as *heuristic programming.*

Operations Research

I will not recount the history of operations research. It is largely the product of efforts that began on a large scale during World War II. Nor will I essay a careful definition, for operations research is as much a social movement—a migration of natural scientists, econometricians and mathematicians into the area of business decision making—as it is a definable body of knowledge.

Operations research attempts to apply mathematics and the capabilities of modern electronic computers to business decision making. By now it is clear that the attempt is going to be highly successful. Important areas of business and engineering decision making have yielded to these techniques, and the area of possible and actual application continues to grow.

Let me be more concrete and show how operations research is affecting management and how it will affect it. I shall ignore business data processing—the automation of clerical activities—and look exclusively at management activities. I can describe the situation by examples, for we are interested in the technical and economic potential of these techniques, not the present extent of their use.

(1) Managers make a whole series of decisions to control inventory and production: purchasing decisions, setting the pro-

duction rate and product mix, ordering stock for warehouses, shipping decisions and the like. Several alternative mathematical techniques are now available for making such decisions; these techniques have been more or less extensively tested in practical situations, and they are being used in day-to-day decision making in a number of companies. The evidence seems to me convincing that decisions of these kinds can now be made, in most situations, with the aid of operations research techniques and with the virtual elimination of managerial judgment, far better than such decisions have been made in the past. Moreover, in most tests that have been made, even at this early stage in the development and application of such techniques, they have shown that they can justify themselves economically. There is little or no excuse for purchasing agents, production control managers, factory managers or warehouse managers intervening in such decisions any more. (I hasten to add that, as with any new technique, a company that wishes to make use of it must be willing to incur some development and training expense.)

(2) The injection of the mathematical techniques just mentioned into the clerical processes involved in procurement, factory production control and filling customers' orders can permit the virtually complete automation of this flow in many situations, with the removal of both clerical and low-level management participation from the day-to-day activity. Customers' orders can be received and filled, the customer invoiced, orders placed on the factory and raw-material stocks replenished—all untouched by human hands and unthought of by human decision makers.

(3) Mathematical techniques for detailed scheduling of factory production, while less far advanced than the techniques just described, will almost certainly have reached within five or ten years the point where scheduling can also be completely automated, both in its clerical and in its decision-making aspects.

(4) In the early years of the computer, one of its main applications was to relieve engineering organizations of the bulk of routine calculations in design. The computer initially was a clerical aid to analysis. Within the past three or four years, we have discovered how the computer can also take over the design-synthesis job in many relatively simple situations. (Though these

situations are "simple," they were complex enough to require the services of college-trained engineers.) To put it simply, computers can now take customers' orders for many types of electric motors, generators and transformers, synthesize devices that meet the design specifications, and send the manufacturing specifications to the factory floor—again untouched by human hands. Where these techniques are now used, it is reported that they yield improved designs at about the same cost as the human design process they replace.

(5) Computers, programmed to carry out linear programming calculations, are now widely used to determine product mix for oil refineries and to determine formulas for commercial feed mixes. The Iowa farmer who tunes in to the morning radio reports of hog prices now learns from the commercial that XYZ feed gives him the best nutrition at the lowest cost because it is blended by electronic computers using modern mathematical techniques.

(6) A large commercial airline has used computers to simulate major parts of its flight and terminal operation and has used the simulation to decide how many reserve aircraft it needed— an investment decision of great magnitude.

The plain fact is that a great many middle-management decisions that have always been supposed to call for the experienced human judgment of managers and professional engineers can now be made at least as well by computers as by managers. Moreover, a large part of the total middle-management job consists of decisions of the same general character as those that have already yielded to automation. The decisions are repetitive and require little of the kinds of flexibility that constitute man's principal comparative advantage over machines. We can predict with some confidence, I think, that persons making such decisions will constitute a much smaller fraction of the total occupied group within a few years than they do now.

Heuristic Programming

The mathematical and computing techniques for making programmed decisions replace man but they do not generally simulate him. That is to say, a computer scheduling a refinery does not make the same calculations as would be made by an experienced refinery scheduler—even if it comes out with a very similar solution.

This fact has led to some misconceptions about the nature of computers and about their potentialities. "Computers are just very speedy morons for carrying out arithmetic calculations," it is often said. "They only do what you program them to do." These statements belong to that class of half-truths that are important just because their implications are so misleading. I shall have to pause long enough to make some categorical statements about computers. I do not have space here to develop them at length.

(1) Computers are very general devices capable of manipulating all kinds of symbols—words as readily as numbers. The fact that computers generally do arithmetic is an historical accident. If a particular decision-making situation is not quantitative we cannot handle it with traditional mathematical techniques. This constitutes no essential barrier to computerization. Much successful research has been carried out in the past five years on the use of computers for processing nonnumerical information.

(2) Computers behave like morons only because we are just beginning to learn how to communicate with them in something better than moronic language. There now exist so-called compiling techniques (e.g., FORTRAN) that instruct computers in general language very similar to the ordinary language of mathematics. With these compilers, we now can program a computer to evaluate a formula by writing down little more than the formula itself, and comparable powers have been developed for nonnumerical computing. They have not reached the point where they permit the programmer to communicate with the computer in idiomatic English, but only in a kind of simple pidgin English.

(3) Computers do only what you program them to do, but (1) you can program them to behave adaptively, and (2) you can program them to improve their own programs on the basis of their experiences—that is, to learn. Hence, the more accurate statement is: Computers do only what you program them to do in exactly the same sense that humans do only what their genes and their cumulative experiences program them to do.

This assertion leaves little room for free will in either computer or human, but it leaves a great deal of room in both for flexible, adaptive, complex, intelligent behavior.

(4) It has now been demonstrated, by doing it, that computers can be programmed to solve relatively ill-structured problems by using methods very similar to those used by humans in the same problem-solving situations: that is, by highly selective trial-and-error search using all sorts of rules of thumb to guide the selection; by abstracting from the given problem and solving first the abstracted problem; by using analogy; by reasoning in terms of means and ends, goals and subgoals; by adjusting aspirations to the attainable. There is no longer reason to regard phenomena like judgment and insight as either unanalyzable or unanalyzed, for, in some forms at least, these phenomena have been simulated—computers have exercised judgment and exhibited insight. The range of capabilities of computer programs of this sort is still extremely narrow, but the significant point is that some such programs have been written, tested and even compared in their behavior with the behavior of human laboratory subjects performing the same tasks.

Computer programs that handle nonnumerical tasks, use humanoid problem-solving techniques (instead of the systematic algorithmic techniques of classical mathematics) and sometimes include learning processes, are called *heuristic programs.* They incorporate, in their processes, one or more aspects of what has been called the art of plausible reasoning, an art that guides us through the numerous, diverse, ill-structured decisions of everyday life.

The engineering design programs I mentioned earlier are really heuristic programs, for they involve inductive reasoning. Heuristic programs have now been written for such tasks as playing checkers, playing chess, finding proofs for geometry theorems and for theorems in elementary symbolic logic, solving trigonometric and algebraic identities, balancing a factory assembly line, composing music (the ILLIAC Suite) and memorizing nonsense syllables. One program, the General Problem Solver, while not as general as its name may suggest, is entirely free from reference to any particular subject matter and is, in fact, a quite flexible scheme for reasoning in terms of goals and subgoals about any subject.

Let me make my point perfectly clear. Heuristic programs do not merely substitute machine brute force for human cunning. Increasingly, they imitate—and in some cases improve upon—human cunning. I can illustrate this by describing briefly the three existing computer programs for playing chess. One of these, the Los Alamos program, depends heavily on machine speed. The program examines, at each move, almost one million alternative possibilities, evaluating them on the basis of simple, crude criteria and selecting the one that appears best. Clearly it is doing something quite different from the human chess player—the human neither could nor would select moves in this way. The second program, Bernstein's program, is much more selective. It examines about 2,500 alternatives, chosen on the basis of rules of thumb a chess player would use and evaluates them in a slightly more complicated way than does the Los Alamos program. The third program, the RAND-Carnegie program, is still more selective. It seldom examines as many as fifty alternatives but selects those to be examined and evaluates them in a rather involved way. All three programs, at present, play about the same level of chess—a very low level, it should be said. But they achieve this result in quite different ways. The Los Alamos program, though it embodies certain heuristic ideas, calls for machine speed rather than machine intelligence. The RAND-Carnegie program begins to approach, in the rules of thumb it embodies, the processes a human uses in choosing a chess move. Bernstein's program lies midway between the other two. Thus, in talking about our increasing capacity to write heuristic programs that simulate human problem solving, I am speaking of programs that lie toward the RAND-Carnegie end of this continuum rather than the Los Alamos end. I am speaking of programs that reason, think and learn.

The microcosm of chess may still appear to you far more structured and programmed than the macrocosm of the everyday world. Perhaps it is, although the point could be argued. However that may be, the microcosm of chess is sufficiently complex, sufficiently rich in alternatives, sufficiently irregular in structure that it poses to the problem-solving organism or mechanism the same *kinds* of difficulties and requirements that are posed—perhaps in higher degree—by ill-structured problems in general. Hence, the fact that chess programs, theorem-proving programs, music-composing programs and a factory-scheduling program now exist indicates that the conceptual mountains have been crossed that barred us from understanding how the human mind grapples with everyday affairs. It is my conviction that no major new ideas will have to be discovered to enable us to extend these early results to the whole of human thinking, problem-solving, decision-making activity. We have every reason to believe that within a very short time—I am even willing to say ten years or less—we will be able technically to produce computers that can grapple with and solve at least the range of problems that humans are able to grapple with and solve—those that are ill-structured as well as those that are well-structured.

If the technical prediction is correct, what about the economics of the matter? Again, we must apply the doctrine of comparative advantage. To what extent, in 1985, will managers and other humans be occupied in thinking about and solving ill-structured problems, as distinct from doing other things? On this point the image in my crystal ball is very dim. I will nevertheless hazard some guesses. My first guess is that man will retain a greater comparative advantage in handling ill-structured problems than in handling well-structured problems. My second guess is that he will retain a greater advantage in tasks involving sensory-manipulative coordination—"physical flexibility"—than in ill-structured problem-solving tasks—"mental flexibility." If this is true, a larger part of the working population will be mahouts and wheelbarrow pushers and a smaller part will be scientists and executives—particularly of the staff variety. The amount of shift in this direction will be somewhat diminished by the fact that as income and general productivity rise, the demand for work involving ill-structured problem solving will probably increase more than the demand for work involving flexible manipulation of the physical environment. The demand for psychiatric work will increase more rapidly than the demand for surgical work—but the rate of automation of the former will be much greater than the rate of automation of the latter.

A Summary: The Automation of Management

Our analysis rests on the assumption that managers are largely concerned with supervising, with solving well-structured problems and with solving ill-structured problems. We have predicted that the automation of the second of these activities —solving well-structured problems—will proceed extremely rapidly; the automation of the third—solving ill-structured problems, moderately rapidly; and the automation of supervision more slowly. However, we have also concluded that, as less and less work becomes man paced and more and more of it machine paced, the nature of supervision will undergo change. There is no obvious way to assess quantitatively all these cross currents and conflicting trends. We might even conclude that management and other professional activities, taken collectively, may constitute about the same part of the total spectrum of occupations a generation hence as they do now. But there is reason to believe that the kinds of activities that now characterize middle management will be more completely automated than the others and hence will come to have a smaller part in the whole management picture.

Some Other Dimensions of Change in Management

There are other dimensions for differentiating management and professional tasks, of course, besides the one we have been using. It is possible that if we described the situation in terms of these other dimensions, the change would appear larger. Let me explore this possibility just a little bit further.

First, I think we can predict that in future years the manager's time perspective will be lengthened. As automated subsystems take over the minute-by-minute and day-by-day operation of the factory and office, the humans in the system will become increasingly occupied with preventive maintenance, with system breakdowns and malfunctions, and—perhaps most important of all—with the design and modification of systems. The automatic factory will pretty much—and subject to all of the qualifications I have introduced—run itself; the company executives will be much more concerned with tomorrow's automatic factory. Executives will have less excuse than they now have to let the emergencies of today steal the time that was allocated to planning for the future. I don't think planning is going to be a machineless function—it also will be carried out by man-machine systems, but with perhaps a larger man component and a smaller machine component than day-to-day operations.

Does this mean that executives will need a high level of technical competence in the engineering of automated factories or data-processing systems? Probably not. Most automation calls for increased technical skills for maintenance in the early stages; but the farther automation proceeds, the less those who govern the automated system need to know about the details of its mechanism. The driver of a 1960 automobile needs to know less about what is under the hood than the driver of a 1910 automobile. The user of a 1960 computer needs to know less about computer design and operation than the user of a 1950 computer. The manager of a highly automated 1985 factory will need to know less about how things are actually produced, physically, in that factory than the manager of a 1960 factory.

Similarly, we can dismiss the notion that computer programmers will become a powerful elite in the automated corporation. It is far more likely that the programming occupation will become extinct (through the further development of self-programming techniques) than that it will become all-powerful. More and more, computers will program themselves; and direction will be given to computers through the mediation of compiling systems that will be completely neutral so far as content of the decision rules is concerned. Moreover, the task of communicating with computers will become less and less technical as computers come—by means of compiling techniques—closer and closer to handling the irregularities of natural language.

I suppose that managers will be called on, as automation proceeds, for more of what might be described as systems thinking. They will need, to work effectively, to understand their organizations as large and complex dynamic systems involving various sorts of man-machine and machine-machine interactions. For this reason, persons trained in fields like servomechanism engineering or mathematical economics, accustomed to dynamic systems of these kinds, and possessing conceptual tools for understanding them, may have some advantage, at least initially, in operating in the new world. Since no coherent science of complex systems exists today, universities and engineering schools are understandably perplexed as to what kinds of training will prepare their present students for this world.

The Broader Significance of Automation

I have tried to present my reasons for making two predictions that appear, superficially, to be contradictory: that we will have the technical capability, by 1985, to manage corporations by machine; but that humans, in 1985, will probably be engaged in roughly the same array of occupations as they are now. I find both of these predictions reassuring.

Acquiring the technical capacity to automate production as fully as we wish, or as we find economical, means that our per capita capacity to produce will continue to increase far beyond the point where any lurking justification will remain for poverty or deprivation. We will have the means to rule out scarcity as mankind's first problem and to attend to other problems that are more serious.

Since, in spite of this increased productivity, the occupations that humans will find in the corporation of 1985 will be familiar ones, we can dismiss two fears: first, the fear of technological unemployment, second, the "R.U.R. fear"—the fear that many people feel at the prospect of fraternizing with robots in an automated world. Fraternize we shall, but in the friendly, familiar way that we now fraternize with our automobiles and our power shovels.

Having dismissed, or dealt with, these two issues, we shall be better prepared to face the more fundamental problems of that automated world. These are not new problems, nor are they less important than the problems of scarcity and peace. But they are long-range rather than short-range problems, and hence seldom rise to the head of the agenda as long as there are more pressing issues still around. Three of them in particular, I think, are going to receive a great deal of attention as automation proceeds: developing a science of man, finding alternatives for work and production as basic goals for society and reformulating man's view of his place in the universe.

A Science of Man

I have stressed the potentialities of the computer and of heuristic programming as substitutes for human work. The research now going on in this area is equally important for understanding how humans perform information-processing tasks—how they think. That research has already made major progress toward a psychology of cognitive processes, and there are no reasons to hope that the potential of the new tools is not limited to cognition but may extend to the affective aspects of behavior as well.

We can predict in the world of 1985 we shall have psychological theories that are as successful as the theories we have in chemistry and biology today. We shall have a pretty good understanding of how the human mind works. If that prediction is correct, it has obvious and fundamental consequences for both pedagogy and psychiatry. We may expect very rapid advances in the effectiveness and efficiency of our techniques of teaching and our techniques for dealing with human maladjustment.

Social Goals

The continuing rise in productivity may produce profound changes, in addition to those already caused by the Industrial Revolution, in the role that work plays in man's life and among man's goals. It is hard to believe—although this may just exhibit the weakness of my imagination—that man's appetite for gadgets can continue to expand at the rate required to keep work and production in central roles in the society. Even Galbraith's proposal for diverting expenditures from gadgets to social services can only be a temporary expedient. We shall have to, finally, come to grips with the problem of leisure.

In today's society, the corporation satisfies important social and psychological needs in addition to the needs for goods and services. For those who do well in managerial careers, it satisfies needs for success and status. For some of these men and for others, it is one of the important outlets for creativity. In a society where scarcity of goods and services is of little importance, those institutions, including the corporation, whose main function is to deal with scarcity, will occupy a less central position than they have in the past. Success in management will carry smaller rewards in prestige and status than it now does. Moreover, as the decision-making function becomes more highly automated, corporate decision making will perhaps provide fewer outlets for creative drives than it now does. Alternative outlets will have to be supplied.

Man in the Universe

It is only one step from the problem of goals to what psychiatrists now refer to as the identity crisis, and what used to be called cosmology. The developing capacity of computers to simulate man—and thus both to serve as his substitute and to provide a theory of human mental functions—will change man's conception of his own identity as a species.

The definition of man's uniqueness has always formed the kernel of his cosmological and ethical systems. With Copernicus and Galileo, he ceased to be the species located at the center of the universe, attended by sun and stars. With Darwin, he ceased to be the species created and specially endowed by God with soul and reason. With Freud, he ceased to be the species whose behavior was—potentially—governable by rational mind. As we begin to produce mechanisms that think and learn, he has ceased to be the species uniquely capable of complex, intelligent manipulation of his environment.

I am confident that man will, as he has in the past, find a new way of describing his place in the universe—a way that will satisfy his needs for dignity and for purpose. But it will be a way as different from the present one as was the Copernican from the Ptolemaic.

Computers in
State Government

Alvin Kaltman

The breadth and complexity of government operations make them obvious candidates for computerization. Preliminary efforts to apply automation in government, however, have often failed through inexperience and poor planning—difficulties also experienced, interestingly enough, in many business efforts to introduce automation. Here a computer consultant outlines the areas of governmental decision-making that can best benefit from the introduction of the computer.

State governments are massive information processors. Forms, records, and reports are constantly being filled out, processed, filed, retrieved, updated, refiled and eventually stored. As state agencies have come to provide more and more services, effective record-keeping by manual clerical procedures has become exceedingly difficult—often impossible. As a result, computers are today being applied in all functional areas of state government. The National Association of State Information Systems estimates that nearly 600 computers are currently installed in state government agencies (excluding higher education).

What are the consequences of this trend? One thinks immediately of financial savings, of improvements in efficiency and speed. In so far as computers have been wisely acquired and used, such benefits are indeed visible, although, as I shall show, most of the possible material improvements remain to be achieved. There are also consequences of other kinds, including political ones.

Start with the economics: state-government automated information processing is a $250-million-a-year industry. However, each individual state's contribution to this total is relatively small, usually representing less than one per cent of the total state budget. From their computer investments, state governments have reaped huge cumulative economic dividends, not to mention greater accuracy, reliability, and responsiveness. Pennsylvania's Bureau of Management Information Systems conservatively estimates that the installation of automated information systems has enabled the state to avoid the cost of 22,000 additional employees—an annual saving of approximately $145 million.

Nevertheless, the costs associated with automated data processing (A.D.P.) in state government have risen at a rate which some consider alarming. The number of computers involved has nearly doubled in the past four years—and fees paid to consultants, in that same period, appear to have increased by a factor of ten.

Studies in some states have revealed a shocking proliferation of computer equipment among the disconnected government agencies, and numerous instances of duplicated development efforts. Moreover, equipment has frequently been under-utilized (which is wasteful), there has been a lack of documentation (so that only a few people know the details of a particular system) and a general lack of standardization in the procedures for acquiring and operating computers, so that quite needless mistakes are common. Agency heads have often failed to realize that the unique characteristics of specific equipment are less important than good systems design and have naively competed with each other for bigger and shinier machines.

Recently, waking up to this situation, most states have indeed begun to establish central control over the acquisition and operation of their computers. A strong, technically competent central authority to oversee state-government automatic data-processing (A.D.P.) operations can make a dramatic difference.

For example, California's State Office of Management Services claims to have: halted the proliferation of unnecessary computers; controlled A.D.P. expenditures; established specific policies on the acquisition and use of computers; increased the sharing of computers (and created a general-purpose shared computer utility); adopted a long range (five-year) A.D.P. plan; and provided A.D.P. training to state employees.

In the following examples of current and potential computer applications in state government, I shall try to show how computers can serve state governments as invaluable tools for decision-making. However, since governmental decision-making is fundamentally a political process, there are and will always be things that computers cannot and—more importantly—should not do.

Administration and Finance

The past few years have brought a continuing sharp rise in the cost of state government: with multi-billion dollar state budgets already a reality, automated appropriations-accounting and budgetary control systems are needed to provide the information necessary for the intelligent allocation of available funds; they can also help an individual agency head discover whether allocated funds are in fact being efficiently used.

Ohio, for instance, has a fiscal-management reporting system which automatically checks the accuracy and validity of each billing before it is accepted. Further, by providing daily reports giving the status of all accounts, the system helps to pinpoint potential fiscal problems before they become critical. It also provides monthly and annual reports on the first day following closing, and enables payments to vendors to be made no later than the date on which they are due. A not-inconsiderable side benefit of computerization has been the development of improved cash control and investment procedures, which have resulted in a three-fold increase in interest income.

Compare this to a state where the governor discovered—too late—that even as he was proposing an all-out fight against water pollution, his Department of Finance had been cutting the telephone expenses portion of his Water Pollution Control Division's budget proposal. As it turned out, this single budget cut of only a few thousand dollars crippled the pollution-reporting program.

With budgetary information obscured—as it often is—both

agency budget requests and finance department recommendations are capricious at best and too often totally unrealistic.

Some states still retain systems of central controls so inhibiting that agency heads require Finance Department approval every time they need even to move a telephone, for example. Such controls are designed to prevent misuse of funds—but they do not help to prevent, or even to spot, other forms of mismanagement, and they tend actually to obstruct the intelligent allocation of resources. Automated program budgeting offers the possibility of relaxing ineffective central controls and replacing them with competent, decentralized operations.

Abraham Lincoln once wrote, "If we could first know where we are and whither we are tending, we could better judge what to do and how to do it." A computer-assisted management information system would have helped him; it can, in a timely and accurate manner, provide reports of expenditures, compare actual expenditures with budget estimates, and note unusual variations in cost. Such a system can not only lead the governor out of the dark; it could take the blinders off the legislature as well. Given the facility of on-line inquiry, legislators would be better able to judge the wisdom of each requested budgetary allocation.

Resources and Development

Departments of Commerce serve as clearinghouses for economic information. On the basis of data published by local, state, and federal agencies, they produce area profiles and statistical abstracts and attempt to do economic planning. A very large number of factors must be considered in the formulation of economic plans; preparing good regional or statewide plans is exceedingly difficult if not impossible without the assistance of a computer. Wisconsin and Alabama are among the states which will soon have operational computer systems for this purpose.

Kentucky is formulating a computerized information system to aid in preparing comprehensive outdoor recreation plans. The system will operate within the framework of an over-all statewide resource control plan, and it should greatly improve feasibility and impact studies of proposed recreation facilities.

Kentucky is also developing an information system to assist in water resource planning by generating supply-and-demand projections for municipal and industrial needs, recreation, power, navigation, and irrigation.

State governments have generally failed to utilize computers effectively in planning and development, but this failure is minor compared with the states' almost total abdication of responsibility in the development of information systems for local governments. Perhaps the best measure of this failure would be the amount of available federal aid which goes un-utilized because local governments are unable to gather and process the information necessary to qualify for the help they need. The federal government has helped some cities in such work, and others have managed to automate certain municipal functions on their own or in cooperative ventures. In Louisiana, for example, an automated federal-aid control system helps to coordinate applications for federal aid by political subdivisions (or state agencies), and to monitor all federal grants.

Even where they exist, the services which state governments provide to local governmental units are in some instances nothing to brag about. In one state the Teachers' Retirement Board is 22 months behind in the recording of information needed to calculate estimated annuitant status. Veterans' Service Office disbursements to cities and towns are over $500,000 in arrears, and as a result some municipalities have had to assume short-term debt in order to meet their obligations. As much as one to two years will elapse between the time a local government seeks to fill a vacant position and the time a state Civil Service Commission prepares a list of eligible candidates for the post.

Throughout the past decade there has been talk of using state data-processing centers to provide services to local governmental units. But even today there are few examples, despite an even greater need for intergovernmental coordination and the cooperative development of data-processing applications. California (through its Intergovernmental Board on Electronic Data Processing) and Pennsylvania (through its Interagency Municipal Information Systems Advisory Committee) have been in the forefront of developing such activities.

As an example of one service that could be provided, consider solid-waste disposal. The creation of centralized disposal facilities and the reduction in available landfill sites imply that solid waste collection, hitherto purely a local matter, will soon have to be considered on a statewide basis. State governments in such circumstances could plan schedules and routes to reduce transport costs—usually the dominant factor in waste disposal— by offering vehicle-scheduling systems to assist and coordinate local waste collection and disposal operations.

Consumer Affairs

While it may be politically expedient for a Commissioner of Insurance to deny a request for higher automobile insurance rates, it is hardly in the public interest for him to do so without supporting data. One Commissioner of Insurance reportedly attempted to freeze certain automobile insurance rates on the basis of a two-paragraph finding; not unexpectedly, a court ruled that the finding was inadequate. Part of the problem was that the rates were determined in the aggregate, whereas the court felt that each type of coverage had to be considered separately. Given the amount of data necessary for such a treatment and the time constraints within which a finding must be made, there would seem to be no alternative to the development of computer systems for such calculations.

California's Public Utilities Commission has already taken some steps in this direction by developing a data bank of rates and costs for common carriers. This should provide a stronger base of factual information for regulatory decisions. Common-carrier tariffs are massive documents, universally regarded as unreadable. Computer-assisted rate analysis might make for more rational rate structures, and, as a side benefit, would yield clearly written tariffs that anyone could understand.

Two further potential computer applications for state governments relate primarily to regulated monopolies: one is measuring the quality of service provided, and the other is monitoring company management performance so as to insure that the general public is not penalized for grossly uneconomical management decisions. If regulation is to be more than a political pretense, then public utilities commissions need to be able to predict accurately the effects of company policies and proposed rate-changes on consumer costs, the quality of service, and company earnings. It is unlikely that such a capability can ever be attained without the use of computers.

Human Services

The Massachusetts Public Health Council in January, 1971, adopted new rules designed to improve the delivery and quality of health services provided by the state's nursing and convalescent homes. This change in nursing-home regulations—the first major revision in 17 years—came about as a result of computer-assisted studies which indicated that a majority of Massachusetts' long-term care facilities were not providing services appropriate to the needs of most patients and that their fees were largely unrelated to the services they gave.

Comparative cost programs for state institutions would greatly improve the ability of institution superintendents and agency heads to pinpoint specific problem areas and would provide the data needed for intelligent resource-allocation decisions. But state governments have in fact generally been quite slow to use computers to improve the efficiency—and hence the quality— of care and services offered by state institutions.

The workload of rehabilitation commissions has increased over the past several years, yet even though their budgets have increased by a factor of five or more, many rehabilitation commissions still make no use of A.D.P. to solve their routine paperwork problems. What this means in human terms is that people needing such help as kidney dialysis treatments may not receive them even though funds are available. In one state nearly $1 million of such funds goes unspent each year due to reliance upon a manual data handling system which has long been overburdened.

Welfare has been aptly described as a growth industry with many ills. One state welfare department discovered in a spot survey that, in the state's largest city, over 25 per cent of the state's medical assistance recipients and nearly 30 per cent of the people on general relief were in fact ineligible. Clearly, the present manual systems, which are already unable to continuously monitor eligibility and prevent abuse, will not be improved by the promulgation of executive orders. Some state governments need to be reminded that computer-assisted case-control systems, to monitor welfare eligibility and eliminate duplicate, excessive, and fraudulent payments, offer the best (probably the only) hope of improving the administration of the welfare system.

The Medicaid program has had an enormous impact upon the welfare picture. In one state it accounts for nearly 65 per cent of the welfare case-load and almost 45 per cent of the welfare dollars spent. Because the state does not have an automated Medicaid payments system, payments have fallen so far behind that some pharmacists claim they have had to borrow money to stay in business because of outstanding bills owed them by the state; some physicians report that reimbursements lag two to three years; and the largest hospital in the state has sought a court order to require the immediate payment of interest on perhaps $10 million in overdue bills.

Florida provides an example of what can be done with an on-line Medicaid payments system. The eligibility of the recipient is first checked, prior to the receipt of medical services. A computer-printed statement is issued within ten days of treatment, verified (as to type of treatment and cost) by the provider of the treatment, and forwarded to the Florida Department of Health and Rehabilitative Services, which pays the bill within 30 days. The system can provide up-to-the-minute daily, monthly, and annual reports on the utilization of Medicaid, categorized by type of service. The ready availability of such information can be most helpful in preventing budgetary crises.

Under the direction of the U.S. Department of Labor, state-wide job-bank programs are being established throughout the country. Missouri's Division of Employment Security provides computer-generated listings of job openings, on microfilm, to its local offices in the St. Louis metropolitan area. Utah has a computerized job-matching system which can handle up to 36 selection criteria. The Utah computer system also monitors the quality of its own service to job applicants—it prints out and sends to the local office a full copy of the application of any individual in the active file who has received no service during the preceding 15 days, or has been selected five times by the computer but never referred to a potential employer, or referred three times but never hired. The system also reminds local office personnel of any selections, call-ins, or referrals that have been pending for three days. Should an applicant who is receiving unemployment insurance or welfare benefits refuse to accept a suitable job, the system immediately notifies the local unemployment insurance claims office or the department of public welfare.

Workmen's compensation boards were among the first state agencies to install punched-card equipment. However, some industrial accident boards still have not discovered that computers can help to reduce compensation backlogs. In one state the Industrial Accident Board is so far behind that workers awaiting settlements are forced on to welfare rolls, at an estimated cost of $1.5 million annually in excess welfare costs alone.

Public Safety

Thanks to the infusion of federal aid, a number of statewide police telecommunications systems have been implemented. A policeman can radio the license number of a vehicle under surveillance to his dispatcher and in a matter of seconds know whether the vehicle has been reported stolen or used as a getaway car in a serious crime. In addition to F.B.I. and police data on vehicles, these systems contain information on stolen parts and equipment, boats, firearms, license plates, stocks, bonds or other securities, and wanted or missing persons.

In some states the police are also able to obtain information on any registered vehicle and licensed driver in the state. The ability of the motor vehicles department to respond to special requests—such as providing a list of light-green two-door sedans with 5 as the last digit of the state license—is critically important to law-enforcement agencies. In some instances the information requested may be simply unavailable; in others police wait six weeks or more while special-purpose computer programs are written and used. Obviously there are states that still need to develop a generalized search-and-retrieval capability for motor vehicle data.

Computers can also be used as laboratory tools providing police with detailed information on such diverse items as fingerprints, fibers, firearms, blood, hair, minerals, vegetables, paper, paint, stains, and tools. In New York State, there are 41 facsimile installations which transmit fingerprints to the State Identification and Intelligence System. Upon receiving and classifying a set of fingerprints, the system conducts an automated search to determine if the individual has a prior criminal history on file. If so, a computer-printed summary of the individual's criminal history is transmitted to the law enforcement agency which requested the fingerprint search. The U.S. Department of Justice has developed a prototype organized-crime intelligence system which it plans to make available to the states.

The growing congestion of both criminal and civil cases in the courts is a widely recognized problem. In one state the Superior Courts are staggering under a backlog of over 18,000 untried criminal indictments or complaints (including more than 100 pending capital cases). On the civil side over 65,000 cases are pending and untried. A 40-month wait for trial is common.

Computer systems cannot substitute for badly needed additional judges and other court personnel, but they can help to reduce the amount of time lost both by witnesses and by the courts due to inadequate information handling and inefficient case scheduling. State governments are coming increasingly to realize that to have a statewide police telecommunications network without having a well administered court system is, in effect, to have very little.

Transportation and Construction

State governments have traditionally equated transportation planning with highway planning. In most of the states, highway departments are using computer models to convert origin/

destination data into highway traffic densities. Indiana's State Highway Commission has used a computer-assisted route location system to generate comparisons of alternative corridors in terms of earthwork, pavement construction and right-of-way acquisition costs. The automated creation of maps from aerial photographs has drastically reduced the amount of field surveying work done by the Texas Highway Department, while in that and other states district engineers are solving routine highway design problems using remote computer terminals and civil-engineering calculation programs such as those developed at the Massachusetts Institute of Technology.

Nevertheless, the states make little use of computers for other kinds of transportation planning. They could well be used for modelling mass-transit, air, rail and port development; indeed, it is unlikely that such models can be developed at all without the use of computers. Manual processing of the data required for fully rational transport planning would be (assuming it were possible) prohibitively expensive.

In a number of states there is a backlog in the disbursement of design and construction funds by bureaus of building construction. One state now requires more than a year longer to disburse appropriated funds than a decade ago, and the backlog is itself costing over $5,000 per day. An automated data processing system could greatly reduce these delays: one proposed system would accurately control accounts, maintain a central file of project records, estimate the cost of construction projects prior to appropriation, prepare and monitor a detailed schedule of all actions required to complete a project, and monitor construction progress. As an aid in the future selection of designers and contractors, the system would also evaluate actual performance.

Computer-based project management could lessen the need for state governments to hire consulting firms to supervise the work of designers and contractors. One state is reported to have agreed to a cost-plus contract that could result in a consulting firm receiving up to $30 million for supervising a project costing an estimated $600 million. While on a percentage basis this fee may not seem unreasonable, it is quite possible that computer-based management could have eliminated or markedly reduced the expense.

The preceding discussion of computer applications in state government has been far from comprehensive. For example, state governments could also use computers in such varied functions as designing buildings, allocating office space, reducing the incidence of lead poisoning, maintaining inventories of capital equipment, preparing purchase orders, allocating civil-defense resources, developing contingency plans for natural disasters, maintaining lists of voters, insuring that automated vote-count systems are protected against deliberate fraud, making publicly available all state-agency regulations applying to the general public, and protecting the public against computer-assisted harassment.

Maintaining Privacy and Security

In many present and potential applications—especially in information systems dealing with criminal history and suspected criminal activity—careful attention must be paid to maintaining security of computerized data. This applies especially to applications directly affecting people.

On the other hand, properly used, the computer can serve as a powerful protector of individual rights. Data now being computerized has often hitherto existed in manual files—sometimes open to view by any staff member or casual visitor, irrespective of his need to know. One state maintains a file of individual court appearances on an estimated five million index cards; in others, arrest histories and court records have been illegally sold to credit bureaus, banks, and brokerage houses. Computerized data, in contrast to legible paperwork, is inherently less accessible to casual inspection; and it can be coded so that information obtained by tapping a data file is indecipherable except to those familiar with the system.

Automated checking on the validity of data, and automatic purging of data, are possible with computer systems. And the computer itself can be programmed to keep track of persons having the right of access to its data, to maintain information on who accessed the data and when, and to automatically check the identification of persons requesting information by means of fingerprint and/or voice-print comparisons.

Towards Real Competence

Although computers are being applied in all areas of state government, the application is often neither efficient nor effective. Among the reasons commonly cited for a state's inability to fully avail itself of the benefits of A.D.P. are lack of competent personnel, lack of central control of A.D.P. work, lack of funds, lack of understanding of the field, unwillingness to share facilities, and resistance to change.

It is true that relatively small direct savings are to be derived from the competent management of a given set of A.D.P. activities (costing only a few million dollars a year). But in many states these apparently modest savings have been confused with the invaluable benefits to be derived from the effective use of computers as a tool for decision-making. Some state officials, underestimating these benefits, have felt unwilling to confront the political costs of establishing effective central control over A.D.P. activities.

But very different reasons have also occasionally prevailed, when state officials understand only too well the implications of establishing central control over the acquisition and operation of their computers. Such officials would rather, for example, that an inept finance-department A.D.P. section spend millions on failing to develop an automated financial information system than that a technically competent central authority should succeed; for the latter would facilitate the auditing of state accounts and expose the actions of agency heads, legislative committee chairmen, and others to public view. Also, a central authority might not respond to political patronage in filling technical positions as readily as the more politically dependent agencies. And a competent state A.D.P. authority would surely insist on open competitive bidding on all contracts for computing equipment, supplies and services. In states where A.D.P. contracts are presently awarded on a sole-source basis with few if any questions asked, such a development might not be welcome.

In some states, a history of incompetent A.D.P. management has made some officials skeptical of ever successfully implementing any but the most routine computer applications. Under these conditions state managements have sometimes become so wrapped up in the intricacies of their computer operations that instead of insisting on visible progress and demanding personal accountability for the achievement of objectives, they have become inured to delays and difficulties. What they fail to see is that if the application of computers in state government is to be effective, a strong, technically-competent central A.D.P. authority is a necessity. Automated information systems alone cannot solve the problems facing state government, but the proper use of such systems can help to make government more responsive and efficient.

Arrival of the
Sales-Counter Computer

Ron Brown

Gradually the computer is becoming more visible to the average consumer in his daily life. One aspect of this unveiling of automation, as a British technical writer explains here, is the computerized cash register. This device is just the tip of an iceberg that promises to produce automated machines for checking credit cards, electronic delivery of cash outside banking hours, and eventually all the software and hardware to produce a genuinely cashless society.

Electronic cash registers are far from being a simple replacement for the mechanical till. Their large scale introduction will bring about a revolution in the running of retail outlets of all kinds. Like mechanical registers, the electronic cash register (ECR) has a set of keys, a cash drawer, a display and a sales recorder; but in an ECR these devices provide many more facilities—and there is much else besides. Despite its complexity, the ECR is, surprisingly, much easier to operate. This is because each sales transaction is electronically controlled. The sales assistant is taken through the transaction step by step and is told what to do next by a lighted display. Incorrect information in wrong sequence cannot be entered because the keys lock and a warning buzzer sounds. The manufacturers claim that, in addition to preventing errors, this approach cuts down the time taken to train new assistants—from 1½ days to under an hour —and this is a great boon in a field where there is a high turnover of staff.

Much more information about the transaction can be entered and recorded, particularly on those ECR's fitted with a so-called automatic reading wand. This is a device that will read information encoded, optically or magnetically, on tags fitted to the goods on sale. Information on a shirt—such as its code number, colour, style, size and price—can be encoded on a tag not much bigger than a conventional price tag. All this information can be entered into the ECR in less than a second and without error by the sales assistant passing a reading wand rapidly across the tag. The information, once entered, is recorded and analysed either immediately or at the end of the day on the store's main computer. Retailers will thus be provided with up-to-date and much more detailed information on how sales of different items are going. This will enable them to keep stocks of goods to a minimum, freeing capital to buy in more exciting lines and for prompt re-ordering of items that are going well.

This improvement in stock control is likely to be the most important advantage of ECR's, but at present it is the most difficult to quantify. The data processing manager of one of Britain's leading stores says that when he applied similar stock control techniques in the electrical industry he obtained a 30 per cent saving. Savings in the retail trade may not be as great as this, but most people in the business are expecting a figure of around 20 per cent. One American retailer even reckons that with his ECR's he will be able to pick up a new fashion craze (like hot pants) three weeks before his competitors using mechanical cash registers.

Manufacturers offer a variety of system configurations, ranging from sophisticated ECR's capable of working completely on their own to terminals with much less logic controlled from a central minicomputer either in the store or at a central location connected to the store by telephone line. There seems to be little doubt that the minicomputer approach is capable of providing many more facilities and is much more flexible—and likely to win out in the end. Most manufacturers will, for the first few years, be offering both "stand-alone" and minicomputer controlled systems until they see which way the market is going to develop.

In the United States, the biggest share of the market—60 per cent—has been captured by Singer-Friden. One market analyst predicts that, in spite of intense competition, Friden's share will still amount to as much as 35 per cent by 1976.

At one time, National Cash Register provided almost all the world's cash registers, but the firm seems to have been a bit too cautious when developing its Type 280 ECR system and is finding the going difficult; it has the weight, experience and market penetration to correct its errors, but at present gives the impression of being a very slow moving organization that will finish up with a small share of the ECR market.

Pitney-Bowes, a newcomer to the cash register field, with still only a small share of the US market, could well be one of the more successful companies. Seven out of the 10 top US retailers are now installing ECR systems and, of these, five have purchased Pitney-Bowes equipment. Department stores in Britain are also reported to prefer the reliability of the twin minicomputer approach used by Pitney-Bowes and the cheapness of their black-and-white optical ticketing system. Cash-and-carry operators are attracted by the fact that the Pitney-Bowes ECR's are also capable of performing the value-added tax calculations needed after April 1973. Pitney-Bowes has already received £750,000 of orders in the first five months' trading in Britain—

more than they expected to pick up in the first year. Total sales over the next 10 years, taking a conservative view, could reach £53 million.

Faster Checkout

Supermarket operators are another group particularly interested in the prospect of electronic point-of-sale terminals. They, too, have an urgent need for some form of electronic cash register. But the technical and operating problems are different and considerably more complex than those in the department store and other shops served by the ECR's already on the market. Supermarkets need what amounts to an automatic or semi-automatic checkout counter. Here the requirement, apart from providing much better control of stock, is to speed up the checkout process itself in order to reduce queues and save expensive floor space.

There appear to be two alternative solutions to the supermarket problem: goods can either be printed with a machine-readable label during manufacture, which can then be scanned by a laser reading head at the checkout counter, or they can be marked with an identifying number which can be read by the assistant at the counter. In both approaches the identifying number, however read, is entered into an electronic cash register which draws out the price from a minicomputer housed somewhere in the store. Prominent among the manufacturers of laser reading heads is the Swiss company Zellweger, which is working with Migros, a big Swiss supermarket chain.

MSI in the United States is pinning its hopes on the alternative approach and has developed an electronic cash register, into which the identifying number can be entered by the assistant touch-typing. She can enter information as fast as she can pick up, read and put down the packets. MSI claims that this is as quick as, and more realistic than, laser reading head systems. The firm installed its first system in the US ten months ago and plans to install one in France during the summer.

The general feeling in the industry is that it will take a couple of years to determine which is the best approach and not until then will the orders really begin to roll in. Once they do, the business could be very substantial. Sales are likely to be faster than in any other section of the electronic cash register industry —$72 million in the US by 1976, and of £50 million in the UK by 1982.

Credit card companies in the United States are suffering substantial losses as the result of the operations of "hot card" merchants. One professional crook claims to be able to fly into a West Coast city early in the morning, purchase three freshly stolen cards, doctor them, and by 5 p.m., having "hit" the banks, radio dealers and airlines, be on his way back to New York $5000 to the good.

American Express sees the on-line credit checking terminal at each retail outlet as the answer—indeed, as the key to profitability in the credit card business. There is even talk of fingerprinted and voice-printed credit cards being checked against data in a central computer via complex satellite communications networks. A Stanford University researcher expects this market to be as much as $500 million in the US by 1980. However, the market in the UK is likely to be very much smaller and much slower to develop, because fraud is nothing like as prevalent in Britain.

For the present, the credit card companies and department stores that issue cards seem to be concentrating on installing credit checking units at central credit verification offices. This, they say, is the only economically viable means at the moment; on-line credit checking terminals at each point-of-sale will probably not make any headway for a few years yet. Within four years, however, sales of credit verification terminals in the US are expected to reach $210 million. In the UK, the prediction is for sales of £2.5 million by 1982.

Cash on Call

Growth in the use of the cash or currency dispenser could well explode sooner than any other terminal device. These units dispense packets of money containing between £2 and £20 when a voucher or magnetically encoded card is inserted and a personal number is typed on a keyboard. Until recently, all dispensers were mechanical ones fitted in the wall of a few branch banks to provide customers with an out-of-hours service. Recently, however, the first electronic dispensers have appeared, and both manufacturers and banks are poised to extend their use to non-banking premises—including railway stations, hotels, places of work, stores and post offices.

Lloyds Bank, which has not used cash dispensers up till now, plans to install IBM on-line units inside the banks themselves to take some of the workload off the cashiers. This is seen by some as the forerunner of the fully automatic branch bank. National Westminster has a dispenser on trial in a Woolco store —an experiment which is proving extremely attractive to the store, bringing in customers who stay to make purchases. National Westminster also has a dispenser in an engineering works in the Bournemouth area. It is possible that all wages will eventually be paid into bank accounts and employees will draw money from a dispenser at the work place as and when required. The National Giro may even install cash dispensers in the 1000 or so main post offices in Britain within the next five years. Interest in cash dispensers in non-banking premises is worldwide, and with each dispenser costing between £5000 and £6000, the total market could be very large—possibly as high as £70 million over the next 10 years.

Perhaps the most futuristic of the terminals now available is the one that will accept the electronic money card developed by Revenue Systems Ltd. One such terminal is already on field trials at a Berkshire garage. Customers buy a card worth £10 for £9.60 and use it to purchase petrol from an automatic pump. Each time a purchase is made the value of the card is reduced electronically by the amount of the purchase until the whole £10 has been used up. The customer then "recharges" his card by paying a further £9.60.

The idea for electronic money cards originated with Bernard Hunn, who set up Revenue Systems with the backing of the National Research Development Corporation and Technical Development Capital who, between them, put up just over £100,000. Development work is virtually complete and the company is now looking for ways of putting the system into production—which will call for a further investment of £125,000 or so. Negotiations are taking place with several companies in Britain and in the United States and Hunn predicts sales of between £150,000 and £200,000 in the next 12 months.

A card such as this, which can be purchased in advance, could be a real winner—as it will bring the cashless society concept to a very large percentage of the population, who would not normally be regarded as credit-worthy enough to qualify for conventional credit cards. It is very difficult to predict how this section will go—a lot depends upon how ready garages and the general public are to accept it. Sales could perhaps reach £10 million over the next 10 years.

A card that can be purchased in advance is also high on the list of priorities of the operators of the world's suburban commuter railway services. "Stored fares" is the name given to this answer to the rising labour costs and problems of fraud. The idea is for regular travellers to purchase a season ticket for, say, £5, which is inserted into an automatic entrance barrier at one station, and in a similar exit barrier at their destination. The equipment at the exit barrier will calculate the cost of the particular trip and deduct it from the value remaining on the card. Discounts similar to those available to purchasers of today's season tickets will apply, and there will be the added advantage that the traveller does not have to pay for days when he is unable to travel because of sickness or holidays or business elsewhere.

Software Problems

However, the rate of introduction of stored fares systems is likely to be slow. Software problems with the most advanced stored fares system in the world—being developed by IBM for the San Francisco Bay area—may be the reason for the recent reversal of opinion among British Rail engineers. Eighteen months ago they were believed to be enthusiastic, but now clearly intend to concentrate on less sophisticated automatic fare collection systems. It seems likely that British Rail will soon introduce an experimental stored fares system on the Southend line as a long term test-bed scheme. For the moment, however, British Rail intends to expand the use of magnetically coded single-trip tickets like those used to open barriers on the Victoria and Piccadilly underground lines in London, and the stored trip ticket system which began operating recently on a Glasgow suburban line. In the latter system, a commuter can purchase tickets valid for, say, 50 rides; each time he leaves the terminal station one of the "rides" is wiped off.

The Glasgow system is excellent for a simple single-line suburban service, but is quite unsuitable for the complex network of suburban rail, bus and underground services in metropolitan areas such as London, where there are a variety of ways that passengers can travel between any two stations in the system; details of all the alternative routes and the relevant fares would have to be available at each terminal point. At present, British Rail believes it would not be feasible to have computers holding all this information at each station. They see the final answer as being a central very high-speed computer, interrogated from each station every time a passenger went through a barrier. When one remembers how many stations there are, how many passengers go through them, and the rate of flow at peak periods, it is easy to see why at least one British Rail executive says there will have to be breakthroughs in both computing and telecommunications before a stored fares system can be introduced in metropolitan areas.

However, not everybody agrees with British Rail. Some manufacturers say that by placing reasonable restrictions on the amount of information stored, a fairly cheap computer suitable for installation at each station could be produced.

Whichever approach finally wins out, the market will clearly be enormous. Apart from the provision of computers and telecommunications facilities, there is the matter of the electronically coded cards themselves for the stored fares, which would have to be produced in vast quantities and would, alone, add up to a very significant annual turnover for the firm manufacturing them.

The Little Railroad That Could

Charles G. Burck

One area of modern living that is undeniably benefiting from the impact of automation is mass transit. Underground riders in London treat the driverless trains of London Transport's Victoria Line as a matter of course; San Francisco commuters are learning to take advantage of the computerized Bay Area Rapid Transit system; and students of West Virginia University are preparing to travel between the scattered parts of their campus in futuristic automated eight-passenger cars. But perhaps the most successful example of automation's application to mass transit is the Lindenwold Line, which links Philadelphia with some of its New Jersey suburbs. Here is its curriculum vitae.

Hundreds of planners and engineers concerned with mass transportation have traveled during the past couple of years to the gray, uninviting city of Camden, New Jersey, across the Delaware River from Philadelphia. They have come from many cities in the U.S. and from numerous foreign countries, including West Germany, Mexico, and Russia. The place they particularly visit in Camden is the headquarters of a commuter railroad called the Lindenwold Line. Many of the technological tourists come back again to study the line in more detail; people from San Francisco's Bay Area Rapid Transit system have returned so often that, in the words of one official, "They don't even announce their arrival anymore."

The Lindenwold Line draws all this attention because it is the first working example in the U.S. of a thoroughly modern,

179

well-planned, and skillfully marketed mass transportation system. The only thing that resembles it, San Francisco's seventy-five-mile BART, will not open for at least six months. The ninety-eight-mile metropolitan system under construction in Washington, D.C., is proceeding fitfully and will not carry passengers before 1974. Transit systems elsewhere are still on the drawing boards: Pittsburgh, Baltimore, and Atlanta are working on plans and engineering studies; seven other cities are thinking seriously about systems of their own. There have been some new transit tracks laid—e.g., Chicago built a line down the median strip of its Dan Ryan Expressway two years ago—but they have been used for conventional, low-speed straphanger transportation, offering nothing in the way of technology that has not been available for fifty years. The Lindenwold Line is unique as a working vision of the future, with lessons for planners, builders, commuters, and critics alike.

The railroad—known to residents as "the Hi-Speed Line"—thrusts through a string of communities in a fast-growing suburban corridor that reaches toward the Jersey shore. It begins as a subway in the center of Philadelphia, and after four stops crosses the Delaware River on the Benjamin Franklin Bridge (which also carries eight highway lanes). After two more subway stops in Camden, it emerges from the tunnels and continues, at grade and on embankments or slender concrete elevated structures, past five suburban stations to Lindenwold, New Jersey, where it terminates. The fourteen-and-a-half-mile journey between the innermost Philadelphia stop and Lindenwold takes twenty-two minutes. Fares range from 30 to 60 cents. Trains are fast, comfortable, and frequent. The system is highly automated, from collection of fares to operation of trains. In two years of operating, the line has built up a daily patronage of some 33,400 riders, so that despite a relatively low fare structure it is breaking even on operating costs.

The most significant thing about the line is that it has measurably reduced automobile traffic. The results are highly visible during rush hours on key arteries. Traffic on the Ben Franklin Bridge, for example, has dropped between 2 and 3 percent, as measured during a twenty-four-hour period. That may not sound like much of a reduction, but it came about despite substantial growth in the numbers of people and automobiles in the region served by the line. Moreover, that decrease—and it amounts to some 1,900 vehicles—is concentrated in peak periods, and traffic that used to crawl across the bridge during rush hour now moves freely.

Instead of a Superhighway

According to surveys taken by the Delaware River Port Authority, which owns the Lindenwold Line, fully 40 percent of the riders are people who formerly drove into the city. (Another 13 percent had not commuted into Philadelphia before.) Now they park their cars in the 8,800 parking spaces at the line's stations. The railroad has functionally substituted for a new superhighway, while sparing Philadelphia the burden of the automobiles brought into town by such a highway. To put it another way, the railroad serves essentially as a remote downtown parking lot and conveyor system. Philadelphia plans to create 10,000 new downtown parking spaces between 1970 and 1980; the railroad has, in effect, already made the city a gift of 8,800.

The significance of that 40 percent switch from automobiles to trains cannot be overstated; there has simply been nothing in North American transit experience to compare with it. Such new transit lines as have been built during the past decade—including the Chicago line and Montreal's beautiful subway system—appear to have won most of their riders at the expense of other mass-transit operations. The results from Lindenwold offer the first conclusive proof that rail mass transit can lure large numbers of people out of their cars .

Since no transit system can offer the door-to-parking-lot convenience of the private automobile, traffic conditions have to be really abominable and the alternative transportation superlative before motorists can be induced to switch. The south Jersey area had successfully met the first condition well before the Lindenwold Line was opened. Buses wheezed into and out of Philadelphia at an average speed of about fourteen miles an hour, and only a sprinkling of commuters rode the three sluggish trains provided each day by the Pennsylvania-Reading Seashore Line.

A motorist driving from the Lindenwold area into Philadelphia could count on spending a minimum of forty-five minutes between Lindenwold and a downtown parking lot—more often an hour.

The alternative was conceived way back in the 1950's after Pennsylvania and New Jersey assigned the Delaware River Port Authority the job of providing a transit line. The authority's first study called for a much larger and costlier three-branch system; a series of subsequent studies scaled the project down to its present dimensions, and it was approved by the two state legislatures in 1962. Capital costs were to be paid out of increased tolls on the Ben Franklin and Walt Whitman bridges, and operating costs were to be covered by revenues. Thus there would be no taxes levied to provide funds for the line.

The Port Authority began construction in 1966, and a year later it formed an operating subsidiary, Port Authority Transit Corp., generally referred to as PATCO. From the outset the planners knew they would have to compete directly with the automobile. Sorely beset though they were, motorists would be reluctant to give up their cars. "There was no captive market," recalls Robert B. Johnston, the engineer who oversaw design and construction. "The system had to be made socially acceptable as a means of travel—and it was the first time any system had been built on that basis."

To Combat the Great Saboteur

With the money available to them, the men who planned the line could not count on any major technological breakthroughs—but they could push the state of the art to its limits and use it thoughtfully. Speed, they decided, was essential. In order to halve the automobile time, they needed an average of forty miles an hour, including stops. That entailed rapid acceleration and high speeds between suburban stations. The second requirement was convenience; service would have to be frequent enough to rival the freedom of choice implicit in automobile travel. Thus there had to be plenty of trains. Finally, the system had to be economical, which meant chiefly that labor costs, the great saboteur of mass transit, had to be minimized.

A ride on the line today shows just how the Port Authority met those objectives. Though built roughly along the right-of-way of the old Seashore Line, the roadbed itself is either new or renovated. Heavy continuous-welded rail provides a quiet, smooth ride. The electric cars, made by Budd Co., are among the most powerful ever built. They accelerate to fifty miles an hour in a little over twenty seconds, which approaches the acceleration of some small automobiles; a little more than a minute after leaving a station the trains are cruising at seventy-five miles an hour. They are air-conditioned, with tinted windows, soft upholstered seats, and insulation against temperature and sound. At top speed the passenger hears only a high-pitched jetlike whine and a well-muted rush of air past the stainless-steel sides. Even outside the train the noise level is so low that PATCO has received few complaints from nearby residents.

The key to low costs is automation. PATCO has 145 riders for each of its employees, janitors and guards included; that figure is unmatched by any other transit line. Passengers enter un-attended stations, buy their tickets from machines, and pass through automated turnstiles. Each train has only one PATCO employee aboard, an attendant who sits at a control panel, opens and closes doors, and pushes a button to start the train after each stop. All other train operations are carried out by a series of onboard electronic packages that accelerate, regulate cruising speed, brake, and halt the train at the right point along each station platform. The attendant is fully schooled in train opera-tion and can take over in an emergency. And if rails are wet with snow or rain, he puts the train under manual operation for better control over acceleration and braking.

The Sum of Many Small Markets

The railroad's nerve center is an unimposing blockhouse on the outskirts of Camden. Here operators control over-all scheduling and scan "mimic boards" that depict train movements and electrical-power conditions in each of the nine substations. The operators keep in touch with train attendants by two-way radio and monitor all of the system's passenger gates through a battery of closed-circuit TV monitors. If something goes wrong at the turnstiles, which happens rarely enough, or if a passenger makes a mistake or becomes confused, he can call the tower on a special phone; by remote control, the operators can let him through or collect any extra fare he owes.

It takes more than up-to-date technology, however, to attract riders and keep them. PATCO's operating officials are profoundly customer-oriented. They have done probably the most thoughtful marketing job in the history of mass transit. "PATCO has no marketing department," as general manager Richard E. Pinkham has said. "PATCO has no department that is not actively engaged in marketing." Schedules provide excess capacity so that even in rush hours there are as few standees as possible—the hope is to give the great majority of riders one of those soft seats. Trains run on a ten-minute headway from 6:00 A.M. to 11:30 P.M., and every five minutes during rush hours, with a couple of extra expresses running on a ninety-second headway. In the small hours of night, PATCO schedules one train each way every hour; no passenger need ever fear being stuck overnight because he missed the last train. On Sunday, trains run every fifteen minutes.

The basic train is a permanently linked, or "married," two-car pair; at peak times there are as many as six cars, and future station expansions will allow for eight. The cars are cleaned inside daily and outside every three days, and stations get scrubbed six nights a week. PATCO has also taken pains to ensure security. The line has its own police force and a squad of K-9 dogs and handlers who patrol regularly. And the closed-circuit TV monitors give the control tower a running check on all turnstile areas.

Officials of the line think especially hard about their off-peak customers. "The transit market is not simply a mass market, as implied by the term mass transportation," says Pinkham. "It is the sum of many small markets, each with its own needs and objectives." The line advertises to shoppers, sports fans, and theatre- and concertgoers. For shoppers in particular, PATCO schedules enough off-hour seating capacity to ensure that passengers have not only a seat for themselves but one for their packages as well. As a further encouragement to midday use, the line drops its 25-cent parking fee at some locations after 10:00 A.M. The result of all these policies is a steadily increasing stream of off-peak users. There are now some 20,000, and Pinkham calculates that four are now added for every new rush-hour rider. PATCO originally anticipated a two-mile "corridor of influence," or drawing area, on either side of the line; the corridor has turned out to be better than four miles wide, and many people drive ten, fifteen, or more miles to a Hi-Speed station.

Mass transit never comes cheap. Originally, the Port Authority estimated it would spend about $67 million to build the line; the final cost, boosted by inflation and by certain added features— e.g., air conditioning in the cars—was about $94 million. Debt service totals $5,400,000 annually, which is handily covered by the bridge tolls. PATCO calculates its operating costs at about 5.9 cents a passenger-mile. But since PATCO regards its cars as capital equipment, it does not include amortization of rolling stock as an operating expense, as do most rail lines. If it did, total operating costs would come to an estimated 7 cents a passenger-mile, which is not at all bad considering the line's youth, the quality of service provided, and the prospects for increased ridership.

The Motorist Is Better Off Too

Revenues for the past year have just about equaled operating costs. PATCO had expected to make a slight operating profit for 1971, owing mainly to a 25 percent increase in electrical costs that took effect at the beginning of the year. There will probably be a 10-cent increase in fares within a year, but at that a ride will still be a bargain. PATCO could pay its capital costs by charging an estimated 12 cents a passenger-mile. It's debatable that the line's riders would pay that much, but some riders on the Long Island Rail Road pay about that much for relatively shoddy service—and the costs of gas, tolls, and parking to a motorist driving into Philadelphia and parking for the day come to at least 12 cents a mile.

As it is, bridge tolls paid by the motorist subsidize the transit rider. Autoists might argue that the increases in tolls constituted an unfair imposition on drivers who use the bridge, but PATCO has some counterarguments. For one thing, says J. W. Vigrass, supervisor of traffic and planning, "the motorist on the bridge is getting more for his money, since peak traffic now moves across it twice as fast." Motorists who have switched, Vigrass thinks, can be said to be saving a total of a million man-hours a year in commuting time.

The benefits of the railroad seem abundantly worth the costs to residents of the Philadelphia area, many of whom want the line to expand. There are several proposals to extend the present route, add stations, and, indeed, build similar lines to other towns. What is built, and when, will be determined by a complex mixture of regional studies now under way, desires of local and state political authorities, and availability of federal and state money. But even if another yard of track is never laid, the Lindenwold Line must be judged a great success. After only two years of operation, it is running at 90 percent of capacity (in terms of rolling stock). Buoyed by this popularity, the line's officials feel they are a part of a pioneering enterprise. "If we keep up with what we're doing," Vigrass says, "we will have definitely solved one kind of urban transit problem." The ultimate accolades, however, come from visitors. Not long ago, after touring the line, a planner who is working on a system for Detroit said, "Don't confuse me with a lot of engineering studies— just show me how to build a carbon copy of PATCO."

Automated Highways:
What Is the Dream and
How Do We Reach It?

Siegfried M. Breuning

Urban transport is one of the most intractable problems of the modern age. Private cars clog city roads with their
presence and city air with their exhausts, while public transportation is rapidly decaying for lack of adequate financing.
The problem of giving personal transportation service to the
maximum number of people seems tailor-made for the computer, and here Siegfried M. Breuning, a Massachusetts Institute of Technology professor with wide experience in transportation policy, assesses the possibilities for computer-controlled cars.

As you approach Boston (or any other metropolis) tomorrow in
your daily commuting or from a weekend trip, you will bring
your car to a halt to receive acceptance at one of the many approach ramps surrounding the city. There, a small door, flush
with the side of your car, will open on a signal from the dash-
board, releasing an arm that will engage the car with a rail on
the ramp. Another signal will register your destination on a
computer. When the access toll has been charged to your credit
card, your car will be drawn up the ramp to enter the new guideway system which traverses Boston. Now, with the two vital
control factors—speed and direction—automated, you are on

your own; you may finish the newspaper, work from your crowded briefcase, watch the sights, catnap. . . . At your destination, you will simply step out of your vehicle and leave its storage to the automated system; or perhaps your computerized vehicle automatically shunts off on a decelerating ramp, the arm retracts behind its door, and you drive your automobile off under conventional power.

Between this "utopia" and today's frustrations lies a complex effort, the barest outline of which appears in the following pages. On the basis of many years of research and planning, we are convinced that better automotive transport is a realizable goal and that it will take the form which this episode suggests.

Our needs clearly include better utilization of whatever area of the earth's surface is devoted to automobile transportation, highways, and parking alike. We need to increase the efficiency and dependability of our transport. We need to simplify the driving task and at the same time assure that the driver does not become correspondingly more reckless with those tasks he still controls. To reduce pollution, we need to substitute a prime energy source, whose emissions of pollutants can be far better controlled, for many local ones. We need to reduce the skill required for driving, to make it possible for a larger segment of the population to drive well for more of the time.

Automation Concepts

This discussion of current issues in automobile transportation suggests almost self-evidently how automation can alleviate or eliminate the problems. And this in turn leads to two approaches: we can continue the gradual process of automating suitable components of the automobile-road system by devising mechanical devices to assume more and more of the driving tasks susceptible to human error; or we can opt for an entirely new and separate, fully automated, individual transportation system. Somewhere in between is the possibility of converting the existing automobile to a dual-mode vehicle capable of operating as a conventional automobile on existing highways or as a fully automated vehicle needing no driver on a controlled access, fully automated guideway system. It is such a dual-mode system which is currently under study at Project TRANSPORT of M.I.T.

The Evolution of Automation

From a practical point of view, it is abundantly clear that we are not likely to scrap today's highway transportation system for an entirely new, unproven alternative, no matter how attractive it may claim to be. Evolutionary procedures are indicated.

The captive-vehicle, closed system is likely to remain for some time a special application for particularly suitable sites such as amusement parks, airports, warehouses, and congested downtown areas. It would make an excellent experiment now, since we still have much to learn about the hardware and software of automated transportation. Eventually, when an extensive guideway system exists, captive vehicles will provide the ultimate of driverless service for people and freight.

For the gradual development of automation, we might expect essentially the process going on now—the addition of automated equipment such as automatic transmissions, speed controls, and headlight dimmers—to continue and to accelerate slightly because of the increasing rate of technological development and the increasing recognition of the value of vehicle automation. The difficulty with this process lies in integrating the components which are being developed into a meaningful totally automated transportation system. Recent progress suggests that this kind of automation of components for vehicles and for highways comes at an excessively high price and is rarely if ever planned with any foresight for later integration with other improvements.

This leads us into the potential for the dual-mode vehicle. The dual-mode system makes possible the use of existing vehicles with modest modifications, and it makes conceivable a gradual development of the guideway and control equipment based upon these vehicles. The initiation problem is even more simplified by the possible use of automated pallets, designed to accommodate a vehicle or perhaps a cargo module for transportation on the automated section of the trip. At the entrance to the guideway, a vehicle drives onto a pallet, records its destination, pays, and is then automatically whisked to its destination exit.

The next logical transition—a guideway system which will accept both pallets and dual-mode vehicles—combines the advantages of both and suggests the flexibility we believe to be inherent in the dual-mode system. We believe that the time is now appropriate for beginning a long-range plan of research and development which will eventually lead to prototypes, then working pilot systems, and ultimately a standard automated guideway system under the configurations we have suggested above.

The Automated Dual-Mode System

An effective guideway must control vehicle direction and speed in accordance with its destination, and it must supply power for moving the vehicle. The system we believe most promising for speed control and steering utilizes two side rails for positive mechanical guidance and constraint of the vehicle and also for power supply. A retractable arm on the vehicle engages the rail and picks up power and control signals, and the same arm also steers the car, either through mechanical linkage to the steering gear or by developing side forces acting upon the moving car.

Other means for steering have been proposed, among them a steel-wheel-on-steel-rail concept for guidance with the rubber wheels used for support. Steering along a buried cable by means of a set of pick-up coils connected to a steering servomechanism has been proposed for conversion of existing roadways to automated guidance. Another notable concept is a vehicle straddling a beam with its wheels cambered inward to engage the two sides of the beam. On conventional roads the wheels return to the normal vertical position. Speed control also can be achieved by many means and the final choice must be based on further experimentation. Conventional speedometers probably cannot be made sufficiently accurate to ascertain proper headway distance on the guideway. Some schemes do in fact propose to allow some small speed differential between successive cars with the expectation that gaps between vehicles will open and close and successive vehicles may in fact occasionally bump. Other proposals for maintaining headways depend on headway detection devices, either between successive cars or along the guideway rail. If precise speed or position control is desired on the guideway, different nonconventional speed and position measurements are necessary, such as a time-related counting and feedback device in the car which measures the rate at which the vehicle passes a series of identifiable points on the guideway, adjusting speed accordingly. A compromise between these concepts might utilize a fairly accurate speedometer with a correction system built into the guideway at given block intervals so that between successive blocks the speeds of the vehicles would be adjusted and an overall average headway maintained.

Guideway Configuration and Construction

Irrespective of what control system is eventually adopted, all cars on the guideway will travel, for all practical purposes, at constant speed and therefore with fixed headways. Thus it will be possible to operate vehicles at much smaller headways than on conventional roads. As a result, we expect at least a fourfold increase in lane capacity over that of a conventional highway. In addition, the reduced width required for the guideway will result in savings in required real estate. Since all traffic will move at constant speed, curves on the guideway can be superelevated to exactly balance the centrifugal force. The larger superelevations will make possible sharper turns and further economies of real estate. Since the guideway structure more closely resembles a railroad than a highway, and can probably be mass-produced and prefabricated, the guideway is likely to be less expensive than a lane of expressway. All these factors combine to make the economics of the guideway for a given traffic capacity very attractive indeed.

Automated System Control and Management

Entrances and exits to the guideway, interchanges, and stations present a more difficult problem. At an entrance, vehicles not acceptable to the guideway must be positively identified and rejected. Acceptable vehicles must then be accelerated and entered into the traffic stream, after it has been determined that the system is not overloaded, not only at the entrance but also at later links over which vehicles will travel. The system's capacity must not be exceeded at any point. Thus, control devices will remove congestion from the guideway system by confining it to its entry point, just as we now propose to meter traffic on expressway ramps.

System control can take many forms. There is a clear trade-off among methods for locating the control apparatus: in the vehicle, on the roadside, or in a central system computer. Undoubtedly the final solution will involve some control equipment in the vehicle and some in a centralized computer, but the best mix has yet to be determined. The centralized computer will likely provide routing, maintain capacity checks on all guideway links, and provide centralized accounting and billing. For each of these processes, various algorithms can be used, depending upon the ultimate objectives of the system.

Stations along the guideway will be necessary to allow vehicles to leave the through-traffic flow and load or unload passengers or cargo. These stations may or may not have associated parking facilities. Since it is possible to run vehicles without drivers on the guideway, it will be possible to provide automated parking facilities in low-cost areas to which empty cars are sent after drivers have left them. But since recall of individual cars from outlying garages will be time-consuming, it is likely that the guideway will foster increased use of rental cars, some of which would be stored bumper-to-bumper on a station lane. Such cars could be used on an overnight basis—rented in the evening for the trip home, stored overnight in the driver's garage, and released into the rental pool the next morning upon his return to his guideway destination.

While the guideway looks very attractive as an economical substitute for heavy-traffic arteries, its ultimate value comes with a fairly complete guideway network, extending even into low-density suburban areas for fully automated passenger and freight service to the individual home. This suggests that guideways may replace streets in new neighborhoods, if prefabricated, standardized, grade-separated guideways can be provided at very low cost.

Problems of Implementation

Some of the biggest problems of developing an automated guideway system are legal and financial. Although clarification may be required of the relation to a new system of many of the existing laws regarding transportation, so far there seem to be no insurmountable problems.

Concerning the question of financing, however, the situation is quite different. Support for research and development in the amounts necessary for meaningful and comprehensive work is lacking. Industry is loath to spend huge sums for risk development in the face of the real possibility that government may step in and support at least the research phase, or that in the end the government may prevent a single developer from reaping the payoff on his risk development if it proves very attractive to the public.

There are also questions of ownership—of vehicles as well as guideways. The restrictive nature of the guideway and the stringent quality requirements for vehicles that will wish to use it seem to suggest private or quasi-private ownership and operation. Governments, either local or state, are not traditionally known to move into innovations such as this one very rapidly, although highway departments or transportation agencies may find this a promising alternative that will ease their ever-growing burdens.

An Approach to Implementation

Enough understanding is now available about automated transportation to move forward actively into areas in which more specific knowledge must be obtained. Most theoretical questions have been amply discussed. It is time to initiate experiments that will advance the understanding of both the hardware and software.

Our first need is for a prototype technical experiment of real automated vehicles on real guideways capable of continuous operation in a controlled environment. Guideway and dual-mode vehicle components necessary for automated operation must be designed, constructed, and fully tested for operational suitability and reliability. The test should also provide clarification of the rather complex control requirements of an automated system, and it should also give some preliminary indications of public reaction.

At the next stage of research and development we will need experiments focusing on the system in continuous operation, and thereafter we will need a pilot system study, exposing the concept to public use and acceptance on a limited scale under controlled conditions.

In parallel with this experimentation, and no less important, is the need to clarify the system *framework* in which an automated dual-mode transportation system can begin to function effectively. A multitude of hardware and software alternatives must be reconsidered and updated at frequent intervals, so that alternatives will be available in case an initial design turns out to be unfeasible or shows signs of obsolescence. If we could not at that time switch quickly and efficiently to an alternative system, we would eventually be saddled with a highly inefficient system.

We must also at this stage develop the legal framework within which automated transportation can function effectively, and we will need to design an effective administrative structure for the development and operation of the new transportation system.

In all this, we must recognize the possibility that automated transportation will attract a larger demand for transportation from those who will drive more because driving is more pleasant and also from that half of our population who cannot now drive. For not least among our aspirations for an improved system is the provision of transportation for millions who do not now drive. They include, particularly, two underserved groups —the poor who cannot now afford cars and the physically handicapped, young and old, who are unable to drive conventional cars. Indeed, we think it entirely conceivable that transportation demand will actually double, perhaps triple, over its current level. People like individualized transportation now and they will like it even more if it can be improved. We must be prepared to meet such potentially drastic changes in demand.

The research must be designed to allow maximum flexibility, both in timing of experiments and in choice among alternatives. Progress in developing automated transportation must always be responsive to the changing needs and tastes of the individual and his society.

Expectations and Recommendations

Further research and development will provide clearer answers to questions related to automated guideway transportation. For the present, we at M.I.T. aim our planning at ultimately providing access even to low-density areas, but we cannot predict when this can be done. Of course, a system that connects all points has substantial advantages. It offers mobility for nondrivers, and it encourages driverless trips and automated travel within neighborhoods. Automated access to individual homes may become a reality much sooner than we now forsee if the public wholeheartedly embraces automatic transportation.

The sum of the implications of automated transportation is a long list of potential improvements: congestion will be minimized and removed from the system's access points; safety will be improved through reducing sources of human error; storage problems will be alleviated since vehicles can be automatically routed to and from automated garages in remote areas; smog will be reduced; and nondrivers will be accommodated on all automated routes. Travel will become substantially more enjoyable and attractive.

Three major tasks are before us now, to prepare for realizing these benefits: we must work out an orderly program for research and development on automated transportation; we must prepare for the possibility of avalanching demand; and we must predict and plan for what will happen to individuals, society, and the economy when confronted with another transportation improvement as startling as that effected by the automobile at the turn of the century.

Education Automation: Freeing the Scholar to Return to His Studies

R. Buckminster Fuller

What will be the long-range effect of computerized learning on education, and on life in general? According to R. Buckminster Fuller, architect, inventor, writer and social commentator, the future is a bright one. He envisions a world of universal learning, with education as the world's prime industry and universities that entice scholars to take up permanent residence to develop more and more knowledge about the whole experience of man.

I have talked to you about solving problems by design competence instead of by political reform. It is possible to get one-to-one correspondence of action and reaction without political revolution, warfare, and reform. I find it possible today with very short electromagnetic waves to make small reflectors by which modulated signals can be beamed. After World War II, we began to beam our TV messages from city to city. One reason television didn't get going before World War II was because of the difficulty in distributing signals over long distances from central sources on long waves or mildly short waves. We were working on coaxial cables between cities, but during the war we found new short ranges of electromagnetic frequencies. We worked practically with very much higher frequencies, very much shorter wave lengths. We found that we could beam these

196

short waves from city to city. Television programs are brought into the small city now by beam from a few big cities and then *rebroadcast* locally to the home sets. That is the existing TV distribution pattern. My invention finds it is now possible to utilize the local TV masts in any community in a new way. Going up to, say, two hundred, three hundred, or four hundred feet and looking down on a community you see the houses individually in the middle of their respective land plots. Therefore, with a few high masts having a number of tiny masers, lasers, or reflectors, each beam aimed accurately at a specific house, the entire community could be directly "hooked up" by beams, instead of being broadcast to. This means a great energy saving, for less than 1 per cent of the omnidirectionally *broadcast* pattern ever hits a receiving antenna. The beaming makes for very sharp, clear, frequency-modulated signals.

In the beaming system, you also have a reflector at the house that picks up the signal. It corresponds directly to the one on the mast and is aimed right back to the specific beaming cup on the mast from which it is receiving. This means that with beam casting you are able to send individual messages to each of those houses. There is a direct, fixed, wireless connection, an actual direct linkage to individuals; and it works in both directions. Therefore, the receiving individual can beam back, "I don't like it." He may and can say "yes" or "no." This "yes" or "no" is the basis of a binary mathematical system, and immediately brings in the "language" of the modern electronic computers. With two-way TV, constant referendum of democracy will be manifest, and democracy will become the most practical form of industrial and space-age government by all people, for all people.

It will be possible not only for an individual to say, "I don't like it," on his two-way TV but he can also beam-dial (without having to know mathematics), "I want number so and so." It is also possible with this kind of two-way TV linkage with individuals' homes to send out many different programs simultaneously; in fact, as many as there are two-way beamed-up receiving sets and programs. It would be possible to have large central storages of documentaries—great libraries. A child could call for a special program information locally over the TV set.

With two-way TV we will develop selecting dials for the children which will not be primarily an alphabetical but a visual *species* and *chronological category* selecting device with secondary alphabetical subdivisions. The child will be able to call up any kind of information he wants about any subject and get his latest authoritative TV documentary, the production of which I have already described to you. The answers to his questions and probings will be *the best information* that man has available up to that minute in history.

All this will bring a profound change in education. We will stop training individuals to be "teachers," when all that most young girl "education" students really want to know is how they are going to earn a living in case they don't get married. Much of the educational system today is aimed at answering: "How am I going to survive? How am I going to get a job? I must earn a living." That is the priority item under which we are working all the time—the idea of *having to earn a living.* That problem of "how are we going to earn a living?" is going to go out the historical window, forever, in the next decade, and education is going to be disembarrassed of the unseen "practical" priority bogeyman. Education will then be concerned primarily with exploring to discover not only more about the universe and its history but about what the universe is trying to do, about why man is part of it, and about how can, and may man best function in universal evolution.

Automation is with us. There is no question about it. Automation was inevitable to intellect. Intellect was found to differentiate out experience continually and to articulate and develop new tools to do physically repeated tasks. Man is now no longer *essential* as a worker in the fabulously complex industrial equation. Marx's *worker* is soon to become utterly obsolete. Automation is coming in Russia just as it is here. The word *worker* describing man as a muscle-and-reflex machine will not have its current meaning a decade hence. Therefore, if man is no longer essential as a worker we ask: "How can he live? How does he acquire the money or credits with which to purchase what he needs or what he wants that is available beyond immediate needs?" At the present time we are making all kinds of economic pretenses at covering up this overwhelming automation problem because we don't realize adequately the larger significance of the truly fundamental change that is taking place in respect to man-in-universe. As automation advanced, man began to create secondary or nonproductive jobs to make himself look busy so that he could rationalize a necessity for himself by virtue of which he could "earn" his living. Take our bankers, for example. They are all fixtures; these men don't have anything to do that a counting machine couldn't do; a punch button box would suffice. They have no basic banking authority whatsoever today. They do not loan you their own wealth. They loan you your own wealth. But man has a sense of vanity and has to invent things that make him look important.

I am trying to keep at the realities with you. Approximately total automation is coming. Men will be essential to the industrial equation but not as workers. People are going to be utterly essential as consumers—what I call *regenerative consumers*, however, not just swill pails.

The vast industrial complex undertakings and associated capital investments are today so enormous and take so long to inaugurate that they require concomitantly rapid regenerative economics to support them. The enterprise must pay off very rapidly in order to be able to refund itself and obtain the economic advantage to inaugurate solution of the next task with still higher technical advantage. In that regenerative cycle of events, the more consumers there are the more the costs are divided and the lower the individual prices. The higher the frequency of the consuming the more quickly the capital cost can be refunded, and the sooner the system is ready for the next wave of better technology. So man is essential to the industrial equation as a consumer—as a regenerative consumer, a critical consumer, a man who tasting wants to taste better and who viewing realizes what he views can be accomplished more efficiently and more interestingly. The consumer thus becomes a highly critical regenerative function, requiring an educational system that fosters the consumer's regenerative capacity and capability.

At present [1961], world economics is such that Russia and China work under an integrated socialist planning in competition with our literally disorganized economic world (for our anti-trust laws will not permit organization on a comprehensive basis). The Communists have high efficiency advantage because of their authoritarianism. We have very little centralized authority, save in "defense." The Communists now have the industrial equation, too, in large scale, and soon complete automation will be with them. They are very much aware of the fact that the more customers there are, the more successful the operation will be, because the unit costs are progressively lower. This is why the Soviets were historically lucky in getting China as customers. They would like also to have, exclusively, India and Africa as customers. If Russia acquires the most customers, we will not be able to compete. They will always have the lower costs on any given level of technology. We are going to have to meet this possibility and meet it vigorously, swiftly, and intelligently. Within the next decade, if we survive at all as an organized set of crossbreeding men on the American continent it will be because we will have suddenly developed a completely new attitude on all these matters. In case you are apprehensive that social and political economics are to be so laggard as to impede your advanced educational programming, it is well to remember that the comprehensive world economics are going to force vast economic reforms of industries and nations, which incidentally will require utter modernization of the educational processes in order to be able to compete and survive.

Every time we educate a man, we as educators have a regenerative experience, and we ought to learn from that experience how to do it much better the next time. The more educated our population the more effective it becomes as an integral of regenerative consumer individuals. We are going to have to invest in our whole population to accelerate its consumer regeneration. We are going to be completely unemployed as muscle-working machines. *We as economic society are going to have to pay our whole population to go to school and pay it to stay at school.* That is, we are going to have to put our whole population into the educational process and get *everybody* realistically literate in many directions. Quite clearly, *the new political word* is going to be *investment.* It is not going to be *dole,* or socialism, or the idea of people hanging around in bread lines. The new popular *regenerative investment* idea is actually that of making people more familiar with the patterns of the universe, that is, with what man has learned about universe to date, and that of getting everybody inter-communicative at ever higher levels of literacy. People are then going to stay in the education process. They are going to populate ever increasing numbers of research laboratories and universities.

As we now disemploy men as muscle and reflex machines, the one area where employment is gaining abnormally fast is the research and development area. Research and development are a part of the educational process itself. We are going to have to invest in our people and make available to them participation in the great educational process of research and development in order to learn more. When we learn more, we are able to do more with our given opportunities. We can rate federally paid-for education as a high return, mutual benefit investment. When we plant a seed and give it the opportunity to grow its fruits pay us back many fold. Man is going to "improve" rapidly in the same way by new federally underwritten educational "seeding" by new tools and processes.

Our educational processes are in fact the upcoming major world industry. This is *it*; this is the essence of today's educational facilities meeting. You are caught in that new educational upward draughting process. The cost of education will be funded regeneratively right out of earnings of the technology, the industrial equation, because we can only afford to reinvest continually in humanity's ability to go back and turn out a better job. As a result of the new educational processes our consuming costs will be progressively lower as we also gain ever higher performance per units of invested resources, which means that our wealth actually will be increasing at all times rather than "exhausted by spending." It is the "capability" wealth that really counts. It is very good that there is an international competitive system now operating, otherwise men would tend to stagnate, particularly in large group undertakings. They would otherwise be afraid to venture in this great intellectual integrity regeneration.

I would say, then, that you are faced with a future in which education is going to be number one amongst the great world industries, within which will flourish an educational machine technology that will provide tools such as the individually selected and articulated two-way TV and an intercontinentally net-worked, documentaries call-up system, operative over any home two-way TV set.

The new educational technology will probably provide also an invention of mine called the Geoscope—a large two-hundred-foot diameter (or more) lightweight geodesic sphere hung hoveringly at one hundred feet above mid-campus by approximately invisible cables from three remote masts. This giant sphere is a miniature earth. Its entire exterior and interior surfaces will be covered with closely-packed electric bulbs, each with variable intensity controls. The lighting of the bulbs is scanningly controlled through an electric computer. The number of the bulbs and their minimum distance of one hundred feet from viewing eyes, either at the center of the sphere or on the ground outside and below the sphere, will produce the visual effect and resolution of a fine-screen halftone cut or that of an excellent television tube picture. The two-hundred-foot Geoscope will cost about fifteen million dollars. It will make possible communication of phenomena that are not at present communicable to man's conceptual understanding. There are many motion patterns such as those of the hands of the clock or of the solar system planets or of the molecules of gas in a pneumatic ball or of atoms or the earth's annual weather that cannot be seen or comprehended by the human eye and brain relay and are therefore inadequately comprehended and dealt with by the human mind.

The Geoscope may be illuminated to picture the earth and the motion of its complete cloud-cover history for years run off on its surface in minutes so that man may comprehend the cyclic patterning and predict. The complete census-by-census of world population history changes could be run off in minutes, giving a clear picture of the demological patterning and its clear trending. The total history of transportation and of world resource discovery, development, distribution, and redistribution could become comprehensible to the human mind, which would thus be able to forecast and plan in vastly greater magnitude than heretofore. The consequences of various world plans could be computed and projected. All world data would be dynamically viewable and picturable and relayable by radio to all the world, so that common consideration in a most educated manner of all world problems by all world people would become a practical event.

The universities are going to be wonderful places. Scholars will stay there for a long, long time—the rest of their lives—while they are developing more and more knowledge about the whole experience of man. All men will be going around the world in due process as everyday routine search and exploration, and the world experiencing patterning will be everywhere —all students from everywhere all over the world. That is all part of the new pattern that is rushing upon us. We will accelerate as rapidly into "yesterday" through archaeology as we do into "tomorrow." Archaeology both on land and under the seas will flourish equally with astronautics.

Technology Is Knocking at the Schoolhouse Door

Charles E. Silberman

One of the strongest arguments in favor of pressing on with new educational technology is the woefully inadequate state of much of the present educational system in the United States. This report focuses on these drawbacks, examines how the computer can improve the situation, and surveys the heated arguments over the teacher's role in the new world of the automated classroom. Its author is a well-known critic of the educational field; his writings on education culminated in a Carnegie Foundation report on the deficiencies of U.S. education.

"Public education is the last great stronghold of the manual trades," John Henry Martin, superintendent of schools in Mount Vernon, New York, recently told a congressional committee. "In education, the industrial revolution has scarcely begun."

But begun it has—slowly, to be sure, but irresistibly, and with the most profound consequences for both education and industry. The past year has seen an explosion of interest in the application of electronic technology to education and training. Hardly a week or month goes by without an announcement from some electronics manufacturer or publishing firm that it is entering the "education market" via merger, acquisition, joint venture, or working arrangement. And a number of electronics firms have been building substantial capabilities of their own in the education field.

Business has discovered the schools, and neither is likely to be the same again. It may be a bit premature to suggest, as Superintendent Martin does, that "the center of gravity for educational change is moving from the teachers' college and the superintendent's office to the corporation executive suite." But there can be no doubt about the long-term significance of business' new interest in the education market. The companies now coming into the market have resources—of manpower and talent as well as of capital—far greater than the education market has ever seen before. They have, in addition, a commitment to innovation and an experience in management that is also new to the field.

The romance between business and the schools began when the federal government took on the role of matchmaker. Indeed, the new business interest in education is a prime example of Lyndon Johnson's "creative federalism" at work. Federal purchasing power is being used to create—indeed, almost to invent —a sizable market for new educational materials and technologies. Until now, the stimulus has come mainly from the Department of Defense and the Office of Economic Opportunity. But the Elementary and Secondary Education Act of 1965 provided large federal grants to the schools for the purchase of textbooks, library books, audio-visual equipment, etc. It also greatly expanded the Office of Education's research-and-development activities and gave it the prerogative, for the first time, to contract with profit-making as well as nonprofit institutions.

The most remarkable characteristic of industry's invasion of the education market is that it has been accompanied by the affiliation of otherwise unrelated businesses. The electronics companies have felt the need for "software," i.e., organized informational and educational material, to put into their equipment and have gone in search of such publishing companies as possessed it. Some of the publishing companies, in turn, particularly textbook publishers, have been apprehensive about the long-range future of their media and willingly joined in such auspicious marriages of convenience. As R.C.A.'s Chairman David Sarnoff explained his company's merger with Random House last May, "They have the software and we have the hardware."

The fact is that, as far as education is concerned, neither side has either—yet. In time, the application of electronic technology can and will substantially improve the quality of instruction. Experiments with the Edison Responsive Environment Talking Typewriter suggest that it has great potential for teaching children to read. I.B.M. has been working on the development of teaching systems since the late 1950's and is now selling its "IBM 1500 instructional system" to a limited number of educators for research, development, and operational use. But a lot of problems—in hardware as well as software—will have to be solved before the computer finds wide acceptance as a teaching device. No computer manufacturer, for example, has begun to solve the technical problems inherent in building a computer that can respond to spoken orders or correct an essay written in natural language and containing a normal quota of misspellings and grammatical errors—and none has promised it can produce machines at a cost that can compete with conventional modes of instruction.

On the other hand, without the appropriate software, a computerized teaching system results in what computer people call a "GIGO system"—garbage in and garbage out. "The potential value of computer-assisted instruction," as Dr. Launor F. Carter, senior vice president of System Development Corp., flatly states, "depends on the quality of the instructional material" that goes into it. But the software for a computer-assisted instructional system does not yet exist; indeed, no one yet knows how to go about producing it. The new "education technology industry," as Professor J. Sterling Livingston of Harvard Business School pointed out at a Defense Department–Office of Education conference in June, "is not being built on any important technology of its own." On the contrary, it "is being built as a satellite of the Information Technology Industry. It is being built on the technology of information processing, storage, retrieval, transmission, and reduction . . . by firms whose primary objective is that of supplying information processing and reproduction equipment and services." And neither these firms, nor the professional educators, nor the scholars studying the learning process know enough about how people learn or how they can be taught to use the computers effectively.

Discovering the Questions to Be Asked

That knowledge is now being developed. The attempts at computer application have dramatized the degree of our ignorance, because the computer, in order to be programed, demands a precision of knowledge about the processes of learning and teaching that the human teacher manages to do without. So far, therefore, the main impact of the computer has been to force a great many people from a great many different disciplines to study the teaching process; they are just beginning to discover what questions have to be asked to develop the theories of learning and of instruction they need.

In time, to be sure, both the hardware and the software problems will be solved, and when they are, the payoff may be large. It will come, however, only to those able to stay the course. And the course will be hard and long—five years, under the most optimistic estimate, and more probably ten or fifteen years. Anyone looking for quick or easy profits would be well advised to drop out now. Indeed, the greatest fear firms like I.B.M. and Xerox express is not that someone may beat them to the market, but that some competitor may rush to market too soon and thereby discredit the whole approach. A number of firms—several with distinguished reputations—did precisely that five years or so ago when they offered shoddy programs to the schools and peddled educationally worthless "teaching machines" and texts door to door.

A lot more is at stake, needless to say, than the fortunes of a few dozen corporations, however large. The new business-government thrust in education, with its apparent commitment to the application of new technologies, is already changing the terms of the debate about the future of American education, creating new options and with them, new priorities. "We have been dealt a new set of cards," Theodore R. Sizer, dean of Harvard's Graduate School of Education, has remarked, "and we must learn how to play with them."

Rarely have U.S. corporations assumed a role so fraught with danger for the society, as well as for themselves, or so filled with responsibility and opportunity. For over the long run, the new business-government thrust is likely to transform both the organization and the content of education, and through it, the character and shape of American society itself. And the timing could not be more propitious. It is already clear that we have barely scratched the surface of man's ability to learn, and there is reason to think that we may be on the verge of a quantum jump in learning and in man's creative use of intellect. Certainly the schools and colleges are caught up in a ferment as great as any experienced since the great experiment of universal education began a century or so ago. Every aspect of education is subject to change: the curriculum, the instruments of education, the techniques and technology of instruction, the organization of the school, the philosophy and goals of education. And every stage and kind of education is bound up in change: nursery schools; elementary and secondary schools, both public and private, secular and parochial; colleges and universities; adult education; vocational training and rehabilitation.

Failure in the Ghetto and the Suburb

The schools have been in ferment since the postwar era began, with the pace of change accelerating since the early and middle

1950's. Until fairly recently they were so deluged with the sheer problem of quantity—providing enough teachers, classrooms, textbooks to cope with the numbers of students that had to be admitted—that they had little energy for, or interest in, anything else. And now the pressure of numbers is hitting the high schools and colleges.

It is becoming clearer and clearer, however, that dealing with quantity is the least of it: most of the problems and most of the opportunities confronting the schools grow out of the need for a broad overhaul of public education. For more than a decade, a small band of reformers—among them Jerome Bruner, Jerrold Zacharias, Francis Keppel, John Gardner, Lawrence Cremin, Francis Ianni—have been engaged in an heroic effort to lift the quality and change the direction of public education. Their goal has been to create something the world has never seen and previous generations could not even have imagined: a mass educational system successfully dedicated to the pursuit of intellectual excellence.

This effort at reform has two main roots. The first, and in many ways most important, has been the recognition—largely forced by the civil-rights movement—that the public schools were failing to provide any sort of education worthy of the name to an intolerably large segment of the population. This failure is not diffused evenly throughout the society; it is concentrated in the rural and urban slums and racial ghettos. The failure is not new; as Lawrence Cremin and others have demonstrated, public education has *always* had a strong class bias in the U.S., and it has never been as universal or as successful as we have liked to believe. But in the contemporary world the schools' failure to educate a large proportion of its students has become socially and morally intolerable.

At the same time there has been a growing realization that the schools are failing white middle-class children, too—that all children, white as well as black, "advantaged" as well as "disadvantaged," can and indeed must learn vastly more than they are now being taught. By the early 1950's it had become apparent that even in the most privileged suburbs the schools were not teaching enough, and that they were teaching the wrong things and leaving out the right things. Where the schools fell down most abysmally was in their inability to develop a love for learning and their failure to teach youngsters how to learn, to teach them independence of thought, and to train them in the uses of intuition and imagination.

The remaking of American education has taken a number of forms. The most important, by far, has been the drive to reform the curriculum—in Jerrold Zacharias' metaphor, to supply the schools with "great compositions"—i.e., new courses, complete with texts, films, laboratory equipment, and the like, created by the nation's leading scholars and educators. This has *not* meant a return to *McGuffey's Reader* or "The Great Books," however. Quite the contrary; the "explosion of knowledge," combined with its instant dissemination, has utterly destroyed the old conception of school as the place where a person accumulates most of the knowledge he will need over his lifetime. Much of the knowledge today's students will need hasn't been discovered yet, and much of what is now being taught is (or may soon become) obsolete or irrelevant.

What students need most, therefore, is not more information but greater depth of understanding, and greater ability to apply that understanding to new situations as they arise. "A merely well-informed man," that greatest of modern philosophers, the late Alfred North Whitehead, wrote forty-odd years ago, "is the most useless bore on God's earth." Hence the aim of education must be "the acquisition of the art of the utilization of knowledge."

Reforming the Teachers

It has become increasingly apparent, however, that reform of the curriculum, crucial as it is, is too small a peg on which to hang the overhaul of the public school. For one thing, the reformers have found that it is a good deal harder to "get the subject right" than they had ever anticipated. And getting it right doesn't necessarily get it adopted or well taught. Five years ago Professor Zacharias was confident that with $100 million a year for new courses, texts, films, and the like he could work a revolution in the quality of U.S. education. Now he's less confident. "It's easier to put a man on the moon," he says, "than to reform the public schools."

Reform is impeded by the professional educators themselves, whose inertia can hardly be imagined by anyone outside the schools, as well as by the anti-intellectualism of a public more interested in athletics than in the cultivation of the mind. The most important bar to change, however, is the fact that the new curricula, and in particular the new teaching methods, demand so much more of teachers than they can deliver. Some teachers are unwilling to adopt the new courses; the majority simply lack the mastery of subject matter and of approach that the new courses require.

It does no good to reform the curriculum, therefore, without reforming the teachers, and, indeed, the whole process of instruction. Under present methods this process is grossly inefficient. One reason is that so few attempts have been made to improve it in any fundamental way. Without question, the schools would be greatly improved if, as James Bryant Conant and others have suggested, they could attract and retain more teachers who know and like their subjects and who also like to teach. A great deal has been accomplished along these lines in recent years, and the experience suggests some kind of reversal of Gresham's Law: raising standards seems to attract abler people into the teaching profession. But something more is needed: teachers have to know how to teach—how to teach hostile or unmotivated children as well as the highly motivated. Until recently, however, most of the creative people concerned with education have been convinced that teaching is an art which a person either has or lacks, and which in any case defies precise description.* Hence their failure to study the process of instruction in any scientific or systematic way. (The collection of banalities, trivialities, and misinformation that make up most of the courses in "method" in most teachers' colleges represents the antithesis of this kind of study.)

---

* There is nothing wrong with the American school system, William James declared some sixty-seven years ago, in a view still being echoed in academic circles, that could not be cured by "impregnating it with genius." But genius, by definition, is always in short supply.

Organized to Prevent Learning

To be sure, teaching—like the practice of medicine—is very much an art, which is to say, it calls for the exercise of talent and creativity. But like medicine, it is also—or should be—a science, for it involves a repertoire of techniques, procedures, and skills that can be systematically studied and described, and therefore transmitted and improved. The great teacher, like the great doctor, is the one who adds creativity and inspiration to that basic repertoire. In large measure, the new interest in the development of electronic teaching technologies stems from the growing conviction that the process of instruction, no less than the process of learning, is in fact susceptible to systematic study and improvement.

Part of the problem, moreover, is that most of the studies of the teaching process that have been conducted until fairly recently have ignored what goes on in the classroom, excluding as "extraneous" such factors as the way the classroom or the school is organized. Yet it is overwhelmingly clear that one of the principal reasons children do not learn is that the schools are organized to facilitate administration rather than learning—to make it easier for teachers and principals to maintain order rather than to make it easier for children to learn. Indeed, to a degree that we are just beginning to appreciate as the result of the writings of such critics as Edgar Z. Friedenberg, John Holt, and Bel Kaufman, schools and classrooms are organized so as to *prevent* learning or teaching from taking place.

The New Concept of Intelligence

The solution, however, is not, as impatient (and essentially anti-intellectual) romanticists like Paul Goodman and John Holt seem to advocate, to abolish schools—i.e., to remove the "artificial" institutions and practices we seem to put between the child and his innate desire to learn. To be sure, the most remarkable feat of learning any human ever performs—learning to speak his native tongue—is accomplished, in the main, without any formal instruction. But while every family talks, *no* family possesses more than a fraction of the knowledge the child must acquire in addition. It would be insane to insist that every child discover that knowledge for himself; the transmission of knowledge—new as well as old—has always been regarded as one of the distinguishing characteristics of human society; and that means, quite simply, that man cannot depend upon a casual process of learning; he must be "educated."

He not only must be educated; he *can* be educated—of this there no longer can be any doubt. The studies of the learning process conducted over the past twenty years have made it abundantly clear that those who are not now learning properly —say, the bottom 30 to 50 percent of the public-school population—can in fact learn, and can learn a great deal, if they are properly taught from the beginning. (These studies make it equally clear that those who *are* learning can learn vastly more.) This proposition grows out of the repudiation of the old concept of fixed or "native" intelligence and its replacement by a new concept of intelligence as something that is itself learned. To be sure, nature does set limits of sorts. But they are very wide limits; precisely what part of his genetic potential an individual uses is determined in good measure by his environment, which is to say, by his experiences.

And the most important experiences are those of early childhood. The richer the experience in these early years the greater the development of intelligence. As the great Swiss child psychologist Jean Piaget puts it, "the more a child has seen and heard, the more he wants to see and hear." And the less he has seen and heard, the less he wants—and is able—to see and hear and understand. Hence the growing emphasis on preschool education.

The abandonment of the concept of fixed intelligence requires changes all along the line. The most fundamental is a new concern for individual differences, which Professor Patrick Suppes of Stanford calls "the most important principle of learning as yet accepted in the working practice of classroom and subject-matter teaching." To be sure, educators have been talking about the need to take account of individual differences in learning for at least forty years—but for forty years they've been doing virtually nothing about it, in large part because they have lacked both the pedagogy and the technology.

Now, however, the technology is becoming available—and at a time when there is a growing insistence that the schools *must* take account of individual differences. Indeed, this quest for ways to individualize instruction is emerging as the most important single force for innovation and reform.

In part, the demand grows out of recent research on learning, which has made it clear, as Professor Susan Meyer Markle of U.C.L.A. has put it, that "individualized instruction is a necessity, not a luxury." In part, too, the demand stems from the conviction, as Lawrence Cremin puts it, that "any system of universal education is ultimately tested at its margins"—by its ability to educate gifted and handicapped as well as "average" youngsters.

The pressure for individualization of instruction is developing even more strongly as a byproduct of the efforts at desegregation of the public schools. Because of the schools'—and society's —past failures, Negro children tend to perform below the level of the white students with whom they are mingled. They need a lot of special attention and help in order to overcome past deficits and fulfill their own potential. Few schools are providing this help; most educators are simply overwhelmed by problems for which their training and experience offer no guide. And so they tend to deal with the problem in one of two ways: by ignoring it (in which case either the Negro or the white students, or both, are shortchanged); or by putting the children into homogeneous "ability groups," in which case they are simply resegregated according to I.Q. or standardized test scores. Neither approach is likely to be acceptable for very long. The need is for a system of instruction in which all students are seen as special students, and in which, in Lyndon Johnson's formulation, each is offered all the education that his or her ambition demands and that his or her ability permits.

Corn for the Behaving Pigeon

Enter the computer! What makes it a potentially important— perhaps revolutionary—educational instrument is precisely the fact that it offers a technology by which, for the first time, instruction really *can* be geared to the specific abilities, needs, and progress of each individual.

The problem is how. Most of the experimentation with computer-assisted instruction now going on is based, one way or another, on the technique of "programed instruction" developed in the 1950's by a number of behavioral psychologists, most notably B. F. Skinner of Harvard. Professor Skinner defines learning as a change in behavior, and the essence of his approach is his conviction that any behavior can be produced in any person by "reinforcing," i.e., rewarding closer and closer approximations to it. It is immaterial what reward is used: food (corn for a pigeon, on which most of Skinner's experiments have been conducted, or candy for a child), praise, or simply the satisfaction a human being derives from knowing he is right. What is crucial is simply that the desired behavior be appropriately rewarded—and that it be rewarded right away. By using frequent reinforcement of small steps, the theory holds, one can shape any student's behavior toward any predetermined goal.

To teach a body of material in this way, it is necessary first to define the goal in precise and measurable terms—a task educators normally duck. Then the material must be broken down into a series of small steps—thirty to 100 frames per hour of instruction—and presented in sequence. As a rule, each sequence, or frame, consists of one or more statements, followed by a question the student must answer correctly before proceeding to the next frame. Since the student checks his own answer, the questions necessarily are in a form that can be answered briefly, e.g., by filling in a word, indicating whether a statement is true or false, or by choosing which of, say, four answers is correct. (Most programmers have abandoned the use of "teaching machines," which were simply devices for uncovering the answer and advancing to the next frame. Programs are now usually presented in book form, with answers in a separate column in the margin; the student covers the answers with a ruler or similar device, which he slides down the page as needed.) If the material has been programed correctly—so the theory holds—every student will be able to master it, though some will master it faster than others. If anyone fails to learn, it is the fault of the program, not of the student. Programed instruction, in short, is a teaching technology that purports to be able to teach every student, and at his own pace.

But teach him what? That's the rub. Most of the applications of programed instruction have been in training courses for industry and the armed forces, where it is relatively easy to define the knowledge or skills to be taught in precise behavioral terms, and where the motivation to learn is quite strong. (One survey of industry's use of programed instruction indicated that 69 percent of the programs used were "job-oriented.") It's a lot harder to specify the "behavior" to be produced, say, by a course in Shakespeare or in American history, and a lot more difficult to sustain the interest of a student whose job or rank does not depend directly on how well he learns the material at hand. And the small steps and the rigidity of the form of presentation and the limitation of response make a degree of boredom inevitable, at least for students with some imagination and creativity.

If programing is used too extensively, moreover, it may prevent the development of intuitive and creative thinking or destroy such thinking when it appears. For one thing, programing instruction seems to force a student into a relatively passive role, whereas most learning theorists agree that no one can really master a concept unless he is forced to express it in his own words or actions and to construct his own applications and examples. It is not yet clear, however, whether this defect is inherent in the concept of programing or is simply a function of its present primitive state of development. A number of researchers are trying to develop programs that present material through sound and pictures as well as print, and require students to give an active response in a variety of ways—e.g., drawing pictures or diagrams, writing whole sentences. Donald Cook, manager of the Xerox education division's applied-research department, has experimented with programs to teach students how to listen to a symphony. And Professor Richard Crutchfield of the University of California at Berkeley is using programed instruction techniques to try to teach students how to think creatively—how to construct hypotheses, how to use intelligent guessing to check the relevance of the hypotheses, etc.

Teaching by Discovery

More important, perhaps, the rigidity of structure that seems to be inherent in programed instruction may imply to students that there is indeed only one approach, one answer; yet what the students may need to learn most is that some questions may have more than one answer—or no answer at all. Programed instruction would appear to be antithetical to the "discovery method" favored by Bruner, Zacharias, and most of the curriculum reformers. This is a technique of inductive teaching through which students discover the fundamental principles and structures of each subject for themselves. Instead of telling students why the American colonists revolted against George III, for example, a history teacher using "the discovery method" would give them a collection of documents from the period and ask them to find the causes themselves.

The conflict between programed instruction and the discovery method may be more apparent than real. At the heart of both (as well as of the "Montessori method") is a conception of instruction as something teachers do *for* students rather than *to* them, for all three methods approach instruction by trying to create an environment that students can manipulate for themselves. The environment may be the step-by-step presentation of information through programed instruction; it may be the source documents on the American revolution that students are asked to read and analyze, but that someone first had to select, arrange, and try out; it may be the assortment of blocks, beads, letters, numbers, etc., of the Montessori kindergarten.

There is general agreement, however, that at the moment, programed instruction can play only a limited role in the schools. Apart from anything else, it is enormously expensive; the cost of constructing a good program runs from $2,000 to $6,000 per student-hour. Because of the costs and the primitive state of the art, Donald Cook believes it inadvisable to try to program an entire school course; programing should be reserved for units of five to fifteen hours of work, teaching specific sets of information or skills that can (or must) be presented in sequence (e.g., multiplication tables or rules of grammar) and whose mastery, as he puts it, offers "a big payoff." In this way teachers can be relieved of much of the drill that occupies so much classroom time; if students can come to class having mastered certain basic information and skills, teachers and students can conduct class discussions on a much higher level.

When the proper limitations are observed, therefore, programed instruction can be enormously useful, both as a means of individualizing instruction and as a research instrument that can lead to greater understanding of the learning and the teaching processes. It is being used in both these ways at the Oakleaf School in Whitehall, Pennsylvania, just outside Pittsburgh, where the most elaborate experiment in the development of a system of individualized instruction is being carried out under the direction of Professors Robert Glaser, John Bolvin, and C. M. Lindvall of the University of Pittsburgh's Learning Research and Development Center.

The Uses of Feedback

Computers and their associated electronic gadgetry offer ways of remedying some of the obvious defects of programed instruction. For example, programs generally involve only one sense—sight—whereas most learning theorists believe that students learn faster and more easily if *several* senses are brought into play. Electronic technology makes it possible to do just that. When a youngster presses one of the keys on the Edison Responsive Environment's Talking Typewriter, the letter appears in print in front of him, while a voice tells him the name of it. When he has learned the alphabet, the machine will tell him—aurally—to type a word; the machine can be programed so that the student can depress only the correct keys, in correct order. And at Patrick Suppes' Computer-Based Mathematics Laboratory at Stanford University, students using earlier versions of I.B.M.'s new 1500 Computer-Assisted Instructional System receive instructions or information aurally (through prerecorded sound messages) or visually (through photographs, diagrams, or words and sentences that are either projected on a cathode-ray tube or presented in conventional typewritten form). Students may respond by typing the answer, by writing on the cathode-ray tube with an electronic "light pen," or by pushing one of several multiple-choice buttons.

To be sure, the 1500 system is still experimental—wide commercial application is five years away—and much richer and far more flexible "environments" are necessary to make the computer a useful teaching device. But computer manufacturers are confident that they can come up with wholly new kinds of input and output devices.

What makes the computer so exciting—and potentially so significant—is its most characteristic attribute, feedback, i.e., its ability to modify its own operation on the basis of the information fed into it. It is this that opens up the possibility of responding to each student's performance by modifying the curriculum as he goes along. This couldn't be done now. Programed instruction currently deals with individual differences in a crude way, chiefly by permitting students to move along as slowly or as rapidly as they can; they still all deal essentially with the same material. But speed of learning is only one relevant dimension of individual differences, and not necessarily the most important. Suppes, among others, is convinced that the best way to improve learning is through "an almost single-minded concentration on individual differences" in the way material is presented to the student.

What this means, in practice, is that a teacher should have a number of different programs at his disposal, since no single strategy of instruction or mode of presentation is likely to work for every student. Second, he should be able to select the most appropriate program for each student on the basis of that student's current knowledge, past performance, and personality. Third and most important, he should be able to modify the program for each student as he goes along in accordance with what the student knows and doesn't know, the kinds of materials he finds difficult and the kinds he learns easily. In time it should be practicable to program a computer to assist in all of these functions.

Games Students Play

Computers lend themselves to the "discovery method" as well as to programed instruction. The exercise of simulating situations and playing games on a computer, for example, can help a student gain insight into a problem by making it possible for him to experiment—and to see the consequences of his (or other people's) actions in much shorter time than is possible in real life. The computer also imposes a strong discipline on the student, forcing him to analyze a problem in a logically consistent manner, while freeing him from a good deal of time-consuming computation.

The armed forces have been using computer simulation and computer games to teach military strategy, and the American Management Association to teach business strategy. Now, a number of researchers, among them Professor James Coleman of Johns Hopkins, are trying to adapt the technique to the instruction of high-school students. Preliminary results suggest that it may be particularly effective in teaching the so-called "disadvantaged" and "slow learners," whose motivation to learn in ordinary classroom situations has been destroyed by years of failure.

As with computer-assisted programed instruction, costs will have to come down dramatically, and techniques for addressing the computer in natural language will have to be developed before widespread application is possible. In the meantime the experiments with computer games have led a number of educational researchers to try to develop non-mechanical games of the Monopoly variety for teaching purposes, especially in the social sciences.

Computers are likely to enhance learning in still another way —by increasing both the amount of information students have at their disposal and the speed with which they can get it. In time electronic storage, retrieval, and presentation of information should make it possible for students or scholars working in their local library—ultimately, perhaps, in their own home—to have access to all the books and documents in all the major libraries around the country or the world. A great many technical problems remain to be solved, however, as everyone working on information retrieval knows through hard (and sometimes bitter) experience.

Thoughts in a Marrow Bone

The biggest obstacle to the introduction of computer-assisted instruction is not technological; it is our ignorance about the process of instruction. Significant progress has been made, however, in identifying what needs to be known before a theory of instruction can be developed. It is clear, for example, that any useful theory must explain the role of language in learning and teaching—including its role in *preventing* learning. It is language, more than anything else, that distinguishes human from animal learning; only man can deal with the world symbolically and linguistically. But verbalization is not the only way people learn or know, as Jerome Bruner of Harvard emphasizes. We know things "enactively," which is to say, in our muscles. Children can be very skillful on a seesaw without having any concept of what it is and without being able to represent it by drawing a balance beam (the use of imagery) or by writing Newton's law of moments (symbolic representation). Present teaching methods, Bruner argues, place too much emphasis on the verbal—a fact he likes to illustrate by quoting these magnificent lines from Yeats:

God guard me from those thoughts men think
In the mind alone;
He that sings a lasting song
Thinks in a marrow-bone

The result is that youngsters too often display great skill in using words that describe words that describe words, with no real feel for, or image of, the concrete phenomenon itself.

Knowing something, moreover, involves at least two distinct processes. The first is memory, the ability to recall the information or concept on demand; and the second is what learning theorists call "transfer," i.e., the ability not only to retrieve the knowledge that is in the memory but to apply it to a problem or situation that differs from the one in which the information was first acquired. We know somewhat more about memory, and recent discoveries in molecular biology hold the promise of vast gains in our understanding of it and our ability to improve it.

Most learning theorists, however, believe that transfer is more important than memory, and that the degree of transfer a student develops depends on how, as well as what, he was taught. For transfer involves a number of specific and distinct traits or skills.

A person must be able to recognize when a problem is present. He must be able to arrange problems in patterns—to see that each problem is not entirely unique but has at least some elements in common with other problems he has solved in the past. He must have sufficient internal motivation to want to solve the problem, and enough self-discipline to persist in the face of error. He must know how to ask questions and generate hypotheses, and how to use guessing and first approximations to home in on the answer. There is reason to think that these skills can be taught. In any case, we must know far more than we do now about both memory and transfer before we can develop the theory of instruction needed to program computers effectively.

Besides that, we need to know more about how the way material is presented—for example, the sequence, size of steps, order of words—affects learning. And we need to understand how to make children—all children—*want* to learn. We need to know how to make children coming from "intellectually advantaged" as well as "disadvantaged" homes regard school learning as desirable and pleasurable. The problem is larger than it may seem, for there is a deep strain of anti-intellectualism running through American life. The notion that intellectual activity is effete and effeminate takes hold among boys around the fifth grade, and becomes both deep and widespread in the junior-high years, when youngsters are most susceptible to pressure from their peers. (Curiously enough, the notion that intellectual activity is *un*feminine sets in among girls at about the same age.) We need to know how to overcome these widespread cultural attitudes, as well as the emotional and neurological "blocks" that prevent some youngsters from learning at all. And we must understand far better than we now do how different kinds of rewards and punishments affect learning.

Interestingly enough, one of the greatest advantages the computer possesses may well be its impersonality—the fact that it can exhibit infinite patience in the face of error without registering disappointment or disapproval—something no human teacher can ever manage. These qualities may make a machine superior to a teacher in dealing with students who have had a record of academic failure, whether through organic retardation, emotional disturbance, or garden-variety learning blocks. The impersonality of the machine may be useful for average or above-average children as well, since it increases the likelihood that a youngster may decide to learn to please himself rather than to please his parents or teachers. And motivation must become "intrinsic" rather than "extrinsic" if children are to develop their full intellectual capacity.

There is reason to think that we may need a number of theories of learning and instruction. For one thing, the process of learning probably differs according to what it is that is being learned. As the Physical Science Study Committee put it in one of its annual reports, "We have all but forgotten, in recent years, that the verb 'to learn' is transitive; there must be some thing or things that the student learns." Unless that thing seems relevant to a student, he will have little interest in learning it (and he will derive little or no reward from its mastery). In any case, different subjects—or different kinds of students—may require different methods of instruction; a method that works wonderfully well in teaching physics may not work in teaching the social sciences.

More important, perhaps, different kinds of students may require different teaching strategies. It is only too evident that methods that work well with brighter-than-average upper-middle-class families fail dismally when used with children, bright or dull, from a city or rural slum. And differences in income and class are not the only variables; a student's age, sex, ethnic group, and cultural background all affect the way his mind operates as well as his attitude toward learning. Differences in "cognitive style" may also have to be taken into account—for example, the fact that some people have to see something to understand it, while others seem to learn more easily if they hear it.

What Knowledge Is Worth Most?

When adequate theories of instruction have been developed, the new educational-system designers will still have to decide what it is that they want to teach. That decision cannot be made apart from the most fundamental decisions about values and purpose

—the values of the society as well as the purpose of education. What we teach reflects, consciously or unconsciously, our concept of the good life, the good man, and the good society. Hence "there is no avoiding the question of purpose," as Lawrence Cremin insists. And given the limited time children spend in school and the growing influence of other educational agencies, there is no avoiding the question of priorities—deciding what knowledge is of most worth.

The answers will be very much affected by the new electronic technologies. Indeed, the computer will probably force a radical reappraisal of educational content as well as educational method, just as the introduction of the printed book did. When knowledge could be stored in books, the amount of information that had to be stored in the human brain (which is to say, committed to memory) was vastly reduced. The "anti-technologists" of antiquity were convinced that the book, by downgrading memory, could produce only a race of imbeciles. "This discovery of yours," Socrates told the inventor of the alphabet in the *Phaedrus*, "will create forgetfulness in the learners' souls, because they will not use their memories; they will trust to the external written characters and not remember of themselves . . . They will appear to be omniscient and will generally know nothing."

The computer will enormously increase the amount of information that can be stored in readily accessible form, thereby reducing once again the amount that has to be committed to memory. It will also drastically alter the role of the teacher. But it will not replace him; as some teaching-machine advocates put it, any teacher who can be replaced by a machine deserves to be. Indeed, the computer will have considerably *less* effect on teachers than did the book, which destroyed the teacher's monopoly on knowledge, giving students the power, for the first time, to learn in private—and to learn as much as, or more than, their masters. The teaching technologies under development will change the teacher's role and function rather than diminish his importance.

Far from dehumanizing the learning process, in fact, computers and other electronic and mechanical aids are likely to *increase* the contact between students and teachers. By taking over much—perhaps most—of the rote and drill that now occupy teachers' time, the new technological devices will free teachers to do the kinds of things only human beings can do, playing the role of catalyst in group discussions and spending far more time working with students individually or in small groups. In short, the teacher will become a diagnostician, tutor, and Socratic leader rather than a drillmaster—the role he or she is usually forced to play today.

The Decentralization of Knowledge

In the long run, moreover, the new information and teaching technologies will greatly accelerate the decentralization of knowledge and of education that began with the book. Because of television and the mass media, not to mention the incredible proliferation of education and training courses conducted by business firms and the armed forces, the schools are already beginning to lose their copyright on the word education. We are, as Cremin demonstrated in *The Genius of American Education,* returning to the classic Platonic and Jeffersonian concepts of education as a process carried on by the citizen's participation in the life of his community. At the very least, the schools will have to take account of the fact that students learn outside school as well as (and perhaps as much as) in school. Schools will, in consequence, have to start concentrating on the things they can teach best.

New pedagogies and new techniques will drastically alter the internal organization of the school as well as its relation to other educational institutions. Present methods of grouping a school population by grade and class, and present methods of organization within the individual classroom, are incompatible with any real emphasis on individual differences in learning. In the short run, this incompatibility may tend to defeat efforts to individualize instruction. But in the long run, the methods of school and classroom organization will have to accommodate themselves to what education will demand.

In the end, what education will demand will depend on what Americans, as a society, demand of it—which is to say, on the value we place on knowledge and its development. The potential seems clear enough. From the standpoint of what people are already capable of learning, we are all "culturally deprived"— and new knowledge about learning and new teaching technologies will expand our capacity to learn by several orders of magnitude. "Our chief want in life," Emerson wrote, "is someone who will make us do what we can."

How Three-Year-Olds Teach Themselves to Read and Write—and Love It

Maya Pines

Despite its publicity, the number of computerized learning schemes actually in operation remains distressingly small. Here is an account of one such scheme—replete with talking typewriters, individual learning booths, and the suspicions of teachers brought up in the old school—which is achieving remarkable results even with retarded children.

Sitting alone in a bare cubicle, a little girl of five happily pecks away at a specially designed automated typewriter and composes a poem. A two-and-a-half-year-old teaches herself to read and write by banging the jam-proof keys of a similar "talking typewriter." Along with several dozen other youngsters, they are taking part in a series of experiments which may have loud repercussions and a surprisingly humanistic effect on education as a whole. The project is the brainchild of a Yale sociologist, Dr. Omar Khayyam Moore.

He believes that the years from two to five are the most creative and intellectually active period of our lives. This is when children first acquire speech and begin to classify their environment. Normally they receive no schooling at this time. And certainly they should not be stuffed with rules and facts. But—says Dr. Moore—they are capable of extraordinary feats of inductive reasoning if left to themselves in a properly "responsive" environment. Furthermore, performing such feats may become a habit and lead to a new breed of highly individualistic, highly imaginative human beings far better prepared than their parents to cope with a complex and unpredictable society.

To Professor Moore—himself highly individualistic and imaginative at forty-three—this is the significance of his "Responsive Environments Laboratory." A man of medium height, with close-cropped hair and deep-set expressive eyes, he is now on sabbatical from his associate professor's post at Yale. He spends most of his time at Hamden Hall Country Day School, a small private school near New Haven, Connecticut. In his laboratory, which is supported by the Carnegie Corporation of New York, Hamden Hall's pupils learn to read, write, type, take dictation, and compose their own stories before they enter first grade. To Dr. Moore this accomplishment is just a happy by-product of his extensive research on culture, learning theory, and "human higher-order problem solving" behavior.

The children who come to his Lab spend no more than half an hour a day there. They may stay away if they wish, or leave after only a few minutes. While the child is in the Lab he is free of all outside pressures. His parents never come in with him and are never told how he is doing. Even his regular teachers, to whom he may be emotionally attached, stay out of the picture. Staff members themselves—half a dozen young wives of Yale graduate students—try to be as impersonal as possible.

The "talking typewriter" consists of a standard-size typewriter keyboard with colored keys, a small speaker, an exhibitor (a frame on which printed matter can be displayed) with a red pointer, a projector which resembles a miniature TV screen, and dictation equipment. Blank paper in the typewriter stands ready to take anything the child types, in jumbo type. There is nothing in the soundproof, air-conditioned booth to distract the child's attention from the machine. Only the keyboard is accessible to the child; all the other gadgets are enclosed in plexiglass or in a wooden cabinet behind the typewriter.

The child discovers immediately that this interesting, adult-looking typewriter is his to play with on his own initiative. The younger the child, the more joyous his response.

The game begins when he presses a key. At once a large letter, number, or punctuation mark appears on the paper, and a soft voice names it through the loudspeaker. The same things happen no matter what part of the keyboard he strikes, as rapidly and as often as he desires. (To test his new-found powers, one two-year-old gleefully struck the asterisk key seventy-five times in succession.)

Joyous Discoveries

When the teacher who has been watching through a one-way mirror sees that the child's interest is waning, she switches a control dial. A curtain lifts over the exhibitor and a red arrow points to a single letter. At the same time the machine's voice names it. Puzzled, the child may try to depress a key, but to his surprise it doesn't work. He tries more and more keys, until he finds the right one. Then the key goes down and prints the letter while the voice names it again. As a new letter pops up on the exhibitor, the child faces an exciting puzzle, a game of "try and find me." Every time a number, letter, or punctuation mark appears on the exhibitor, he hunts for it amid the blocked keys until he hits the jackpot.

From stage to stage, the rules of the game keep being changed for the child, who must constantly adapt himself to fresh situations.

Meanwhile he is learning to touch-type without effort. Each set of keys to be struck by a particular finger has its own identifying color, and the group meant for the right hand responds to a slightly different pressure from that meant for the left. He is also learning to recognize different styles and sizes of type as they appear on the exhibitor, and handwritten letters which may be flashed on the projector's screen.

About once a week the child plays with a blackboard and chalk in a booth which has little automated equipment. (Only one "talking typewriter" is fully automated at present, and the children are assigned to booths at random.) Under ordinary circumstances, when you give a child a piece of chalk, he will scribble or draw pictures. But there are horizontal lines on this blackboard which discourage art work, and eventually the child tries to make letters. At this point, the teacher helps by putting a letter on the projector and suggesting that he draw one like it. Soon the child learns to write the letters he has begun to read and type.

The teacher's role depends on the degree of automation in the booths. Sometimes she takes over the machine's voice part, speaking as gently and patiently as the "talking typewriter." Sometimes she operates the exhibitor by hand. When using the fully automated booth, she merely watches the child through a one-way mirror and comes to his rescue if he raises his hand for help. This may happen if the machine gets stuck (until now the Lab has had only an experimental model to work with) or if the child needs a handkerchief or human company.

As the child advances he finds that the exhibitor suddenly shows him a series of letters, such as "CAT." By now he may be able to pick out a "T" right away, but when he tries this the key is blocked. "A" is blocked, too. When he strikes "C" however, the machine responds by typing it and saying, "C." The exhibitor's red arrow, which had been pointing to "C," then moves to the right over "A." As he strikes all three keys in the proper sequence, the machine prints them, names them one by one, and then says, "Cat." From now on, letters appear only in series—but to the child they are still letters, not words. Then one day, although no one has been "teaching" him, the child suddenly realizes that the letters he knows so well determine words. Overwhelmed by the revelation, he is likely to run out of the booth ecstatically—a reaction the Lab has witnessed over and over again.

This joy in discovery, Professor Moore believes, is sadly lacking in most methods of early childhood education. "By the time a child is three, he has achieved what is probably the most complex and difficult task of his lifetime—he has learned to speak," he points out. "Nobody has instructed him in this skill: he has had to develop it unaided. In bilingual or multilingual communities, children pick up several languages without accent at a very early age. There's plenty of information-processing ability in a mind that can do that."

I visited his "Responsive Environments Laboratory" a few weeks ago. It is a modest, green, prefabricated structure with a narrow corridor, five cubicles with "talking typewriters" in various stages of automation, and a few offices.

At 8:30 in the morning I watched a very small girl enter the building, trailed by a few slightly older children. After being helped to remove her coat and muffler, she walked over to a long table on which stood open jars of bright-colored paints and let a teacher paint her fingernails different colors, to match the color code on the typewriter keys. Then she went into the automated booth and sat down at a chair facing the typewriter. First she pressed the carriage-return key a couple of times, seeming satisfied with the noise it made and the voice which said, each time, "carriage return." Then she banged on "C" and listened to the machine's response, "C." For a while she hummed a tune. Next she fiddled with a side lever. Finally she began to type a few letters rapidly, glancing up at the characters she produced and alert to the voice which came from the loudspeaker. After eighteen minutes in the booth, she suddenly raised her hand. A teacher came in to help her off the chair. "Bye-bye," said the little girl, and walked out.

She was exactly two years and eight months old. In less than two months she had taught herself all the letters in the alphabet, both upper and lower case, and could also write some of them on the blackboard.

Most children pay little attention to the adults in the Lab—they are too fascinated by the machine. The only exceptions are some older ones who have learned to be careful before they start work at the Lab. Thus one newcomer, a little boy of six, would go into his booth and hesitantly press a few keys, then run out to ask the teacher, "Am I doing it right?" He could not get used to the idea that *anything* he did was all right.

Watching the children in the nursery group, mostly four-year-olds, I saw that several who had been in the Lab no more than four months were writing full sentences.

"Barry is a RAT," one little boy typed in complete, silent concentration. He had ranged all over the keyboard, typed the numbers from 16 to 20 in proper sequence, played with the quotation marks, and written several nonsense words before producing his gem, to which he suddenly added, "and a cat." He was using correct fingering technique. Later on, checking his records, Professor Moore told me that while the boy was bright, he did not test in the "gifted" range, which begins above an IQ of 140. He did have one incalculable advantage, however: permissive parents who laid heavy emphasis on intellectual skills, thus giving him much to relate to what he learned in the Lab.

Because of their individual differences, I found it hard to gauge the progress of the kindergartners, the next group, who had been in the Lab for a year and four months. But the first graders were impressive. Two of them—aged six—were busy in one of the offices editing a newspaper which they and a few classmates had dictated into the tape recorder and then typed. It contained little stories, poetry, and riddles: "Why is grass like a mouse?—Answer: because the cat'll eat it (cattle)." One poem by a girl of five was entitled "A Duck" and read as follows:

> There was a duck,
> Who could kick.
> He had good luck,
> Because he was quick.
> He could run in a race,
> He would win.
> He would get some lace
> And a magic pin.

When I met the pint-sized poet she was engrossed in her daily session with the "talking typewriter." From the projector she fluently read a story about Aladdin's lamp. Then she questioned the teacher about the plot and answered the teacher's questions about the meaning of certain words and the story. When she came out of the booth, she sat down with me in an empty office. I asked her whether she wanted to be a poet when she grew up. "No," she replied without hesitation, "I want to be a house-wife." Writing poetry was fun, she said, but the really nice part was being able to work on the newspaper "with Jeff," one of the editors. Did she prefer the Lab when a teacher was there, as today? She liked it best when she was alone in it, she replied emphatically, "so I can do *exactly* what I like."

The most advanced children in the Lab are the two young editors. One is Professor Moore's gifted daughter, Venn, who started playing with the "talking typewriter" when she was two years and seven months old and could read first-grade stories before she was three. Jeffrey, who is the same age, joined her in Professor Moore's early experiments at Yale, and now both children read seventh-grade books with pleasure. To test their skill, I opened a copy of *Scientific American* at random and asked them whether they could read it. They did so exuberantly, taking turns. Although they stumbled over some words which they did not understand, they could clearly handle anything phonetically.

The Crucial Years

People have an idealized version of the playpen as happy and *mindless,* Professor Moore observes. "They say, 'Life is hard enough as it is, let's leave the early period alone.' But we're using only half an hour a day! And with the one hundred two children we've seen so far, we have yet to run into one who'll come in, explore the place, and not want to come back. Of course the children still have their sandbox and paints and so on—in fact, the Lab actually allows us to prolong some of these things.

"As traditionally handled now in the reasonably good nursery schools, at least the children are free, though they receive little intellectual stimulation. But comes the first grade, and the game is over. At the very time when he is becoming interested in the wider world around him, the child must divorce himself from such matters and confine himself to squiggles. He must learn the alphabet, learn to print, and because of his low skill, read baby stories that are not appropriate for him. All of this takes so long that many important things are dropped as frills—painting and music, for instance.

"No wonder so many children develop a hatred for intellectual work early in school. Yet intellectual things are as natural as anything else."

The human mind is extraordinarily open between the ages of two and five. The problem, Dr. Moore believes, is not to miss this critical period. Researchers have found that even rats and monkeys have an inborn curiosity which impels them to seek new territory for its own sake. Experiments have also demonstrated that the key to a rat's learning ability is what happens to it during infancy—which lasts only a few weeks. If rats are exposed to a stimulating environment during this crucial period, they acquire skills with ease later. If not, their whole subsequent performance is impaired.

"If animals are comfortable and have free time, then they will explore," says Professor Moore. In human beings, behavioral scientists have begun to recognize this same "competence drive" as a major motivation along with the drives of hunger, thirst, and sex. But often the drive is stifled. "Every year we lose hundreds of thousands of children who have the ability to learn but who don't go on to college," Professor Moore says. "They have made a nearly irreversible decision very early in life, long before they reach the guidance people in the last year of high school."

For this reason he feels that our educational spending habits are topsy-turvy. "If I had a certain sum to spend on twenty Ph.D. candidates and twenty nursery-school children, I'd use most of it on the youngest children," he says. "They're the ones who need it most." But generally, he points out, schools provide only minimum equipment and teachers for nursery school and kindergarten.

"We're going to have to change our whole notion of how much capital investment should go into education, especially in the early years," Dr. Moore says. "If necessary, we can cut down on expense later; older students should be able to make use of more community facilities, and anyway they can do more on their own."

Dr. Moore has recently set up additional experimental centers in Boston, Massachusetts, and Freeport, New York. Another is being established in Cooperstown, New York. He wants to find out whether his methods work equally well with children in other settings and also to explore the problem of cost.

The matter of expense is possibly the major objection voiced by visitors to his Lab. And indeed it does present a problem. The first production model of his fully automated typewriter (called "A.R.E." for "Automated Responsive Environments") cost an estimated $400,000 to develop. Built by the Thomas Edison Research Laboratory of West Orange, New Jersey, it is a cross between an analogue and a digital computer, new enough to have been patented, and small enough to be portable. The computer co-ordinates the action of the typewriter keyboard, the voice, the dictation equipment, the exhibitor, and the projector. Even on a mass-production basis, this combination would not be cheap. An effort is now being made to develop a low-cost, only partially automated device that can do many of the same things.

But even so, the Moore program cannot be a bargain. The "talking typewriter" actually increases the need for skilled teachers. There must be several monitors in the Lab, at least for young children. In addition, regular classroom teachers must be able to deal with unusually inquisitive, individualistic youngsters. This requires teachers who are not wed to routines.

More Fun for Father

At Hamden Hall, as the Lab produced more and more small children who could read, write, and think independently, some teachers were upset. All their past training seemed threatened when first the kindergarten, then the first grade, were reorganized to make use of the children's skills. One dogged conservative simply refused to face facts. Although nearly all her charges could read and take dictation, she insisted on the standard "reading readiness" exercises.

"That's like giving young children a 'talking readiness' test, and not letting them speak until they pass it," scoffs Professor Moore. "It would mean never saying anything in front of a child that he can't understand, when actually he bathes in speech from the time he is born, and eventually catches on to its patterns."

It was Edward I. McDowell, Jr., headmaster of Hamden Hall, who three years ago took the initiative in bringing Professor Moore and his experiment to the school, in which 340 boys and girls attend classes running from nursery through twelfth grade. Like some of the teachers, a few of the trustees have not been happy about the consequences and last year they tried to oust McDowell. With the backing of parents whose children were directly involved in the experiment he fought back and won out.

This year the first-grade class is reading fourth-grade geography books, going on field trips (to a bakery and other nearby points of childhood interest), and enjoying other extras usually called "enrichment." The children are also plodding—with considerably less enthusiasm—through penmanship practice and the standard school workbooks (the latter at third- and fourth-grade level).

Mr. McDowell foresees far more drastic changes in the kind of school that might in the future evolve from these experiments. "It's going to lead to an ungraded school system all the way up the line," he says. "Educationally this is nothing new, but administratively it's quite a problem. It means the children won't stay in the same room all day long; when it's time for math, for instance, they'll have to split up. In general they'll remain with their own age groups. But in reading-writing, math, and science, they will be grouped according to achievement."

Before starting in the Moore program, each child is given a battery of intelligence and projective tests by a clinical psychologist, as well as physical and eye examinations and hearing tests. A speech expert evaluates his ability to make sounds and a sociologist takes a look at his parents and his home. The clinical psychologist checks up on the children at various stages of the program. So far, there have been no negative results, and according to the psychologist the children's Rorschach tests show "greater richness and better balance" as they advance in the program. Some of their parents report that their children become more interesting.

"Now that letters and numbers are her friends, everything

has more meaning for her," commented one mother. Another child's father admitted, "I was waiting for my boy to grow up before I spent time with him. Now, I'm sorry when he goes to bed."

Many aspects of the program are specifically designed to give the child an early grasp of reality. When the child learns to read into the recording equipment and then take his own dictation, for instance, he becomes his own judge of what constitutes adequate reading. If his original reading from the projector is unclear, he realizes that he is the source of his difficulties; if he reads well, he will find that he is helping himself. Such objectivity presumably should help children to think better and develop a more adequate "social self."

"However, we keep watching for other, negative consequences," Professor Moore says. "Maybe they will show up in time."

Meanwhile, Dr. Moore hopes that the less gifted children will benefit even more than the brighter ones from their sessions with a "responsive environment." Because they are alone with the machine, those who don't understand quickly need not be embarrassed or suffer from constant comparison with the faster learners. In the standard classroom, the gifted child often supplies virtually all the central principles, interpretations, and key facts; thus slower students are deprived of exhilarating discoveries. This may be one of the reasons why slower students come to resent the gifted child, he suggests: they intuitively associate him with their loss.

A "talking typewriter" has infinite patience. It plays no favorites. It does not hold out bribes or threats, nor need the child feel anxious about losing its love. For these reasons, it seems ideally suited to teaching retarded children and others with severe handicaps.

Last year, five retarded boys and girls who had been rejected by public kindergartens because of their low IQ's and behavior problems came to the Lab, tried out the gadgets, and liked them. After seven weeks of work their attitude improved enough for their schools to agree to take them back conditionally. After a year of work in the Lab, all had learned to read simple material. Their IQ's ranged from 59 to 72, classifying them as "educable" retarded who, with the best of standard methods and three to four years of painstaking drills, might begin to read around the age of nine. Yet here was a six-year-old boy (IQ 64) typing away, "The goose laid a golden egg." Although it might take them five or six times as long to reach the same stage as a normal child, they made steady progress at their own pace.

Had these five children been institutionalized or simply deprived of further education, they would probably have become wards of the state for the rest of their lives. In this case the cost of the machine was clearly justified.

Professor Moore plans to concentrate his future research on the deaf, the retarded, and others with severe handicaps. The Responsive Environments Foundation, Inc., a nonprofit organization he has set up with Mr. McDowell, will open its doors to such children next fall.

These experiments with children evolved from Professor Moore's earlier work for the Office of Naval Research. For the past nine years he has dealt with the kind of "human higher-order problem solving" involved in mastering artificial symbolic languages. As his emphasis shifted from deductive to inductive processes, his research with adults became more and more difficult. What he needed was a research lab in which an entirely new order of things had to be discovered.

"Rather than create a whole new environment that was strange enough," he said, "I decided to go in for ignorant subjects."

The most ignorant subjects, of course, are newborns. The most practical time to start experimenting was when these children were up and about, at two-and-a-half or three.

Learning Machines or Teaching Machines?

Unlike parrots, young children don't learn item by item, but by overall search—they absorb whole patterns, Dr. Moore believes. Instead of just repeating a word or phrase over and over, they make up their own sentences. This is the key difference between the "responsive environments" approach and usual "programed instruction" or "teaching machines." Some children explore the

keyboard systematically, others scatter their efforts—they are
not all sent along a pre-set path from A to B to C.

This flexibility may make it possible to program the "talking
typewriter" for six languages simultaneously. The teacher can
then select the language she wants by the flick of a switch. She
can program the projector to show, for instance, a picture of a
cat with the word "cat" in a foreign language. After the student
has seen the word, typed it, and heard it pronounced, the machine may ask him to repeat it, and then play back his own
and the correct pronunciation. If the dials are set correctly, anybody can insert his own program simply by typing and talking
into the machine. Unlike other computers, this machine does
not require a mathematician to translate commands for it.

All kinds of unfamiliar subjects can be presented in this
fashion. A system for teaching basic arithmetic, using an electric calculator, has been worked out in a preliminary way. The
Navy and Air Force plan to try out the "talking typewriter"
with adult illiterates as soon as enough machines are available.
The city of Freeport, New York, has passed a special bond issue
to build a new-model "Responsive Environments Laboratory"
for its kindergarten and first-grade pupils next year; circular in
design, it will consist of ten booths monitored by a yet unde-
termined number of teachers in the center of the Lab. And
Israel—despite the problems involved in converting to a different alphabet—expects to put several machines on trailers in the
near future and send them out to far-flung kibbutzes, to help
new immigrants learn Hebrew.

Meanwhile the machines which already exist represent a
unique "learner-tracking system," in the words of P. Kenneth
Komoski, President of the nonprofit Center for Programed Instruction, Inc., which is supported by the Carnegie Corporation.
Very little is known about how children actually learn; most of
our theories on the subject really deal with performance, rather
than the learning process. Yet here are some machines—Mr.
Komoski prefers to call them "learning machines," rather than
"teaching machines"—which keep records of every relevant
or irrelevant path their subjects take while learning.

"Suppose we discover that children with certain kinds of
background learn in a certain, restricted way," he speculates.

"Eventually it may become possible to open up such closed systems and show these children other ways. Studying the tracks they leave, one might figure out some exercises which would help them break out of overly limited patterns of thought."

Even more important is the impact Professor Moore's work may have on programed instruction as a whole, according to Mr. Komoski. "Programing today takes the best we already know about teaching and puts it into a more efficient means of communication," he says. "It makes the students come up with the right answers, but it is very didactic, with all the little pieces in a preconceived sequence. And because of the tremendous commercial activity in the field, a lot of unimaginative programing is being sold—or oversold. Professor Moore's work is the only real attempt, in automated teaching, to keep alive the student's curiosity and ability to deal with new problems."

Tomorrow's Thinkers

If future experiments prove as successful as those to date at Hamden, what passes for early-childhood education in most nursery schools may come to seem a terrible waste. Professor Moore, however, declines to be drawn into the controversy that is almost certain to result. He has wisely steered clear of an area where slogans like "Why Johnny Can't Read" can arouse the nation, where proponents of the "look-see" method of reading instruction can wage a sterile fight for years with teachers of "phonics," and where the very age at which children should be taught reading is an explosive issue.

"We've been trying very hard to develop an adequate technology and test it carefully. We do not advocate that other people use it," he says. "We don't yet have a finished program. We want to keep the atmosphere free for further experimentation." When the Department of Agriculture wished to convince farmers to shift to hybrid corn and contour farming, he points out, "they simply put up a few model farms here and there, where farmers could come and watch. They did not argue." Professor Moore hopes similarly to proceed by example.

The one issue on which this quiet man speaks with undisguised emotion is the need to develop the next generation's inductive processes. "Modern society is evolving so dynamically that we can no longer depend on child-rearing methods which were adequate before," he says. "We have no time. We can't stand pat. We have more new problems today than we can even name, and we must turn out larger and larger numbers of youngsters who can make fresh inductions about our world.

"A new kind of person is needed to handle the present rate of change. This is our chief trouble today: Technological change but intransigent behavior. It's too late for us—our generation can't make it. At best, we are just the transition group."

The Computer's Role in Health Service Research

G. Octo Barnett, Jerome H. Grossman,
Robert A. Greenes

Medicine has been one of the last bastions of the professional world to yield to the encroachment of automation, and even in the early 1970's the computer has carved out little more than a small niche in the vast field of health delivery. Part of the reason is the natural reluctance of doctors to allow a situation to develop in which it will appear that a machine is diagnosing and treating patients; but another important factor is the lack of penetrating cost analyses relevant to the use of automation in the health industry. A group of experts from Harvard Medical School and the Massachusetts General Hospital reviews the state of the art.

The application of computers in the space-age race for the moon and the application of computers to the care of patients began at about the same time. The former has been spectacularly successful, the latter a stumbling effort still in its primitive stages. The difference is obviously related in part to the quite different nature of the objectives and support available. But there are other reasons. This paper will describe in part the current state of the art of applying computer technology to patient care and discuss some of the ways in which this field is unique.

Such a discussion is always a dangerous venture, for in medical computing the difference between realistic possibility and hopeful fantasy can be quite subtle. Computer-assisted patient care is a particularly hazardous subject because the potential for change seems truly global.

The delivery of health care is essentially a problem-solving activity, depending heavily on the processing of information. A physician's work entails collecting accurate information, precisely formulating hypotheses and testing them, and efficiently managing many individuals and large amounts of data. As medical care comes to depend less on the individual physician and more on the coordinated activity of several professional and auxiliary personnel, timely and productive communication becomes increasingly important. The geographic mobility of people in general—among them, our patients—and a growing concern with the prevention of illness and the management of chronic disease make the long-term storage and ready availability of data essential.

There have been a number of productive applications of computers in patient care, which have begun to reveal the importance of the new technology and to shed light on the processes whereby it is assimilated into the health-care world.

However, the casual reader should not be deluded by the flamboyant claims of the enthusiasts. Experts in this field are renowned for their failure to anticipate the implications of their innovations for patient care, administration, and labor.

There are several fundamental issues which need emphasis, as they are frequently misunderstood or ignored by engineering consultants, by the computer industry, and by hospital administrators.

(1) Most important, computer technology cannot be viewed as an isolated entity, important in its own right. Highly sophisticated instruments—for example, new and more elaborate pressure transducers, or special-purpose computers for detecting cardiac rhythm abnormalities—have played an important role in advancing medical knowledge and have resulted in better care for a limited number of patients. However, they have had no great impact on the day-to-day problems of patient care.

Medical care is a series of intense interpersonal experiences, which can be fully understood only when viewed within a complex social-political-economic context. Technological issues must be considered in terms of the total problem: it is foolish to design a technological solution in the abstract or for an irrelevant "problem."

(2) The extent to which computers can be applied to patient care is limited only in part by the cost and power of available computer systems. Equal or greater limitations are: our inability to state explicitly our problems and objectives; the lack of an easy medium of communication between people who are not computer-trained and the computer; the fact that medical practitioners are unsophisticated about computer usage; and the inadequacy of the manpower available for computer development.

(3) The application of computers is a development problem. Even though we may be sure that a job can be done, if it has in fact never been done before all kinds of unknown difficulties are sure to emerge. Development is expensive and always seems to take twice as long as it should.

(4) The belief that computer techniques can be easily transferred from one field to another must be abandoned. One of the most damning fabrications perpetrated by the computer industry is that application systems can be independently developed for a new kind of user as a marketing service.

Fundamentally, the use of the computer in medicine can be widespread and successful only to the extent that the medical care experts themselves come to understand the machine and find out how to apply it to their needs. Patient care has its own kinds of information-processing tasks, which are unique, no matter how similar they seem to those of other fields on the surface. To be successful, the computer must function as part of the everyday operation of a hospital. Until that happens, applications remain isolated and peripheral, and have little impact.

(5) The approach that begins with a total systems analysis must be reevaluated. Only through considerable experimental effort—developing and evaluating a number of alternatives—is it possible to arrive at realistic specifications for a computer system and requirements for information-handling procedures. We do not accept the assumption that we require a system for fulfilling our needs as we presently define them.

As Galbraith has pointed out, the successful application of technology requires the division and subdivision of the overall task into component parts, to the point where each subdivision matches up with some established area of scientific or engineering knowledge. The implication for medical care is that we must decide upon specific objectives, and then divide the tasks into component parts with explicit definitions. The most appropriate approach would therefore be to concentrate attention on such partial computer-system modules as can be made operational now—not on total systems that may exist sometime in the future.

The Score So Far

Computer technology has already had an impact on the medical system in several areas. The four most widespread applications have been in accounting, scheduling, patient monitoring, and automated laboratories.

The business functions of the hospital were the first to be automated, and almost any hospital of any size has some type of computer-based billing, mostly employing simple modifications of approaches and equipment used in industrial settings. There has not been much of the sort of innovation that would help to reveal (for example) the true cost of specific hospital services; there has been virtually no effort to measure the costs of alternative ways of organizing treatment.

This kind of information is desperately needed: any significant cost/benefit analysis of medical care is *still* impossible, not just for lack of tools to measure benefits, but also because we have little documentation of costs. (It is often suggested that computer-based information systems may help to moderate the spiraling costs of medical care, but this has been almost impossible to demonstrate because of the paucity of information on the costs of the present manual methods.)

Scheduling in most large hospitals is, to paraphrase Churchill, anarchy surrounded by confusion and wrapped in chaos. Lack of coordination in the scheduling of admissions, operating rooms, X-rays, discharges, and ambulatory visits is undoubtedly one of the most wasteful aspects of hospital operations. Certainly it is a prime source of irritation and frustration to both physicians and patients.

But it is no use applying the computer for scheduling before the conflicting interests of the various hospital power groups are reconciled and ground-rules for the allocation of resources are defined. Thus far, experiments in computer-assisted scheduling have amounted to little more than the mechanization of bookkeeping. They have not involved any significant reexamination of how the scheduling of a particular function interacts with the rest of the medical care system.

Consider for example the automation of the instruments and procedures of clinical laboratories. Largely as a result of today's automated laboratory systems, medical care is becoming increasingly based on chemical or physical analysis of body components and characteristics of body function. Computers are being used on an expanding scale, both in private hospitals and commercial laboratories, and soon every clinical laboratory of any size will have access to some sort of computer system. The relative success of this particular application was aided by several circumstances. The laboratories' objectives are relatively simple. The data are numerical. And laboratory staff are technical to begin with. However, it also helped that the clinical laboratory in most hospitals is an income-producing activity, and its director is thus in a position to command funds for the latest and most sophisticated equipment. If any of the work of the nursing staff were an equally obvious income-producer, the automation of medication would be much more advanced than it is at present.

Patient monitoring attracted the interest of computer-oriented engineers early in the game, probably because the signals are easy to measure and the analysis techniques superficially simple. However, development actually went very slowly for the first decade, and only recently has there been any evidence of improved patient care. This delay was due in part to physicians' and engineers' failure to understand the need for close and continuing collaboration. The most spectacular failures occurred when an engineering group developed a system independent of a critical and continuing medical contribution. Some of those early commercial ventures made the Edsel seem a rousing success.

The recently successful patient monitoring developments have one interesting characteristic: they are among the few applications with any significant transferability from one hospital to another. Monitoring deals with patients, and patients at different hospitals are much the same; whereas in administration, a particular unit of a specific hospital will have its own peculiarities. The computer can undoubtedly improve the functioning of a unit or service in a given hospital, but it is unlikely that other hospitals will be able to take over such a development directly.

In summary, innovations that use computer technology are most successful and best accepted where there is cooperation between computerniks and health care experts, with clearly identified needs and well-defined objectives. Such criteria are not often satisfied in health care research; indeed, projects in this area can almost uniformly be characterized by poor communication, diffuse purposes, and grandiose objectives.

The Stress of Technology

Our most productive approach will be to design modular systems for present needs within a structure that can be gracefully expanded. Two agencies have the power to bring significant change to the health care delivery system. One of these is government, through regulation of licensing practices and payment for services. The other is technology.

It has been repeatedly demonstrated that technical innovation of a widespread or radical nature inevitably leads to organization change. As Victor Fuchs has stated: "The medical profession, or at least a significant portion of it, seems to believe that there can be rapid and far-reaching technical change without disturbing the traditional organization of medical practice. This belief is irrational." It may well be that the resistance to change which permeates so much of the power structure of the American medical scene will be broken not by governmental action or by guidance from professional societies, but by the internal contradictions and resulting stresses caused by technological innovation.

Health system research currently places great importance on planning and on evaluating theoretical models, but little on experimentation with operational systems. There is obviously a need for planning to identify specific objectives; it would be foolish to develop technological innovations without a clear understanding of the process of delivering health care.

However, most of the problems are already known, and our highest priorities are not for another model of the theoretical application of queuing theory, or for a new master plan for a health care delivery system in some urban or rural area. What we need now is extensive experimentation on many levels.

Pure ivory-tower research has its place, but so does experimental research. We talk and write exhaustively about the use of auxiliary medical personnel, about how to organize physicians to optimize the use of professional time, about how to motivate hospitals to provide more efficient services, about how technology can make the care of patients more effective. The ratio of theory to experimentation seems disproportionately high. Fundamentally, the provision of health care is not a problem that will be solved by graduate student theses in industrial management, or by changing linear functions to quadratic functions.

The action is not in theoretical research. It is in the delivery of health services in urban hospitals, the provision of services to neighborhoods without physicians, and the increasingly effective utilization of physicians and auxiliary medical personnel. The problems are in the medical care establishment of today, and it is here that the problems must be confronted and solved.

We will never be able to modify the attitudes or change the behavior of physicians, hospitals, patients, and probably not even of politicians, by learned papers or impassioned polemics. Bringing computers to the health services is not an end unto itself; its purpose is to provide an approach and a tool to assist in the experimentation that is so badly needed.

Computer technology alone is a distracting and expensive toy. Computer technology when used by a sophisticated group working on a realistic need with well-defined objectives, in an appropriate medical care delivery environment, has almost unlimited potential.

Medical Transition

Michael Crichton

Medical computers are still in the experimental stage, but some of those experiments are remarkably comprehensive. Here a medical writer who has gained prominence as a science-fiction novelist envisions the computerized treatment of one particular patient.

Flight 404 from Los Angeles to Boston was somewhere over eastern Ohio when Mrs. Sylvia Thompson, a fifty-six-year-old mother of three, began to experience chest pain.

The pain was not severe, but it was persistent. After the aircraft landed, she asked an airline official if there was a doctor at the airport. He directed her to the Logan Airport Medical Station, at Gate 23, near the Eastern Airlines terminal.

Entering the waiting area, Mrs. Thompson told the secretary that she would like to see a doctor.

"Are you a passenger?" the secretary said.

"Yes," Mrs. Thompson said.

"What seems to be the matter?"

"I have a pain in my chest."

"The doctor will see you in just a minute," the secretary said. "Please take a seat."

Mrs. Thompson sat down. From her chair, she could look across the reception area to the computer console behind the secretary, and beyond to the small pharmacy and dispensary of the station. She could see three of the six nurses who run the station around the clock. It was now two in the afternoon, and the station was relatively quiet; earlier in the day a half dozen people had come in for yellow fever vaccinations, which are given every Tuesday and Saturday morning. But now the only other patient she could see was a young airplane mechanic who had cut his finger and was having it cleaned in the treatment room down the corridor.

A nurse came over and checked her blood pressure, pulse, and temperature, writing the information down on a slip of paper.

The door to the room nearest Mrs. Thompson was closed. From inside, she heard muffled voices. After several minutes, a stewardess came out and closed the door behind her. The stewardess arranged her next appointment with the secretary, and left.

The secretary turned to Mrs. Thompson. "The doctor will talk with you now," she said, and led Mrs. Thompson into the room that the stewardess had just left.

It was pleasantly furnished with drapes and a carpet. There was an examining table and a chair; both faced a television console. Beneath the TV screen was a remote-control television camera. Over in another corner of the room was a portable camera on a rolling tripod. In still another corner, near the examining couch, was a large instrument console with gauges and dials.

"You'll be speaking with Dr. Murphy," the secretary said.

A nurse then came into the room and motioned Mrs. Thompson to take a seat. Mrs. Thompson looked uncertainly at all the equipment. On the screen, Dr. Raymond Murphy was looking down at some papers on his desk.

The nurse said: "Dr. Murphy."

Dr. Murphy looked up. The television camera beneath the TV screen made a grinding noise, and pivoted around to train on the nurse.

"Yes?"

"This is Mrs. Thompson from Los Angeles. She is a passenger, fifty-six-years old, and she has chest pain. Her blood pressure is 120/80, her pulse is 78, and her temperature is 101.4."

Dr. Murphy nodded. "How do you do, Mrs. Thompson."

Mrs. Thompson was slightly flustered. She turned to the nurse. "What do I do?"

"Just talk to him. He can see you through that camera there, and hear you through that microphone." She pointed to the microphone suspended from the ceiling.

"But where is he?"

"I'm at the Massachusetts General Hospital," Dr. Murphy said. "When did you first get this pain?"

"Today, about two hours ago."

"In flight?"

"Yes."

"What were you doing when it began?"

"Eating lunch. It's continued since then."

"Can you describe it for me?"

"It's not very strong, but it's sharp. In the left side of my chest. Over here," she said, pointing. Then she caught herself, and looked questioningly at the nurse.

"I see," Dr. Murphy said. "Does the pain go anywhere? Does it move around?"

"No."

"Do you have pain in your stomach, or in your teeth, or in either of your arms?"

"No."

"Does anything make it worse or better?"

"It hurts when I take a deep breath."

"Have you ever had it before?"

"No. This is the first time."

"Have you ever had any trouble with your heart or lungs before?"

She said she had not. The interview continued for several minutes more, while Dr. Murphy determined that she had no striking symptoms of cardiac disease, that she smoked a pack of cigarettes a day, and that she had a chronic unproductive cough.

He then said, "I'd like you to sit on the couch, please. The nurse will help you disrobe."

Mrs. Thompson moved from the chair to the couch. The remote-control camera whirred mechanically as it followed her. The nurse helped Mrs. Thompson undress. Then Dr. Murphy said: "Would you point to where the pain is, please?"

Mrs. Thompson pointed to the lower-left chest wall, her finger describing an arc along the ribs.

"All right. I'm going to listen to your lungs and heart now."

The nurse stepped to the large instrument console and began flicking switches. She then applied a small, round metal stethoscope to Mrs. Thompson's chest. On the TV screen, Mrs. Thompson saw Dr. Murphy place a stethoscope in his ears.

"Just breathe easily with your mouth open," Dr. Murphy said.

For some minutes he listened to breath sounds, directing the nurse where to move the stethoscope. He then asked Mrs. Thompson to say "ninety-nine" over and over, while the stethoscope was moved. At length he shifted his attention to the heart.

"Now I'd like you to lie down on the couch," Dr. Murphy said, and directed that the stethoscope be removed. To the nurse: "Put the remote camera on Mrs. Thompson's face. Use a close-up lens."

"An eleven hundred?" the nurse asked.

"An eleven hundred will be fine."

The nurse wheeled the remote camera over from the corner of the room and trained it on Mrs. Thompson's face. In the meantime, Dr. Murphy adjusted his own camera so that it was looking at her abdomen.

"Mrs. Thompson," Dr. Murphy said, "I'll be watching both

your face and your stomach as the nurse palpates your abdomen. Just relax now."

He then directed the nurse, who felt different areas of the abdomen. None was tender.

"I'd like to look at the feet now," Dr. Murphy said. With the help of the nurse, he checked them for edema. Then he looked at the neck veins.

"Mrs. Thompson, we're going to take a cardiogram now."

The proper leads were attached to the patient. On the TV screen, she watched Dr. Murphy turn to one side and look at a thin strip of paper.

The nurse said: "The cardiogram is transmitted directly to him."

"Oh my," Mrs. Thompson said. "How far away is he?"

"Two and a half miles," Dr. Murphy said, not looking up from the cardiogram.

While the examination was proceeding, another nurse was preparing samples of Mrs. Thompson's blood and urine in a laboratory down the hall. She placed the samples under a microscope attached to a TV camera. Watching on a monitor, she could see the image that was being transmitted to Dr. Murphy. She could also talk directly with him, moving the slide about as he instructed.

Mrs. Thompson had a white count of 18,000. Dr. Murphy could clearly see an increase in the different kinds of white cells. He could also see that the urine was clean, with no evidence of infection.

Back in the examining room, Dr. Murphy said: "Mrs. Thompson, it looks like you have a pneumonia. We'd like you to come into the hospital for X rays and further evaluation. I'm going to give you something to make you a little more comfortable."

He directed the nurse to write a prescription. She then carried it over to the telewriter, above the equipment console. Using the telewriter unit at the MGH, Dr. Murphy signed the prescription.

Afterward, Mrs. Thompson said: "My goodness. It was just like the real thing."

When she had gone, Dr. Murphy discussed both her case and the television link-up.

"We think it's an interesting system," he said, "and it has a lot of potential. It's interesting that patients accept it quite well. Mrs. Thompson was a little hesitant at first, but very rapidly became accustomed to the system. There's a reason—talking by closed-circuit TV is really very little different from direct, personal interviews. I can see your facial expression, and you can see mine; we can talk to each other quite naturally. It's true that we are both in black and white, not color, but that's not really important. It isn't even important for dermatologic diagnoses. You might think that color would be terribly important in examining a skin rash, but it's not. The history a patient gives and the distribution of the lesions on the body and their shape give important clues. We've had very good success diagnosing rashes in black and white, but we do need to evaluate this further.

"The system we have here is pretty refined. We can look closely at various parts of the body, using different lenses and lights. We can see down the throat; we can get close enough to examine pupillary dilation. We can easily see the veins on the whites of the eyes. So it's quite adequate for most things.

"There are some limitations, of course. You have to instruct the nurse in what to do, in your behalf. It takes time to arrange the patient, the cameras, and the lighting, to make certain observations. And for some procedures, such as palpating the abdomen, you have to rely heavily on the nurse, though we can watch for muscle spasm and facial reaction to pain—that kind of thing.

"We don't claim that this is a perfect system by any means. But it's an interesting way to provide a doctor to an area that might not otherwise have one."

Boston's Logan Airport is the eighth busiest in the world. In addition to the steady stream of incoming and outgoing passengers, there are more than 5,000 airport employees. The problem of providing medical care to this population has been a difficult one for many years. Like many populations, it is too large to be ignored, but too small to support a full-time physi-cian in residence. Nor can a physician easily make the journey back and forth from the hospital to the airport; though only 2.7 miles away, the airport is, practically speaking, isolated for many hours of the day by rush-hour traffic congestion.

The solution of Dr. Kenneth T. Bird, who runs the unit, has been to provide a physician when the patient demand is heavi-est, and to provide additional coverage by television. The sys-tem now used, called Tele-Diagnosis, is frankly experimental. It has been in operation for slightly more than a year. At the present time, eight to ten patients a day are interviewed and examined by television.

The Logan TV system is probably the first of its kind in the country, but Bird refuses to discuss priority. "The first to have it," he says, "was Tom Swift, in 1914."

Certainly there is a science-fiction quality about the station's equipment, for along with the Tele-Diagnosis apparatus, there is also a time-sharing station linked to the hospital's computer. Among other things, this computer can be used to take a pre-liminary history—to function as a doctor in questioning the patient about his symptoms and their nature. Some 15 per cent of the patients examined by Tele-Diagnosis have had their med-ical history taken by computer before they see the doctor him-self. Like the cardiogram, the computer history can be sent directly to the physician.

Being interviewed by a machine is less bizarre than it sounds. Indeed, like the TV link-up, it is remarkable for the ease with which patients accept it. The most common complaint is bore-dom: the machine sometimes pauses three or four seconds between questions, and the patients get fidgety.

To be interviewed, one sits in front of a teletype console. The computer asks questions, which are printed out, and the patient punches in his answers. Whenever the computer gets a "yes" answer to some question, it follows it up with more questions on the same subject. If it gets a "no" answer, it goes on to the next topic. At the conclusion of the question, the com-puter writes out a medical summary. Unlike the questions, the summary is phrased in medical terminology. The entire process takes roughly half an hour.

The result of one such interview is reprinted in part below. The computer was given the same presenting complaint as that of Mrs. Thompson: chest pain. In an attempt to confuse it, the machine was first fed some false but suggestive information, namely, that there was a family history of cardiovascular disease, and that the patient was taking digitalis. However, in later questions, the machine was given a straightforward history for the type of chest pain most common among medical students— that of psychogenic, or musculoskeletal, origin.

A sample of the questions and answers ran as follows:

```
68  HAS YOUR VOICED CHANGED (BECOME ROUGH, SCRATCHY OR
HOARSE) DURING THE PAST YEAR?

▪9 NO

69  DO YOU HAVE A COUGH?

▪8 YES

70  HOW LONG HAVE YOU HAD THE COUGH?
1.  A FEW DAYS
2.  A FEW WEEKS
3.  A FEW MONTHS
4.  A FEW YEARS

▪3.

67  DO YOU HAVE THIS COUGH EVERY DAY?

▪8 YES

71  DO YOU BRING UP ANY MATERIAL (SUCH AS SPUTUM,
PHLEGM, OR MUCUS) FROM YOUR CHEST?

▪9 NO

74  HAVE YOU EVER COUGHED UP BLOOD?

▪9 NO
```

At the conclusion of these and other questions, the computer printed the following summary:

```
MEDICAL HISTORY SUMMARY     DATE: MAY 27, 1967

NAME: MICHAEL CRICHTON      UNIT#: DEMO
```

AGE: 26   SEX: MALE

CHIEF COMPLAINT: CHEST PAIN

COMMUNITY PHYSICIAN: NONE

OCCUPATION: MEDICAL STUDENT

MEDICATIONS: DIGITALIS

DRUG REACTIONS: PAN ALBA

HOSPITALIZATIONS: NONE

FAMILY HISTORY: HEART ATTACK, HYPERTENSION.

SOCIAL HISTORY
    PT. IS MARRIED, HAS NO CHILDREN. COLLEGE GRADUATE.
PRESENTLY A STUDENT, WORKING 50-60 HRS/WK. HAS BEEN
SMOKING 5-10 YRS, 1 PACK/DAY. ALCOHOLIC CONSUMPTION:
1 DRINK/DAY. FOREIGN TRAVEL WITHIN THE LAST 10 YEARS.

REVIEW OF SYSTEMS

GENERAL HEALTH
    NO SIGNIFICANT WEIGHT CHANGE IN PAST YEAR. SLEEPS
6-8 HRS/NIGHT. HEAD INJURIES: NONE WITHIN PAST 5 YRS.
EYE SYMPTOMS: NONE. HAS BEEN TOLD BY MD OF NO EYE
DISEASE. NO TINNITUS. NO EPISTAXIS. NOTES SINUS
TROUBLE. DENIES CHANGE IN VOICE.

RESPIRATORY SYSTEM
    PT. NOTES COUGH OF SEVERAL MONTHS DURATION, WHICH
OCCURS DAILY. DENIES SPUTUM PRODUCTION. DENIES
HEMOPTYSIS. NOTES NO DYSPNEA. HAS HAD HAY FEVER.
HAS HAD NO KNOWN CONTACT WITH TUBERCULOSIS. LAST
CHEST X-RAY ∎2 YRS AGO.

CARDIOVASCULAR SYSTEM
    PT. NOTES CHEST PAIN OCCURRING LESS THAN ONCE A
MONTH. LOCATED "ON BOTH SIDES". WHICH RADIATES TO
NEITHER ARM NOR NECK. PAIN IS NOT AFFECTED BY DEEP
BREATHING, IS NOT ASSOCIATED WITH EATING, EMOTION,
OR EXERCISE. PAIN IS NOT RELIEVED BY RESTING.
PT. NOTES PALPITATIONS ON RARE OCCASIONS, DENIES
ORTHOPNEA. DENIES PEDAL EDEMA, DENIES LEG PAINS,
DENIES VARICOSE VEIGNS, DENIES PERIPHERAL REACTION
TO COLD. CARDIAC MEDICATIONS: NONE. HAS BEEN TOLD
BY MD OF NO COMMON CARDIAC DISEASE. NO ECG IN PAST
2 YRS.

This is only half the total report. Analysis of gastrointestinal,
musculoskeletal, genito-urinary, hematologic, endocrine, dermatologic, and neurological systems followed. This particular com-

puter program draws no conclusions about diagnosis; it only summarizes answers to its own questions, and it does not cross-check itself. Thus, while the computer was told the patient took digitalis, it later accepted the conflicting statement that the patient took no cardiac medications.

This program, which was devised at the MGH, is a rather simple example of the way that computers can and almost certainly will be used in the future. But it is the least sophisticated of the medical-history programs available; more complex ones already exist.

When Mrs. Thompson arrived at the MGH emergency ward, which had been expecting her, she was taken down to the EW X-ray department. In doing so, she passed a door near the front of the EW which is unmarked, without a label. Over the door is a lighted sign that says, incongruously, "On Air."

Dr. Murphy was behind that door, sitting in a corner of a small room, surrounded by equipment. Directly in front of him was a camera and a large TV screen, on which he watches the Logan patients. Built into his desk were two other screens: one, a small monitor of the larger screen, the other, a monitor that showed him his own image being transmitted to the patient. This second monitor allowed him to check his own facial expressions, the lighting in the room, and so on.

To his right was a panel of buttons that controlled the various remote cameras—two in the examining room and one in the laboratory. The examining-room remote camera is operated by a joystick: by pushing the stick right or left, up or down, the camera moves accordingly. In addition, there are buttons for focusing and zoom control.

Before going out to check on Mrs. Thompson, Dr. Murphy continued a study of Tele-Diagnosis capability: reading a series of 120 chest X rays that are set up for him at Logan. He planned to read these by TV and later reread them in person, to compare the accuracy and consistency of his diagnosis.

The nurse at Logan set up the next X ray.

"What's this one?"

"Jay-nineteen," the nurse said, reading off the code number.

"Okay." He moved the joystick and touched the buttons. The camera tracked around the X ray, examining the ribs, then scanning the lung fields. "Wait a minute." He zoomed in to look closely at the right-upper lobe; he watched the little monitor, because resolution was better, but by glancing up at the large screen, he could also get a magnified view. "No. Well, on second thought . . ." He zoomed back for an over-all view. He zoomed in on another part of the upper lobe. "Looks like a small cavitation there . . ." He zoomed back, touching the buttons. He turned to the joystick, panned across the rest of the lung field, occasionally pausing to look at suspicious areas. "Nothing else, not really . . ." He finished his scan, and returned to the right-upper lobe. "Yes, there's cavitation. I'd have to call it moderately advanced tuberculosis. Next, please."

He was working with considerable rapidity. "You get to be pretty good at this," he said. "At first, it all seems clumsy, but as you get more accustomed to the equipment, you move faster."

The average time for a patient interview and examination by Tele-Diagnosis is now twelve minutes, less than half the average figure a year ago.

"What I'm doing now," he said, "is really just a test of our capability. It has no immediate practical use, because we can't take X rays at Logan—that's one of the main reasons we brought Mrs. Thompson into the hospital. But it's important to know if X rays can be read at a distance with accuracy. Our impression is that you can read them as well on TV as you can in person.

"Jay-twenty," the nurse said, putting up another film.

Murphy began his scan. "Ah. What's this? Looks like a rib fracture . . ."

One can argue that for the past twenty years technology has defined the hospital, has made it what it is today. That is, once a range of expensive, complex therapeutic and diagnostic machinery became available, the hospital assumed the role of providing a central location for such equipment. This was inevitable: private practitioners and even large group practices could not afford to buy such equipment, nor maintain it, nor pay the personnel to operate it. Only the hospital could do this. It was the only institution in existence that could possibly absorb the expense. Other possible institutions, such as nursing homes, were wholly inadequate.

Furthermore, because the hospital was already oriented toward acute care of critically ill patients, the technology that it absorbed was precisely that which helped in this area. Monitoring machines and life-support equipment are clear examples. Thus technology reinforced an already existing trend.

Now, however, the pressures and forces acting upon the hospital are social and of a nature that is changing the meaning of technology within the hospital. As C. P. Snow has said, "We have been letting technology run us as if we had no judgment of our own." But such judgment is now required, and one can argue that in the next twenty years the hospital will define technology. That is, it will create a demand for new technological applications—and in certain ways will itself produce the new technology.

By doing this, the hospital will be extending its newest and most striking trend, which is to foster innovation, later to be picked up by other, nonacademic institutions. The absurd endpoint of such a trend would be for the hospital to direct personally the diagnosis and therapy of a patient who never enters the hospital. Absurd as it may be, it is already happening in the case of many patients treated at Logan Airport. It will happen more often, in other ways, in the future.

Of the almost limitless spectrum of potential technological advance, we can concentrate here on two areas of imminent advance, television and computers. One ought to say that they have been imminent for a long time; a decade ago one heard that computers were about to revolutionize medicine, and one still hears it today. It obviously hasn't happened yet. Indeed, neither television nor the computer has made much difference yet to routine hospital functioning. Television is employed on occasion for student teaching; it is used in a small way for dispatching blood samples and other items; it has some application in X-ray technology, in terms of image-intensification systems. Computers remain primarily the plaything of researchers. At the MGH there is now a computer program to help in running the clinical chemistry lab, and a computer to help in billing and patient record-keeping, but the computer and television as direct aids in patient care have not made their appearance.

In contrast, the Tele-Diagnosis system at Logan Airport uses computers and TV in direct confrontation with the patient.

The system is expensive and in some ways primitive. Also, its present thrust is diagnostic; therapy, the steps following diagnosis, will still be directly carried out by a doctor, nurse, or the patient himself. There are no machines to do this, unless one stretches the definition to include renal-dialysis machines, exercise machines, and the like.

In general, diagnostic automation appears much closer than therapeutic automation—and is much more readily acceptable to physicians. Consider, then, diagnostic automation first.

The first and most striking feature of the Logan system is that diagnosis can occur at a distance. The doctor's stethoscope is three miles long. But, oddly, that is the least original aspect of the situation. In medicine, diagnosis at a distance is very old and has some humorous elements. Beginning around A.D. 900, for example, the practice of uroscopy, or "water casting," came into vogue. It was felt that the amount of information obtainable from inspection of urine was unlimited. The urine of a sick man was often sent many miles to be examined by a prominent physician.

David Riesman cites a typical medieval interpretation of urine:

> The urine is pale pink, thick above, thin below, becoming gray or dark toward the surface. The grayness and obscurity is caused by overheating of the material. The symptoms are these: pain in the head, especially in the temples, sourness of the breath, pains in the back from bile descending to the loins and kidneys, with paroxysms every day or every second day, usually coming on after dinner time.

In medieval literature there are many discussions of the hazards to the physician of uroscopy; even in those days, diagnosis at a distance had its risks. The Spanish physician Arnold of Villanova, who lived in the thirteenth century, wrote:

> With regard to urines, we must consider the precautions to protect ourselves against people who wish to deceive us. The very first shall consist of finding out whether the urine be of man or of another animal or another fluid.
> The second precaution is with regard to the individual who

brings the urine. You must look at him sharply and keep your eyes straight on him or on his face; and if he wishes to deceive you he will start laughing, or the color of his face will change, and then you must curse him forever and in all eternity.

The third precaution is also with regard to the individual who brings the urine, whether man or woman, for you must see whether he or she is pale, and after you have ascertained that this is the individual's urine, say to him: "Verily, this urine resembles you," and talk about the pallor, because immediately you will hear all about his illness. . . .

The fourth precaution is with regard to sex. An old woman wants to have your opinion. You inquire whose urine it is, and the old woman will say to you: "Don't you know it?" Then look at her in a certain way from the corner of your eye, and ask: "What relation is it of yours?" And if she is not too crooked, she will say that the patient is a male or female relation, or something from which you can distinguish the sex. . . . Or ask what the patient used to do when he was in good health, and from the patient's doing you can recognize or deduce the sex. . . .

The list continues through nineteen precautions, all designed to enable the physician to pry information from the person bringing the urine, and to prevent deception. Arnold was not above a little deception himself, however:

You may not find anything about the case. Then say that he has an obstruction of the liver, and particularly use the word, obstruction, because they do not understand what it means, and it helps greatly that a term is not understood by the people.

The modern counterpart of this medieval guessing game over urine is the telephone conversation between physician and patient. For years after the telephone became common, physicians resisted making telephone diagnoses, and they still frown on them. But every practicing doctor now spends a substantial part of his day talking to patients on the phone, and he is resigned to making a large number of decisions, some of them uneasily, by phone.

Closed-circuit television, while far from the ideal of a personal examination, is vastly superior to the telephone alone, and in many cases it is surprisingly adequate. This does not mean that future patients will all be seen by closed-circuit television, with neither doctor nor patient leaving home. What it does mean is that television will probably work in certain very special applications. One of these is the Logan application —providing a doctor to a clinic during low-use periods. Another obvious use would be specialist consultations. A hospital or clinic that needs a neurologist only a few times a year cannot afford to staff one. Nor could it find one, even if it could afford it. Television is perfectly suited to such consultation.

At the same time, a system such as that at Logan makes possible a routine physical examination, but goes no further— and there are suggestions that technology will ultimately change the very nature of physical examination. Here the historical trend is clear.

Consider the innovations in physical diagnosis. In the nineteenth century, there were three of great importance—the stethoscope, the blood-pressure cuff, and the thermometer. Each of these is really nothing more than a precise way to determine what can be inaccurately determined by other means. Thus the thermometer is superior to the hand on the forehead; the stethoscope superior to ear against the chest*; and the blood-pressure cuff superior to a finger compressing the artery to test its pressure.

Now, the first two advances of the twentieth century were quite different: the X ray and electrocardiogram provided new information not obtainable by physical contact. No amount of squeezing and touching the patient will tell you anything directly about the electrical currents in his heart. You may deduce this information from other findings, but you cannot extract it directly. Similarly, X rays represent a new kind of vision, providing a new kind of information.

At the present time a variety of examination procedures are being tested. These include thermography, ultraviolet light, ultrasonic sound, as well as mapping electrical currents in the

* For the purposes of this argument, I will ignore the fact that the stethoscope really initiated auscultation as a useful examination procedure. In truth, ears were not pressed against the chest with much regularity before Laënnec invented the stethoscope and described auscultation.

skin. Except for thermography, these all represent "new" sensory information for the doctor.

Thus the initial trend was to measure the patient more exactly, and later, to measure the patient in new ways. The first approach has been to find new sorts of measurements and new sensory information. But a second approach, now in its infancy, concerns translation of old information into new forms. The computer will be helpful here in a number of ways, in producing what is called "derivative information."

In a simple way, this is already being done. The human computer* and the electrocardiogram are a clear example. The electrocardiogram measures electrical currents within the heart muscle—the current that makes it contract and beat. Often, when a physician looks at an electrocardiogram, he wants specific electrical information. He wants to know about rate and rhythm, about conduction of impulses, and so on. At other times, he wants non-electrical information. He may want to know how thick a part of the heart wall is, for instance. In this case, he derives the information from the electrical information.

But there are more complex forms of derived information. A physician examining a patient with heart disease may be interested in knowing the cardiac output—exactly how much blood the heart is pumping per minute. This is the product of heart rate (easily determined) and volume of blood ejected per beat (very difficult to determine). Because cardiac output is so hard to assess, it is not much used in diagnosis and therapy. However, by measuring heart rate and the shape of the arterial pulse (both easily done) a computer can calculate cardiac output and can perform these calculations continuously over a period of days, if necessary. If a physician needs to know cardiac output, he can have this information. He can have it for as long as the patient is connected to the computer.

Does the physician really need cardiac output? At the moment, he can't be sure. For centuries he's had to content himself with other information. There is reason to believe, however, that cardiac output will be useful in a variety of ways, as will other derived information.

---

* Defined as the only computer that can be produced by unskilled labor.

An interesting technological application concerns the reverse of the coin: determining which information the physician already has but does not need. This is not to say that the information is inaccurate, but only that it does not have diagnostic significance and is therefore not worth obtaining. At present, the physician naturally tries to avoid gathering useless information, but in certain circumstances he cannot perform as well as a computer. Multiple discriminant analysis is a case in point. As one observer notes, "There is a limitation on the human mind regarding the speed, accuracy, and ability to correlate and intercorrelate multiple variables with all possible outcomes and treatment consequences." There is a limitation on the computer, too. Practically speaking, there are many limitations. But in purely mathematical capability, the human mind is much inferior to the computer in multiple-discriminant analysis.

This is a function vital to diagnosis. It refers to the ability to consider a large body of facts, and on the basis of those facts to assign a patient to one diagnostic category or another on the basis of probability. Consider a simple set of categories: appendicitis versus no-appendicitis. (This is a simplification of what is, practically speaking, a larger problem in diagnostic categories, but it will serve to explain the principle.) Let us assume that a surgeon seeing a patient with pain on the right side must make only this decision. How does he make it? No single piece of information will tell him the answer (except, perhaps, the fact of a previous appendectomy). Certainly such routine data as sex, age, white count, degree of fever, duration of pain in hours will not tell him. But considered all together, they permit him to arrive at a decision.

This is all very familiar. But the point is that it is not very precise. A discriminant function can be produced that weights each variable—age, sex, white count—on the basis of how important each variable has been in the past. Thus the discriminant function has two uses. First, it can make a diagnosis and act as a consultant to the surgeon.* Second, it can determine

---

* Several discriminant functions have been made and shown to be as accurate as the surgeons, though interpretation is made more complex by the fact that these functions are generated from data on previously diagnosed patients.

which variables are most significant, which account for the greatest proportion of the variance, in making a diagnosis. This can sometimes be surprising. For example, one study of women undergoing gynecologic surgery indicated that the age of the patient had great diagnostic importance, and that notation of last menstrual period, biopsy of smear, pre-operative hemoglobin, and urine-sediment study were all much less important to making a diagnosis.

These applications of the computer are designed to be diagnostic aids to the doctor, rather than a replacement. One hears, for example, that "even though computers can be programmed to make diagnoses, it takes the physician to perform the physical examination, and it takes the personal contact of the doctor-patient relationship to gather the information needed for the identification process."

For better or worse, this is not quite true. History-taking, long the province of the physician and a keystone to his "art," is partially amenable to automation. The Logan station utilizes a simple program, which is not so much a conversation with the computer as a quiz. But more sophisticated programs exist, and still better ones are being planned.

Some years ago, Joseph Weizenbaum of MIT designed a program to conduct psychiatric interviews. Although in some senses the program can be regarded as a "trick," it can nonetheless achieve impressive results. Dr. Andrew T. Weil has reported one interaction between the computer and a human psychiatrist as follows (the computer writes in upper-case letters; mere humans, in lower-case).

doctor, i have terrible news
YOU SAY YOU HAVE TERRIBLE NEWS
yes, there is a computer program at m.i.t. that'll ruin us
WHY DO YOU SAY THAT
i have seen it working
YOU SAY THAT YOU HAVE SEEN IT WORKING
it's frightening—you must see it
YOU THINK I MUST SEE IT

you sound depressed to me
IN YOUR FANTASY PERHAPS WE SOUND DEPRESSED TO
EACH OTHER

yes—perhaps
I UNDERSTAND
i do too
YOU SAY YOU DO TOO
we are both in the same boat with respect to the computer
LET'S CONTINUE TO TALK ABOUT YOU--SHALL WE
you are a comfort
WHAT MAKES YOU THINK I AM A COMFORT
at a time like this you want to talk about me
WHY DO YOU THINK I WANT TO TALK ABOUT YOU
because you share my feelings about that damned computer
WHAT DOES THAT SUGGEST TO YOU
that, of course, you hate computers too
YOU THINK I HATE COMPUTERS TOO
why not, they're hardly human, are they
PERHAPS THAT'S WHAT WE ARE HERE TO FIND OUT
no computer could converse as you can, for example
OH
i can't understand how anyone could be fooled by a mere
machine
CAN'T YOU REALLY
no, after all, there is nothing creative about a computer program
YOU ARE BEING NEGATIVE
i am convinced i am correct
ARE YOU WORRIED TO HAVE BEEN CONVINCED YOU ARE CORRECT
no, not in the least. not at all. not even a little
YOU ARE BEING NEGATIVE
you said you agreed with me, didn't you
IS THAT WHAT YOU HEARD ME SAY
why don't you try to dissuade me—computers diddle with numbers that's all
YOU WISH ME TO TRY TO DISSUADE YOU
you can't
YOU THINK I CAN'T
for example, could a computer in conversation like this raise a
new topic

YOU SEEM TO HAVE AVOIDED SPEAKING OF YOUR PARENTS
ALTOGETHER
precisely as you just did
YOU THINK I JUST DID
yes, and that's what shows the difference between a man and a
computer
I SEE

This kind of interaction is suggestive, at least of the ways computers can be utilized in the future. And as the hospital reaches out into the community, these may be increasingly important. According to Jerome Grossman of the MGH Computer Sciences Laboratory, "A large part of history-taking is directed toward finding out how sick a person really is. The first question is always whether a patient needs to see a doctor at all. That's the biggest decision doctors make over the phone now— talking to the patients, trying to decide whether they're sick enough to be seen now, or whether it can wait. The patients want to know the same thing, so they spend all night or all week-end trying to get hold of the doctor, who's off duty, or out of town, or something. . . .

"In the near future, when the home computer and television set is practical, you're going to be able to plug right into the hospital computer without ever leaving your home. The computer will flash questions on the screen, like 'Do you have a cough?' and you answer by touching the screen with your finger at the appropriate place. We've just developed a screen like this. It doesn't require any special gadgets or light pens or anything, just your finger. Touch the screen, and the information is recorded. Eventually, the computer will flash back some directions, like 'Come to the hospital immediately' or 'Call your doctor in the morning' or 'Have a check-up within six weeks,' or 'Someone will come on the screen, if further classification is necessary.' So there you have it. That first big decision—who needs to be seen—is settled by the computer, without ever having required the doctor's presence."

The idea is interesting not because it is an imminent practical development—it is not*—but rather that it represents a further extension of the hospital into the community—not only into clinics via TV, but into the home of many individuals, via computer. One can argue, in fact, that those who predict the hospital's role as "primary physician" or "first-contact physician" is declining are wrong. It will, ultimately, increase with the use of computers.

Automated diagnosis is one thing; automated therapy, quite another. It is probably fair to say it is feared equally by both patients and physicians. It is also important to state firmly that the following discussion is largely speculative; automated diagnosis is in its infancy, but automated therapy has hardly been conceived. Its modern forerunners are the monitoring systems that check vital signs and the electrocardiogram. These monitors are not computers at all, in any real sense; they are just mechanical watchdogs, about as sophisticated as a burglar alarm.

At the present time, there are serious problems facing anyone who wishes to automate the therapy of even a circumscribed class or category of patient. To automate the therapy of all patients, with the full spectrum of disease, would be an enormous undertaking. Whether or not it is done will depend largely upon the demand for it, which in turn depends upon the availability of physicians. In assuming that it will be done, at least to some extent, I have also assumed that the shortage of physicians in this country will increase in the forseeable future, necessitating a practical change in the doctor's functions.

Partially automated therapy is already desirable. The reasons are twofold. First, modern therapy makes necessary an enormous amount of paperwork; one hospital study concluded that 25 per cent of the hospital budget was devoted to information processing. The usual hospital systems for collecting, filing, and retrieving information consume great quantities of time for nearly everyone working in the hospital, from the physician who must spend time thumbing through the chart, to the nurses who

---

* What *is* imminent is the use of computer stations to take a portion of routine history and to advise the doctor on further tests. Such consoles are already in use experimentally in the MGH medical clinics and in certain private doctors' offices.

must record routine data, to the personnel who work full time in the chart-record storage rooms. One consequence of the present methods, aside from the expense, is the number of errors that occur at various points along the line. And the possible advantage of putting all data through computers is the ability to check errors. For instance, if medications are ordered by the physician through a computer, that computer can tirelessly review orders for drug incompatibilities, inappropriate dosages, and so on.

The second reason comes from experience with present monitors in intensive-care units. These monitors "watch" the patient more carefully than any group of physicians could; the patient's condition is sampled continuously, rather than just during rounds. Such monitoring has already changed many ideas about the nature of disease processes* and it has renewed consideration of therapy at intervals. For example, most drugs are now given every six hours, or every four hours, or on some other schedule. But why not continuously, in an appropriate dose? And in that case, why not have a machine that can correct therapy on the basis of changes in the patient's condition?

Seen in this light, automated therapy becomes a more reasonable prospect. It will require adjustment, of course, by both doctors and patients. But that adjustment will be no more severe than in other sectors of society.

In the past fifty years, society has had to adapt to machines that do mechanical work—in essence, taking over functions of the musculoskeletal system. It is now quite accepted that almost nobody does anything "by hand" or "on foot," except for sport or pleasure. But what is coming is what Gerard Piel calls "the disemployment of the nervous system," in a manner comparable to the disemployment of the musculoskeletal system. Man has accepted the fact that there are machines superior to his body; he must now accept the fact that there are machines in many ways superior to his brain.

---

* One example: the incidence of cardiac arrythmia following myocardial infarction is now suspected to be virtually 100 per cent; it is thus an almost certain consequence of heart attack—this is useful information, since the arrythmias are the most common cause of sudden early death from heart attack.

The image of the patient, lying alone in bed, surrounded by clicking, whirring stainless steel is certainly unnerving. It is easy to agree with the doctors who fear automation as leading to depersonalized care, and the computer, as psychologist George Miller notes, as "synonymous with mechanical depersonalization." But that is probably because we are so unfamiliar with them, and, in any event, man has found ways to personalize machines in the past—the automobile is a baroque example— and there is no reason to think he cannot do it in the future.

One example of an attempt to computerize some elements of patient therapy is the computer-assisted burns treatment project being carried out, with the Shrine Burn Institute, in Dr. G. Octo Barnett's Laboratory of Computer Science at the MGH. The project director, Kathleen Dwyer, notes that "there's no theoretical reason why you couldn't build a program to carry out some functions of a doctor, at least for certain kinds of patients. But, practically speaking, it's a long way off."

In trying to find out why, precisely, it is a long way off, one gets two kinds of answers. The first is that nobody is really interested in working very hard, at the moment, to duplicate a doctor on magnetic tape. The second answer is that doctors don't know themselves precisely how they operate; until doctors figure it out, no one can program a machine to carry out the same functions. The classic situation is that of the physician who enters the room of a person with normal temperature, heart rate, blood pressure, and electrocardiogram, takes one look at him and says: "He looks sick." How did the physician arrive at that conclusion? If he can't tell you the signals he used, then the programmers can't computerize them.

This situation is often held up as a kind of limit on the application of machines to medicine. How can one imitate the "unconscious" or "instinctive" or "intuitive" or "experiential" functions of a doctor? But, in fact, as Kirkland and others have pointed out, the argument is really more damaging to the reputations of physicians than machines. For, unless the doctor is flatly guessing when he says, "The patient looks sick," he is drawing a conclusion on the basis of some input, presumably visual. One need only identify that input—and then plug it into the computer. But if the input is truly unidentifiable, one must strongly suspect that the doctor is guessing or expressing a prejudice.

In any event, there is considerable interest in knowing how a doctor decides that a patient looks sick, or looks better, for, as Dr. Jerome Grossman says: "Working with computers has made us look closely at how people think."

But at the moment computer-assisted programs are all that are being used. Dwyer's program, which will be in pilot use by the end of 1970, is specifically designed to help in a major management problem—the burned pediatric patient. These young patients require close monitoring and frequent changes in therapy. This in turn produces an enormous amount of paperwork and accumulated data that is hard for a physician to summarize in his own mind simply by reading the chart. Dwyer anticipates that a computer-assisted program would "facilitate the orderly collection and retrieval of information [and] would not only improve patient care . . . but would also lead to the development of optimal therapeutic models and a better understanding of the disease process."

The first phase of the project will be a simple bookkeeping function: storing information about the patient and his treatment and displaying it on command on a teletype, or a cathode-ray tube (essentially, a TV screen), whenever the physician requests it. A hypothetical example of such a display follows:

```
FLUID 1-O                                        SMITH, JOHN
2/2/68 11.30AM                                   123-45-67


TIME      RINGERS     ORAL      URINE      WT (KG)    OTHER IV
_____

TODAY
2/2/68

8AM       300/300      -        100/100     32          -

9AM       250/550    100/100    100/200     32.5        -

10AM      100/650    200/300    135/325     33         100B

11AM      200/850     50/350    122/447     32.5        -

FLUID TOTALS     INPUT: 1300    OUTPUT: 447    WT. CHANGE: +.5

YESTERDAY
2/1/68

8AM       100/100     50/50      75/75      31          -

9AM       200/300     -/50       50/125     31          -
```

TIME	RINGERS	ORAL	URINE	WT(KG)	OTHER IV
YESTERDAY 2/1/68					
10AM	300/600	100/150	75/200	31.5	300P
11AM	300/900	100/250	100/300	31.7	-
12PM	200/1100	76/325	100/400	32	-
1PM	150/1250	-/325	150/550	-	-
'					
'					
'					
11PM	. . . .				
12AM	. . . .				
'					
'					
6AM	100/2500	-/700	200/1200	32	-
7AM	75/2527	50/750	100/1300	32	-
FLUID TOTALS	INPUT: 3325		OUTPUT: 1300	WT. CHANGE: +1	
1/31/68	3000(200)/3200		1100	-1.5	B.P
1/30/68	300(-)/3000		1000	-.5	-
1/29/68	4200 100/4300		900	-1	-

Here the computer is summarizing intravenous (Ringers) and oral fluid intake, urine output, and weight change over a five-day period. This achievement will not be very exciting to anyone who has not spent half an hour going through a patient's chart attempting to extract this information—which the computer can provide in milliseconds.

But the second stage is rather different. It is called "computer-generated treatment regimen," and what it means is that the computer will itself advise future therapy, which the physician is free to accept or ignore. Another hypothetical example, for a new patient admitted to the unit:

```
ADMISSION DATE T 05/08/69   ADMISSION TIME N 11.22AM
ADMITTING DOCTOR'S INITIALS...KRD
PATIENT'S NAME...SMITH,JOHN
BIRTH DATE...4/20/65
UNIT NUMBER...1234567
   THIS UNIT NUMBER IS ALREADY ASSIGNED. TRY AGAIN OR
   USE TEMP.
UNIT NUMBER...123456
LOCATION...SB1
WEIGHT (LB OR KG?)...20KG
HT (IN OR CM?) ...110   IN/CM?   CM
BURN DATE T      TIME 8AM
TOTAL PERCENT BURN...36
PERCENT 1ST DEGREE...0   2ND DEGREE...9
   2ND-3RD DEGREE...27
BURN SURFACE COMPUTED TO BE 0.27 SQ METERS
TREATED PREVIOUS TO EW
   NO
EW THERAPY
   YES  ENTER TOTALS (ML)
LAC RINGERS...200    N/S...0   PLASMA...0   BLOOD...0
URINE...0    VOMITUS...0

SUGGESTED INITIAL REPAIR AND MAINTENANCE
   1440 ML RINGERS BEFORE 4.00 PM 05/08/69
   RATE: 315 D/M PED (80 AD)
   1640 ML RINGERS BEFORE 8.00 AM 05/09/69
   RATE: 100 D/M PED

SUGGESTED INITIAL REPAIR AND MAINTENANCE
   1440 ML RINGERS BEFORE 4.00 PM AT A RATE
   OF 310 D/M (PED)
   1640 ML RINGERS BEFORE 8.00 AM ON 05/09/69 AT A RATE
   OF 100 D/M (PED)
```

Now this is not really so ominous. The suggestions for therapy are actually based on principles that come from John Crawford, chief of pediatrics at the Burns Unit. In essence, they represent (assuming no error in the program, and no variables that he would take into account but the machine does not) his therapeutic program were he personally treating the patient.

Thus the computer is at best as clever as a single clever man, and at worst considerably less astute than that one man.

Once in use, the MGH burns project will be analyzed by doctors, and adjustments made to refine the program. And as the program improves, it may become more and more difficult for a physician to ignore the computer's "advice."

In the future, it may be possible to have a computer monitor the patient and carry out therapy, maintaining the patient within certain limits established by physicians—or even by the computer itself.

The major consequence, indeed the avowed aim, of computer therapy in any form will be to reduce the routine work of patient care done by doctors. Other elements of that care are already disappearing; nurses have taken over several of these, and technicians have taken over others. Thus, during the week, the MGH has routine blood samples drawn by technicians and routine intravenous maintenance—starting IV lines and keeping them running—done by specially trained IV nurses. These programs were quite radical a few years ago, when doctors thought nurses constitutionally incapable of dealing with intravenous lines or drawing blood from a vein. But a startling consequence of this new specialization of nonphysician health personnel has been better care, in certain areas, than the physician himself could deliver. Even if doctors don't believe this, the patients know it well. On weekends, when the IV nurses and the blood technicians are off duty, the patients complain bitterly that the physicians are not as skilled in these tasks.

As for the special skills still reserved to physicians, such as lumbar punctures and thoracic and abdominal taps, it is only a matter of time before someone discovers that these, too, can be effectively delegated to other personnel.

It would thus appear that all the functions of a doctor are being taken over by other people or by machines. What will be left to the doctor of the future?

Almost certainly he will begin to move in one of two directions. The first is clearly toward full-time research. The last fifteen years have seen a striking increase in the number of hospital-based physicians and the number of doctors conducting research in governmental agencies. This trend will almost surely continue.

A second direction will be away from science toward the "art" of medicine—the complex, very human problems of helping people adjust to disease processes; for there will always be a gap between the illnesses medicine faces and science's limitations in treating them. And there will always be a need for people to bridge that gap.

Physicians moving in either direction will be helped by a new freedom from the details of patient care; and physicians now emotionally attached to those details, such as those doctors who religiously insist on doing their own lab work, are mistaking the nature of their trade. Almost invariably, they would do better spending their time talking with the patient, and letting somebody else look at the blood and urine or count the cells in the spinal fluid—especially if that person (or machine) can work more rapidly and accurately than the physician himself.

One can argue that this presages a split among physicians, between those with a scientific, research orientation, and those with a behavioral, almost psychiatric orientation. That split has already begun and some bemoan it. But, in reality, art and science have rarely merged well in a single individual. It is said that Einstein would have starved as a cellist, and it is certainly true that the number of doctors in recent years who have been both superb clinicians and excellent laboratory researchers is quite small. Such men certainly can be found, and they are always impressive—but they are distinctly in the minority. In fact, the modern notion that the average physician is a practitioner of both art and science is at best a charming myth, at worst a serious occupational delusion.

In the final analysis, what does all this mean for the hospital and for the patient in the hospital? One may look at the short-term possibilities, as represented by the burns treatment program.

It will reduce the mundane work of ward personnel, both doctors and nurses, and leave them more time to spend with the patient. For doctors, it should mean more time for research as well. And for the patient, that should ultimately be a good thing.

Furthermore, as an extension of the hospital, a computer program offers quite extraordinary possibilities. Any hospital in the country—or even any doctor's office—could utilize the program, by using existing telephone lines. A community hospital could plug into the MGH program and let the computer monitor the patient and direct therapy. As a way to utilize the innovative capability of the hospital, and its vast resources of complex medical information, this must surely represent a logical step in 2,500 years of evolution. And for the patient, that, too, should ultimately be a good thing.

Myoelectric Control

D. S. Halacy, Jr.

The ultimate achievement of cooperation between men and machines would be their conjunction in one body. Expressed that way, the prospect has a mild science-fiction ring to it, but in fact such mergers, of a rudimentary sort, already exist, in the form of amputees fitted with prosthetic devices which operate from the healthy nerves that used to control the amputated part of the body. In this excerpt from *Cyborg, Evolution of the Superman,* D. S. Halacy traces the progress of such developments to date, and looks towards the refinement of man-machine cyborgs in the future.

> *There is a second class of machines with which we have also been concerned which has a much more direct and immediately important medical value. These machines may be used to make up for the losses of the maimed and the sensorily deficient, as well as to give new and potentially dangerous powers to the already powerful. The help of the machine may extend to the construction of better artificial limbs; to instruments to help the blind to read pages of ordinary text by translating the visual-pattern into auditory terms; and to other similar aids to make them aware of approaching dangers and to give them freedom of locomotion.*

Norbert Wiener
The Human Use of Human Beings
Houghton Mifflin, 1950.

The term "mechanical man" is understandable in view of the many mechanical principles the human body makes use of in its operation. The fact that the nervous system operates somewhat like an artificial electrical control system suggests a fascinating new approach. In an age of electronics it is logical that this new science be put to work with living systems that are susceptible to the flow of electrons.

Electricity has two main uses in artificial systems: as a control, and as a source of power. We may roughly divide body electricity into the same two categories and we will look at them in this order, taking the idea of nerve "signals" first.

Myoelectric Signals

In 1963 poet Robert Graves of Oxford and Majorca delivered the Arthur D. Little Lecture at Massachusetts Institute of Technology. In his talk, which concerned his wish to discover the mystique behind modern science, Graves applauded "Dr. Norbert Wiener's brilliant use of severed nerve-ends to give a man whose leg has been amputated control of an artificial one." This tribute touched off a controversy concerning research at MIT and Harvard on the use of "myoelectric signals" to operate prosthetic devices, a sophisticated cyborg technique already exploited by Russian workers.

John Lear, science editor for *Saturday Review,* noted Graves's mention of Dr. Wiener's cybernetic application wedding man and machine. Lear himself was aware of such experimental work going on, having discussed it with Wiener a year earlier. However, he had withheld mention of it in his science columns because of the highly experimental nature of the work, and the feelings of Wiener and others involved that such disclosure before publication in a scientific journal would compromise the men working with myoelectric artificial limb applications. Now that mention *had* been made of the work, and distorted mention at that, Lear felt justified in commenting briefly on Graves's address and setting the record straight.

True, Dr. Wiener should have been applauded for the feat, but mostly for encouraging a younger scientist, Dr. Melvin J. Glimcher, associate professor of orthopedic surgery at Harvard and director of the orthopedic research laboratories at Massachusetts General Hospital. Glimcher typifies the new breed of cyberneticist, or bionicist, combining knowledge of physics and mathematics with mechanical engineering and biology. His doctorate is in biophysics.

Researching the literature on artificial limbs, Glimcher came on descriptions of a British type incorporating "feedback" principles stemming from cybernetics. However, this device did not operate very successfully. A better prosthetic hand seemed to have been produced by the Russians, and Glimcher made a trip to Moscow to see it used and be further convinced he was on the right track. Impressed with the Russian myoelectric hand, Glimcher returned to this country determined to design and build a better one.

Enthusiastic, he visited Dr. Wiener, who was then laid up in the hospital with a broken hip sustained in a fall. Wiener was impressed by Glimcher's project and suggested men who would be valuable on the team.

Half a dozen of the people involved in the project took strong exception to Lear's article, pointing out he was raising false hopes in amputees—even though Lear plainly credited Glimcher only with *probably* picking up signals from a nerve, and pointed out that actual use of these signals to operate an artificial limb might be decades away. And there the controversy rested. Dr. Wiener died shortly thereafter, before he could see the flowering of this phase of the science he launched more than two decades ago.

As with Sputnik, the Russians seem to have stolen a march on their American scientific brethren in the field of myoelectric control. Like Mr. Yesalis of the S. H. Camp Company, who was quoted earlier as saying that the Russian device did indeed operate as its inventors claimed and that it was the only such artificial hand he knew of, Dr. Glimcher was much impressed. Lear had written that Glimcher considered the Russian hand crude, but the letter of protest signed by Glimcher, Wiener and others refuted this, and said that despite some technical difficulties it was more advanced than any similar device they were aware of. Surely the father of cybernetics should be quite cognizant of developments in his own field.

The Russians refer to their hand as a "cybernetic forearm prosthesis activated by muscle nerve impulses." Such a method is obviously far superior to such techniques as cineplasty, in which the patient's muscle mechanically operates a cable. The

Russians claim their system "is most convenient because the command is transmitted from the cerebral cortex to the hand by the beaten track which was severed by the trauma." Simply "thinking about it" operates the hand.

When the brain signals the hand to move, the muscles to be used produce a tiny charge in electrical potential at the site. Electrodes of metal foil glued to the skin over the muscles can detect this change in voltage and measure its amplitude. Given this basic signal to work with, Kobrinsky and Gurfinkel used it in the manner described in a Russian document:

> The information obtained from the continually measured bio-electrical potentials of the muscle is processed into a set of standard impulses whose repetition frequency is proportional to the power of the biocurrents.
>
> To reproduce any movement, biocurrents are tapped from two antagonistic muscles, for instance, flexor and extensor, and accordingly two channels of converting the information are used. As a result two groups of program signals are simultaneously fed to the input of the servodrive.
>
> The servodrive which carries out the program of control is a mechanical step motor operating in the differential regime, a condition allowing for control with biocurrents from two antagonistic muscles. . . .

Interestingly, in 1964, it was reported that Germany's Thalidomide Trust was negotiating for rights to quantity production of the Russian myoelectric limb in Germany.

While the Russians were achieving this success, American researchers were also busy. At UCLA's Department of Engineering, Drs. Weltman, Groth, and Lyman published a report entitled "Analysis of Bioelectric Prosthesis Control" in 1959. Well aware of the benefit in using the patient's own nerve signals to control an artificial limb, researchers were simply not able to extract reliable signals from the welter of myoelectric activity present in the body.

Instrumentation was one of the problems. Placing of electrodes of metal foil above the pertinent nerve area was generally successful in picking up tiny electrical signals, but the slightest movement of the electrode relative to the body introduced false signals. New, lighter, and better-attached electrodes were designed and eliminated this part of the difficulty.

In August 1962, an International Symposium on Application of Automatic Control in Prosthetics Design was held in Opatija, Yugoslavia, and the UCLA scientists presented a paper entitled "Electrical and Mechanical Properties of New Body Control Sites for Externally Powered Arm Prostheses."

Application of the myoelectric control idea to another field came about this time. Astronauts were being hurled into space, and while the bugaboo of weightlessness seemed little problem, there was much concern over man's ability to operate controls properly during the extreme acceleration environment of blast-off and reentry. At times these forces reached as high as 8g, with the result that a man's body "weighed" more than half a ton, and his arm alone might weigh close to 100 pounds. Lifting such a burden and using it precisely is an impossibility, so the idea of tapping myoelectricity to operate a booster for the arm was a natural.

Working under contract to the Air Force, Spacelabs, Incorporated, a California firm, got busy on the design and construction of a myoelectric "muscle booster" for astronauts and others subject to extreme conditions of acceleration. Results of this work were detailed in a paper presented at the third Bionics Symposium, held in March, 1963, at Wright-Patterson Field, Dayton, Ohio. Authors were Drs. Weltman, Martell and Sullivan, and Dean Pierce of Spacelabs.

The researchers investigated the myoelectric signals available in an average-size muscle and found that the total "bandpass" was from 3 to 1,000 cycles per second, with maximum signal power in the region from 10 to 200 cycles per second. The amplitude of the signals ranged from 1 to 3 millivolts, about 1/1000 the voltage in a flashlight cell.

Only the voluntary contraction of a muscle can be successfully detected; relaxation signals are buried in electrical "noise" always found at the body's surface. Two kinds of muscular activity result in myoelectric signals at the detecting electrodes: normal muscular activity, and learned or trained activity.

Electrodes were glued in place over the anterior deltoid, medial deltoid, and posterior deltoid, and also the pectoralis muscle. A training period of only one or two minutes was found sufficient for the subject to effect control of the servo booster.

Subjects were trained to use the myoelectric boost system to operate a switch on a simulated spaceship control panel. With the arm artificially weighted to 80 pounds, the subjects carried out their tasks successfully, proving they could effect in and out movements simultaneously with up and down. Speed of the booster was normally 6.8 degrees per second and no difficulty was experienced at this slow rate of movement. Above 13.5 degrees per second subjects were unable to hold the hand steady at the desired position, and the booster displayed "oscillatory hunting" of a type common in electromechanical equipment.

Another use of myoelectric control is in the training of muscles in the rehabilitation of patients. Since electrical signals can be displayed visually on an oscilloscope or audibly heard on a loudspeaker, a subject can see or hear when the proper signal is being generated. Although the sound from the loudspeaker is simply so much noise, it is interesting to speculate on the possibility of using voluntary myoelectric signals to permit a speechless person to "talk."

Much of the difficulty reported by American scientists working on the problem of using electromyographic signals for control of artificial limbs continues to be the distinguishing of the desired signal in the midst of all the "noise" or irrelevant electrical activity surrounding it. A sneeze, for example, might raise havoc with a piece of equipment monitoring muscles for control functions. However, progress is being made and evidence on the potential of precise control possible through electromyography is encouraging.

Workers at Queen's University in Kingston, Ontario, in Canada have been able to elicit a response not from just a particular bundle of nerve fibers, as the Russians do in their artificial hand, but from an individual "motor unit" amongst the thousands. John V. Basmajian at Queen's inserts a fine wire electrode into a small muscle at the base of a subject's thumb and connects the electrode to two oscilloscopes, a loudspeaker and a tape recorder. By watching the oscilloscopes and listening to the popping sounds muscular activity makes in the loudspeaker, the subject learns to completely relax the muscle in question, and then to actuate single motor units in the muscle bundle, a feat impossible without feedback not normally associated with muscular activity. Some subjects were able to summon up responses of individual and coded nerves, as many as five. Further training led to the production of a "galloping" rhythm in the loudspeaker, and drumbeats on order! Coupling of such signals to some artificial device could lead to a delicacy of control to make the Russian prosthesis resemble an old-fashioned hook.

A greater refinement of the muscle training technique has recently been reported by Dr. John Lyman and his associates at U.C.L.A. Feeling that the oscilloscope training method was not ideal, particularly with a naive subject, and that the loudspeaker method left similar shortcomings, the researchers devised a visual display board showing the schematic diagram of a man. Lights placed at appropriate muscle sites lit up when the proper muscle action was made by the subject. Performance of subjects seemed to bear out the theory back of the new training method. At the beginning of the training, no desired response could be made by an amputee subject. At the final training period, involving 101 cycles of muscular activity, scores ranging from 97 percent to 100 percent were recorded for the various muscles involved. And it was demonstrated that contractions of desired muscles could be made at the rate of one per second.

Bernard Wolfe's novel, *Limbo*, describes the training of athletes fitted with "pros" of a type much like the Russian artificial hand. These men learn a delicate control impossible to people with natural limbs, strangely reminiscent of present-day experiments in refining elicited muscle responses. *Limbo* was written in 1952, several years before actual work was begun on myoelectric exploitation, but with an eye on Norbert Wiener's predictions for cybernetics.

"All right, fellows." It was Theo's voice. "That's enough horsing around. Let's do some dexterities and discernments."

It was easy to follow the vaulting bodies, as they rose and fell the tubes in their limbs blinked agitated semaphores; the clearing looked like an enormous telephone switchboard gone berserk. And there was more illumination than that. The amps seemed to be carrying powerful searchlights—no, Martine saw now that the index finger of each amp's right hand was itself a searchlight, from its tip projected a beam of light.

"Come on, you guys," Theo said. "This isn't getting us anywhere. Your jumping's fine—it's your d-and-d's that are ragged—"

Shouts of protest from the playful athletes: "Follow the leader! Let's play follow the leader!"

The last suggestion seemed to appeal to everybody. "Great idea!" "Follow the leader!" "Come on, Theo, you be leader!" A dozen index fingers pointed at Theo, his bulging-skulled head was bathed in light.

"All right, men," he said humorously. "All *right*. This is no way for humanists to pass the time, but I guess you deserve a little relaxation."

The beams of light were still on him. He bent his legs. "Here goes!" he called, and took off from the ground. Up he rocketed, thirty feet or more, caught hold of a raffia branch and whirled around it, the tubes in his limbs leaving trails like miniature comets. Then he let go and dropped, his body twisting so fast that it could be seen only as a twinkling blur. There were whistles, shouts of approval.

Now the athletes followed suit: one by one they jumped, pinwheeled, spun back to earth.

Theo laughed. "What a bunch of duds!" he said. "Not one of you made it. Haven't you noticed anything about my sweat shirt?"

The lights flashed on him again. He turned around slowly, the young men gasped in surprise: the "M" that had been on his chest was now on his back.

"Let that be a lesson to you," he said. "That shows you what you can do when you really concentrate on your dexterities—as I was dropping from the tree I slipped my arms out of my sleeves, twisted my shirt around, and put it on again backwards. You'd better do some woodshedding on your discernments too—if you'd been a little more discerning you would have noticed it. . . ."

Researchers have not yet achieved the virtuosity of *Limbo's* artificial limb makers, but progress of a modest sort is being made. At Cleveland's Case Institute of Technology a three-year, forty-man project funded by the Department of Health, Education, and Welfare has resulted in a computer-controlled myoelectric hand.

Instead of the atomic power used in the fictional limbs, the Case device is actuated by carbon dioxide gas at a pressure of 600 pounds per square inch. Myoelectric signals from the trapezius muscle in the shoulder are amplified and fed to a stimulator situated over paralyzed muscles of the subject's lower arm.

This stimulation makes it possible for him to open and close his hand. The gas-powered splint that moves the whole arm is computer-controlled, with the program initiated and halted by eyelid movements! An override system consists of an infrared light source in the wearer's spectacles, beamed as needed toward photocells on the arm splint.

This prototype artificial hand is too expensive for anything except use as a research tool but it is hoped that it will lead to a practical, moderately priced replacement for handicapped people.

Biopower

Thus far we have talked of using electrical signals generated in the living body for *controlling* electronic equipment. Such signals are at best of the order of a few thousandths of a volt and obviously do not represent very much power generated. To use them even for control signals necessitates amplifying them many thousandfold. In light of this it may seem fantastic to investigate the living body for sources of electric *power*. But then, the whole idea of the cyborg is fantastic.

Familiar with electricity from early childhood, we come to take it much for granted. Electricity powers our homes, some of our transportation, and much industry. It comes out of the wall socket, or from storage batteries. There is a new device being developed into a practical power source—the fuel cell, a sort of battery with a gas tank. Most living things, from bacteria upwards, are fuel cells of a special kind—biochemical fuel cells.

Oxidation of a fuel, such as the burning of wood in the presence of air, produces energy in the form of heat. A chemical battery oxidizes a fuel, but suppresses the heat production and produces a flow of electrons instead. Part of the food we eat is turned into electricity inside our bodies, as we have seen in considering brain waves, myoelectric nerve signals and so on. A new branch of biological science now is investigating the phenomenon of "biopower," the production of appreciable quantities of electricity in living things.

Fifty years ago a biologist named Potter put together a number of yeast "cells" to make a biobattery with an output of a tiny fraction of a watt. He discovered that his living cells had a voltage of about half a volt. For half a century this remained an interesting laboratory curiosity. Then in the late 1950's a number of researchers picked up the ball and began to run in all directions. As a result the Navy developed "marine biocells," in which microorganisms obligingly converted marine matter into modest amounts of electricity to power small pieces of electronic equipment needed on buoys and other floating gear.

Another group demonstrated a radio powered by a test tube full of sea water and bacteria, and operated a model boat on a similar biocell taking its fuel from the water. There was the standard amount of loose talk of converting the Black Sea into a huge biobattery to bring a kind of TVA to underprivileged Asiatics who had never before known the blessings of electric power.

There are more achievable uses for biopower, particularly in closed-cycle systems for spaceships where living organisms could function to produce power, purify water and air, and even grow food! This in itself is surprising enough, but the biopower people have much more to demonstrate. Scientists at General Electric's Space Sciences Laboratory in Pennsylvania moved from bacteria to a more advanced form of life in the search for bioelectricity. Working with rats, they found that appreciable amounts of power were generated in the muscles of these animals. At a symposium in 1962, J. J. Konikoff and L. W. Reynolds reported on their progress.

They called their work "bioelectrogenesis," the generation of electricity in living matter. Part of their research concerned yeast cells such as Potter had pioneered in 1911. But they also investigated the production of bioelectricity in rats. After anesthetizing the subjects, they attached electrodes of platinum black to the coelom and the skin of the brachial region. The rodent power plant produced 300 microamperes of current at 3/10 of a volt. A flashlight cell produces far more current, of course, but only about 1½ volts.

Given this new power supply, General Electric researchers

built a small oscillator operating at 500 kilocycles and designed for the low voltage available. This was operated successfully by the rat power supply for periods up to eight hours.

There are a number of ways of generating electricity, even in living things. One is by connecting electrodes to sites in the body at different galvanic levels, as was done with General Electric's rat. Another is to implant a cylindrical platinum electrode in a vessel, such as the cecum passing intestinal fluid. This would be a fuel cell in the sense of an artificial type, except that it is implanted in a living thing and uses organic "fuel," generating current from fluid passed through the ring electrode.

In addition to the task of operating an implanted electronic pacemaker, bioelectricity might also power a transmitter like G.E.'s "rat radio" to telemeter information to remote stations. There are two important phases of this work. In laboratory research it is helpful to know what is going on inside the body of the subject. If this could be done without the nuisance and technical disadvantages of wires, it would be most helpful and accurate. Scientists also like to know what is happening to experimental subjects at a distance, whether they be wild geese whose mating instincts are being studied, or astronauts under the stress of space flight.

Something approaching this was announced by the Veterans Administration in Boston in May, 1964. Dr. Irving R. Levine described the system in which a patient living in Braintree, some twenty miles from the VA center, was monitored and treated by remote control. Signals from a bioelectric amplifier attached to the patient, suffering from a neurospastic disorder, were relayed to the VA by telephone company Dataphone equipment. The system is called Telemedography.

An implanted transmitter, powered by bioelectricity, could automatically send information to a central receiver on the condition and whereabouts of wild life and astronauts, as well as medical outpatients on whom the doctor wishes to keep tabs. Exercising the imagination a bit, the scheme could work in reverse, and radio a signal back to the subject to adjust his pacemaker as needed, signal a wandering duck to come home, or tell a space traveler that he was dangerously near the end of his endurance.

Articles have appeared in the popular press that extended General Electric's bioelectrogenesis studies to fantastic extremes: Electrodes from a battery in the body producing electricity from muscle, blood or whatever, are led to a plug-in socket in the wrist, or head or other handy location so that the wired individual could plug in his personal electric fan, hearing aid, transistor radio or even Dick Tracy's new wrist television! Tape recorders, television cameras for spies and radar sets for the blind are envisioned by wide-eyed reporters who also foresee the day man recharges his biobatteries by plugging himself into a socket!

The human heart is a powerful mechanism. Where the rat-powered radio operated on 90 *micro*watts of power, the heart requires a motor of about 35 watts or 1/30 horsepower to replace it. This makes it about 400,000 times as powerful as the rat battery. This power source potential is behind the idea of using muscles to generate electricity via the piezoelectric method. This scheme, mentioned earlier and used by one research team to power a pacemaker in a dog, converts pressure into electrical current.

The future of bioelectrical power is intriguing. The Navy envisions schemes for operating weapons remotely and with no time lag as is common with conventional firing techniques. There are already experimental weapons systems in which the soldier merely looks toward his target and flicks his eyes to fire the gun. This seemingly sophisticated concept is crude by contrast with the newer myoelectric method of doing something by merely "thinking about it."

This possibility, and the need from which it stems, were accurately foreseen by Bernal in 1929 when he wrote, "On the motor side we shall soon be obliged to control mechanisms for which two hands and feet are inadequate. *Volition* would simplify its operation." (The italics are mine.)

Because of parallels between the body's control system and the technology of electronics, which parallels are surely more than fortuitous, by the way, the cyborg seems sure to be increasingly electrical and electronic in nature. Engineers will exploit human nervous systems more and more in a fashion similar to the juggling performed on artificial circuits to achieve desired results.

Bernal also wrote, "We badly need a small sense organ for detecting wireless frequencies, infra-red, ultra-violet, and X-rays, ears for supersonics, temperature detectors, electrical detectors, and chemical organs. We may train a number of hot and cold and pain receptors to take over." No one yet has "X-ray eyes" but achievements are in the offing that seem a prelude to just this sort of creation of new sensors.

The Uses of Computers in Science

Anthony G. Oettinger

No sooner had the computer been invented than it was put to work in a scientific laboratory. Its effect on science has been startling—stretching man's understanding of a multitude of disciplines in much the same way that the telescope extended man's visual knowledge of the universe. Here Anthony G. Oettinger, a computer specialist and professor at Harvard University, reviews the computer's contributions to the sciences, from particle physics to psychology.

In its scientific applications the computer has been cast in two quite distinct but complementary roles: as an instrument and as an actor. Part of the success of the computer in both roles can be ascribed to purely economic factors. By lowering the effective cost of calculating compared with experimenting the computer has induced a shift toward calculation in many fields where once only experimentation and comparatively direct measurement were practical.

The computer's role as an instrument is by far the more clear-cut and firmly established of the two. It is in its other role, however, as an active participant in the development of scientific theories, that the computer promises to have its most profound impact on science. A physical theory expressed in the language of mathematics often becomes dynamic when it is rewritten as a computer program; one can explore its inner structure, confront it with experimental data and interpret its implications much more easily than when it is in static form. In disciplines where mathematics is not the prevailing mode of expression the language of computer programs serves increasingly as the language of science. I shall return to the subject of the dynamic expression of theory after considering the more familiar role of the computer as an instrument in experimental investigations.

The advance of science has been marked by a progressive and rapidly accelerating separation of observable phenomena from both common sensory experience and theoretically supported intuition. Anyone can make at least qualitative comparison of the forces required to break a matchstick and a steel bar. Comparing the force needed to ionize a hydrogen atom with the force that binds the hydrogen nucleus together is much more indirect, because the chain from phenomenon to observation to interpretation is much longer. It is by restoring the immediacy of sensory experience and by sharpening intuition that the computer is reshaping experimental analysis.

The role of the computer as a research instrument can be readily understood by considering the chain from raw observations to intuitively intelligible representations in the field of X-ray crystallography. The determination of the structure of the huge molecules of proteins is one of the most remarkable achievements of contemporary science. . . . The labor, care and expense lavished on the preparation of visual models of protein molecules testify to a strong need for intuitive aids in this field. The computational power required to analyze crystallographic data is so immense that the need for high-speed computers is beyond doubt.

The scope and boldness of recent experiments in X-ray crystallography have increased in direct proportion to increases in computer power. Although computers seem to be necessary for progress in this area, however, they are by no means sufficient. The success stories in the determination of protein structures have involved an interplay of theoretical insight, experimental technique and computational power. . . .

The metaphor of the transparent computer describes one of the principal aims of contemporary "software" engineering, the branch of information engineering concerned with developing the complex programs (software) required to turn an inert mound of apparatus (hardware) into a powerful instrument as easy to use as pen and paper. As anyone can testify who has waited a day or more for a conventional computing service to return his work only to find that a misplaced comma had kept the work from being done at all, instant transparency for all is not yet here. Nevertheless, the advances toward making computer languages congenial and expressive, toward making it easy to communicate with the machine and toward putting the machine at one's fingertips attest to the vigor of the pursuit of the transparent computer.

A few critics object to the principle of transparency because they fear that the primary consequence will be atrophy of the intellect. It is more likely that once interest in the *process* of determining molecular structure becomes subordinate to interest in the molecule itself, the instrument will simply be accepted and intellectual challenge sought elsewhere. It is no more debasing, unromantic or unscientific in the 1960's to view a protein crystal through the display screen of a computer than it is to watch a paramecium through the eyepiece of a microscope. Few would wish to repeat the work of Christian Huygens each time they need to look at a microscope slide. In any case, computers are basically so flexible that nothing but opaque design or poor engineering can prevent one from breaking into the chain at any point, whenever one thinks human intuition and judgment should guide brute calculation.

It is essential, of course, for anyone to understand his instrument well enough to use it properly, but the computer is just like other commonplace instruments in this regard. Like any good tool, it should be used with respect. Applying "data reduction" techniques to voluminous data collected without adequate experimental design is a folly of the master not to be blamed on the servant. Computer folk have an acronym for it: GIGO, for "garbage in, garbage out."

X-ray crystallography is the most advanced of many instances in which similar instrumentation is being developed. Four experimental stations at the Cambridge Electron Accelerator, operated jointly by Harvard and M.I.T., are currently being connected to a time-shared computer at the Harvard Computing Center to provide a first link. A small computer at each experimental station converts instrument readings from analogue to digital form, arranges them in a suitable format and transmits them to the remote computer. There most data are stored for later detailed calculation; a few are examined to instruct each of the small machines to display information telling the experimenter whether or not his experiment is going well. Heretofore delays in conventional batch-processing procedures occasionally led to scrapping a long experiment that became worthless because poor adjustments could not be detected until all calculations were completed and returned.

This type of experiment is described as an "open loop" experiment, since the computer does not directly affect the setting of experimental controls. Closed-loop systems, where the experiment is directly controlled by computer, are currently being developed. Their prototypes can be seen in industrial control systems, where more routine, better-understood devices, ranging from elevators to oil refineries, are controlled automatically.

The problem of "reading" particle-track photographs efficiently has been a persistent concern of high-energy physicists. Here the raw data are not nearly as neat as they are in X-ray diffraction patterns, nor can photography as readily be bypassed. Automating the process of following tracks in bubble-chamber photographs to detect significant events presents very difficult and as yet unsolved problems of pattern recognition, but computers are now used at least to reduce some of the tedium of scanning the photographs. Similar forms of man-machine interaction occur also in the study of brain tumors by radioactive-isotope techniques. Where the problem of pattern recognition is simpler, as it is in certain types of chromosome analysis, there is already a greater degree of automation.

Let us now turn from the computer as instrument to the computer as actor, and to the subject of dynamic expression of theory. To understand clearly words such as "model," "simulation" and others that recur in this context, a digression is essential to distinguish the functional from the structural aspects of a model or a theory.

A robot is a functional model of man. It walks, it talks, but no one should be fooled into thinking that it is a man or that it explains man merely because it acts like him. The statements that "the brain is like a computer" or that "a network of nerve cells is like a network of computer gates, each either on or off," crudely express once popular structural theories, obviously at different levels. Both are now discredited, the first because no one has found structures in the brain that look anything like parts of any man-made computer or even function like them, the second because nerve-cell networks were found to be a good deal more complicated than computer networks.

A functional model is like the electrical engineer's proverbial "black box," where something goes in and something comes out, and what is inside is unknown or relevant only to the extent of somehow relating outputs to inputs. A structural model emphasizes the contents of the box. A curve describing the current passing through a semiconductor diode as a function of the voltage applied across its terminals is a functional model of this device that is exceedingly useful to electronic-circuit designers. Most often such curves are obtained by fitting a smooth line to actual currents and voltages measured for a number of devices. A corresponding structural model would account for the characteristic shape of the curve in terms that describe the transport of charge-carriers through semiconductors, the geometry of the contacts and so forth. A good structural model typically has greater predictive power than a functional one. In this case it would predict changes in the voltage-current characteristic when the geometry of the interfaces or the impurities in the semiconductors are varied.

If the black box is opened, inspiration, luck and empirical verification can turn a functional model into a structural one. Physics abounds with instances of this feat. The atom of Lucretius or John Dalton was purely functional. Modern atomic theory is structural, and the atom with its components is observable. The phlogiston theory, although functional enough up to a point, evaporated through lack of correspondence between its components and reality. Although the description of the behavior of matter by thermodynamics is primarily functional and its description by statistical mechanics is primarily structural, the consistency of these two approaches reinforces both.

The modern computer is a very versatile and convenient black box, ready to act out an enormous variety of functional or structural roles. In the physical sciences, where the script usually has been written in mathematics beforehand, the computer merely brings to life, through its program, a role implied by the mathematics. Isaac Newton sketched the script for celestial mechanics in the compact shorthand of differential equations. Urbain Leverrier and John Couch Adams laboriously fleshed out their parts in the script with lengthy and detailed calculations based on a wealth of astronomical observations. Johann Galle and James Challis pointed their telescopes where the calculations said they should and the planet Neptune was discovered. In modern jargon, Leverrier and Adams each ran Neptune simulations based on Newton's model, and belief in the model was strengthened by comparing simulation output with experiment. Computers now routinely play satellite and orbit at Houston, Huntsville and Cape Kennedy. Nevertheless, there is little danger of confusing Leverrier, Adams or a computer with any celestial object or its orbit. As we shall see, such confusion is more common with linguistic and psychological models.

The determination of protein structures provides an excellent example of how computers act out the implications of a theory. Finding a possible structure for a protein molecule covers only part of the road toward understanding. For example, the question arises of why a protein molecule, which is basically just a string of amino acid units, should fold into the tangled three-dimensional pattern observed by Kendrew. The basic physical hypothesis invoked for explanation is that the molecular string will, like water running downhill, fold to reach a lowest energy level. To act out the implications of this hypothesis, given an initial spatial configuration of a protein chain, one might think of calculating the interactions of all pairs of active structures in the chain, minimizing the energy corresponding to these inter-actions over all possible configurations and then displaying the resultant molecular picture. Unfortunately this cannot be done so easily, since no simple formula describing such interactions is available and, with present techniques, none could be written down and manipulated with any reasonable amount of labor. Sampling more or less cleverly the energies of a finite but very large number of configurations is the only possibility. An un-supervised computer searching through a set of samples for a minimum would, more likely than not, soon find itself blocked at some local minimum—unable, like a man in a hollow at the top of the mountain, to see deeper valleys beyond the ridges that surround him.

The close interaction of man and machine made possible by new "on line" time-sharing systems, graphical display techniques and more convenient programming languages enables Levinthal and his collaborators to use their intuition and theoretical insight to postulate promising trial configurations. It is then easy for the computer to complete the detail work of calculating energy levels for the trial configuration and seeking a minimum in its neighborhood. The human operator, from his intuitive vantage point, thus guides the machine over the hills and into the valley, each partner doing what he is best fitted for.

Even more exciting, once the details of the interactions are known theoretically, the X-ray diffraction pattern of the mole-cule can be calculated and compared with the original observa-tions to remove whatever doubts about the structure are left by ambiguities encountered when going in the other direction. This closing of the circle verifies not only the calculation of molecu-lar structure but also the theoretical edifice that provided the details of molecular interactions.

In this example the computer clearly mimics the molecule according to a script supplied by underlying physical and chemi-cal theory. The computer represents the molecule with a suffi-cient degree of structural detail to make plausible a metaphori-cal identification of the computer with the molecule. The metaphor loses its force as we approach details of atomic struc-ture, and the submodels that account for atomic behavior are in this case merely functional.

The remarkable immediacy and clarity of the confrontation

of acted-out theory and experiment shown in the preceding example is by no means an isolated phenomenon. Similar techniques are emerging in chemistry, in hydrodynamics, and in other branches of science. It is noteworthy, as Don L. Bunker has pointed out, that computers used in this way, far from reducing the scientist to a passive bystander, reinforce the need for the creative human element in experimental science, if only because witless calculation is likely to be so voluminous as to be beyond the power of even the fastest computer. Human judgment and intuition must be injected at every stage to guide the computer in its search for a solution. Painstaking routine work will be less and less useful for making a scientific reputation, because such "horse work" can be reduced to a computer program. All that is left for the scientist to contribute is a creative imagination. In this sense scientists are subject to technological unemployment, just like anyone else.

In the "softer" emerging sciences such as psychology and linguistics the excitement and speculation about the future promise of the computer both as instrument and as actor tend to be even stronger than in the physical sciences, although solid accomplishments still are far fewer.

From the time modern computers were born the myth of the "giant brain" was fed by the obvious fact that they could calculate and also by active speculation about their ability to translate from one language into another, play chess, compose music, prove theorems and so on. That such activities were hitherto seen as peculiar to man and to no other species and certainly to no machine lent particular force to the myth. This myth (as expressed, for example, in *New Yorker* cartoons) is now deeply rooted as the popular image of the computer.

The myth rests in part on gross misinterpretation of the nature of a functional model. In the early 1950's, when speculation about whether or not computers can think was at the height of fashion, the British mathematician A. M. Turing proposed the following experiment as a test. Imagine an experimenter communicating by teletype with each of two rooms (or black boxes), one containing a man, the other a computer. If after exchanging an appropriate series of messages with each room the experimenter is unable to tell which holds the man and which the computer, the computer might be said to be thinking.

Since the situation is symmetrical, one could equally well conclude that the man is computing. Whatever the decision, such an experiment demonstrates at most a more or less limited functional similarity between the two black boxes, because it is hardly designed to reveal structural details. With the realization that the analogy is only functional, this approach to the computer as a model, or emulator, of man loses both mystery and appeal; in its most naïve form it is pursued today only by a dwindling lunatic fringe, although it remains in the consciousness of the public.

In a more sophisticated vein attempts continue toward devising computer systems less dependent on detailed prior instructions and better able to approach problem-solving with something akin to human independence and intelligence. Whether or not such systems, if they are achieved, should have anything like the structure of a human brain is as relevant a question as whether or not flying machines should flap their wings like birds. This problem of artificial intelligence is the subject of speculative research described in an article by Marvin L. Minsky. Once the cloud of misapplied functional analogy is dispelled the real promise of using the computer as an animated structural model remains.

Mathematics has so far made relatively few inroads in either linguistics or psychology, although there are now some rather beautiful mathematical theories of language. The scope of these theories is generally limited to syntax (the description of the order and formal relations among words in a sentence). Based as they are on logic and algebra, rather than on the now more familiar calculus, these theories do not lend themselves readily to symbolic calculation of the form to which mathematicians and natural scientists have become accustomed. "Calculations" based on such theories must generally be done by computer. Indeed, in their early form some of these theories were expressed only as computer programs; others still are and may remain so. In such cases the language of programs is the language of science; the program is the original and only script, not just a translation from mathematics.

Early claims that computers could translate languages were vastly exaggerated; even today no finished translation can be produced by machine without human intervention, although machine-aided translation is technically possible. Considerable progress has been made, however, in using computers to manipulate languages, both vernaculars and programming languages. Grammars called phrase-structure grammars and transformational grammars supply the theoretical backdrop for this activity. These grammars describe sentences as they are generated from an initial symbol (say S for sentence) by applying rewrite rules followed (if the grammar is transformational) by applying transformation rules. For example, the rewrite rule $S \rightarrow SuPr$, where *Su* can be thought of as standing for subject and *Pr* as standing for predicate, yields the string *SuPr* when it is applied to the initial symbol S. By adding the rules $Su \rightarrow$ John and $Pr \rightarrow$ *sleeps* one can turn this string into the sentence "John sleeps." Transformations can then be applied in order to turn, for example, the active sentence "John followed the girl" into the passive one "The girl was followed by John."

Under the direction of Susumu Kuno and myself a research group at Harvard has developed, over the past few years, techniques for inverting this generation process in order to go from a sentence as it occurs in a text to a description of its structure or, equivalently, to a description of how it might have been generated by the rules of the grammar. Consider the simple sentence "Time flies like an arrow." To find out which part of this sentence is the subject, which part the predicate and so on, a typical program first looks up each word in a dictionary. The entry for "flies" would show that this word might serve either as a plural noun denoting an annoying domestic insect or as verb denoting locomotion through the air by an agent represented by a subject in the third person singular.

The specific function of a word in a particular context can be found only by checking how the word relates to other words in the sentence, hence the serious problem of determining which of the many combinations of possible functions do in fact fit together as a legitimate sentence structure. This problem has been solved essentially by trying all possibilities and rejecting those that do not fit, although powerful tests suggested by theory and intuition can be applied to eliminate entire classes of possibilities at one fell swoop, thereby bringing the process within the realm of practicality.

A grammar that pretends to describe English at all accurately must yield a structure for "Time flies like an arrow" in which "time" is the subject of the verb "flies" and "like an arrow" is an adverbial phrase modifying the verb. "Time" can also serve attributively, however, as in "time bomb," and "flies" of course can serve as a noun. Together with "like" interpreted as a verb, this yields a structure that becomes obvious only if one thinks of a kind of flies called "time flies," which happen to like an arrow, perhaps as a meal. Moreover, "time" as an imperative verb with "flies" as a noun also yields a structure that makes sense as an order to someone to take out his stopwatch and time flies with great dispatch, or like an arrow.

A little thought suggests many minor modifications of the grammar sufficient to rule out such fantasies. Unfortunately too much is then lost. A point can be made that the structures are legitimate even if the sentences are meaningless. It is, after all, only an accident of nature, or for that matter merely of nomenclature, that there is no species of flies called "time flies." Worse yet, anything ruling out the nonexisting species of time flies will also rule out the identical but legitimate structure of "Fruit flies like a banana."

Still more confusing, the latter sentence itself is given an anomalous structure, namely that which is quite sensible for "Time flies . . ." but which is nonsensical here since we know quite well that fruit in general does not fly and that when it does, it flies like maple seeds, not like bananas.

A theory of syntax alone can help no further. Semantics, the all too nebulous notion of what a sentence means, must be invoked to choose among the three structures syntax accepts for "Time flies like an arrow." No techniques now known can deal effectively with semantic problems of this kind. Research in the field is continuing in the hope that some form of man-machine interaction can yield both practical results and further insight into the deepening mystery of natural language. We do not yet know how people understand language, and our machine procedures barely do child's work in an extraordinarily cumbersome way.

The outlook is brighter for man-made programming languages. Since these can be defined almost at will, it is generally possible to reduce ambiguity and to systematize semantics well enough for practical purposes, although numerous challenging theoretical problems remain. The computer is also growing in power as an instrument of routine language data processing. Concordances, now easily made by machine, supply scholars in the humanities and social sciences with tabular displays of the location and context of key words in both sacred and profane texts.

Psychologists have used programming languages to write scripts for a variety of structural models of human behavior. These are no more mysterious than scripts for the orbit of Neptune or the structure of hemoglobin. The psychological models differ from the physical ones only in their subject and their original language. Convincing empirical corroboration of the validity of these models is still lacking, and the field has suffered from exaggerated early claims and recurrent confusion between the functional and the structural aspects of theory. Psychology and the study of artificial intelligence are both concerned with intelligent behavior, but otherwise they are not necessarily related except to the extent that metaphors borrowed from one discipline may be stimulating to the other.

In actuality it is the languages, not the scripts, that are today the really valuable products of the attempts at computer modeling of human behavior. Several languages, notably John McCarthy's LISP, have proved invaluable as tools for general research on symbol manipulation. Research on natural-language data processing, theorem-proving, algebraic manipulation and graphical display draws heavily on such languages. Nevertheless, the computer as instrument is rapidly making a useful place for itself in the psychology laboratory. Bread-and-butter applications include the administration, monitoring and evaluation of tests of human or animal subjects in studies of perception and learning. . . .

It is also interesting to speculate on the use of on-line computers as tools for the investigation of the psychology of learning and problem-solving. Experiments in this area have been difficult, contrived and unrealistic. When the interactive computer serves as a problem-solving tool, it is also easily adapted to record information about problem-solving behavior. Here again the problem will not be the collection of data but rather devising appropriate experimental designs, since an hour's problem-solving session at a computer console can accumulate an enormous amount of data.

In short, computers are capable of profoundly affecting science by stretching human reason and intuition, much as telescopes or microscopes extend human vision. I suspect that the ultimate effects of this stretching will be as far-reaching as the effects of the invention of writing. Whether the product is truth or nonsense, however, will depend more on the user than on the tool.

Computers in the Library: Project Intrex and Its Planning Conference

Carl F. J. Overage and R. Joyce Harman, editors

The fully automated library is unlikely to become a reality for many years, but library facilities largely based on computers are quite likely to be in operation by the mid-1970's. Here is a report on one of the most advanced projects in quest of that goal—an automated scientific reference library at the Massachusetts Institute of Technology. The two editors, leaders of the project team, describe the hardware and the software of the facility, and provide a "how-to" guide for the library user.

Among the many difficulties caused by the growing complexity of our civilization, the crisis faced by our great libraries is one of the most distressing, for these libraries have long been regarded as outstanding manifestations of our culture. But they will become increasingly ineffectual agencies for the transfer of information, and they could become lifeless monuments, unless we can find new methods of managing the enormous mass of books, periodicals, reports, and other records produced by our expanding intellectual activities.

The spectacular advances of the last decade in data processing and in document copying have given us good reason to hope that a way can be found out of the library crisis by the imaginative use of new technology.

In the university of the future, as it is visualized at MIT, the library will be the central resource of an information transfer network that will extend throughout the academic community. Students and scholars will use this system not only to locate books and documents in the library, but also to gain access to the university's total information resources, through Touch-Tone telephones, teletypewriter keyboards, television-like displays, and quickly made copies. The users of the network will communicate with each other as well as with the library; data just obtained in the laboratory and comments made by observers will be as easily available as the text of books in the library or documents in the departmental files. The information traffic will be controlled by means of the university's time-shared computer utility in much the same way in which today's verbal communications are handled by the campus telephone exchange. Long-distance service will connect the university's information transfer network with sources and users elsewhere.

Today we do not know how to specify the exact nature and scope of future information transfer services. We believe that their design must be derived from experimentation in a working environment of students, faculty, and research staff.

Moreover, the rapid pace of scientific and technological research and development introduces a factor of substantive obsolescence in many kinds of literature. This reduces the frequency with which such literature must be consulted. However, society is unwilling to erase the record of the past, for historians and other investigators find the serious study of the past illuminating and valuable in the better understanding of many aspects of contemporary civilization. Because so much of the record of

contemporary civilization has been published on wood pulp
paper that is subject to rapid deterioration, research libraries
have the added obligation of finding means of preserving these
records. New methods of preserving old paper and filming or
otherwise preserving the content of crumbling documents are
being put into effect while concurrently specifications for improved papermaking are being developed.

Fortunately, the modern evolution of science and technology,
with very heavy Federal financial support, has not only produced new demands for scientific and technological information,
but also a technology that can be applied in the solution of
information-handling problems facing almost all parts of society.

The Impact upon the University Library and Its Response

Increased emphasis on research and the steadily growing volume
of publication have combined to accelerate the growth rate of
university library collections. Some of the larger university
libraries are growing at the rate of 3-4 per cent per year, many
of the smaller ones at even higher rates. Present policies and
prospects for research support and for the extension of educational opportunities suggest that this trend will continue upwards. The number of books published in this country alone is
increasing about 10 per cent per year, and the same is true of
other major publishing nations. In addition, many new and
smaller nations are developing substantial publishing programs,
under both private and governmental auspices. The number of
current scholarly journals, now estimated at 70,000 to 75,000
titles, is also growing steadily. The resultant output of published
items is perhaps not properly characterized as an explosion, but
it is very large and it becomes larger each year.

The university library not only acquires a substantial portion
of this published material but organizes it for use, primarily
through subject classification and cataloging. The experience of
scholars and students who have used foreign as well as American libraries is that the systems of subject classification and
cataloging currently provided by American university libraries
make them far easier to use than comparable collections in other

countries. Stack access to a large book collection classified by subject is both a sobering and an enlightening experience for a reader who encounters it for the first time, as many foreign visitors testify. Similarly, the dictionary catalog, with author, title and subject approaches, is a versatile tool for bibliographic access to the collection.

There is a dramatic extension of the diversity of materials to be acquired in language, country of origin, and form. As research in all disciplines is evermore concerned with enquiries pertaining to every corner of the globe, so there is no quarter in which libraries must not seek out publications and reports, and there is no language in which raw material for study is not issued. Serious research is being conducted and its results are being published in countries and languages in which only a few years ago no significant scholarly investigation took place. The difficult undertakings of acquisition and bibliographic organization of such materials are being handled by university libraries, either singly or cooperatively, with growing effectiveness.

As regards the diversity in the forms in which research materials are being produced—and accordingly collected and used— it is sufficient to mention only a few to indicate the current involvement of libraries with physical forms of information that have necessitated marked departures from traditional practices. The broad array of audio-visual materials is symptomatic. Libraries now collect sound recordings on discs, tapes, and sound tracks. Microreproductions and publications issued initially in microimages appear in more and more different forms. Motion pictures and still photographs have become essential elements in research collections. And, finally, there are video tapes, which potentially constitute the most numerous, bulky, and potent arm in the whole of the audio-visual arsenal.

Technical report literature has become a major element in university libraries only since World War II. No matter how this material is handled, whether in central collections or in scattered special-project files, ultimate disposition for historical purposes must be a serious concern of librarians. In addition to bibliographic complexities inherent in this type of literature, security classification adds a further complication.

The newest forms of research material are products of electronic data processing which require treatment radically different from those of any previous library practices. Data banks and computer programs are sure to proliferate at a very rapid rate, and they will have to be maintained and controlled in a manner that will make them readily available for current use and manipulation, as well as for historical purposes. Fortunately, such materials are singularly adaptable to mechanized handling.

Libraries have traditionally shared their resources, services, professional tools, and administrative development. This continuing cooperation has given flexibility and viability to libraries, enabling them to survive inadequate support, increasing work loads, and an apathetic public.

The Library of Congress report on automation points out: "Cooperation among libraries exists in acquisition, cataloging, particular bibliographic projects, library lending, and in many other areas. This cooperation is an attempt to make maximum use of limited resources." For most of the 20th century, the high points of cooperation were in cataloging (furnished by the Library of Congress) and in widespread interlibrary loan of publications. These activities have been carried out on a nationwide basis and have brought economy and efficiency to library programs. They have enabled specialized and small libraries to bring to their users the widest range of the world's printed information.

During the past 10 years, however, a serious dilemma arose from the inability of the Library of Congress to keep up with the cataloging needs of American libraries, and also from the inability of libraries generally both to serve their own users and to share their resources with others. Restrictions on interlibrary loan have developed in research libraries in all parts of the country, as a result of increasing demands for service from those outside as well as users in the immediate university locale.

Research libraries now face an aggregate of responsibilities and problems including: a doubling in the output of scientific information every 10 years; the impact of technical-report publications; a variety of new demands for service; increases in the number of languages of publication, as well as the quantity and quality of foreign-language materials; the proliferation of new and changing scientific disciplines; a complex range of forms of publication; and the need to coordinate their work with an unstructured system of information sources and information and library centers.

When it became apparent that these problems were not limited to a small group of libraries but affected all research and university libraries, attention was directed toward expanded cooperation as a possible alleviation. Administrators, librarians, Government officials and information specialists proposed a variety of patterns for cooperative systems.

Networks

Network success rests upon elements beyond traditional library cooperation which has been informal and variable in its scope and services. Moving from cooperative to network activities will necessitate: a strong, well-supported center; establishment of firm participant responsibilities; agreements among libraries, and standardization in cataloging, subject headings and other library procedures.

Libraries will be strengthened by network support to furnish their clientele with services beyond the competence of a single library. Information will include not only traditional books and journals, but also current indexing, abstracting, state-of-the-art studies, unpublished papers and symposia reports, standard data, and translations. In addition, the resources of the numerous NASA, AEC and Defense information centers will be available. Special files such as project information in the Science Information Exchange will also be part of the system.

The Library of Congress automation report pointed out that the extension of library cooperation would require major changes in library organization and attitudes. These are two important elements that thus far have not been treated in discussions of library networks. In order to avoid disruptive changes in library organization and unanticipated personnel problems, it is imperative that all network experiments include special studies to determine new library organization patterns and needs for retraining of library staff and users.

A Look at the Future

Assuming the traditionalists have accepted a new tradition of togetherness, how do we visualize the library network of 1975? There will be a large number of specialized information centers in different fields. Each center will have the responsibility for monitoring the literature in its particular field or subfield, for collecting necessary experts to do that monitoring and for providing service to users of the network in that specialized field. Each center will have a storage and computation facility, and will provide bibliographic and reference services for all users.

There will also exist a time-shared network with various nodes distributed around the country. People with access to this network will interrogate any of the information centers attached to the network. Each center will control the bibliographic information for all classes of literature in its field—monographs, journal articles, reports. One can now imagine a really interesting result: the possible disappearance of the local catalog in fields where such bibliographical control exists.

Imagine a typical user at a local console attempting to find a relevant document (not an idea at this point). He would interrogate the net and be referred to one or more suitable information centers. He would engage in discourse with that center, until his request had a sufficient degree of specification. He might then have to wait for a while or he might get immediate service. In any case, the result of this process would be a specific citation or citations.

Now imagine that there is also a national facility that contains a catalog of the holdings of books, reports, and serial titles in all major libraries. Within the network, one can then call on a national facility with a citation, and find out where some copy of the document might exist. Thus, the local user would press a "find" key on his console with reference to a particular citation, and would receive an answer that (happily) the document was indeed available locally. Or a slightly less happy answer might be that it was available nearby. Then, as another possibility, the user might press a "local" button and be given some indication by the local system as to how and when he can get a copy of the document. Thus, the local system might say that the document was available in both microfilm and hard copy; did he wish hard copy of the microfilm for personal retention? Alternatively he might get an immediate picture of some portion of the text on the cathode-ray tube on his console.

Note that this process does not involve at any time the use of the local catalog. All bibliographical information is stored in decentralized centers having to do with each specialty; the document location may be in a separate local or national store. It is evident that, given a specific citation, one may then need to proceed to ascertain:

Where is it?

What is the local address or call number?

What is the local availability status or capability? and, finally, request it.

An immediate objection today to the idea of decentralized centers on this scale is the cost of communications. However, if we imagine that there are less than 500 such centers, and if we now imagine that they are connected to time-shared networks, the number of actual connections that would have to be made to tie all such centers to the net might not be so very large. They would no doubt group themselves in a number of geographical regions and one then might connect them together via coaxial cable or some other reasonable broad-bandwidth connection.

A Central Computer

The flow of information in the system of 1975 will be controlled by means of a time-shared digital computer. Sharp distinctions must be drawn among at least four different ways in which computers are now being used and certainly will be used by the university of 1975. An early discussion is required to avoid confusion on the extent to which these different applications can or should share common computational facilities, either during the development phase or operationally.

Four applications which are already clearly distinguishable are related to (1) the needs of the universities for computational and data-handling facilities in the conduct of their organizational businesses, such as payrolls, scheduling classes, and so forth; (2) the computational needs of the members of the university community in the pursuit of their intellectual endeavors; (3) the use of computers for what has now come to be called computer-aided instruction (CAI); and, finally, (4) the use of the computer for information retrieval. All four of these applications can and will make use of computers operating in a time-sharing mode and, in principle, they all could share a single common facility. While this might seem to be a desirable state of affairs in the interest of economy, it seems highly unlikely that all four different groups of users could work together satisfactorily, particularly in the early, developmental stages.

The Information Store

A university has access to a great many sources of information. Much of the information is recorded in books, pamphlets, and so forth, and resides in the present-day library. Some of the information is retained in the minds of the community itself, and is communicated to the student body in the normal teaching processes, and to colleagues via seminars and informal discussion. The information transfer system of 1975 might have provisions for tapping this latter source of knowledge just as it obviously must have facilities for tapping the information stored in the library.

In predicting the form in which the "recorded" portion of the information will be stored, we have assumed that by 1975 we shall be roughly half-way in the transition from the library of the present time to a completely on-line intellectual community —at least so far as the science and engineering holdings are concerned; that is, approximately half the scientific information actually transmitted to the user would be stored in books or on microfilm, and half in some computer-accessible form. A word of caution: We are talking here not about the total information available but that portion of the information that the user actually makes use of. Obviously, the heritage of the existing library will not be easily duplicated or replaced, and most of the archival type of information will still exist in printed form.

A large portion of library information will be available in image microform. This main image store will be accessed by address only. Microfilm copies of equal size or of larger format (for inexpensive viewers) and hard copy will be available locally within seconds on demand. Although local viewing of the microform may possibly be done by mechanical transport of the microform, remote viewing will be possible by high-resolution facsimile or CRT display.

Certainly, we are not going to take the present library holdings and transfer them *en masse* into a machine-readable form by 1975, if, in fact, this is ever done. Much of the material that is created between now and 1975 will be produced in hard-copy form. However, it is not at all unreasonable to assume that the most often-used portion of this information will either be initially produced in machine-readable form or be converted into machine-readable form and will be available to an on-line intellectual community through terminals of some sort. And since a large part of the scientific community is concerned with recent information rather than archival information, we will assume that up to 50 per cent of the *active* information will be stored, transmitted or reproduced in coded form. This coded material will consist of source documents in the present-day sense and of derived material in the form of card catalog information, abstracts, indices, bibliographies, concordances, critical reviews, summary information and condensations. There is, of course, a present-day tendency to consider such information as being distinct from the documents themselves, but we will assume that by 1975 the amount of such material will have grown disproportionately and that it will no longer be considered separately. We can anticipate that it will be necessary to index, abstract, and condense the normal indexing and abstracting documents themselves.

Access Techniques

Physical Aspects

In the information transfer system of 1975, the user will have a choice of means by which he can obtain access to the information stored in the system. It is highly unlikely that he will borrow books from the library as he does at present. If he needs the actual document itself, he will obtain a copy of it. This copy may be prepared by the publisher in the usual fashion, and we can think of the bookstore and the library as having coalesced, at least in the university community. If the desired document is out-of-print at the time of the request, the library will duplicate it by one of the many duplicating facilities that it will then possess. We are, of course, assuming that progress will have been made toward resolving the legal aspects of the situation, and toward developing methods of fairly reimbursing the authors and publishers.

Because of the difficulties of handling books of different sizes, one might think that the leading libraries will have standardized on a fixed book size both for storage and for distribution. But this could have been done with profit at any time within the last 300 years, and it seems that a general law may be at work, the consequence of which is that it is easier to introduce a distinctly new system than to modify slightly an old one. We have little confidence that the actual format of ordinary books will be very much modified by 1975. Books for storage purposes could be produced with high-quality materials which would no longer be subject to the high deterioration rates which affect our present materials.

As a second type of service, we will assume that many users will want to read specific pages of a given document but will not have any need for the possession of the actual document. These users will be served through a variety of consoles with cathode-ray tube or other method of presentation of page material. It seems reasonable to assume that the costs of such consoles will be still quite high and that they will not have wide distribution. However, in a community the size of MIT, it would not be unreasonable to assume that there may be as many as 50 to 200 such terminals scattered around the campus at strategically located positions, in branch libraries or student reading rooms and places of that sort.

A third class of service to be provided will be that of producing hard copy by typewriters or printers (mechanical and non-mechanical) at remote locations, quite analogous to the typewriter output now obtainable through the MAC computer, but at a higher output speed. Again, making an estimate as to the magnitude of this service, it would seem not unreasonable to assume that substantially every faculty member would have such a terminal available to him and there might be between 100 and 1000 available to the student body.

A fourth form of service will be through the medium of terminals designed primarily for CAI use. This service will resemble that provided by the third class of terminals with, however, serious restrictions on the speed of output printer, dictated by cost considerations as noted earlier. There may be 1000 of these terminals in use at MIT by 1975.

And as a final form of output, we will certainly have available a Touch-Tone push-button input and voice-answer-back system. By 1975 we can expect that each student will have a telephone available either on his own study desk or, at worst, shared with another student in his dormitory room. In effect, access by telephone and by any of the other terminals would be independent of geographical location and there would be as many terminals on the information transfer system as there are telephones.

Intellectual Aspects

We have talked about access in terms of physical devices. Now let us turn our attention to the intellectual aspects of providing access to stored information.

In the information transfer system of 1975, an augmented catalog (author, subject, title, table of contents, abstract, citations, etc.) will be available via the computer in machine-readable form. In addition, the Touch-Tone telephone with voice-answer-back could, of course, be used for obtaining certain types of catalog information. It is not unreasonable to assume that by 1975 a fairly elaborate voice-answer-back technique will have been developed, based on the "twenty-question" idea so that the input required of the user will be minimized and limited to occasional pushing of one of the ten buttons that will then exist on many telephones.

This same system would, of course, be employed extensively in instructional use. We can envision the situation by 1975 in which all lectures are stored, at least temporarily, and that the student who has missed a lecture in person can have it repeated to him over the telephone. Implied in all this, although not stated so far, is the assumption that this telephone answer-back service—and, indeed, all the mechanized aspects of the library —will be available on a 24-hour basis, so that the student at any time during the preparation of his next assignment could refresh his memory as to the exact happenings in the class the day before.

The typewriter output service which now bulks so large in on-line systems such as Project MAC will, probably by 1975, have ceased to have so large a significance, although here again it may well be that very rapid printers, facsimile printers, and the like will have been developed as of this time, in which case this service will still be important. This service will be used to obtain extracts of documents, abstracts, condensations, and material which requires detailed study on the part of the student. The absence of effective graphics will, however, be a serious drawback as of 1975 unless major developments are made which cannot at the present be fully anticipated.

Turning now to the most elaborate form of terminal which, as indicated earlier, will probably contain both typewriter input and rapid output, and a cathode-ray tube display with a light pen or some other graphic input device, we note there are essentially no limits to the intellectual scope of the activity that can be carried on by means of these terminals. The user will be able to have displayed, on his scope, catalog information, extract information, or complete portions of complete documents, depending on his needs at the moment.

From what has been said, it is evident that we anticipate a situation in 1975 in which the on-line intellectual community will, in effect, have come into existence, still with terminals inadequate because of economic considerations. It is also highly unlikely that the system will be able to serve all the potential users or that it will contain a completely adequate corpus of information in machine-readable form, but it will be a start. This would provide the evolutionary aspect of the system, enabling it to expand to provide all the desired services at some future time.

The conventional library as a storehouse for books would, of course, continue to exist and will continue to be extremely useful to the user of 1975, although it seems possible that, by this time period, character-reading equipment may have been developed such that most archival information could be translated on demand into machine-reading form. However, we will assume that this would not be done on a routine basis but only on a request basis.

The routine operational procedure in the book aspect or document-storage aspect of the complete information transfer system would consist largely of making and distributing repro ductions, either page reproductions or entire volume reproductions, to requesting users. These reproductions would, however, not necessarily be in full-size copies. It is uncertain at the present time what these forms will ultimately be and what the mechanism of their enlargement for ultimate use will be but, again, it seems reasonable to assume that we will be in a transition stage with most forms of services presently available, or conceptually available today, in rather widespread use. Many users will desire that the documents be delivered to them in their full size. For storage reasons, the library will, however, probably not save all source documents in their full size but will be well along in an orderly process of converting a large share of source material into microforms. The user who then requests full-size copies will have the enlargements made for him at the library and they will be delivered to him in this form. Other users, of course, will want to retain a larger volume of material. These users will ask for the material to be delivered to them in a microform package and will then have locally available enlarging equipment for viewing.

The viewing equipment of 1975 will undoubtedly provide for rapid page-turning of microdocuments in such a fashion that the user will be able to thumb through a book, in much the fashion that he now thumbs through a physical book, and to make use of all the quick-scanning procedures that users employ today.

The Role of the Librarian

Naturally, collections of art books, posters, original manuscripts and letters, photograph records, etc. will have to be maintained, acquired and loaned—much as they are at present. It will be wrong to imagine, however, that the librarian's only function in the 1975 environment will be to care for the more recalcitrant members of the collection. Certainly, the librarian of 1975 will be less involved than now with the individual transaction between user and book, but our whole purpose is to increase very greatly the utility of the information-transfer system. The librarian will be of primary importance in the acquisition of new material, in cooperative cataloging, in organizing the collection, instructing users of the library, and in modifying the rules and programs to maximize the services provided to the user over the long run. The librarian will be able to operate with greater freedom by having control over advanced machinery. The librarian will be much involved with the arrangement of channels with other libraries and facilities and with the presumption and provision to users of proper and economical terminals or other means of access to the system. Vastly more material than now will be available to the user of the library, and there will be a need for professional librarians at all levels in the system. It seems likely that to be a librarian in 1975 will be very fruitful and exciting.

Computers and the Muse of Literature

Stephen M. Parrish

The arts have long been regarded as the last bastion against the encroaching machines. And indeed, although computers have been programmed to compose music and write poetry, their artistic endeavors are hardly guaranteed to garner the acclaim of the critics. But computers are well fitted to the more mechanical tasks of the specialist in the arts—such as compiling bibliographies, analyzing texts and producing concordances. Dr. Parrish, a pioneer in the use of computers for humanistic research at Cornell, assesses their value for arts scholars.

To a certain kind of sensibility, poetry and electronics seem incompatible, and to put lines of verse into a computer seems grotesque, something like putting neckties into a Waring Blender. It would, I imagine, be painful to this sort of sensibility to watch a book of poems being manufactured—the messy inks, coarse rolls of paper, heavy, laboring presses, the sweaty, brutish printers. The same sort of pain and disquiet must have been felt by people who thought of poetry in terms of illuminated letters on parchment, when they watched the arrival of Gutenberg with his clumsy blocks of movable type.

The sources of this anguish are easy enough to understand. In certain important ways, the humanist is always wedded to the past, and the march of events on any of his horizons is disturbing to him. This particular kind of event, the development of literary data processing, is especially disturbing, and not only because poems, novels, and plays are converted by it into "literary data." The humanist is likely to feel himself threatened by the advent of machines which can do things that are beyond his own capacities. If the computer can do the work of a scholar, he will ask fearfully, what is to stop it from becoming a critic? We already know it can write poetry. And if its poems resemble rather the work of a drunken poet than a sober poet, who can tell the difference in modern poetry?

Innocence of this sort is charming in its way, and we can tolerate it with good humor in our turn. At the same time, I think, we ought to recognize the ingredients of it. One of them, ironically, is a species of anti-intellectualism. There is a kind of critic—let us speak plainly—who does not want to know too much, who fears that facts may overwhelm his judgment. This kind of critic has always tended to deprecate the scholar and take his contributions lightly. He now regards with dismay the massive support offered to scholarship by computers. I am thinking here of the sort of critic who recently reviewed a concordance by telling how painful it was to have to praise it: "Though it will certainly be of use to serious students of the poet, in deference to his spirit I cannot help remarking that I am sorry to say I am glad to have this book." To people of this sort, critical response seems more honest, more sensitive when unencumbered and unembarrassed by masses of "evidence."

Another element of the humanist's characteristic hostility to the computer is a little more admirable and deserves to be taken more seriously. It consists of the feeling that criticism as a qualitative measure of a work of literature can never be truly affected by quantitative measurement, the only kind a computer is capable of making. The real questions in the humanities, as a critic has recently put it, are always qualitative and always unanswerable. What, then, could a data processing machine contribute to their analysis? Another critic has pointed up our dilemma by describing the barrier that lies between the realms of measurement and of judgment. He called it the quantitative-qualitative barrier.

Without striking very deeply into literary theory, we ought to be able to see that this problem is not a new one, and has nothing to do with computers. It is not even distinctive to the field of literary study. Consider the problem faced by the psychologist, who has to relate human emotion on one side of his barrier to human behavior on the other side. Or the biologist, who has to find out whether his barrier, in fact, exists: that is, whether life in the laboratory is anything more than the sum of a number of physical factors. In the study of literature, the barrier lies, as it has always lain, squarely across some of our central preoccupations. It lies, that is, between the black marks of ink on sheets of white paper, which are quantitative things, and the emotions and ideas that produced those marks, which are qualitative. Or between the marks and the values they embody. Or, depending on one's critical stance, between the marks and the emotions and ideas they arouse in the reader.

The material on the qualitative sides of these several barriers is a good deal more complex than the material on the quantitative side, but the critic's job is always somehow to find connections across the barrier. One of the commonest forms in which he meets the barrier is simply in the shape of metaphor. When we construct a metaphor we are ordinarily connecting an abstract, intangible thing with something concrete and tangible for the purpose of making it clear. (There are other purposes, but this is the central one.) We are trying, that is, to render a qualitative thing in quantitative terms. Thus we speak of courage as steely, of love as a rose or a flame, of truth as a great rock. One of the finest metaphors I ever met was uttered by an English critic who was trying to convey the peculiar qualities of American writing. "Reading American prose," he said, "is like eating blankets." (Never has the qualitative-quantitative barrier been so gracefully leaped.) Underneath the problem of metaphor lies the problem of language. In using language we try to represent something qualitative and complex, like an idea or a value, in terms of something measurable and concrete, like a word. And here the quantitative-qualitative problem is commonly expressed in the psycho-linguistic inquiry whether there can be any thought without language.

If this barrier is familiar, as I think it should be, to most of us under various analogical forms, we ought not to shy at it in the form it takes when we process literary texts on a computer. Up to a point at least, we are only doing with the computer what we have been accustomed to doing ourselves, except more slowly and clumsily and a little less accurately—that is, enumerating the physical properties of a literary text. From counts and comparisons and analyses of these physical properties, we draw inferences and make judgments about the qualitative values that lie in or behind the text, just as we do when we act as critics, using the materials we collect as scholars. We are not asking the computer to be a critic. We are asking it to help us be better critics, and this it can do by helping us be better scholars, by putting before us swiftly, information, relationships, patterns, and the like, which we would have had to work long hours or years to get for ourselves, or which might have eluded us altogether. I take it as axiomatic that scholarship, while not equivalent to criticism, is essential to it, just as quantitative measurement is essential to qualitative judgment.

I should perhaps add that we are not asking the computer to

be a poet any more than a critic, but only to help us understand poetry better. It is, I confess, fascinating to think about the computer poet, because he puts our critical principles to some hard tests. Consider the question of intention, much argued in recent years. The intention of the author of a literary work, we are assured by some critics, is wholly irrelevant to the critical response. The work reveals its own intention, and the critic's job is to discover it from the work. Now it seems clear that this principle makes one kind of sense for poetry when an intelligence is assumed ordering the elements of the poem, and quite another kind of sense if the elements are allowed to collect at random or under mechanical control. The same problem arises when we talk of irony in the literary work, or satire. While irony may technically be looked upon as a property of the work, it clearly originates in the mind of the author, when the author has a mind, and depends upon that mind for its validity. One begins therefore to wonder if the first question we need to ask of any new poem is whether or not it was written by a computer. Perhaps only another computer could tell. But that way madness lies. And fascinating as these speculations are, we must turn to more serious things.

The most widely talked about and probably the most widely practiced use of computers in literary research is the making of verbal indexes. There are two main forms which an index of the words of a text can take. It can be simply an alphabetical list of the words, showing the frequency of each and its location, or either frequency or location, sometimes with the very common words omitted. This style of index is practical for really large texts—novels, series of novels, the entire works of Voltaire or Aristotle, or Shaw (I mention lightly three authors whose work has not been indexed but needs to be). The value of such indexes ought to be obvious. By imposing order upon the vocabulary of a great writer and thinker, they would give us fresh access to his ideas, not to speak of his literary art—symbols, images, personifications, and the like. Without an index we simply cannot be certain that we know, without tracking down all the instances, everything that Voltaire said about virtue or Aristotle about value or Shaw about women. I choose half-serious examples, but the principle ought to be clear. The frequency list moreover—and the computer can rank the words in order of frequency as easily as it can rank them alphabetically—might show us terms and concepts whose importance to our author we had underestimated. The student of language will easily devise more sophisticated uses for a verbal index; the maker of dictionaries will find it invaluable.

The other main form of the verbal index, called the concordance, again lists all the words alphabetically, but shows each word in its context—for verse, ordinarily the entire line in which the word occurs. The making of concordances on the computer is by now a relatively simple, routine process. It is, at any rate, in theory; it is often difficult and time consuming in practice as we develop techniques for eliminating bugs. The photoelectric scanner being still some way from production, although models are in operations, we ordinarily have to fall back on the punching of texts on IBM cards on a keypunch machine, line by line for verse, one line per card. Once the text is transferred from cards to tape, the computer simply indexes the words in the list by listing under each word the lines of text in which it occurs, together with appropriate identifying information. This list, called the "output," can then be cut into pages and photographed by an offset process. An alternative form of output, called by IBM the KWIC Concordance, Key Word In Context, shows the word being indexed running in a column down the center of the page and fore and aft of it as much context as the page will contain. This is clearly a better output for prose; the line of context seems in most instances better for verse.

The procedures for making concordances by these means have been described in several places, among them my own preface to the first concordance we made at Cornell, of Matthew Arnold. I invite you to compare these tactics to the tactics that were set down some fifty years ago by Lane Cooper at Cornell, when he prepared the Wordsworth Concordance published in 1911. By lashing on squadrons of graduate students, discontented Ithaca housewives, and junior colleagues (incidentally three of these people died during the operation), Cooper accomplished the immense labor of cutting and pasting, stamping and alphabetizing, hundreds of thousands of slips of paper in less than a year. It was a labor that might have taken one man twenty years.

He set a record, and devised a system that was widely followed, but it is doubtful that anyone will follow it again for a project of any size. In this realm of literary research, the computer has pretty clearly taken over. Although we lack a central clearing house of information, word does often come in to Cornell of projects that are underway around the country. Dylan Thomas, we learn, is being punched in Pittsburgh, Byron in Texas, Racine in Virginia, and the movement is worldwide. At a literary data processing center outside of Milan, Italy, indexing of Greek and Latin texts has been going forward since shortly after World War II under the direction of Roberto Busa, S. J. In time he will have achieved some massive indices which ought to revolutionize study of the church fathers. In England, Holland, and Germany computer indexing is being used to support philological and linguistic study. In France an effort is being made to collect on punched cards all important French literary texts from the Sixteenth to the Twentieth Centuries, and a newly established center at Nancy is beginning to transfer these texts to magnetic tape.

It is this last venture that points most boldly toward the future. A number of verbal indices of French plays have been produced, some of them published by Larousse in a lengthening series, some available for reference only in the single copy that came as output from the computer. The main force of these ventures is now being mounted behind the making of a great new dictionary of the French language on historical principles. Comparison with the *Oxford English Dictionary,* which took 60 years to complete and involved hundreds of contributors, is instructive. The French come late to a game which they ought logically to have played out centuries before the English, but they come equipped with computers, and they field a winning team. No longer will a great national dictionary rest upon the frail memories of Oxford dons, country clergymen, and gentlemen of letters, with a few American scholars thrown in to season the mix. No longer will the accumulation and sorting of the little handwritten slips of paper consume years of effort. The French will have ready access to the full range of their best literature and can establish meanings with clear certainty, and dates at which meanings shifted or words came into or passed out of common use. These advantages are so overwhelming it is improbable that anything of this sort will ever again be undertaken by hand. Here, too, the computer now rules the field, and this is a fact at which we can only rejoice.

The next large area of use for the computer in literary research lies in enumerative bibliography. Here we are in the field known as information retrieval. As knowledge in the modern world grows exponentially—or as the humanists might prefer to put it in their quaint language of metaphor, astronomically—our ability to keep up with it and get access to what we need of it falters. There are close to 100,000 technical journals of one sort or another, appearing currently in sixty-odd languages. New journals are being founded at the rate of two or more per day. The archaic and inefficient retrieval systems we have devised for books—that is, the library catalog with its systems of classification—simply will not accommodate the floods of new information that overwhelm the technician and the scholar in every major field of research. The humanist is probably less hurt by this deficiency than the scientist, for knowledge in the humanities is not always cumulative. But the difficulty is a real one even for us, as anyone knows who has tried to read up on his subject. Faced in particular with mountains of periodical literature indexed only by author and by title, if it is indexed at all, we are as though in the presence of a great library without a catalog. Somewhere inside, we suspect, is just the information we want, but we have no way of finding it save running the aisles and tumbling the books at random.

The scientists have moved more swiftly than the humanists to solve these difficulties. The KWIC index of titles is one device used by chemists to provide ready access to the mountains of journal literature in that field. However, this tactic breaks down in humanistic studies because our titles are not descriptive. We have books like *The Fields of Light, The Mirror and the Lamp, The Road to Xanadu, Minnow Among Tritons,* and the like. Other systems of automatic indexing will clearly have to be devised to provide for humanistic titles. In the meantime, a possible solution would be to provide descriptive subtitles to articles and books, these to be attached by the author, preferably, or by a reader if the author is unwilling to do it.

Some of the other systems might be briefly reviewed. The most costly and the most comprehensive would involve transcribing the entire text of articles onto tape, and this becomes feasible, clearly, only when we have the photoelectric scanner to pick up print. Several moves would be possible once you have these texts on tape. The computer can be instructed to pick out the significant high-frequency words in the article and to index it under each of those words. It could even provide an intelligible abstract of the article by printing automatically all sentences in which these significant high-frequency words cluster. Another rough but successful abstracting tactic would be to print up the first, the second, and the last sentences of each paragraph.

But to run all articles onto tape is not a program for this week, or even for next week. Less automatic, but more modest and more realistic at this stage of our technology, is the simple tactic of summarizing articles either in the form of subtitles or in the form of abstracts, as is now being done in *Abstracts of English Studies,* and then indexing these subtitles or these abstracts in, perhaps, KWIC format. Something like this tactic is being developed now by a team of bibliographers at the University of Colorado. They have bitten off ten years of periodical articles in American literature and propose to experiment with various ways of indexing them.

We may still be years from that fine day when a scholar can push buttons in his office and have flashed on a screen before him all references that touch on the subject he is asked about. But the day is surely not very far away when large-scale bibliographies of secondary literature will be automated in some degree. To extend the toil and drudgery of compiling by hand lists and indexes of references—even now we have fallen hopelessly behind the waves of this information that wash over us— would be senseless when the computer is at hand waiting only for us to program and feed it. It is sobering but somehow typical that scientists are ahead of us here, that the humanist has lagged behind in learning to free himself for creative research.

The two or three broad areas of computer use I have so far touched on are areas in which the computer can do better and faster things which we have been accustomed to doing for ourselves. But there is another area, to my mind vastly more exciting, because I think I am prepared to argue that in it the computer is capable of doing things which we could scarcely have done for ourselves, let alone even have visualized. This, then, is the area of what I shall call loosely textual analysis. One very important activity which the computer can undertake here is simply the massive comparison or collation of texts. Any scholar who has two editions, or two copies of the same edition, or two manuscripts to compare, will find it easy enough to read one against the other and tally the differences. But the scholar who has 40 texts to compare faces a problem of a different order. Forty factorial comparisons would run to more than a single lifetime, though one might normally hope that fewer would be needed. The scholar would still have a sufficient labor on his hands comparing the first text to each of the other 39. If all 40, however, are put on tape, the computer could be programmed to collate them remorselessly, swiftly, and to order and list the variations, arranging them in any designated format. For the editor of a family of manuscripts or the bibliographer searching for stop-press corrections, undertakings which have hitherto been beyond reach now seem to move within it.

A more sophisticated sort of textual analysis can be brought into play in the tactical attack on attribution problems, as for instance, by Mosteller and Wallace in their important article on the authorship of the Federalist Papers. One might hope that the tactics developed there could be applied to an increasing degree in the ranges of eighteenth-century journalism and elsewhere in English literature. The analysis of style is a province in which the computer can make significant advances over our own capacities. We are accustomed to using metaphors for style simply because we haven't got any better way of describing style. We call Swift's style muscular, Dickens' style robust, Henry James' languid, American style blanket-tasting, or whatever. What we are describing, of course, is not the style itself but our feelings about it. We are trying, that is, to provide an objective correlative by means of which we can communicate the impressions the style makes upon us. To describe the style itself in objective terms is a very different matter, only rarely achieved and then in ways that do not command wide assent. Some recent advances on this front in what we have come to call computational stylistics have to my mind been spectacularly promising. I cite only one of a number of instances. Mrs. Sally Sedelow, now at the University of North Carolina, has ingeniously devised some parameters of style, some objective measurements of every measurable feature of a piece of prose: the elements of form, rhythm, texture, schematic structure, and the like, all ordered and collated by the computer. This breathtaking achievement may cause a special anguish to humanists who have been taught that style is the man, his reason, his *logos*—and who would venture to build parameters of man? But our sentimental attachment to nineteenth-century propositions ought not to blind us to the extraordinary value of this advance. Close, objective, even scientific description of language is something critics have rarely achieved, and the uses of this new tool, once it is sufficiently tested and refined, may be imagined by anyone who has ever tried to say anything about language.

I wonder if I have sounded too hopeful, too positive, too visionary. Skeptics and realists will point out that I have consistently made the best of my examples. I have glossed over the immense, unpredictable difficulties that always dog and foul computer operation. I have avoided mentioning costs in computer time, of achieving what we have done pretty cheaply in the past by hand. Of all these charges I am a little guilty, but I should like to say a word in answer to them.

First, as to costs: We must distinguish clearly between developmental costs and production costs. A great deal of expensive computer time is needed to devise and to test a program. The programs that I have been describing require relatively little time to run. It is, therefore, highly uneconomical to build a computer program for one run, wholly reasonable to build it for a sequence of runs. The most recent concordance at Cornell University involved a computer run of less than two and a half hours on an IBM 7090. The publication of the output, like those of the earlier volumes, was simplified, and the costs were strikingly low because typesetting was avoided by merely photo-offsetting the sheets that came out of the printer.

But there is another way of looking at cost. It is easy enough to reckon the dollars and cents paid for computer time, punch typing, and the like. However, who will "cost out" the hours, days, and years of a scholar's life (the coin of investment of generations before our own). Was the Arnold Concordance, I wonder, which three or four of us made on a computer in a couple of hundred hours, including man and computer time, really more costly than the Wordsworth Concordance which took Lane Cooper and his legions a couple of years? I know what my own answer would be, and it is, I think, time that we began to value the scholar's time at its true worth, that we began to insist on the human use of human beings.

About the other objections: When we talk about computers we have to distinguish between possibilities that lie in the present or in the immediate future—the next five years—and the possibilities that lie in the distant future, the next 50 years. We need to remember that we are only a bare 20 years into what has been described as the computer revolution. I would argue that we cannot surely foresee what computers will be able to do 50 years from now; and, incidentally, that because we cannot, we probably ought to assume that they will be able to do practically anything it might occur to us to ask them to do. I have, therefore, confined myself to what I think computers are likely to achieve in the next five years. If anything, I have been conservative, as computer people will recognize, if the humanists don't. We are in the early stages of a scientific revolution, an explosion that cannot fail to affect us all in everything we do. This revolution is something we could have seen coming in our own field. (I speak here as a critic and scholar in the field of English literature.) It really began shortly after the turn of the century. Some of the significant advances that we might cite were the sharply improved standards of textual editing that began to prevail in the early 1900's; the immense thrust forward given to analytical bibliography by Greg, Pollard, and McKerrow in England, and people like Hinman and Bowers in America; the growth in America from roots in England of the New Criticism which has stubbornly attempted to focus our critical attention on the literary text, to standardize criteria of objective judgment, to reduce and suppress subjective, purely emotional responses that always precede or accompany the act of criticism.

In very recent years we have, simply, opened a new dimension of this revolution by learning to process literary data on mechanical and electronic devices. If we are sometimes slow to understand, let alone accept, the wider revolution that explodes about us—and that is going to spread relentlessly whatever we do—I would guess that nearly all of us have learned to understand and accept the narrower revolution in our own special fields. We want accurate texts. We want a close understanding of the origins of the text. We want objective criticism. We want to be able to analyze and rearrange rapidly large masses of data. The thing which we may not understand, though we are going to have to soon enough, is that in a revolution of this sort, there is no holding back and no turning back. The successful completion of a computer concordance makes the making of concordances by hand old fashioned, obsolete; the making of dictionaries or large bibliographies by hand will soon enough in the same way become obsolete. And not only the making but the using of them is involved. As a scholar has recently observed, when all libraries, or at least all pertinent bibliographical references, are readily available on tape or in a core memory, there will be no excuse for ignorance. More ominous, some of us may think, but just as inevitable, the perfection of attribution study, source study, or influence study by computer tactics will make obsolete studies that rely on the judgment and the memory of one poor fallible human scholar. Who would venture to match his analytic powers, his powers of measurement, his memory against those of a computer! Who will come along after Mosteller and Wallace and make subjective judgments about characteristic verbal patterns! Who will follow Mrs. Sedelow with personal opinions about the properties of style!

I don't believe that any of these fearsome events need cause us disquiet provided that we guard against the one real danger, which is, I think, that we might allow the usefulness of computers in certain areas of research to steer scholarship towards those areas and away from other important areas. We have, as humanists, nothing to fear and everything to gain from coming to terms with the revolution which is the greatest single event of our time. Indeed only by understanding it rightly and turning it to our support can we really serve the cause of the humanities in the modern world.

III

The Computer's Impact on Society

Introduction
to Section III

Hardly more than a quarter of a century after the first computer was built, computerization is affecting the life of virtually every man, woman and child in the United States. Computers are on their way to an inevitable state in which they will totally permeate our life styles, and possess the ability—with little control by man—to change our society for good or ill. Thus, the basic question we must ask is not: shall we allow further developments of computers and automation technology? Rather, we must seek the best means of controlling computerization to insure that it serves man, and not vice versa. The selections in this section represent the views of a number of authors on the likely impact of automation on what we are wont to call the human side of our lives, and on the means of controlling that impact.

One critical aspect of this broad area is our own view of the computer and its potentialities. Many people, impressed by the predictive abilities of computers in calling political election results from an apparently minimal number of returns and their astonishing accuracy in guiding spacecraft to the moon, Mars and beyond, see the machines as latter-day witches, whose decisions are *ipso facto* incontrovertible. Less sanguine critics persist in the notion that a computer is no better than its programmer. The truth probably lies somewhere between these two extremes, but for the moment, as Donald Mackay points out, present-day computers do face a number of basic limitations.

Even with its limitations, however, automation has already

had, and will continue to have, remarkable impact on a number of critical areas of our society. Probably the area that first springs to mind when one considers the influence of computerization on society is the job market. The exact nature of that influence, however, is often a matter for heated argument. What is clear is that the simple picture that envisions entry of a computer into a factory, followed immediately by exit of the majority of the human working force, is simply wrong. In many ways, the effect of automation on labor is likely to be felt more strongly by the customer than by the men in the machine shop, and the articles by Paul Einzig, Dennis Gabor and Tom Alexander plot out a rough schedule for the increasing influence of automation in the lives of the consumers and workers; Einzig starts with the present, Gabor moves on to the near future, and finally, Alexander envisions the approach to real automation as defined by the computer experts, involving robots, thinking machines, and perhaps a few human engineers to keep a paternal eye on the process of computerized production.

Back in the present, even the limited capacity for automation now available has contributed to one of the darker sides of the computer—its threat to the privacy of the individual. In early 1967 a scheme was proposed by a number of U.S. bureaucrats and computer men to institute a national data center—a computerized network that would contain in one location all the information about Americans that is now spread among a vast number of different federal agencies. Immediately the scheme was attacked by civil libertarians as the first step toward an American 1984. By collating all the known facts about individuals, the critics argued, the network might be able to produce personality profiles that might compromise a large number of innocent people. Eventually, under Congressional pressure, the bureaucrats backed down, still protesting their innocence of conspiratorial motives, and in his account "Data Banks and Dossiers," Carl Kaysen, himself a promoter of the data-bank scheme, explores the sorry history of the project.

Another threat presented by the computer is somewhat less distinct than that of data banks, but no less dangerous. This is the erosion of human values in the face of a machine-dominated society. The late sixties and early seventies saw a worldwide reaction against the dehumanizing influence of technology, the crux of the protest being the argument that modern technological undertakings have no place for the individual. Implicit in this argument is the assumption that as computers—the flagships of technology—get better, those values we regard as essentially human will gradually disappear. To some extent, that problem was foreseen in the earliest days of time-sharing computers by experts who tried to overcome it by humanizing their machines. Thus, a group headed by Professor Robert Fano at the Massachusetts Institute of Technology programmed its machines to say "please" and "thank you" in their interactions with humans. Here, two respected commentators on the social scene—Margaret Mead and Kenneth Boulding—argue that man's theology will manage to survive the impact of his technology.

A strikingly different view of man's future vis-à-vis the machine comes from scientist and science-fiction writer Arthur C. Clarke, who suggests that the computer is a continuation—and in fact the last straw—of the threat that science has presented to religion since the Middle Ages. Before the Reformation, the earth was the center of the universe and man was the center of creation, at least in the view of the church authorities. Then came Copernicus, and gradually the earth was relegated from the center of all things to the status of a small planet revolving around a minor star in an unremarkable galaxy. Now, developments in molecular biology and exobiology suggesting that life may be more than the one-in-a-billion throw of the dice that it was once believed to be are pushing man's prerogative as God's only chosen creature further toward oblivion. And here, argues Clarke, is where the computer comes in, with its promise of outthinking man. Two facts should be borne in mind while reading Clarke's contribution: (1) science-fiction writers have frequently proved more accurate in their forecasts of the future than scientists, and (2) Clarke suggests that the dominant computers of the future may look upon man with a benevolent eye.

Machines and Societies

D. M. Mackay

As we know from the computerized election returns, machines can appear to have an almost supernatural knowledge of voting habits, often calling results before many people have had the opportunity to use their votes. It is tempting to wonder whether this predictive ability can be extended into the manipulation of society's attitudes. Dr. Mackay, a prominent British cyberneticist, examines this question, and finds some hopeful limitations on the abilities of the machines.

A "machine", in the classical sense of the term, represents the antithesis of all that is characteristically human. Certain functions in society—its hewing of wood and drawing of water—might be delegated to mechanical devices; but any implied resemblances between these and human agents are trivial.

The past few decades, however, have seen a radical change in our whole conception of machines and their possibilities. With the growth of the science of communication and control, the idea of a machine has been so enlarged that few, if any, specifiable characteristics are in principle outside its scope. It becomes meaningful to ask not only what function machines may perform for society, but also how far societies themselves can be regarded as machines, and whether well-tried remedies for the ills of machines can be applied to corresponding disorders of society. Since the notion of mechanism is never far from that of manipulation, this quesion in turn raises a crop of others which go to the roots of our traditional conceptions of social responsibility.

329

Have Machines Any Limitations?

Is there any foreseeable limit to the competence and power of machines in these new rôles? I am not a prophet, nor the son of a prophet, and the present symposium will have its fill of prognostication. Routine aspects of information-processing in such fields as science, medicine, law, commerce, transport, and even criminal identification are obvious candidates for mechanization. Translation from one language to another may have an irreducible residue of obstacles to full automation; but no one doubts that in fields with sufficiently restricted contexts mechanical translation will evenually be with us if we want to pay for it. At present the chief benefit of research in this area has been to our understanding of the structure of language.

Electronic and other computing analogues of economic or political situations become rapidly more expensive and cumbrous as they are refined to allow for the interactions of real life; but already, as we have seen, they have thrown some light (in simple cases) on the mechanisms subserving the stability of social functions. Applications to the mechanics of business strategy and of politico-military gamesmanship are confidently proposed.

In fact, wherever the social function of human beings or groups can be reduced to a formula (if not too complex), there seems no reason to doubt that mechanistic thinking and mechanical computing devices will find increasing application.

What I want to discuss now, however, is rather the implications of such possibilities than their fulfillment. If societies are in some respects like machines, would it be possible in principle to predict and manipulate the behaviour of societies as we can that of machines? What new kinds of responsibility have now to be recognized? And who, in this case, are "we"?

Societies As Cognitive Information-Systems

There can be no question that an accurate information-flow model of a society could be a powerful tool in the hands of anyone, in government or elsewhere, who wanted to predict or manipulate social processes to his ends. If the predictor himself were sufficiently isolated from that society, and could gain the information to keep his model up to date without significantly disturbing it, then his power might in principle seem unlimited.

Is such a society then as helpless before its predictor as a piece of clockwork? It is not, for a reason which has been hard to ignore at various points already. However mechanical may be the information-system embodied by a social structure, the significant fact is that its units are themselves cognitive information systems. This does not necessarily mean that the individual human organism, as a mechanism, is inexplicable in terms of an information-flow model. On the contrary, the logical relationship between physical, personal and even religious ways of talking about man requires no such "postulate of impotence" at the mechanical level.

What it does mean is that the behavioural characteristics of the units of a human society are sensitive to information, including information about that society, if it comes their way. A notorious current illustration of such sensitivity is the way in which the publication of an opinion poll before an election can affect people's voting behaviour, so strongly as to invalidate predictions based on it, even though the same poll, kept secret, would have given an accurate forecast. The very process of sampling public opinion can often change it significantly. The same considerations expose what Popper has called the "fallacy of historicism", namely the idea that human history is inevitably predictable by extrapolation from its past, so that all a wise man need do is to discern its direction and mount the appropriate band waggon. As Popper points out, there are many human situations where such extrapolating is logically impossible, since the attitude of the predictor himself to his prediction is one of the data needed to complete that prediction. In other words, no matter how scientific the basis of an alleged prediction of the course of history, it may still be possible for an individual or society confronted with it to make nonsense of it, by taking the opposite attitude to the one assumed when the calculation was made.

Self-Validating Descriptions

The mechanically-minded reader may now be impatient. "Surely" he may ask "it must be possible, with a sufficiently complex predictive model, to trim the prediction in such a way that when published it ensures its own fulfillment?" There are, indeed, circumstances in which it is possible to "adjust" a poll result, for example, so that its publication brings about its own fulfillment. But in the field of human attitudes such circumstances are exceptional.

There is, moreover, an obvious objection to such a procedure at a more fundamental level. Suppose we assume that the adjusted forecast is confirmed by events, so that nobody who believed it feels himself to have been deceived. But suppose it had not been published? Then (*ex hypothesi*) the result would have been different—perhaps even reversed. Thus publication here was not primarily informative, but manipulative. And although a large computer may not always be essential to this end, the more powerful the predictive apparatus used, the more subtle and wide-ranging will be the manipulation of social attitude possible under the guise of scientific prediction.

Here, I believe, is a threat to society far more serious than any from the growth of automation. If any future use of computers wants watching on behalf of mankind, it is this; for our society's insatiable thirst for information about itself and its future has now laid it wide open to the most subtle bondage of all, in which major decisions can in principle be taken for it (wittingly or otherwise) by those whom it asks to predict them; and in an age that takes verification as its chief criterion of truth the manipulators could have the strongest possible defence: "We were right, weren't we?"

The Limits to Machines as Models

Behind this curious situation there is in fact a basic logical impasse. Any complete description of a cognitive information-system must include, or depend on, the information possessed by the units of the system. Any change in the information possessed by a unit must, in general, require a change in the complete description. It follows that in general, *no complete description exists which would be equally valid whether or not the units were informed of it.* In other words, no complete machine-model (nor any other complete predictive model) of a society is possible, which would be equally valid before *and* after any member of that society learned of it. In this area, then, there is a fundamental incompatibility between two of the normal aims of science—to observe facts, and to spread knowledge of those facts as widely as possible.

The implications of this could take us far afield. Here we must simply note a few consequences. In the first place, the situation of society is not quite as desperate as it might seem, for any would-be predictor of society who is sufficiently involved in that society must find his calculations frustrated by ignorance of his own (future) reactions to his own (as yet incomplete) conclusions. No improvements in his computing facilities can obviate this fundamental limitation. Moreover, even if he were to isolate himself for a time, his potential victims could indefinitely embarrass him by equipping themselves with a similar predictive model.

Secondly, on many questions of social attitude now open to scientific study, it is fallacious to suppose that there must exist *neutral* scientific knowledge to be publicly acquired. The declared aim of science is to propound conclusions which are true regardless of the attitude people take to them. It is now abundantly clear that many questions being asked of applied social science even today *have no such answers.* To recognize the ineradicably instrumental character of public scientific enquiry here is to lay emphasis on a new dimension of the responsibility of the scientist, at present barely acknowledged. It is not simply that we are able to alter people's opinions predictably, which all propagandists can. What seems objectionable is our unrecognized and unavoidable power to do so when we are asked (and believed) to supply only "objective" information. Any situation that can give one man an effective voting power of thousands, without being held proportionately responsible, needs watching. If, as scientists, we feel it to be an undemocratic one, the remedy lies largely in our own hands.

Thirdly, this of course presses upon us the question suggested earlier. Who, in all our discussion of the matter, are "we"? We here assembled are scientists; but without intolerable hubris we cannot divorce ourselves from the very society about which we have been speaking—whose ills we would like to remedy. What differentiates us is not any special competence to decide that society should pursue one goal rather than another, but only a certain skill in calculating what may happen if it does.

Here we face a current growing point in our understanding of social phenomena. What can justifiably be believed by a group (in the first person plural) must obviously be related to what can justifiably be said by each of its members (in the first person singular). Yet as Michael Foster pointed out in the symposium *Faith and Logic,* the logic of this relation (between talk of "I" and talk of "We") is still surprisingly little understood. Our present discussion has uncovered only one of its peculiarities, but it is sufficient to show the need for fresh and urgent thought on the special limitations of the scientific method and of the scientist when functioning as a guide to the evolution of social attitudes.

It is equally important, on the other hand, not to exaggerate these limitations; for great benefits, as we have seen, may be expected to accrue from a better understanding of the social mechanism. To establish that scientific investigation can only illuminate, and not replace, human valuation and commitment, is not to belittle but to defend the proper dignity of our scientific enterprise.

What it does emphasize is the important part that extrascientific judgments of value must inevitably play in our social applications of science. The chief object of society should be the fulfillment of the human individual—on this Sir Julian Huxley and Jesus Christ are agreed. Any disagreement must be on what constitutes fulfillment. Is it to "love God, and our neighbour as ourselves"? Or is it something else? To such questions we dare not pretend that science can give an answer; yet, as several speakers have pointed out, they are of crucial practical importance at the outset of any planning to better the lot of our fellows. To allow them to go by default, when we rightly devote so much concentrated thought to all other phases of the problem, would be to betray our calling.

My personal hope, if I may express it in conclusion, is that in years to come we shall work realistically for a more constructive relationship between scientific and religious thought on such problems. We are emerging from a period of confused conflict between "science" and "religion", revolving chiefly around what I believe were mistaken ideas of the nature and scope of both. It is in a proper working partnership between the two—ideally in the same persons—that I see the best hope for the future of man.

Must Automation Bring Unemployment?

Paul Einzig

The proponents and opponents of automation have taken their positions at extreme ends of the spectrum. While the former see only minimum effects on employment patterns as a result of introducing the machines, the latter see doomsday levels of unemployment higher even than during the depression. In this analysis Paul Einzig examines these arguments and finds them both specious.

I will examine whether automation is likely to go beyond relieving overfull employment and whether it is likely to bring about large-scale unemployment. In this respect we are confronted with two diametrically opposite views. One of them was expressed, in its most extreme form, by Dr. Norbert Wiener in his book *The Human Use of Human Beings*. In the revised second edition of that book, published by Doubleday in 1954, he made the forecast that the unemployment that would be caused in the United States by automation would overshadow the experience of the thirties. This view found supporters, though in a less extreme form, among many labor union leaders and their followers within and outside the United States.

The other extreme has been voiced by the numerous enthusiasts of automation. In order to make out the strongest possible case against labor union resistance to automation, they do their utmost to minimize its possible adverse effects on employment. Most of their arguments are, on the whole, sound, so far as they go. But they present only one side of the picture. Both supporters and opponents of automation always have technological unemployment in mind—that is, dismissals through redundancy created by the installation of labor-saving equipment.

It is of course understandable that, under the influence of some isolated instances of staff reductions resulting from automation, the possibility of wholesale replacement of men by machines should dominate the minds of most people interested in the economic consequences of the system. Supporters of automation are, however, nearer the truth than its opponents when they seek to prove that, in the balance, technological unemployment is likely to be moderate. What they as well as the opposite camp overlook is that automation is liable to cause *nontechnological* unemployment. Nor has the possibility of *delayed* technological unemployment that may arise not immediately after the installation of labor-saving equipment, but only on the occasion of the next trade recession, been adequately examined.

Unemployment may be classified according to its causes into the following categories:

(1) Technological unemployment arises through the replacement of men by machines.

(2) Unemployment through bottlenecks arises through curtailment of production because of lack of raw materials, semi-products, fuel, electric power, transport facilities, or skilled labor in key positions.

(3) Unemployment through obsolescence arises through loss of markets as a result of being undersold by firms using more up-to-date equipment.

(4) Financial unemployment arises when production has to be curtailed through credit squeezes or other causes leading to inadequacy of financial resources, or to unduly high interest rates.

(5) Deflationary unemployment arises when deficiency of purchasing power leads to a decline in consumer demand for goods.

(6) Underinvestment unemployment arises from a decline in capital expenditure.

(7) Unemployment through rationalization arises as a result of redundancy through amalgamations of firms, or their reorganization on more efficient lines.

(8) Change of demand unemployment arises from changes in consumer tastes, or from a diversion of purchasing power in new directions, or from changes in production methods leading to changes in requirements of capital goods.

(9) Imported unemployment arises from loss of overseas markets through a decline of demand in other countries, through depression or import restrictions in the importing countries, or to an overvaluation of the currency of the exporting country, or to increased imports competing with the national products on the domestic market.

The term "technological unemployment" was coined by that greatest of wishful thinkers, Karl Marx, who believed that capitalism was doomed, among other reasons, because there was bound to be an increase in the amount of capital per head of labor employed in production, and that, deprived of earnings, the laborers would be unable to buy the output produced with the aid of the growing volume of capital.

The static theory, according to which there is only a certain amount of work to be done, and any labor-saving device is therefore bound to reduce the number of workers who can be employed for the execution of that work, may have been roughly correct during periods of decline, of prolonged stagnation, or of very slow expansion. In the thirties automation would undoubtedly have created technological unemployment in addition to the existing deflationary unemployment. Amidst the conditions then prevailing the new devices would have been used for reducing the total cost of the existing output, rather than for increasing the output at the same total cost.

Today automation operates against an entirely different monetary, economic, social and political background. In conditions such as prevailed most of the time during the postwar period, amidst an expanding economy accompanied by an inflationary trend, large-scale technological unemployment was virtually inconceivable, at any rate so long as the trend continued. Industrial firms were determined to increase their output on the assumption that the inflated demand was bound to continue indefinitely, or that at any rate the government could not possibly afford to allow the development of a recession of sufficient dimensions to cause large-scale unemployment. For years the production plans of many firms had been handicapped by scarcity of labor. They would now seize the opportunity of increasing their output while retaining their existing staffs which they would not dare to reduce for fear of being left without an adequate labor force for further expansion. There was "hoarding" of labor instead of resorting to redundancy dismissals.

Moreover there was usually strong and successful resistance by the unions and by their members to such attempts at dismissals of redundant workers as occurred. Frequently they insisted on "feather-bedding" and make-work practices in order to prevent dismissals, in spite of the reduced requirements of labor resulting from the installation of labor-saving equipment. Only firms which were able to use the new machinery for increasing their output instead of for reducing their labor cost could proceed with automation unhampered. Firms which did not expect to be able to sell a larger volume of goods had to abstain, in many instances, from automation aimed at labor-saving, because in the circumstances of the postwar period labor refused to be saved. It is probable, however, that in the large majority of companies there was no such resistance to automation, because it could be affected without redundancy dismissals.

Although automation tends to reduce direct labor requirements for an unchanged output, it tends to create employment in other directions. Until the system has reached maturity there is bound to be an additional demand for capital equipment to replace the old machinery. Owing to the more intensive use of machinery by several small shifts, it is likely to wear out more quickly. In any case, new inventions are liable to make the automatic equipment obsolete in a relatively short time. Larger profits earned through the reduction of cost per unit of output enables the firms to replace obsolescent equipment earlier.

The electronics industry itself provides a fair amount of new employment. It is an expanding industry with wide possibilities. In his evidence before the Congressional Subcommittee on Economic Stabilization Walter Reuther of the UAW pointed out, however, that "even automation is being automated," so that employment in the electronics industry is not expanding at anything like the same rate as its output. Between 1947 and 1952 its output increased by 275 per cent, but the number of its employees increased by 40 per cent only.

On the other hand, new industries, which owe their existence to automation, have come into being. Apart from the production of atomic energy and of isotopes, which could not have been achieved by hand methods and close human contact, the Congressional Subcommittee's Report on Automation and Technological Change quotes the instance of polyethylene (a new and very useful product increasingly employed in everyday household items) which could not have been produced without applying automation methods. The number of similar examples is likely to grow in the course of time. Automation will create new industries in which the use of direct human labor would be too dangerous, or which call for a degree of precision that is beyond human capacity. Even after allowing for such possibilities, however, the Congressional Report pointed out that "it would be unwise to overemphasize the employment potentials in these new industries and assume that their growth will be sufficient to take care of displacements in the older industries."

Taking a long view, automation is likely to be accompanied by a progressive reduction of working hours. This should go a long way towards offsetting unemployment. Moreover, longer leisure would create new occupations and would accentuate the existing trend towards the relative expansion of service industries as distinct from goods industries. As automation tends to raise the standard of living, there would be an increased demand not only for goods whose prices have been reduced through automation, but for other kinds of goods as well, so that the industries producing them would employ additional labor. It is, perhaps, not unduly optimistic to hope that more leisure, together with the higher standard of living, will mean an increase in the demand for artists of every kind and for others catering to cultural requirements.

So long as postwar circumstances remain substantially unchanged, automation would be proceeding in an atmosphere of inflationary boom. Given an adequate degree of flexibility of labor, any employee who has become superfluous through automation should easily find some kind of new job. There would be a reversal of the postwar flow of labor from rural to urban districts, from nonproductive to directly productive occupations, from the household and from retirement to the factories. Automation would be accompanied by an increase in the prices of raw materials, so that mineworkers and agricultural laborers could be paid higher wages. It is true that farmers would not be able to outbid those manufacturers who benefit by automation, but workers who have become redundant in towns could pursue a tolerable existence by taking up farm labor.

There would be inevitably a certain amount of transitional unemployment. Pockets of unemployment might arise through automation in offices. But a reduction in the number of office workers through the use of computers and other automatic machinery for routine work would be a step in the right direction. There has been for some time an unmistakable trend towards the relative increase in the number of office workers. In the United States during the thirty years ending in 1950 the number of factory workers increased by 53 per cent, that of office workers by 150 per cent. In Britain there has been a similar trend. In 1951 there were 2¼ million clerks. As Dr. Bowden observed at the Conference of the Institute of Management in 1955, Britain was becoming "a nation of clerks." A reversal of this trend, during a period when the redundant clerks could easily find alternative occupations, should not be regarded as a major tragedy from a national point of view, even if it is bound to cause inconvenience and hardship to many individuals.

In any case there is room for two opinions even about the effect of automation on office employment. The official American view is that it does not necessarily reduce the demand for clerical labor. Giving evidence before the Congressional Subcommittee, Mr. James P. Mitchell, U.S. Secretary of Labor, quoted the instance of an insurance company which, after installation of electronic data machines continued to face a clerical labor shortage, because of the ever-expanding volume of business. And Mr. Robert W. Burgess, Director of the Department of

Commerce Bureau of the Census, stated that, on the basis of past experience, there is every reason to believe that the development of cheap and versatile electronic data-processing machines will not be accompanied by a major reduction, if any, in the number of office jobs. He believed that "the lower costs and increased possibilities for timely information have made it possible to meet more of the demand for increased facts to guide decisions by American businessmen and governments." Instead of causing unemployment among office workers, automation tends to increase the requirements of better service, which necessitates large office staffs side by side with electronic computers. Although it would be inadvisable to generalize about the validity of the conclusions reached by the two officials, their opinions should go some way toward counteracting the alarmist view that electronic computers will necessarily mean large-scale unemployment among clerical workers. In this respect too, as in other respects, a great deal depends on whether the economy remains expansionary or not.

Taking everything into consideration, it seems that fears of technological unemployment are grossly exaggerated. To reduce these fears to absurdity, the National Association of Manufacturers pointed out in its evidence before the Congressional Committee that, if technological progress really resulted in unemployment, the United States would have in 1955 some 40 million unemployed, because it is now possible to produce goods with about two-fifths as much labor per unit as in 1910.

Those who recall the large-scale unemployment of the interwar period in support of their arguments against automation are guilty of the logical fallacy of arguing on the basis of false analogy. They should be reminded that unemployment during that period was not due to any noteworthy extent to technological progress. The slump in the early twenties was a reaction from the exaggerated post-armistice boom. Inadequacy of consumers' purchasing power, over-saving resulting from the unequal distribution of national incomes, and a restrictionist monetary policy, were the main causes of unemployment in various countries between the wars. The heavy unemployment in the United States during the thirties was brought about by the slump which resulted mainly from overspeculation.

The only technological cause of unemployment during the

interwar period was the adoption of tractors and combines in agriculture. In addition to displacing some agricultural labor it led to an increase in output with no corresponding expansion in the purchasing power of the masses. But this mechanization occurred mainly during a period when the economic climate was distinctly deflationary so that it was bound to produce a deflationary effect.

Admittedly, even though automation does not cause large-scale technological unemployment during a period of inflationary expansion, it may produce deferred effects if and when, for no matter what reason, a deflationary trend should develop. Labor-saving equipment installed before the turn of the trend would then enable industrial firms to reduce the number of their employees without having to curtail their output too drastically.

The conclusion inferred from this argument is not to delay automation, because by doing so we are liable to incur unemployment through obsolescence, leading to deflation. The remedy is to proceed with automation at a reasonable pace as a means of eliminating one of the possible causes of deflation.

Apart from technological unemployment, automation may cause unemployment as a result of bottlenecks resulting from shortages of raw materials, electric power, or fuel. Should automation proceed at a very high rate, increased demand may cause such bottlenecks which may hold up production and would cause passing unemployment. There is even a possibility of a complete exhaustion of some irreplaceable raw materials, leading to unemployment of a more lasting character.

Hitherto we have been dealing with unemployment arising from a very rapid progress of automation. But unemployment is likely to arise also through inadequacy of such progress, if other producers at home or abroad proceed with automation at a higher rate; they may be able to undersell the less progressive producers, and the latter may then have to curtail their output and may even have to close down if they lose their markets. The cumulative effects of a large number of bankruptcies would be deflation and unemployment on a large scale.

It may well be asked why such a situation has not already arisen as a result of the uneven rate at which automation is proceeding in various countries, and within the same countries as between various firms. The explanation is that in an inflationary climate producers are not prepared to pass on to the consumer the benefits derived from automation. They do not cut their prices, for the time being, and the less progressive firms are thus given a chance to catch up with the more progressive firms. But sooner or later the latter might decide to cut their prices, and this would mean unemployment through obsolescence. The difference between technological unemployment created by automation and obsolescence unemployment created by inability to keep pace with the progress of automation is that obsolescence unemployment is more liable to be self-aggravating. Amidst an inflationary background technological unemployment is bound to be temporary and relatively moderate. For one thing, care is taken for social considerations, that the spending power of the victims of automation is not unduly reduced. If, however, a firm is compelled to dismiss its workers, not because they have become redundant through labor-saving equipment, but because it has lost its markets, it cannot afford to pay generous compensation, or retain them until they have found some other employment, or re-train them for other jobs.

If obsolescence unemployment is the result of price-cutting by automated foreign rivals, the effect of the losses incurred will become aggravated, from a national point of view, by the deterioration of the balance of payments. A nation which lags behind its commercial rivals in the sphere of automation is likely to have a perennial adverse balance of payments. This would mean a depletion of its gold reserve to an extent that would not be offset by the expansion of other firms within the country.

From the foregoing it appears that the problems of unemployment, as a direct or indirect consequence of automation, though not nearly as grave as is suggested by Dr. Wiener, is in fact not so negligible as it is claimed to be by enthusiasts of the new system. The gravest danger arises not through an unduly high rate of automation but through an unduly slow rate of automation. Those who are opposed to automation for fear of technological unemployment do not realize that if their policy were followed their country would be exposed to much more extensive and intractable nontechnological unemployment.

Automation is bound to proceed sooner or later, whether we like it or not. Our choice does not rest between automation and full employment but between prompt automation with the possibility of moderate temporary unemployment and delayed automation with the certainty of grave perennial unemployment, until our progress has caught up with that of our competitors.

The only circumstance that is likely to mitigate the threat to those countries which have not proceeded with automation as fast as their rivals, is that during a period of expansion and inflation the more advanced firms are not likely to lower their prices unduly, if at all. Their desire to earn bigger profits, or to take the line of least resistance by yielding to wage demands, instead of lowering their prices in accordance with the reduction of their costs, may give the less advanced countries a breathing space during which they have a chance of catching up with the progress of their more dynamic rivals. But the first business recession would be accompanied by price cuts, and the backward firms would then feel the full weight of the disadvantages of being left behind in the "automation race."

In his evidence before the Congressional Subcommittee, John Diebold draws a distinction between the effect of automation on employment while it is in process of being established, and that when it has become a settled part of the economy. He believes that, since automation tends to increase the amount of capital per head of labor employed, once it is completed it will tend to reduce rather than increase the dismissal of employees. Their pay will represent a relatively small item in the expenditure of automated firms, compared with the charges on the increased fixed capital, so that it will not be worth while to dismiss them. Even though Mr. Diebold quotes with approval Keynes's flippant wisecrack that "in the long run we are all dead," he attaches, rightly, great importance to this essential difference between the short-run and long-run effect of automation.

The Challenge of Automation to Education for Human Values

Margaret Mead

Many prominent leaders of opinion who are not connected with the computer business have joined the chorus bewailing the ills that unchecked automation can bring. Here, however, Margaret Mead, the prominent anthropologist and social critic, argues that the long-term benefits of automation far outweigh the short-term inconveniences. The problem, she points out, is how to get through the transition period.

Technological advances are themselves neutral. Each technological advance is, therefore, just what the civilization in which it is made can make of it. At present, there is a tendency to treat automation as a devil that is responsible for unemployment at best and for dehumanization of mankind at worst. This attitude is a retreat from the traditional American welcome to technological change. Unlike our European contemporaries, Americans did not conduct vendettas against machines or describe them as soul destroying. Instead, machines that could be substituted for human hands, human legs, or human backs were welcomed. It is worth while asking why we welcomed labor-saving devices and the assembly line that made it possible to mass-produce

345

things that everyone needed, at a price that a majority of the people could afford, and now are balking at devices which save not only heavy physical labor, but mental labor as well. Why are we more concerned with the immediate transitional stage from partly automated to completely automated industry than we are with the ultimate benefits? Why do we not welcome the end of routine factory labor which made no demand for imagination or spontaneity? Why are we not thinking about the other things that people who work can do once some of the tasks they now do have been rendered unnecessary?

There are, I believe, several answers. With the advent of automation we have come face to face with the truth of what social prophets have been predicting for over a quarter of a century—that the problems of a society as productive as ours, with such extensive natural resources and such a large internal market, were bound to become problems of distribution rather than production. While a good part of the rest of the world is struggling with problems of production, we, in the United States, have to face affluence, which means that our task is not to get people to work under threat of starvation, but how to distribute buying power so that the wheels of our highly productive economy can continue to turn productively. Thus, we are facing today a second phase of the moral revolution that began during the Depression, when we abandoned the century-old notion that individuals should be penalized because the industrial society has slowed down. During the Depression we accepted, in practice if not in principle, the idea that society was responsible for the subsistence of all its members and that failure to have a job no longer was to carry with it the penalty of starvation for oneself, one's wife, and one's children. We did not recognize, however, that we would have to disassociate still further the ability to find properly paid work in a free labor market and the right to a decent standard of living. Although it is clear now that this second principle—the right to live well—will have to be accepted also, first in practice and later in principle, we have not yet begun to do so. Welfare still is regarded as a burden carried by society for its improvident and unfortunate members and is kept to minimum standards often well below either health or decency. There is little recognition that the price of preserving our own affluence will be giving up of the old insistence of an industrializing society that in order to share in the society's wealth, one must do productive work.

A second reason why automation is being viewed with suspicion is because the transitional adjustments, which cut down on the labor needed in industry, are being made at the expense of the least well-educated members of the community, and especially of minority groups. Instead of looking ahead to a world in which, with high productivity implemented by machines, we may have enough people at last to care for other people, our imaginations are stymied by the spectacle of the contemporary unemployed, who are pictured as permanently unemployable in a society where only the highly educated will be needed and where there will be a steadily increasing group of unskilled people to be supported.

A third reason lies in the coincidence of automation and the development of a series of technical devices which are pictured as robbing people of privacy, reducing them to cyphers, and subjecting them to decisions made by computers. Automation possibilities and these other developments have coincided and are in many ways interdependent, as when a computer is programmed to invent a better computer than itself, or when the checking of income taxes or registration of university students are said to be "done by a computer." The way in which all of these subjects have been handled in the press has suggested to many people that machines were taking over, Big Brother was equipped with long-distance listening devices, and all individuality was lost. Not nearly enough stress has been put on the importance of the questions that are asked of machines, on the inability of machines to do anything for which they have not received full instructions, and the extent to which all these devices facilitate living in the modern world.

A fourth reason lies in our inability to think of a responsible role in society which is not evaluated as a job, paid for with money, which individuals seek freely, from which they can be fired, and at which they must work or else, if not starve, they will live in humiliation and deprivation. We can look forward to a day in which the privilege of working will be open to all but under no threat of starvation.

We can look forward to a day when all the dull, unrewarding, routine technical tasks can be done by machines, and the human tasks—caring for children, caring for plants and trees and animals, caring for the sick and the aged, the traveler and the stranger—can be done by human beings. We can look forward to a day when we never will ask a human being to do something that a machine can do better, but will reserve for human beings our requests and demands for those things which machines cannot do. Just as jobs multiplied when production and consumption depended upon factory work, we may expect the number of tasks for human beings to perform humanly to multiply once it is recognized that we will need a device by which each member of society can validate his right to share in its productivity. Instead of the old economy of scarcity, in which the product was limited, we will have a new economy which is limited neither by the available workers nor by the available market for the goods produced.

The problem then of putting automation in perspective involves a substitution of long-term goals for concentration on short-term effects, attention to our peculiar American situation of educational contrasts and racial and cultural diversity, and a far better public understanding of the way in which machines can serve human purposes rather than merely create problems.

We then can ask: How will automation permit us to make our society more human? Is it more or less human for mothers and daughters, separated by hundreds of miles, to be able to dial each other cheaply? Is it more or less human to have a machine to help a child review a rote learning lesson, or calculate the milk money, while a trained teacher is free to teach? Is it more or less human to provide a bed-ridden patient with a self-regulating bed? Is a child who can rent earphones in a museum and walk about at his own speed more or less human than one herded in a group of 50? Is it more or less human for a people to be able to share the entire ritual of mourning for a martyred president than for them to read a few short lines in a newspaper printed on a hand press?

Making the post-automation world human will demand new educational measures: an immediate interpretation of the relationship between human instruction and machine execution;

new programs which will prepare children for a world in which they will work, not under threat, but as part of their membership in their society; emphasis on human skills rather than upon routine machine tending skills; and greater attention to the development of individual interests and talents to use the greater leisure which everyone may expect to have.

Technology, Life and Leisure

Dennis Gabor

Although the exact effect of automation on employment is debatable, there is general agreement that the people most affected by automation will be those with the lowest intelligence quotients, who today perform society's most menial and tedious tasks. Here Dennis Gabor, inventor and physicist, advocates a reorganization of employment patterns designed to overcome the exclusion of such people from the labor market of the future.

In our society the technologist is a man who minds his own business. He is a link in the long chain of production which streches from the scientist over the inventor or innovator, through the production engineer to the salesman—but not beyond. So long as his products can be sold, he is not supposed to be interested in the impact of his work on society. Like a good soldier he does his duty and 'does not reason why'.

For the last two hundred years, since the birth of the industrial society, the technologist and his master, the industrial director or promoter, have served society well. When the industrial society came into being, first in this country, life had not changed much since Roman times. Of the world population, which was about a quarter of the present, by and large 80 per cent lived on the land and were engaged in producing food. By far the greatest part were illiterate, and unless they were soldiers or sailors seldom got further from their birthplace in all their lives than to the next town or village. By present-day standards their lives were poor and monotonous beyond imagination. A small minority had stately town and country homes, with droves of servants, everything was within their reach—except that when they had toothache, they had to have the tooth extracted without any better anaesthetic than brandy!

Technology, in which we must of course include medical technology, has changed all this. The world population has trebled in a little more than a hundred years, and is now increasing at a rate at which it doubles in forty. In the industrial countries less than 10 per cent of the population produce more than sufficient food for the rest. The average man or woman is several inches taller than a hundred years ago, and has a chance at birth to reach seventy years or even more. We have every reason to be proud and happy when we look backward—but none whatever when we look forward!

Fifty years ago an engineer could have a perfectly good conscience when he bent over his job, fully satisfied that he was a benefactor of humanity when he produced more or cheaper machines and all sorts of consumable goods. He can still have his good conscience if he happens to be a Russian, an Indian or a Chinese. But in the Western industrial countries at the present time such myopic self-satisfaction amounts almost to blindness.

Trying to look into the future is a more difficult task now than it ever was. It is true that we have carefully compiled statistics of the past to help us, but the task is aggravated by the enomously enlarged range of future contingencies. When a statesman of the past contemplated the possibility of a war, the worst contingency he could think of was defeat in the field, an angry monarch dismissing his ministers, and a sizeable tribute to be paid out of the coffers of the merchants. Today he would have to contemplate total annihilation. I believe though that in this one respect the modern forecaster has an advantage. Science and technology, through the invention and wholesale manufacture of thermonuclear bombs and intercontinental missiles, *have taken victory out of war*. I therefore believe that we can reasonably discard this greatest of all possible worries. We can with some confidence look forward to a world without wars between the great industrial countries. For a thinker, such as H. G. Wells 50 years ago, this would have been an as good as perfect assurance of a happy and glorious future. It may be indeed, but only if we consciously and determinedly set our face against the other dangerous trends of our civilization, which are quite bad enough to nip any facile optimism.

When a weather forecaster wants to make his job easy, he will announce 'no change'—and he will be about 70 per cent right. The social forecaster in a changing world cannot have it quite as easy, but for him 'no change in the rate of progress' will be the next best thing. Technically this means plotting statistical figures of the past on a logarithmic scale against time, and drawing a tangent to the curve. This was the method followed by three American authors, H. H. Landsberg, L. L. Fischman and J. L. Fisher in a recent 1000-page report on *Resources in America's Future* (Johns Hopkins Press, 1963). They illustrate the past growth and the projections of the population, the gross national product, the personal expenditure, the steel production and the number of motor cars up to the year 2000 in the United States. In brief the forecast is that, between A.D. 1960 and 2000, in the United States:

Population	will grow from 180 million to 331 million		
Labour force	"	" 73 " to 142 "	
Gross national product	"	" $504 billion to $2200	
Personal consumption			billion
total	"	" $329 " to $1320 "	
Personal consumption *per capita*	"	" $1825 " to $4000 "	
Steel ingot production	"	" 99 million tons to 294 million tons	
Motor cars in use	"	" 59 million to 244 million	

The authors do their best to prove that these projections are possible, that is to say compatible with the mineral and land resources of the United States, though in several important raw materials the U.S. will have to rely heavily on imports.

I do not doubt that this is a possible world, but I deny that it is a desirable one. Voices such as those of Landsberg, Fischman and Fisher are of course sweet music to those new Conservatives, Tory or Labour, who do not want to conserve things as they are but progress as it is. Against this I venture to voice the heretical opinion that exponential curves grow to infinity only in mathematics. In the physical world they either turn round and saturate, or they break down catastrophically. It is our duty as thinking men to do our best towards a gentle saturation, instead of sustaining the exponential growth, though this faces us with very unfamiliar and distasteful problems.

Chief of these is the problem of leisure. I have tried to face this in a recent book and have come to the conclusion that we must devote the next forty years to a gentle transition towards the Age of Leisure. The estimate of forty years I took from a very wise man. Moses showed the Promised Land to his people, but then he led them for forty years through the wilderness, until a new generation grew up, worthy of it.

The growth addicts do not like to hear of leisure. In their 1000-page book Messrs. Landsberg, Fischman and Fisher devote just four lines to the question of working hours, and forecast a working week of 37 hours by A.D. 2000. Their forecast, if it came true, would in fact leave not more time for leisure but less. If the present tendency continues and for instance New York and Los Angeles continue their essentially linear growth (parallel to the coastline) the commuter in A.D. 2000 will spend not two hours on the way to and from his work, but four. If this is so, we need have no fear of the impact on society of mechanization, automation, leisure and boredom, of which another American author, Donald Michael, has painted a terrifying picture. We can then dismiss with a smile the recent estimate that, at the present rate, automation (which means of course mechanization *and* automation) makes every year two million workers redundant in the United States.

From these contradictory voices we can draw one solid conclusion, and this is that, for good or for bad, the development of technology will be an even more powerful force in the future than it was in the past. The 'optimistic' estimates of the growth addicts presume new inventions and techniques which will save us from the shortage of raw materials. The Cassandras of leisure presume a progress which will outrun the shortage in resources, so that men can work shorter hours at a higher level of material welfare on an impoverished Globe.

The technologist, as a good back-room boy, can say to these people: 'I can give you either. I can give you your exponential growth for a while, with flyovers on top of flyovers on which hundreds of millions of motor cars will race to and from your city centres, and I can provide power for these cars even when the last barrel of natural oil will be exhausted. But I cannot guarantee the exponential growth for ever. On the other hand, I can also give you a world in which nobody need live at more than walking distance from his work, and where people use fast transport only for pleasure. A world in which people will have to work only as much or as little as is good for them'.

I do not think that with those bold promises I have over-rated the power of science and technology. There are absolute limits to what technology can ever do, and these have been authoritatively reviewed by the Past-President of S.I.T., Sir George Thomson. But almost unilimited power, by burning the sea or by burning the rocks and plentiful substitutes for the vanishing high-grade ores are well within the reach of the science and technology of the near future, as well as means of communication which make it unnecessary to move people bodily about every day.

Let me ask now: With such potential powers, need the technologist remain only an obedient tool, who like the genie out of the bottle does the bidding of others? Is he not also a man, who can opt for one way into the future or the other? I do not advocate technology; I do not want technologists on top, though I would certainly welcome more scientists and technologists in high advisory positions. What I am hoping for is more modest, but also, I believe, achievable. I should like the young, gifted technologists to look into the future, make their choice, and give their talents and their enthusiasm to those industries and tendencies which aim at a smooth transition into the Age of Leisure,

instead of stiffening the exponential curve until it breaks down
—as one day it must!

When an engineer plans an operation, he must first visualize
the end product. In the present case, I am afraid, this is next to
impossible. It is perhaps more difficult for the engineer, with his
non-humanistic and unphilosophical education, than for other
educated men to visualize a society whose success is not measured in tons of pig-iron per year, and whose chief values are
love and laughter.

One cannot visualize the final steady state, but there need not
be a steady state! What we must be aiming for is a state of
steady evolution which continues the thousand million years
long story from the amoeba to man. But economically this may
well appear as a steady state, at any rate as compared with the
frantic exponential growth of the last half-century, and this is a
matter for quantitative discussion. Also, while we cannot foresee the end, we can foresee the next steps. We can, following
Karl Popper, adopt the principle of 'piecemeal social engineering' fighting the greatest evils rather than fighting for the greatest
ultimate good. The greatest evils and the most dangerous trends
are not difficult to recognize.

The most dangerous trend is, of course, over-population, not
only in the under-developed countries but also in the West. One
might say that this is not a matter for technology, but I consider
it as absurd to exclude the pharmaceutical industry from technology. It would be even wrong to say that instrument technology has nothing to do with The Pill, because electronic
instruments have now a solid foothold in biochemistry and in
pharmacology.[1]

But population control is also a political and religious question, and here the technologist or scientist has only one advantage over others; that he has a more vivid conception of the
absurdity of unlimited exponential growth than people unused
to quantitative reasoning.

---

[1] I saw a brilliant example of this at a recent visit to Prof. Ernest B.
Chain's Institute in Rome, where chromatograms with radioactive isotopes are read out by scintillation counters and recorded by automatic
typewriters, enormously speeding up and refining the study of metabolism.

Unlike most authors, I do not consider a dramatic decrease in the birth-rate of the under-developed countries as impossible. This may happen immediately after the first impact of industrialization; as soon as the people just emerging out of hopeless poverty realise that there is a possibility of a 'good life'. This has actually happened in Japan, in Hungary and in Rumania (supported by appropriate legislation at the right time). It may well be that the growth of population will stop much slower, if at all, in the Western countries where parents can rear large families without great sacrifices. (This may, of course, also come about in the at present under-developed countries, once they have risen sufficiently above the starvation level.) But having large families is just the one luxury our civilization cannot afford, at a time when only 2.3 children per family are required for a static population. This is a typical case when science grants one wish to man, only to deny him another. One cannot have a long life and many babies! It may well be that this trend will stop only by another technological frustration when the overcrowding of motorways has made it finally impossible for famiies to move about in the family car.[2]

At this point the technologist is in a dilemma; a dilemma very typical of our times. What is the use of building more motorways if there will be more families and more motorways and in the end the whole country turns into a Kingston By-pass? This is a repetition, though on a less tragic scale, of the dilemma of the physician in the East who stops child mortality so that the babies shall starve during adolescence, or when they grow to adult age. Unless and until the populations reach a steady level, all planning will be a two-edged sword!

Let us turn now to what is more properly our business; to the problems of technological change. It will be useful to divide this into mechanization, rationalization and automation. Mechanization is the replacement in production processes of muscle power by machine power, but leaving the control of the operations to human intelligence. Rationalization I will use for the simplifica-

[2] Some people, like Dr. Matthews, think that only heavy taxation of the third baby can prevent this. The imaginative writer, Arthur C. Clarke (*Profiles of the Future,* Harper and Row, New York, 1962), even thinks of 'antiheterosexual legislation'.

tion of operations, manual or clerical, the cutting out of unnecessary motions (which used to be called Scientific Management and is chiefly connected with the names of F. W. Taylor and L. M. Gilbreth), and the cutting out of unnecessary paperwork, and I would include with it also the lopping-off of dead branches of the national economy. Automation, a term mostly attributed to John Diebold or, to a lesser extent, to Del Harder, Vice-President of Ford's, 1946, is, in the first place, an extension of mechanization by taking the controls away from the human operator, and embodying them in the machine. The distinguishing characteristic of modern automatic machines is that they contain some sort of sensing organ, and a feedback path from the sensing organ to the actuator. In an extended sense automation comprises all methods of production in which human intelligence is replaced by machines.[3] By another term, introduced by Professor Norbert Wiener, these can be called 'cybernetic' processes.

I cannot think of a better or briefer characterization of the present stage of our material culture than as a war between mechanization, rationalization and automation on the one side

---

[3] Automation has become a horrah-word for some, a bogey-word for others; one must therefore take some care in its definition. It is natural to go back for this to its author, John Diebold, President of the Diebold Group of Management Consulting Companies, and in particular to his Congressional Testimony, 1960 (reprinted in *Automation,* a Vintage Book, New York, 1962). Unfortunately, he gives not one definition but many, of which a few may be quoted: 'Automation is a philosophy of technology—a set of concepts' (p. 17). 'If automation means anything at all, it means more than a mere extension of mechanization' (p. 25). '. . . automation as a *new* way of analyzing and organizing work . . . (p. 25). '. . . the fundamental importance of automation is not so much the connecting of machines as it is the ability to create automatic information and control systems' (p. 27).

The author plainly contradicts himself when in his classification of automation together with computers, process control systems and numerical control, he includes as a fourth 'Detroit' automation, which is the linking together of machines by automatic transfer devices, and nothing but an extension of mechanization. One gets the impression that 'any thing new in production or management' would be the only sufficiently comprehensive definition of automation to satisfy John Diebold.

and Parkinson's First Law[4] at the other. But I would call it a Gentleman's War, in which neither side wants to annihilate the other, for very good reasons. If Parkinson's Law were to win, that is to say, the proliferation of bureaucrats and office workers of all sorts, the result would be the misery of inefficiency. But if mechanization, rationalization and automation were to win, the result would be unemployment, unless we learn something about what to do with leisure and with the redundant workers, and this would be the misery of efficiency. For the time being both contestants have done well. In the United States between 1947 and the end of 1961 the labor force has expanded from 60 to 71 million. In this time the number of production-line workers has decreased by 7 per cent while the total production has increased by 57 per cent. The labor force has expanded by the addition of 15 million office workers, bringing the ratio of 'white collar' to 'blue collar' workers close to 2:1, and the number of unemployed has risen only slightly. Parkinson's Law and automation have kept the balance almost perfectly!

The representatives of the automation industry and of the management consulting companies contest hotly that automation need not bring unemployment, and of course there are circumstances in which they are right. For instance, the British shipbuilding industry can hardly be saved from ruin and consequent unemployment without some measure of rationalization and automation. But it is absurd to deny that all three lines of technological change have the primary purpose of employing less workers in the production process, at maintained or increased production level. And this means of course not only manual workers but clerical. For the time being the rationalization of clerical and sales work has lagged behind production, and it is natural that the increased product could be sold only by an increased effort in selling. But can anybody imagine a world in which automatic factories turn out all the industrial products with hardly any workmen in them, in which automatic lorries

[4] 'Work expands so as to fill the time available for its completion. Subordinates multiply at a fixed rate, regardless of the amount of work produced'.

358 / The World of the Computer

without drivers transport the goods to their destination, in which automatic machines do all the accounting, and the redundant population are engaged in high pressure salesmanship? Or, if it can be imagined, is there anybody who finds such a world desirable?

Let us not deceive ourselves; the offices cannot forever take up the masses which have become redundant on the shop floor. It would be an equally bad self-deception if we believed, what is said so often, that automation will produce more jobs for computer-programmers, engineers, technicians and draughtsmen than it will eliminate on the production line. This would be indeed a travesty of automation. If this were so, automation could be adopted only by philanthropic societies, not by industry or commerce. And, most important of all, we must face the fact that automation will make the lowest intelligence-brackets unemployable on a profit-basis. One cannot make a computer-programmer out of the average unskilled worker who has been eliminated on the assembly line. Attempts at re-training, such as have been made in particular by Armour's in the U.S., had the disappointing result which could be expected beforehand.

We must face the dilemma squarely. We cannot stop automation, because it is a powerful means for increasing the wealth and well-being of our industrial civilization. But if we do not stop automation, we cannot stop the lowest intelligence brackets from becoming unemployable on the production line. We have then the choice of bracketing them with the lunatics and feeble-minded, whom our society already maintains at the taxpayers' expense. If we pay them just enough to live on, as we pay the unemployed, we destroy their purchasing power, apart from making them miserable and forcing a good proportion of them into alcoholism and crime. If we pay them well, while they are not taking part in the production process, we create a dangerous attraction for those who have the intelligence to work, but do not like it much, who may well be a large majority. Besides, I am not sure whether good pay in idleness would be a very healthy thing just for the least intelligent, who are least able to make good use of their leisure.

There is only one way out of this dilemma, and this is that we must find work even for the least intelligent; work in which they can feel useful and keep their self-respect. The only major outlet is in the services. I will not go as far as Michael Young who suggested the return of personal service. But I can well imagine a world in which cafeterias and supermarkets are prohibited by law, and the job of the dustman, the night watchman, the milkman, the postman, and many others are protected by law against automation.

I have tried to take a first shot at a quantitative treatment of the employment problem with the aid of the 'Intelligence-Occupation Matrix' shown on page 361. This is a two-entry table or matrix, in which the columns represent ability or intelligence, and the rows represent occupations. For lack of something better I have taken the intelligence quotient (IQ) as the measure of ability. This need not be taken too literally. The IQ may be a good measure of the ability of schoolchildren, but it is hardly an adequate measure of the suitability of an adult to fill a job, as it leaves out ambition, stamina and ethical qualities. But until we have something better, we may as well take the IQ as the measure of that quality of men which cannot be altered at will so that people in different columns cannot be interchanged.

The rows in the matrix represent different lines of occupation, and I tried to arrange these roughly in the order of intelligence which they required, from scientists, artists and members of the learned professions down to service operatives. The division which I have used is not exactly what is found in the statistical yearbooks, and this matters little for the moment, because we have no statistics for the time being of the IQ in the various professions. All I could do was to make a likely guess for a present-day industrial country on the basis that there is full employment for all but the lowest 5 percentiles in the intelligence scale (those below an IQ of 73.5).

Whether we have a fully reliable estimate of the present distribution or not, we can play on such a matrix a game of 'full employment and social justice around A.D. 2000 in a technologically advanced society'. The rules of this game are as follows: People can be shifted only in their own columns. Social justice requires that they shall be raised as high as possible, so that nobody is employed in a job much below his intelligence level, but they cannot be shifted above the slanting line, which represents the highest occupation which can be satisfactorily filled by an IQ class. On the other hand, the national economy has only a limited number of vacancies to offer in the productive jobs. I have assumed that both the manual and the clerical jobs have fallen to one-half of their present proportion in the productive industries, with the exception of technicians (draughtsmen, servicemen), where I have allowed a 50 per cent rise. This is a small class, but I have given it a special entry as so much nonsense is talked about this type of profession. It is believed by some people that the more and more complicated machines, such as computers, will require a large number of highly trained specialists to tend and mend them. But in any reasonable society it will not be necessary to re-design the machines because of 'built-in obsolescence' every few years, and computers are already eliminating hundreds of draughtsmen in the 'lofting rooms' of the shipbuilding and aircraft industries. As regards servicemen, they must indeed have high intelligence so long as they have to repair many dozen different types of radio sets, without instructions, and with nothing but a screwdriver, a soldering iron and a test lamp. On the other hand, most modern and complicated computers or electronic instruments carry with them a detailed instruction book for trouble-chasing, and a test set. It has turned out, to the dismay of benevolent people, that the moronic fringe is more suitable for mechanically following the instructions and making a good job of it than the more intelligent, who will soon get bored. I have, therefore, lowered the average intelligence of technicians in the forecast instead of raising it, with a moderate increase in their numbers.

I have assumed that automation will release a considerable number of people between the upper 10-40 percentiles of intelligence (in the IQ range of 120.7-104.1), almost one half of them, and these I have mostly shifted into education below university level. This means that almost one sixth of the population will become educators, which I think is enough to satisfy anybody who is complaining about the present shortage of teachers. I have cut down a little in the upper intelligence brackets of educators, as social justice requires that these should rise to university level.

We cannot, however, upgrade the lowest intelligence bracket

INTELLIGENCE—OCCUPATION MATRIX

	133.1	126.5	120.7	113.6	104.1	91.5	73.5	Sums
IQ higher than:	133.1	126.5	120.7	113.6	104.1	91.5	73.5	
lower than:		133.1	126.5	120.7	113.6	104.1	91.5	
(% of population)	2	3	5	10	20	30	25	
Science, arts and learned professions	**1.6**	**2.0**	**2.4**					**6.0**
	1.0	1.2	1.8					4.0
Higher administration	**0.4**	**0.8**	**1.0**	**1.8**				**4.0**
	0.3	0.6	1.0	3.1				5.0
Education (below university level)		**0.2**	**1.6**	**7.0**	**7.0**			**15.8**
	0.4	0.7	1.2	2.0	0.5			4.8
Clerical				**1.0**	**3.0**	**6.0**		**10.0**
	0.2	0.2	0.6	3.0	10.0	6.0		20.0
Technicians				**0.2**	**2.0**	**2.8**		**6.0**
	0.1	0.2	0.2	0.4	3.1	1.0		4.0
Production operatives (incl. farming)					**7.0**	**11.0**	**2.0**	**20.0**
		0.1	0.1	1.2	6.4	17.0	15.0	39.8
Service operatives					**1.0**	**9.2**	**23.0**	**33.2**
			0.1	0.3	1.0	6.0	10.0	17.4
								95.0%

Lower figures: As it is now in a highly industrialized country.
Bold figures: As it may be around A.D. 2000.

91.5-73.5 which represent the lowest still employable 25 per cent of the population, and these I have shifted into the services which do not require skills, with the result that this class of employment will now have to take about one-third of the whole labor force. This is the class of which I said before that it *must* be employed, for its own good and for the good of society, even if it means legislative restriction of automation.

By a gradual re-distribution of employment, on the lines as indicated, it will be possible for a while to restrict the spread of unwanted leisure, and to maintain a society in which an employment scheme such as I have tentatively forecast, with about one third of the populaion in low-skill services, represents about the limit of what can be obtained from re-distribution. When automation advances further, when the automatic factories, capable of 24-hours' operation, can turn out goods in plenty with less than one fifth of the labor force engaged in direct production, a decision, perhaps the most important ever to be made, can no longer be delayed. By that time either humanity will be psychologically prepared to have leisure and work in about the inverse proportion as today—or else there is nothing left but to arrest technological progress, and retain work as occupational therapy! I refuse to contemplate the third alternative, which is that the growing population and the exhausted resources of the globe will make it just possible for humanity to survive by incessant work and effort.

Can the technologist do anything to promote the well-being of men and women in an age of leisure? The answer is that technology has already done much, and will be able to do more. By the invention of printing, of the phonograph, the cinema, the radio and television, technology has lifted the masses out of the brutish stupor in which they spent their all-too-short spells of rest—unless they were enjoying cock-fights, bull-baiting, or (as J. B. Priestley writes) 'the cartwheel round the village idiot's neck'. But passive entertainment has perhaps gone as far as it can go. Technology has also given the averagely gifted man modest means of self-expression, such as photography, amateur cinematography and a multitude of 'do-it-yourself' hobbies. It may well be that a more developed technology will be able to go much further along this line. I am thinking of the new development of computers, which are just coming out of the stage of being slaves, with foreseeable results, and which in some cases have produced real surprises. Perhaps mechanical means of self-expression will be invented which will act as amplifiers of the artistic power? (Action painting, the random spraying of colors on a canvas may be a very primitive precursor of such pastimes.)

Education is of course the time-honoured means for making leisure not just bearable but creative. While the education of the feeble-minded has made some progress, far too little attention has been devoted so far to the science of higher education. No wonder, because it requires a very rare combination of gifts; an abstract mathematical talent allied to psychological insight. Progress on these lines is somewhat hypothetical, and there is probably more prospect in the development of intelligence-enhancing drugs. Rats have been observed to learn much faster when they were treated with minute doses of nicotine. Not even the strongest opponents of the anti-smoking campaign would claim that nicotine has the same effect on men, but it is more than likely that chemical intelligence-enhancing agencies suitable for humans will be discovered in the not too remote future.

And finally, just as Parkinson's First Law has come to the rescue of our economic and social equilibrium at the first impact of automation, I believe that we can expect much help in the future from Parkinson's (as yet unwritten) N-th Law: 'Healthy people find absorbing interest in whatever they are doing! They will create values to suit the social frame in which they are living'. Let us see that the young generations shall be healthy in body and mind, with abundant vitality, and we need not have fear about the future. In that future the ironmongering technologist of the past and present will have yielded his leadership to a new class of creative men. The wealth and the material welfare which the technologist has created will be taken for granted, like the air which we breathe. The pursuit of happiness, which in our world is mostly a by-product of hard work, will have taken different pathways, still unknown to us. We can be certain only of one thing, and this is that it will not be a direct, shortest-way approach, because this is the one way in which happiness can never be reached.

The Hard Road
to Soft Automation

Tom Alexander

The first wave of automation in industrial production left much bitterness among unions, who felt that it had put too many of their members out of work; among customers, who believed that it had cut down on their flexibility of choice; and among managers, who lamented that it had penetrated too few of the musty corners of their plants. The next wave will represent in many ways a more revolutionary development in using the computer. Here an award-winning science writer sets the scene for the forthcoming robot era.

It now seems surpassing innocence that only a few years ago Americans regarded automation as a menace. In 1962, President Kennedy asserted that "the major domestic challenge of the Sixties is to maintain full employment at a time when automation is replacing men." Now, in 1971 unemployment is once again a problem, but few economists blame it on automation, and a number of union leaders are pushing for the acceptance of *more* automation. Even in a year of recovery from a recession, many college students and young blue-collar workers proclaim their intention to shun tedious, unpleasant tasks, no matter what the wages. When asked how these jobs are going to get done. workers and intellectuals alike reply blithely, "Let the machines do them." Gradually, in fact, the willingness to replace men with machines is being transformed from the status of a threat to something like a social necessity.

But this new set of attitudes will not of itself bring results.

For the unpleasant fact is that automation has reached something of a roadblock in the U.S., just as it is becoming socially desirable. In industries ranging from autos to apparel, there now appear to be serious economic barriers to pushing conventional mechnization much further. Companies that ventured boldly into automation during the huge capital-spending spree of the late Sixties have recoiled in confusion and disillusion. Those tedious jobs on the assembly line have changed hardly at all, and there now is deep concern about U.S. productivity, which has not been growing at a healthy rate over the past few years. With the economy improving, the figures have turned up after a dismal showing last year. But such factors as the diversion of capital and effort into environmental and other "quality of life" concerns are bound to be a permanent drag.

It is obviously essential that the U.S. get moving again on automation—and not just to please its young who would like more interesting jobs. For a nation that neglects productivity becomes less competitive, less able to sell its goods internally or abroad, and therefore becomes less affluent, less able to afford such amenities as health, education and a decent environment. What seems most ominous is that the slowdown in U.S. productivity is occurring simultaneously with rapidly increasing productivity in most other countries and particularly in those countries such as Germany and Japan whose high-technology goods are the primary competition for our own. While our gain in manufacturing productivity over the past five years has averaged 2.1 percent, for example, Japan's has averaged 15 percent.

To some degree, the gains in Japan and elsewhere are a matter of their catching up with the U.S., which still has a considerably higher average output per worker than any other nation. But there is also evidence that other nations are already looking well beyond the time of simply catching up and are plotting long-term strategies. Japan, for example, is becoming a world leader in research on exotic measures for improving productivity, including the substitution of robots for assembly-line workers.

A Nineteenth-Century Flavor

One of the reasons that automation is now at something of a standstill is simply the fact that it has already come so far. In many industries, mechanization has proceeded to the point where the cost of labor is not the primary determinant in the cost of the finished product. The total amount of labor left in the manufacture of an American automobile is around a hundred hours, considerably more than in some foreign autos that do not undergo frequent model changes.

A second problem is that recent trends in production volume have not been running in favor of increased efficiency. On the typical factory floor, automation to date has been based on expensive, fixed-purpose machinery operated for the long-run, high-volume manufacture of many identical items. It is no exaggeration to say that much of present automation has a decidedly nineteenth-century flavor. The automobile industry is generally accepted as the bellwether in applied automation, but if Henry Ford I were to step into one of today's auto plants, he would not be unduly startled by what he saw. He would find that auto assembly still involves a large number of people doing a lot of handling of materials and tools. He would find that most of the automatic machinery consists basically of the kinds of motors, cams, cogs, and conveyers that he himself could have assembled. The epitome of "Detroit automation" is the transfer machine for the automatic machining of engine blocks. It was actually invented in Britain in 1926. Only high-volume production can justify the tremendous cost of such custom-built machinery, which simply gets discarded when car models or engines change.

This approach may have just about reached its economic limits. Sales volume is no longer expanding at a rate that encourages further mechanization founded simply on economies of scale. In fact, the opposite trend is apparent, rooted in a steadily increasing demand for variety in quality and style. Much of the appeal of foreign cars, for example, whether Volkswagen or Mercedes-Benz, seems to spring from a desire for a greater range of product choice. But the needs to increase variety and respond to changing tastes necessarily fragment the production run and compromise the rationale for conventional automation. Thus the auto companies have been pacing back and forth along this economic barrier, alternately proliferating models and styles to satisfy demand and then cutting them back to satisfy production economy.

Any number of industries are faced with the same dilemma. Appliance manufacturers note that in some lines their product mix has jumped from about 75 different models to 200. Comments Westinghouse Vice President Gordon C. Hurlbert, "We are switching from the production of large numbers of identical items to the production of large numbers of individually different, yet similar, items. Industry is becoming a large-scale job shop."

Corporations are also getting trapped by shifting priorities. It usually takes from a year up to get delivery on a piece of custom-fabricated production machinery, and by that time the product it was meant for is often no longer interesting. Owens-Illinois, Inc., for example, has spent $40 million and six years' time adapting light-bulb-making machinery to the production of lightweight throwaway bottles at the rate of 700 per minute. The impetus was to counter the invasion of metal cans into the soft-drink market. But already the ecology movement has made returnable containers desirable again.

Design by Electronics

Most further developments in laborsaving machinery are likely to emerge from exploitation of the electronic computer and its peripheral apparatus. Unlike "hard" or "Detroit" automation, with its cams and gears operating in fixed relationships to produce an unvarying product, computers potentially furnish some of the versatility of the human artisan who handcrafts exclusive items to order. This "soft" automation is accomplished through software—programming that can, in effect, convert a cabinet full of electronic components into a new machine on short notice. Until fairly recently, computers were judged too expensive to be scattered around through factories doing varied production jobs. But the cost of electronics has been undergoing one of the most dramatic declines of any commodity in industrial history. An analysis by Dr. Lawrence Roberts of the Defense Department's Advanced Research Projects Agency finds that the price per computation has been falling by a factor of ten every 5.6 years. Roberts sees no sign of this trend bottoming out, either. Some of today's "mini-computers" selling for between $5,000 and $10,000 have more speed and power than machines that sold for $125,000 only a decade ago. Digital Equipment Corp. has recently come out with a small $800 computer that can control a machine tool.

To be sure, the cost of electronics is not the only barrier. The development of new software is still very much an art, akin to the art of the nineteenth-century inventor before mechanical engineering became routine enough to be taught in schools. But libraries of prewritten programs are quite extensive by now, and mini-computers and computer terminals are gradually becoming a common sight amid the dirt and clamor of the factory floor.

Already, the computer has shown a lot of what it can do in the way of improving productivity. It has made a huge impact in the process industries; some oil refineries and chemical plants are now virtually run by computers and a few technicians whose responsibility consists mostly of checking up on things. Some facets of industrial production, such as the machining of individual components, have lent themselves readily to "custom manufacturing." The techniques have evolved from the original breakthrough of numerical control, which employs punched tape to guide machine tools. The tape specifies what is *supposed* to happen, but tool wear and metal hardness tend to introduce variations in the finished product. The newer "adaptive control" computers can measure what is actually happening and make adjustments accordingly.

Computers can also connect several different processes to produce fairly complex components. At least one company will soon be able to supply on an off-the-shelf basis the computerized equivalent of an entire machine shop. Starting with plain metal stock or castings, these machines can be programmed to turn out practically any shape of part with economies that approach, if not match, products fabricated on high-volume, special-purpose transfer machines. The new programmable machines will have tracks or conveyers that run past several different kinds of tools. The piece is simply clamped into a mobile jig or pallet, which then races around the track to the various machines that perform programmed operations.

Machines Command, People Work

But the fallacy of judging the state of automation by such sophisticated developments is that the available menu of technology is unbalanced. It serves little purpose to buy the latest marvel in high-production machinery if its prolific output is simply going to pile up on the factory floor while the rest of the plant lags behind. Other essential links in the manufacturing chain, such as the movement of materials and parts to and from machines, their assembly into finished products, and the inspection of these products, have proved far more difficult to automate, largely because they involve activities that have customarily demanded the versatility and judgment of humans. But, in principle at least, some of these other operations are amenable to computerization. Companies such as Jervis B. Webb now install entire systems that stow different items away in bins and retrieve items upon request. Many companies now keep track of inventory and reorder by computer. Some of the auto manufacturers' computers go even one step further: they follow changing tastes, as reflected in car buyers' orders, and stock up with extra supplies of parts that seem to be in particular demand.

In fact, the largest single contribution of the computer to manufacturing over the near term may lie not so much in mechanization as in this sort of systemization of processes. It has become obvious that the computers that control fabrication, materials handling, and inspection functions, plus those in charge of orders, inventory, and distribution, could all be tied together. The result would not be a people-less factory but rather what has been called "the programmed responsive plant." Here people would be found doing many of the things they do now, but largely under the direction of machines. The aim is to provide the industrial equivalent of what the biologists call "homeostasis" in higher animals—i.e., automatic adjustments within the organism to meet widely varying and interacting internal and external conditions.

The Humanoids Are Coming

That will still leave the assembly lines, as well as a lot of random hand labor, beyond the reach of automation. But some of the attempts to invest machines with manlike versatility and flexibility are already invading these areas, too. For a decade now, limited numbers of machines, called robots by some, have been toiling away in industry. Though they bear little resemblance to humans, they do possess vaguely anthropomorphic hands and arms and can be set to work on a wide variety of tasks. Close to 500 of the machines are now used in industry, performing such routine and laborious tasks as feeding presses and machine tools, stacking bricks, shot-peening aircraft parts, and welding auto bodies.

The two principal robot makers in the U.S. are Unimation, Inc., jointly owned by Condec Corp. and Pullman, Inc., and the Versatran Division of AMF Inc. Recently, I.B.M. also entered the field, while Sundstrand Corp. is considering doing so, fueling speculation that robots, after a decade of on-again, off-again enthusiasm, may finally be turning the corner into exponential growth. Costing anywhere between $20,000 and $30,000, depending upon its versatility and capability, a robot is usually considered economically worthwhile when it can substitute for one man on each of two shifts, or when the work is particularly dangerous or arduous. "Some 55 percent of all blue-collar work consists simply of 'putting and taking,' " says Joseph F. Engelberger, the articulate and confident president of Unimation. "And literally millions of such distasteful jobs are potential jobs for robots."

The biggest purchasers of the machines to date have been the auto manufacturers. General Motors has some ninety of the devices scattered throughout its installations working at various tasks. G.M.'s largest robot force is at its new Lordstown assembly plant, where twenty-six "Unimate" robots have taken over some of the welding of Vega automobiles. Ford bought its first robot in 1962 to feed a press that stamped out body brackets; some twenty of the machines are now at work and Ford recently placed an order for sixty more.

One can easily see what there is about the robot that fascinates the auto men and almost everyone else who has lots of blue-collar workers doing routine tasks. In principle, such "universal automation" could be purchased off the shelf, saving the delay and expense of custom machinery. Moreover, it could be easily reprogrammed for a model change in a half-hour or so, saving the months required to design and build new special-purpose automation.

Even so, few production men in the auto industry or elsewhere appear to share Engelberger's confidence that robots are going to take over a substantial number of blue-collar jobs anytime soon. For one thing, the robots have a long history of reliability problems. Bugs, of course, can be worked out, but the robots have other fundamental limitations. One is that special-purpose automation can be built to do many jobs faster than a general-purpose device, and if the production run is long enough, the economics still favor special-purpose machines. So is all that versatility really worth the price? General Motors' Lordstown plant is a noteworthy embodiment of this perplexity, for the plant is simultaneously an experiment in trying to get a long production run of one vehicle especially designed for manufacturing economy and an experiment in trying to get some versatility into the machinery. Both the line and the car were designed so that Vegas could be turned out at the high volume of about a hundred vehicles an hour for several years to come. But G.M. also has four body styles of the Vega going down the line. Some of the Unimates are hooked up to sensing switches that can tell which style—say, station wagon or fast-back—is coming next. The Unimates then change their welding patterns accordingly.

Talents for Menial Jobs

The fundamental limitation that today's robots have in common with all conventional automation is that they are both blind and stupid. The Vega line, for instance, includes a large investment in high-precision jigs and "accuracy rails" for positioning the car bodies exactly. These, together with stop-and-go movements of the assembly line, ensure that an auto body presented to a Unimate is stationary and in exactly the right spot. Otherwise the blind Unimates might simply bang their hands against the auto body or execute their precise stitchwork of spot welds in empty air.

An irony of automation has been that the machines often take over the more skilled jobs, such as machining or welding, leaving the menial tasks for humans. At Lordstown people pick up the sheet-metal panels and clamp them into position in the welding fixtures. At one time the G.M. engineers considered robotizing this job too. But the panels would have to be presented to the robot's clutching hands exactly the same way every time, and the machinery to accomplish this was judged prohibitively expensive. Similar problems of recognition, orientation, and alignment are the basic technical barriers everywhere to the extension of soft automation. In principle, for example, body measurements and style and fabric preferences could be fed into a computer that could then proceed to control the cutting of cloth for "tailor-made" garmens on a volume basis. But no one yet knows how to design a machine that can replace the seamstress, who takes these variable and flexible pieces of cloth, aligns the seams, and stitches them all together.

So, along with hands and versatility, tomorrow's machine should ideally have vision, hearing, and sufficient "intelligence" to act on what it sees or hears. In some respects the progress toward this goal has already been remarkable. In Stanford's mechanical-hand experiment, for example, the machine was programmed to understand a number of spoken commands, recognize simple objects, and carry out tasks that called for assembling these objects in various configurations.

Already, too, there are devices on sale that can read limited amounts of handwriting, or recognize and sort up to 2,000 different paperback books by the appearance of their covers. Other off-the-shelf computers can control machinery in response to spoken orders. Almost unobtrusively, all such machines are making inroads into the realm called "artificial intelligence," which was considered quite far-out only a decade or so ago.

The Stanford machine, a similar one at M.I.T., and the mobile robot Shakey, are actually all experiments in solving problems through the techniques of "scene analysis."

Scene analysis is an approach to what many scientists believe is an essential challenge in both human and machine intelligence: the ability to create some kind of internal representation or model of the real outside world. This model might take the form of recorded information that can be called up to generate a "mind's eye view" of what a machine has witnessed. It might be abstract generalization in the form of theories or mathematical equations. Or it might be simply a series of internal connections that respond to stimuli in mimicry of the conditioned reflexes in biological organisms. In any event, once this internal microcosm has been constructed, the brain or computer can perform "thought experiments" on the model and thereby predict the consequences of actions taken in the real world.

So far, it has required much dedicated programming effort and fairly large computers to arrive at the point where Shakey or the various mechanical hands can look at a pattern of light against dark, say, and decide whether the pattern represents a cube. Recognizing randomly shaped objects in the real clutter of a factory is a much more formidable task. Three-dimensional and color vision will certainly help, and these approaches are now being tried.

Learning How to Balance a Motorcycle

Other researchers are approaching the challenge of machine intelligence from a different direction, one that seems to correspond more nearly to the way that nature itself approached learning in biological evolution and also to the way that individual biological organisms learn. Called the "adaptive" or "goal-oriented" approach, it does not attempt to compute and store all the positions and interactions of all relevant objects and physical principles. Instead, it relies on relatively simple computer programs or even "self-programming" networks of computer-like logic circuits that simulate some of the functions of the neuron cells in biological brains.

Adaptronics, Inc., a tiny firm in McLean, Virginia, actually sells general-purpose "adaptable networks" that can learn to control industrial processes and even aircraft. They do this either by noting the reactions of an experienced human operator to changing circumstances or by performing small experimental movements of the controls to reach some optimum goal. Lewey O. Gilstrap Jr., executive vice president of Adaptronics, illustrates the difference between the adaptive technique and the computer-programmed technique by comparing the way each would handle the "motorcycle hippodrome problem," frequently given to students in mechanics courses.

The problem, essentially, is how to balance a motorcycle racing around the vertical walls of the "hippodromes" sometimes found at fair grounds. The computer-programming approach, says Gilstrap, would begin with writing a program that includes Newton's equations of motion, measurements of the radius of the hippodrome, and the speed and weight of the motorcycle. The necessary angle of bank of the cycle could then be computed. An adaptive control device would master the problem in the same way the motorcyclist does, simply by riding the machine around the hippodrome. What the rider does through constant experiments and adjustments is try to keep the influence of gravity and centrifugal force balanced out to zero.

In the long run the adaptive-control and computer-programming experiments may prove to be complementary. Each concerns a different aspect of the over-all problem of machine intelligence. Adherents to both views admit that any effective general-purpose robot might have to use both techniques, just as humans need both reflexes and analytical abilities to perform anything other than trivial tasks.

Few experts in the field would care to guess how close we are to the general-purpose robot that could handle jobs involving vision and judgment. Dr. Charles Rosen, staff scientist at Stanford Research Institute, believes that the time is now ripe to begin trying to apply artificial intelligence in robots to simple industrial problems. Nevertheless, he believes that real economic benefits from these techniques will have to wait for the perfection of a lot of computer programs and techniques. These things, he says, may take ten or twenty more years.

Gilstrap, however, is already willing to venture out on a limb. "Given the amount of money G.M. spends on a model change and a few years' time," he says, "I'm pretty sure we could design and build a robot that would understand spoken instructions and go about doing, say, most of the tasks in a household. And given a big enough market, the household robot could sell for between five and ten thousand dollars."

A Japanese Manipulator with TV Eyes

Some American researchers have been impressed and others downright puzzled by the Japanese infatuation for robots and artificial intelligence. In Japan robots are being sold or developed by some thirty-four companies, including two that have licenses from Unimation and Versatran. Hitachi, Ltd., has under development an "intelligent" manipulator with TV eyes that provide binocular vision. No American company is known to be doing such work. Dr. John McCarthy, who heads the Stanford Artificial Intelligence Project, recently paid a visit to Japanese laboratories and came back talking about the eagerness with which the work is pursued. "There is one important difference between their work and ours," observes McCarthy. "Ours is basic research and theirs is oriented toward industrially useful machines that can take over part of the assembly process."

It is possible, of course, that these eager Japanese companies will spend large sums and then find that the product has only a very limited commercial utility. The Japanese do not think so, however, and the point that comes across to foreign visitors is that Japanese industry is pursuing these exotic notions with some of the same outpourings of enthusiasm and money characteristic of the fruitful U.S. aerospace endeavor in the Fifties and early Sixties. In Japan, corporations function in a climate of "administrative guidance" from the government. At the government's discretion, companies engaged in expensive or risky research or development can borrow a great deal of long-term money from the Japan Development Bank. Many small high-technology firms carry debt levels six or seven times as high as invested capital. In assigning high priority to automation, the Japanese Government appears to have its eyes on various econometric models of the national economy that forecast manpower shortages in manufacturing of from four to eight million workers by 1975.

The Japanese remain eager to profit from U.S. technology in fields where Japan still lags. Teams of intent Japanese businessmen and engineers are almost monthly visitors at such leading technology research centers as the Battelle Memorial Institute and Stanford Research Institute. By now, furthermore, many an

American company has learned to its sorrow what it means to let the nose of the Japanese camel under the tent. Since 1950 the Japanese have spent some $2.5 billion for licenses to manufacture goods that were the fruit of expensive American R. and D. Many of the American licensors have discovered that for the mess of pottage thus obtained they had set up their most damaging competitor.

But as the robot research indicates, the Japanese are also proceeding to develop new technology of their own. For example, the Japanese Government has identified the electronic computer as "the pivotal strategic industry upon which future economic growth will largely depend." In 1966, chafing under the necessity of importing some 70 percent of its computers from the U.S., Japan launched a crash program to develop a "super high-performance electronic computer" and associated software that would rank with the biggest and best in the U.S. In doing so, the government divided the program into eight main tasks, each of which was assigned to a separate industry team, aided by government and university labs.

Who Will Pursue Production?

Just what should be done to remedy the failing position of the U.S. in the productivity sweepstakes is far from clear. According to capitalist doctrine, we should be able to assume that corporate enterprise will mend the gaps in competitiveness. From the record of ships, steel, textiles, and electronics—and now perhaps automobiles, as well—this has not been happening.

Until about World War II the primary sources of innovation in American production technology were private individuals or companies. But later, business began leaving the responsibility for increasing the state of the art of productivity more and more to the government—or to chance—and concentrating its innovative efforts upon the search for new consumer products.

This dependence upon government has been characteristic even of those industries whose business *was* production technology. The best example of this is the machine-tool industry. Numerical controls, which have been called the greatest advance in manufacturing since Henry Ford's assembly line, are a notable example. In 1952 the Air Force sponsored a contract with M.I.T.'s Servo-Mechanisms Laboratory to devise ways of controlling machine tools with punched tape. These techniques were subsequently perfected in a number of airframe companies building warplanes and missiles. Most of the other recent advances in machining, including electro-chemical machining, electrical-discharge machining, explosive forming, and the emergent adaptive control, have also been primarily responses to aerospace industry requirements and funding.

Similar government incentives led to the development of the first electronic computer, built near the end of World War II as a tool for making artillery calculations. The current technology of large-scale integrated circuits, which are bringing the cost of computers down at such a rapid rate, is largely the fruit of defense-space demand for compact computers in rockets and aircraft. Even the emerging techniques for using computers to achieve homeostasis in industrial processes had government origins in the space program.

It is not necessary to assert that spending on military or space R. and D. was either a particularly efficient or a particularly desirable way to improve productivity. The only point is that it did, and that the investment will certainly pay for itself many times over in contributions to the G.N.P. But in recent years the ground rules have begun to change in a number of important ways. Not only has there been the well-publicized over-all decline in government-funded R. and D., but there has been a much sharper decline in funds going into the kinds of high-technology activities that have led to higher productivity. Whereas military and space R. and D. amounted to 55.7 percent of the total in 1964, it now amounts to only 39 percent. The major increases have been in such realms as health, pollution, and education. Desirable as these may be, they are likely to yield relatively little spin-off that will improve productivity.

Some, to be sure, have taken comfort from the way companies have increased their own R. and D. recently, as the government level has declined. But according to a recent McGraw-Hill survey, some 88 percent of this industry effort is still being devoted to the old pursuit of new or improved products, not to better methods of making them.

A Choice of Incentives

Most of those who have considered the question of where new productivity will come from believe that some form of government action will be required. Some, like Dr. Myron Tribus, research-engineering vice president for Xerox, suggests that a special tax credit be enacted for industries that increase their R. and D. budgets to a specified percentage of sales, say 5 percent. Others would place the emphasis on results. Roger Bolz, president of the consulting firm Automation for Industry, advocates revising present tax laws to provide larger credits and depreciation write-offs to companies that invest in equipment yielding measurable improvements in productivity. "As things stand now, companies have little incentive to develop or buy technology that won't show a payoff within two or three years," says Bolz. "But the long-term economic well-being of the nation as a whole is far too important to leave to corporate decisions about short-term gain."

Dr. Robert U. Ayres, vice president of International Research & Technology Corp., a consulting firm, proposes that federal money simply be allocated to sponsoring R. and D. in small private firms. Even relatively small sums, he believes, could play a "pump-priming" role by reducing risk and thereby triggering bank loans to carry ideas through to development. Still others have discussed the equivalent of a national research-and-development institute to mine the multifold but now idle talents that were developed in past aerospace work.

Any course forceful enough to be effective is likely to encounter political objections. However laudable the motive, tax breaks or subsidies for business are not very popular in Congress this year. But the stakes on productivity involve far more than corporate interests. They underlie all the "quality of life" concerns of everyone in the U.S. as well.

Data Banks and Dossiers

Carl Kaysen

One of the first concrete moves toward creating a large computerized data network was a proposal that began to circulate around U.S. government departments in the mid-sixties. It envisioned a computerized national data center that would contain all the information about the American population known to any government agency. The ostensible purpose of the center was to produce fast and accurate statistical information for harried bureaucrats involved in planning national policies. But the proposal was no sooner aired than it was savagely attacked by civil libertarians, who saw in it thinly veiled threats to the privacy of every single American. The attacks eventually caused the idea to be dropped, to the dismay of many of its proponents. Here, Carl Kaysen, chairman of the commission that recommended the data center, and president of the Institute for Advanced Study in Princeton, defends its aims and intentions.

Both the intellectual development of economics and its practical success have depended greatly on the large body of statistical information, covering the whole range of economic activity, that is publicly available in modern, democratic states. Much of this material is the by-product of regulatory, administrative, and revenue-raising activities of government, and its public availability reflects the democratic ethos. In the United States there is also a central core of demographic, economic, and social information that is collected, organized, and published by the Census Bureau in response to both governmental and public demands for information, rather than simply as the reflex of other governmental activities. Over time, and especially in the last three or

379

four decades, there has been a continuing improvement in the coverage, consistency, and quality of these data. Such improvements have in great part resulted from the continuing efforts of social scientists and statisticians both within and outside the government. Without these improvements in the stock of basic quantitative information, our recent success in the application of sophisticated economic analyses to problems of public policy would have been impossible. Thus, the formation last year of a consulting committee composed largely of economists to report to the Director of the Budget—himself an economist of distinction—on "Storage of and Access to Federal Statistical Data" was simply another natural step in a continuing process. The participants were moved by professional concern for the quality and usability of the enormous body of government data to take on what they thought to be a necessary, important, and totally unglamorous task. They certainly did not expect it to be controversial.

The central problem to which the group addressed itself was the consequences of the trend toward increasing decentralization in the Federal statistical system at a time when the demand for more and more detailed quantitative information was growing rapidly. Currently, twenty-one agencies of government have significant statistical programs. The largest of these—the Census, the Bureau of Labor Statistics, the Statistical Reporting Service, and the Economic Research Service of the Department of Agriculture—account for about 60 percent of a total Federal statistical budget of nearly $125 millions. A decade ago, the largest four agencies accounted for 71 percent of a much smaller budget. By 1970, the total statistical budget of the Federal Government will probably exceed $200 millions and, in the absence of deliberate countervailing effort, decentralization will have further increased. Yet, it has already been clear for some time that the Federal statistical system was too decentralized to function effectively and efficiently.

The Drama Begins

Such is the background of the report which recommended the creation of a National Data Center. Here, Congressman Cornelius Gallagher (D., 13th District, N.J.) entered the scene, with a different set of concerns and objectives. He was Chairman of a Special Subcommittee on Invasion of Privacy, of the Government Operations Committee of the House, which held hearings on the proposed data center and related topics in the summer of 1966. To some extent the hearings themselves, and to a much greater extent their refraction in the press, pictured the proposed Data Center as at least a grave threat to personal privacy and at worst a precursor to a computer-managed totalitarian state. Congressman Gallagher himself saw the proposal as one more dreary instance of a group of technocrats ignoring human values in their pursuit of efficiency.

It now appears as if the public outcry which the Committee hearings stimulated and amplified has raised great difficulties in the way of the proposed National Data Center. To what extent are they genuine? To what extent are they unavoidable? Are they of such a magnitude as to outweigh the probable benefits of the Center?

In answering these questions, it appears simplest to begin with a further examination of the proposal itself. The inadequacies arising from our over-decentralized statistical system were recognized two decades ago; since then they have increased. The present system corresponds to an obsolete technology, under which publication was the only practical means of making information available for use. Publication, in turn, involved summarization, and what was published was almost always a summary of the more basic information available to the fact-gathering agency. In part, this reflected necessary and appropriate legal and customary restrictions on the Federal Government's publication of data on individuals or on single business enterprises. In part, it reflected the more fundamental fact that it was difficult or impossible to make use of a vast body of information unless it was presented in some summary form.

Any summarization or tabulation, however, loses some of the detail of the underlying data, and once a summary is published, retabulation of the original data becomes difficult and expensive. Because of the high degree of decentralization of the statistical system, it is frequently the case that information on related aspects of the same unit is collected by different agencies, tabulated and summarized on bases that are different and inconsistent, with a resultant loss of information originally available, and a serious degradation of the quality of analyses using the information. The split, on the one hand, between information on balance sheets and income statements, as collected by the Internal Revenue Service, and, on the other hand, the information on value of economic inputs and outputs as collected by the Census, is one example of this situation.

The result of all this is the substitution of worse for better information, less for more refined analysis, and the expenditure of much ingenuity and labor on the construction of rough estimates of magnitudes that could be precisely determined if all the information underlying summary tabulations were available for use. This, in turn, limits the precision of both the policy process, and our ability to understand, criticize and modify it.

These effects of the inability of the present system to use fully the micro-information fed into it are growing more and more important. The differentiation of the Federal policy process is increasing, and almost certainly will continue to do so. Simple policy measures whose effectiveness could be judged in terms of some overall aggregate or average response for the nation are increasingly giving way to more subtle ones, in which the effects on particular geographic areas, income groups, or social groups become of major interest. The present decentralized system is simply incapable of meeting these needs.

It is becoming increasingly difficult to make informed and intelligent policy decisions on such questions in the area of poverty as welfare payments, family allowances, and the like, simply because we lack sufficient "dis-aggregated" information—breakdowns by the many relevant social and economic variables—that is both wide in coverage and readily usable. The information the Government does have is scattered among a dozen agencies, collected on a variety of not necessarily consistent bases, and not really accessible to any single group of policy-makers or research analysts. A test of the proposition, for example, that poor performance in school and poor prospects of social mobility are directly related to family size would require data combining information on at least family size and composition, family income, regional location, city size, school performance, and post-school occupational history over a period of years in a way that is simply not now possible, even though the separate items of information were all fed into some part of the Federal statistical system at some time.

A secondary, but not unimportant gain from the creation of the data center, is in simple efficiency. At present, some of the individual data-collecting agencies operate at too small a scale to make full use of the resources of modern information-handling techniques. The use of a central storage and processing agency —while maintaining decentralized collection, analysis, and publication to whatever extent was desirable—would permit significant economies. As the Federal statistical budget climbs toward $200 million annually, this is not a trivial point. Even more important than prospective savings in money are prospective savings in the effort of information collection and the corresponding burdens on individuals, business, and other organizations in filling out forms and responding to questionnaires. As the demand for information grows, the need to minimize the costs in respondents' time and effort becomes more important. The present statistical system is only moderately well-adapted to this objective; a data center would make possible a much better performance on this score.

What It Is and Isn't

So much for the purpose of a data center; how would it function? First, it is important to point out that a data center is *not* the equivalent of single centralized statistical agency which takes over responsibility for the entire information-gathering, record-keeping, and analytical activity of the Federal government. Rather, it deals with only one of the three basic functions of the statistical system—integration and storage of information in accessible form—and leaves the other two—collection of information, and tabulation, analysis, and publication—in their present decentralized state. To be sure, if the Data Center is as efficient as some of its proponents expect, some redistribution of the last set of tasks between the agencies presently doing them and the Center would probably occur. This, however, would be the result of choice on the part of the using agencies, if they saw an opportunity to do a better and less costly job through the Center than they could do for themselves.

The crucial questions, of course, are (a) what information would be put into the data center, and (b) how would access to it be controlled? In the words of the Task Force Report, the "Center would assemble in a single facility all large-scale systematic bodies of demographic, economic and social data generated by the present data-collection or administrative processes of the Federal Government, . . . integrate the data to the maximum feasible extent, and in such a way as to preserve as much as possible of the original information content of the whole body of records, and provide ready access to the information, within the laws governing disclosure, to all users in the Government, and where appropriate to qualified users outside the Government on suitably compensatory terms."

The phrase "large scale systematic bodies of demographic economic and social data" translates, in more concrete terms, into the existing bodies of data collected by Census, the Bureau of Labor Statistics, the Department of Agriculture, the National Center for Health Statistics, the Office of Education, and so on. It also includes the large bodies of data generated as a by-product of the administration of the Federal income tax and the Social Security system. It does *not* include police dossiers from the FBI, personnel records of the Civil Service Commission or the individual government agencies, or personnel records of the armed services, and other dossier information, none of which fits what is meant by the phrase "large-scale, systematic bodies of social, economic, and demographic data."

For the data center to achieve its intended purposes, the material in it must identify respondents in some way, by Social Security number for individuals, or an analogous code number now used within the Census for business enterprises called the Alpha number. Without such identification, the Center cannot meet its prime purpose of integrating the data collected by various agencies into a single consistent body. Whether these Social Security or Alpha numbers need in turn to be keyed to a list of respondents which identifies them by name and address within the data center itself, or whether that need be done only within the actual data collecting agencies, is a technical detail. That it must be done someplace is perfectly clear, as it now is done within the several agencies that collect the information.

On the other hand, it is not in general necessary that the

central files in the data center contain a complete replica of every file on every respondent who has provided information to the original collectors. In many cases—e.g., the Social Security files—a properly designed sample would serve the same purposes more economically. To this extent, then, the data center will not contain a file on *every* individual, *every* household, *every* business, etc., but a mixture of a collection of samples—some of them relatively large—and complete files of some groups of reporting units which are particularly interesting and important from an analytical point of view. But here again, the significance of the difference between reproducing for the data center a complete file which already exists in some other agency, and reproducing only a sample therefrom, can easily be over-emphasized.

Anxieties

It is neither intemperate nor inappropriate to observe that the merits of the proposed data center have hardly been discussed in the tones that ordinarily mark consideration of a small change in government organization in behalf of greater effectiveness and efficiency. The anxieties stimulated by or crystallizing around the proposal can be divided into six groups: (1) the center will contain information that should not be in it; (2) the information can be improperly used by those within the government who have access to it; (3) the "bank" will be subject to cracking, so to speak, and data on individuals will be used to their detriment in any way from blackmail to gossip; (4) an enterprise of this sort is inherently expanding in nature, and no matter how modestly it begins, it will grow to include more and more, and eventually too much; (5) it both represents and encourages meddling and paternalistic government, trying to do too much in controlling the lives of its citizens; and (6) at a deeper level, it stands for a notion of an omniscient government, which is in some fundamental way inconsistent with our individualistic and democratic values. These categories are overlapping in part and hardly all on the same logical level of discourse, but they seem to contain broadly all the criticisms that have been made.

To what extent are these problems real and new; to what

extent are they simply translations into a new technical mode of familiar and persistent problems in the relation of citizens and government? And, if the latter, how well can variants of familiar mechanisms be adapted to deal with them? In what follows, I argue that while the fears raised by critics have real content, the problems are neither entirely novel, nor beyond the range of control by adaptations of present governmental mechanisms.

The first two questions go to the fundamental problem of government: *quis custodiet ipsos custodes?* The content of information now in the inventory of government agencies is controlled ultimately by the Congress, operating through the appropriations process; and more immediately by the separate bureaucratic hierarchies of each data collecting agency, subject to the overall review of the Director of the Budget. He has a specific statutory responsibility for reviewing all governmental questionnaires directed to the public, with a view to eliminating duplication and keeping the total burden on respondents at a reasonable level. If this process seems to be working ineffectively, in the sense of ignoring persistent complaints, then the Appropriations Subcommittees that deal with the budget requests of each data-collecting agency are readily able to exercise a further control. In practice, the existence of this restraint operates to reinforce powerfully the caution of the collecting agencies in expanding their requests.

A new data center would operate within the same framework of controls. Indeed, the Congress, in authorizing its creation, should define the kind of information which it would assemble, and could follow the line of demarcation of large-scale systematic demographic, economic, and social statistics suggested above. The inclusion of dossier information could be specifically prohibited. A clear distinction between a "dossier" and "statistical data file" on an individual can be made in principle; namely, for a dossier, the specific identity of the individual is central to its purpose; while for a file of data it is merely a technical convenience for assembling in the same file the connected set of characteristics which are the object of information. The purpose of the one is the assembly of information about specific people; the purpose of the other, the assembly of statistical frequency distributions of the many characteristics which groups of individuals (or households, business enterprises, or other reporting units) share. In practice, of course, this distinction is not self-applying, and administrators and bureaucrats, checked and overseen by politicians, have to apply it. But so is it ever.

A similar set of observations is relevant to the question of the control over the use of data in the center. The present law and practice governing the Census Bureau offer a model for this purpose. The law provides that information contained in an individual Census return may not be disclosed either to the general public or to other agencies of the government, nor may such information be used for law-enforcement, regulatory, or tax-collection activity in respect to any individual respondent. This statutory restriction has been effectively enforced, and the Census Bureau has maintained for years the confidence of respondents in its will and ability to protect the information they give to it. The same statutory restraint could and should be extended to the data center, and the same results could be expected of it. The data center would supply to all users, inside and outside the government, frequency distributions, summaries, analyses, but never data on individuals or other single reporting units. The technology of machine storage and processing would make it possible for these outputs to be tailored closely to the needs of individual users without great expense and without disclosure of individual data. This is just what is *not* possible under our present system.

Temptations

However, it may be argued that the greater richness of the data file on any single reporting unit in a new data center as compared with those presently existing in the Census, the Social Security Administration, the Internal Revenue Service, and elsewhere would greatly increase the temptation for those with legitimate access to the data to use it improperly. The same argument goes to the third point listed above—the "cracking" of the center by outsiders ranging from corrupt politicians to greedy businessmen and organized criminals. It is clearly the case that centralized storage in machine-readable form of large bodies of information makes the rewards of successful abuse or "penetration" relatively large—compared to what they would be in a more decentralized, less mechanized system. It is not at all clear, however, that the cost of successful misapplication or penetration cannot be increased even more sharply than the rewards. In detail this is a technical problem of great complexity, but it seems clear from experience with a variety of secrecy-preserving techniques that a well-designed system of record storage and use could make "penetration" highly costly and to a large extent self-announcing. It is not difficult, for example, so to organize and code the basic records that programs for retrieving information routinely record the user and the purpose for which it was used. Any continued improper use would thus leave a trail that would invite discovery. Or, to mention another aspect, identifying numbers could be specially coded, and the key to that code made available on a much more restricted basis than were other codes. While no security system can be made perfect, it is feasible to make the costs of breaking it sufficiently high so as to keep the problem within tolerable bounds. The same kinds of safeguards would prevent misuse of the data by those with legitimate access to it.

The last three kinds of objections are similar in that they reflect a certain stance toward the government, and toward the evolution of its role in the larger society, and are not tied to any specific concrete problems. Indeed, the concrete problems underlying these broader concerns are those already examined. How will the contents of the data bank be controlled? Who will determine to what uses it may be put? How can we prevent the stock of information from being abused, misused, or simply misappropriated? But there appears beyond these specifics an attitude hard to discuss because of its intangible nature.

On the broadest level, one can simply reject the notion that there is an ineluctable ever-expanding process of governmental "intrusion" which must be resisted at every turn, yet inevitably overcomes whatever resistance the public offers. After all, this is the stuff of right-wing ideology. Opposed to this is the pragmatic liberal view that the public calls in the government, with more or less deliberation, when there are social problems to be solved which require governmentally-organized efforts and legally-enforceable obligations for their solution. Indeed, many proponents of this view see the restraints on government action built into our political systems as too high, rather than too low, and action as typically too little and too late. On this view we have suffered more, at least in matters of domestic policy, from the feebleness of our government than from its overweening strength.

Without decisively choosing one over the other of these ideological stances, and with full recognition that a government too feeble for the welfare of its citizens in some matters may be too strong for their comfort or even their liberty in others, it is possible to believe, as I do, that the present balance of forces in our political machinery tends to the side of healthy restraint in matters such as these. After all, the very course of discussion on these problems, since the Center was first considered, supports this view. Accordingly, I conclude that the risky potentials which might be inherent in a data center are sufficiently unlikely to materialize so that they are outweighed, on balance, by the real improvement in understanding of our economic and social processes this enterprise would make possible, with all the concomitant gains in intelligent and effective public policy that such understanding could lead to.

The Wisdom of Man
and the Wisdom of God

Kenneth E. Boulding

On frequent occasions in the history of science advances in man's understanding of natural phenomena and his application of that understanding through technology have threatened the foundations of his religious beliefs. Automation and cybernation with their overtones of machine intelligence are no exception.

We live in an age of enormous and unprecedented change. This fact has been dinned into our ears to the point of boredom; yet it can hardly be repeated too often. If we are to survive as a human race, we must learn to ride this enormous hurricane of change which we have created and are still creating. In many areas of human knowledge and activity the change in the last fifty years has been as great as in all previous human history.

To put the matter even more dramatically, the date that divides many aspects of human history into two equal parts lies well within the lifetime of those now living. There are no signs, furthermore, that this rate of change is slowing down; indeed, if anything, it is speeding up, and the next fifty years are likely to see even greater changes than the last fifty years. This puts a strain of unusual magnitude on man as a person and on his social organization. Though his ability to meet the strain has increased greatly as a result of the very changes which are happening, one is tempted to view the present era as a neck-and-neck race between increase in strain and increase in ability to cope with it.

If the strain on us increases faster than our ability to cope with it, we may be in a bad way. If, however, our ability to cope increases fast enough, we may get over this transition and enter into a future which it is not absurd to describe as glorious, a future indeed which has been foreseen, however dimly, by saints, sages, and prophets in many times and places. This image of a glorious future, and indeed a glorious future for man here on earth, has been particularly important in the Biblical tradition. From Judaism on into Christianity it has carried over into the modern secular idea of progress on both sides of the Iron Curtain.

All change is fundamentally a change in the system of information and knowledge. This is one of the great generalizations which is finally emerging from the whole study of the evolution of the universe. This is because matter and energy, taken together, are conserved; that is, if there is more in one place or in one system, there must be less in another. They are subject to the inexorable iron law of exchange, in which things are transferred and shuffled around, but not created. There is no similar law of the conservation of information and knowledge, even though there may be ultimate limitations on its growth. In exchange, what one gets, the other gives up. However, when a teacher teaches a class, the class knows more at the end of the hour and the teacher knows more too. The knowledge possessed by the transmitter is not lost in transmission. It is lost only by aging and death. The very act of printing disseminates information without appreciable loss of the structure contained in the type, at least in the short run. We now know that the gene acts as a printer, that it imprints its own pattern on the matter around it, and hence is able to multiply its own structure many billion times.

In the beginning, indeed, is always the Word. The seed of anything, of a man, of a nation, of a church, of a society, or of a whole new world, is always a body of coded information. The modern view of the world, therefore, is very different from that of the crude materialism of the nineteenth century. In the great vision of the universe which the last three hundred years has opened up to us, we detect in the whole evolutionary process, from the very formation of the elements themselves, the building up of more and more complex structures of knowledge. One stands finally in awe of the ultimate supremacy of Spirit.

Ethics and Religion

One of the most interesting and at the same time most difficult questions regarding the developed society or the spaceship Earth is the nature of the ethical and religious systems which will be compatible with such a very different order of human life and society. Man's existing ethical and religious systems were developed for the most part in what might be called the age of civilization. We might almost call this the Biblical Age, for the Bible is perhaps its greatest and most representative work. Nevertheless, the Bible, though it is a product of the age of civiliza-

392 / The World of the Computer

tion, clearly looks beyond it. It is a work of prophecy as well as of history. The prophetic vision, both of the Old and of the New Testaments, looks forward to a Messianic age in which the promise that is implicit in the very nature of man is to be fulfilled. This surely is at least one interpretation of the idea of the Covenant which is so fundamental to the Old Testament, that man had in himself a promise which he is destined one day to redeem. In the New Testament, this takes perhaps a more eschatological form; nevertheless, the hope of a Messianic age in the future is continued in the Christian doctrine of a Second Coming.

Furthermore, the Biblical ethic, especially of the New Testament, is more appropriate to the developed society than to the age of civilization. In the age of civilization in which war is a normal state of man, in which the threat system dominates human relations, and in which whatever order there is is maintained precariously by the legitimizing of violence, the ethic of the Sermon on the Mount has remained a counsel of perfection, to be followed only by the specialized religious orders or the separated sect. In the spaceship Earth, we had better learn to love our enemies, or we will destroy each other. Indeed, we had better learn to love ourselves, and our neighbors as ourselves; otherwise, again, we will destroy ourselves, either through conflict or through sheer boredom and ennui. We will have to learn to be poor, or at least parsimonious, in spirit, even in the midst of material affluence. We will have to learn how to mourn, or we will be gobbled up in egotism and pride. We will have to learn how to be meek, or we won't inherit the earth at all. We will have to learn how to hunger and thirst after righteousness, for there will be no effective sanctions. We will have to learn how to be merciful, for we all have to live at each other's mercy. We will have to learn how to be pure in heart, or the corruption of affluence will engulf us. We will even perhaps have to learn how to be persecuted if we are to maintain creatively the kind of tensions which will be necessary if the world is simply not to go to sleep. Tennyson's vision of the time when "the kindly earth shall slumber, lapped in universal law," represents not so much a utopia as a very real danger; and the problem of how to maintain conflict creatively without allowing it to destroy us may be perhaps the most crucial issue facing mankind a thousand years from now.

One of the acute problems which is already beginning to face us is the removal of sanctions for what in the past age has been regarded as sin. Many of the ethical problems of the present period of transition arise out of this. In the developed society or even in the present transitional state, we can already perceive a situation in which we can indulge in lechery without fear of physiological consequences, either in pregnancy or disease; we can indulge in gluttony without getting fat (no-calorie food must be just around the corner) and in drunkenness without getting any hangovers; in avarice without restricting our consumption; in sloth without getting poor; in anger without getting into trouble. There will be no occasion for envy, when everyone can get all he wants; and the whole system, of course, will be able to indulge in pride without even a fall. The fear of earthly consequences, therefore, largely disappears as a motivation towards what has hitherto been regarded as virtue. In the developed society it is the pure heart or nothing.

Ecumenicity and Ecology

Another of the ethical consequences of the spaceship society will be the development of an ethic of extreme conservation to support the material parsimony which we have already seen will be necessary. The historical bases for this are more likely to be found in Eastern religions than in the Judeo-Christian tradition, and it may be precisely at this point that ecumenicity must lead us beyond the stream of history in which we in the West have grown up, and should lead to a genuine dialogue with the religions of South and East Asia. It may be that India, for instance, had to adjust to a highly conservationist economy before the West had to do it, simply because the West was always more expansionist geographically and hence could preserve the illusion of the illimitable plane for a longer period. There is a paradox here, in that the scientific revolution could probably have taken place only in the West, precisely because of the Western expansionism and aggressiveness and the concept of man as the conqueror of nature. The East has never had any illusions about being able to conquer nature, and has always regarded man as living in a somewhat precarious position, as a guest of doubtful welcome, shall we say, in the great household of the natural world.

In the West, our desire to conquer nature often means simply that we diminish the probability of small inconveniences at the cost of increasing the probability of very large disasters. We see this, for instance, in flood control, where the army engineers with their ideology of "conquering" the river actually build up the probability of major disasters, and we see this also in national defense, where we obtain a temporary security at the cost of inevitable long run disaster. Western man, therefore, must learn to live within nature as a member of a great ecological system, and not as a conqueror. Perhaps we can say in the words of St. Paul that we must become "more than conquerors"; man must learn not to enslave the natural order to his own will and his own whims, but to love the natural order and to find his place in it as one member of a great family. This idea, perhaps, is a little uncomfortable in the Judeo-Christian tradition, where God often is set sharply off against nature. Nevertheless, we now live in an age of inevitable contact and cross-fertilization of religious ideas in the whole world, and if we are to move successfully towards a spaceship society, then the Judeo-Christian tradition must learn from the other great tradition of mankind, of South and East Asia, and must learn to develop an ethic of conservation rather than of conquest.

Automation and Cybernation

A problem that weighs heavily on many minds in the more developed countries is that of cybernation and automation. There are a good many prophets of doom who see in this development a profound change, perhaps for the worse; who fear enormous unemployment; who see man beset with leisure on his hands which he will not be able to use productively; who see him enslaved to an enormous and complicated machine, the workings of which he does not understand, and which may break down in utter disaster.

These forebodings are not to be dismissed lightly. Nevertheless, much that has been written on this subject is exaggerated, and fails to place the development of cybernation and automation in the setting of a long process of technical change and growth in knowledge. Cybernetics is derived from the Greek word for steermanship; it refers to the development of systems which are self-regulating and goal-seeking. Such systems are very old; indeed it is this quality which more than any other distinguishes life from inanimate matter, so that in biological evolution, systems of this kind were invented eons ago. Even the most primitive human societies have possessed certain social mechanisms for dealing with environmental change and preserving an internal environment which was more stable than the external environment. The escapement mechanism of a medieval clock, the governor of the eighteenth century steam engine, the pianola roll in the Victorian player piano, the early twentieth century thermostat, are all examples of cybernetic mechanisms.

Cybernation is not something, therefore, which has burst upon us unannounced. It has to be seen as an integral part of a long process of technological change, originating far in the past and continuing far into the future. Neverless, it is true that it is only within the last twenty years that the theory of cybernetic systems has been worked out explicitly and that they have been applied to a very large range of mechanical operations, replacing and supplementing the biological cybernetic operations involved in mechanical and manual human skill, or even the more routine and mechanical operations of human intelligence. The impact of these changes has been felt mainly in manufacturing and white collar industries. There is no evidence, however, that this has produced an abnormally large rate of increase of overall productivity of labor, even though there are some spectacular special cases. The operations which are most affected by rapid technological change represent a relatively small segment of developed economies such as the United States, and the more development there is indeed, the smaller the rapidly developing sectors of the economy tend to become, and the larger the relatively stagnant sectors.

The Obsolescence of Man

Arthur C. Clarke

The amazing rate at which computers have developed over the past quarter-century—from sophisticated adding machines to systems that possess at least rudimentary intelligence —has inevitably caused the philosophers of science to rethink man's own role in the world. In the view of Arthur Clarke, one of the world's foremost writers of science fact and science fiction, such introversion may lead to a chilling discovery: that man is really no more than a stepping stone in evolution, a staging post on the route to a brave new world dominated by intelligent machines. Eventually, Clarke suggests, man may end up as a pampered specimen in some biological museum.

About a million years ago, an unprepossessing primate discovered that his forelimbs could be used for other purposes besides locomotion. Objects like sticks and stones could be grasped—and, once grasped, were useful for killing game, digging up roots, defending or attacking, and a hundred other jobs. On the third planet of the Sun, tools had appeared; and the place would never be the same again.

The first users of tools were *not* men—a fact appreciated only in the last year or two—but prehuman anthropoids; and by their discovery they doomed themselves. For even the most primitive of tools, such as a naturally pointed stone that happens to fit the hand, provides a tremendous physical and mental stimulus to the user. He has to walk erect; he no longer needs huge canine teeth—since sharp flints can do a better job—and he must develop manual dexterity of a high order. These are the specifications of Homo sapiens; as soon as they start to be filled, all earlier models are headed for rapid obsolescence. To quote Professor Sherwood Washburn of the University of California's anthropology department: "It was the success of the simplest tools that started the whole trend of human evolution and led to the civilization of today."

Note that phrase—"the whole trend of human evolution." The old idea that man invented tools is therefore a misleading half-truth; it would be more accurate to say that *tools invented man*. They were very primitive tools, in the hands of creatures who were little more than apes. Yet they led to us—and to the eventual extinction of the ape-men who first wielded them.

Now the cycle is about to begin again; but neither history nor prehistory ever exactly repeats itself, and this time there will be a fascinating twist in the plot. The tools the ape-men invented caused them to evolve into their successor, Homo sapiens. The tool we have invented *is* our successor. Biological evolution has given way to a far more rapid process—technological evolution. To put it bluntly and brutally, the machine is going to take over.

This, of course, is hardly an original idea. That the creations of man's brain might one day threaten and perhaps destroy him is such a tired old *cliché* that no self-respecting science-fiction writer would dare to use it. It goes back, through Čapek's *R.U.R.*, Samuel Butler's *Erewhon*, Mary Shelley's *Frankenstein*, and the Faust legend to the mysterious but perhaps not wholly mythical figure of Daedalus, King Minos' one-man office of scientific research. For at least three thousand years, therefore, a vocal minority of mankind has had grave doubts about the ultimate outcome of technology. From the self-centered human point of view, these doubts are justified. But that, I submit, will not be the only—or even the most important—point of view for much longer.

When the first large-scale electronic computers appeared some fifteen years ago, they were promptly nicknamed "Giant Brains" —and the scientific community, as a whole, took a poor view of the designation. But the scientists objected to the wrong word. The electronic computers were not *giant* brains; they were dwarf brains, and they still are, though they have grown a hundredfold within less than one generation of mankind. Yet even in their present flint-ax stage of evolution, they have done things which not long ago almost everyone would have claimed to be impossible—such as translating from one language to another, composing music, and playing a fair game of chess. And much more important than any of these infant *jeux d'esprit* is the fact that they have breached the barrier between brain and machine.

This is one of the greatest—and perhaps one of the last—breakthroughs in the history of human thought, like the discovery that the Earth moves round the Sun, or that man is part of the animal kingdom, or that $E = mc^2$. All these ideas took time to sink in, and were frantically denied when first put forward. In the same way it will take a little while for men to realize that machines can not only think, but may one day think them off the face of the Earth.

At this point you may reasonably ask: "Yes—but what do you mean by *think*?" I propose to sidestep that question, using a neat device for which I am indebted to the English mathematician A. M. Turing. Turing imagined a game played by two teleprinter operations in separate rooms—this impersonal link being used to remove all clues given by voice, appearance, and so forth. Suppose one operator was able to ask the other any questions he wished, and the other had to make suitable replies. If, after some hours or days of this conversation, the questioner could not decide whether his telegraphic acquaintance was human or purely mechanical, then he could hardly deny that he/it was capable of thought. An electronic brain that passed this test would, surely, have to be regarded as an intelligent entity. Anyone who argued otherwise would merely prove that he was less intelligent than the machine; he would be a splitter of nonexistent hairs, like the scholar who proved that the *Odyssey* was not written by Homer, but by another man of the same name.

We are still decades—but not centuries—from building such a machine, yet already we are sure that it could be done. If Turing's experiment is never carried out, it will merely be because the intelligent machines of the future will have better things to do with their time than conduct extended conversations with men. I often talk with my dog, but I don't keep it up for long.

The fact that the great computers of today are still high-speed morons, capable of doing nothing beyond the scope of the instructions carefully programmed into them, has given many people a spurious sense of security. No machine, they argue, can possibly be more intelligent than its makers—the men who designed it, and planned its functions. It may be a million times faster in operation, but that is quite irrelevant. Anything and everything that an electronic brain can do must also be within the scope of a human brain, if it had sufficient time and patience. Above all, it is maintained, no machine can show originality or creative power or the other attributes which are fondly labeled "human."

The argument is wholly fallacious; those who still bring it forth are like the buggy-whip makers who used to poke fun at stranded Model T's. Even if it were true, it could give no comfort, as a careful reading of these remarks by Dr. Norbert Wiener will show:

> This attitude (the assumption that machines cannot possess any degree of originality) in my opinion should be rejected entirely. . . . It is my thesis that machines can and do transcend some of the limitations of their designers. . . . It may well be that in principle we cannot make any machine, the elements of whose behaviour we cannot comprehend sooner or later. This does not mean in any way that we shall be able to comprehend them in substantially less time than the operation of the machine, nor even within any given number of years or generations. . . . This means that though they are theoretically subject to human criticism, such criticism may be ineffective until a time long after it is relevant.

In other words, even machines *less* intelligent than men might escape from our control by sheer speed of operation. And in fact, there is every reason to suppose that machines will become much more intelligent than their builders, as well as incomparably faster.

There are still a few authorities who refuse to grant any degree of intelligence to machines, now or in the future. This attitude shows a striking parallel to that adopted by the chemists of the early nineteenth century. It was known then that all

living organisms are formed from a few common elements—
mostly carbon, hydrogen, oxygen, and nitrogen—but it was
firmly believed that the materials of life could not be made from
"mere" chemicals alone. There must be some other ingredient—
some essence or vital principle, forever unknowable to man. No
chemist could ever take carbon, hydrogen, and so forth and
combine them to form any of the substances upon which life
was based. There was an impassable barrier between the worlds
of "inorganic" and "organic" chemistry.

This *mystique* was destroyed in 1828, when Wöhler synthe-
sized urea, and showed that there was no difference at all
between the chemical reactions taking place in the body, and
those taking place inside a retort. It was a terrible shock to those
pious souls who believed that the mechanics of life must always
be beyond human understanding or imitation. Many people are
equally shocked today by the suggestion that machines can
think, but their dislike of the situation will not alter it in the
least.

Since this is not a treatise on computer design, you will not
expect me to explain how to build a thinking machine. In fact,
it is doubtful if any human being will ever be able to do this in
detail, but one can indicate the sequence of events that will lead
from H. sapiens to M. sapiens. The first two or three steps on
the road have already been taken; machines now exist that can
learn by experience, profiting from their mistakes and—unlike
human beings—never repeating them. Machines have been built
which do not sit passively waiting for instructions, but which
explore the world around them in a manner which can only be
called inquisitive. Others look for proofs of theorems in mathematics or logic, and sometimes come up with surprising solutions that had never occurred to their makers.

These faint glimmerings of original intelligence are confined
at the moment to a few laboratory models; they are wholly lacking in the giant computers that can now be bought by anyone
who happens to have a few hundred thousand dollars to spare.
But machine intelligence will grow, and it will start to range
beyond the bounds of human thought as soon as the second
generation of computers appears—the generation that has been
designed, not by men, but by other, "almost intelligent" com-

puters. And not only designed, but also built—for they will have far too many components for manual assembly.

It is even possible that the first genuine thinking machines may be *grown* rather than constructed; already some crude but very stimulating experiments have been carried out along these lines. Several artificial organisms have been built which are capable of rewiring themselves to adapt to changing circumstances. Beyond this there is the possibility of computers which will start from relatively simple beginnings, be programmed to aim at specific goals, and search for them by constructing their own circuits, perhaps by growing networks of threads in a conducting medium. Such a growth may be no more than a mechanical analogy of what happens to every one of us in the first nine months of our existence.

All speculations about intelligent machines are inevitably conditioned—indeed, inspired—by our knowledge of the human brain, the only thinking device currently on the market. No one, of course, pretends to understand the full workings of the brain, or expects that such knowledge will be available in any foreseeable future. (It is a nice philosophical point as to whether the brain can ever, even in principle, understand itself.) But we do know enough about its physical structure to draw many conclusions about the limitations of "brains"—whether organic or inorganic.

There are approximately ten billion separate switches— or neurons—inside your skull, "wired" together in circuits of unimaginable complexity. Ten billion is such a large number that, until recently, it could be used as an argument against the achievement of mechanical intelligence. About twenty years ago a famous neurophysiologist made a statement (still produced like some protective incantation by the advocates of cerebral supremacy) to the effect that an electronic model of the human brain would have to be as large as the Empire State Building, and would need Niagara Falls to keep it cool when it was running.

This must now be classed with such interesting pronouncements as, "No heavier than air machine will ever be able to fly." For the calculation was made in the days of the vacuum tube (remember it?), and the transistor has now completely altered the picture. Indeed—such is the rate of technological progress today—the transistor itself is being replaced by still smaller and faster devices, based upon abstruse principles of quantum physics. If the problem was merely one of space, today's electronic techniques would allow us to pack a computer as complex as the human brain on to a single floor of the Empire State Building.

Interlude for agonizing reappraisal. It's a tough job keeping up with science, and since I wrote that last paragraph the Marquardt Corporation's Astro Division has announced a new memory device which could store inside a six-foot cube *all information recorded during the last 10,000 years.* This means, of course, not only every book ever printed, but *everything* ever written in *any* language on paper, papyrus, parchment, or stone. It represents a capacity untold millions of times greater than that of a single human memory, and though there is a mighty gulf between merely storing information and thinking creatively —the Library of Congress has never written a book—it does indicate that mechanical brains of enormous power could be quite small in physical size.

This should not surprise anyone who remembers how radios have shrunk from the bulky cabinet models of the thirties to the vest-pocket (yet much more sophisticated) transistor sets of today. And the shrinkage is just gaining momentum, if I may employ such a mind-boggling phrase. Radio receivers the size of lumps of sugar have now been built; before long, they will be the size not of lumps but of grains, for the slogan of the microminiaturization experts is "If you can see it, it's too big."

Just to prove that I am not exaggerating, here are some statistics you can use on the next hi-fi fanatic who takes you on a tour of his wall-to-wall installation. During the 1950's, the electronic engineers learned to pack up to a hundred thousand components into one cubic foot. (To give a basis of comparison, a good hi-fi set may contain two or three hundred components, a domestic radio about a hundred.) At the beginning of the 1960's, the attainable figure was about a million components per cubic foot; in the 70's, thanks to developments in solid-state engineering, it was heading for 100,000,000.

Fantastic though this last figure is, the human brain surpasses it by a thousandfold, packing its ten billion neurons into a *tenth* of a cubic foot. And although smallness is not necessarily a virtue, even this may be nowhere near the limit of possible compactness.

For the cells composing our brains are slow-acting, bulky, and wasteful of energy—compared with the scarcely more than atom-sized computer elements that are theoretically possible. The mathematician John von Neumann once calculated that electronic cells could be ten billion times more efficient than protoplasmic ones; already they are a million times swifter in operation, and speed can often be traded for size. If we take these ideas to their ultimate conclusion, it appears that a computer equivalent in power to one human brain need be no bigger than a matchbox.

This slightly shattering thought becomes more reasonable when we take a critical look at flesh and blood and bone as engineering materials. All living creatures are marvelous, but let us keep our sense of proportion. Perhaps the most wonderful thing about Life is that it works at all, when it has to employ such extraordinary materials, and has to tackle its problems in such roundabout ways.

As a perfect example of this, consider the eye. Suppose *you* were given the problem of designing a camera—for that, of course, is what the eye is—which *has to be constructed entirely of water and jelly*, without using a scrap of glass, metal, or plastic. Obviously, it can't be done.

You're quite right; the feat is impossible. The eye is an evolutionary miracle, but it's a lousy camera. You can prove this while you're reading the next sentence.

Here's a medium-length word:—photography. Close one eye and keep the other fixed—repeat, *fixed*—on that center "g." You may be surprised to discover that—unless you cheat by altering the direction of your gaze—you cannot see the whole word clearly. It fades out three or four letters to the right and left.

No camera ever built—even the cheapest—has as poor an optical performance as this. For color vision also, the human eye is nothing to boast about; it can operate only over a small band of the spectrum. To the worlds of the infrared and ultraviolet, visible to bees and other insects, it is completely blind.

We are not conscious of these limitations because we have grown up with them, and indeed if they were corrected the brain would be quite unable to handle the vastly increased flood of information. But let us not make a virtue of a necessity; if our eyes had the optical performance of even the cheapest miniature camera, we would live in an unimaginably richer and more colorful world.

These defects are due to the fact that precision scientific instruments simply cannot be manufactured from living materials. With the eye, the ear, the nose—indeed, all the sense organs—evolution has performed a truly incredible job against fantastic odds. But it will not be good enough for the future; indeed, it is not good enough for the present.

There are some senses that do not exist, that can probably never be provided by living structures, and that we need in a hurry. On this planet, to the best of our knowledge, no creature has ever developed organs that can detect radio waves or radioactivity. Though I would hate to lay down the law and claim that nowhere in the universe can there be organic Geiger counters or living TV sets, I think it highly improbable. There are some jobs that can be done only by vacuum tubes or magnetic fields or electron beams, and are therefore beyond the capability of purely organic structures.

There is another fundamental reason living machines such as you and I cannot hope to compete with nonliving ones. Quite apart from our poor materials, we are handicapped by one of the toughest engineering specifications ever issued. What sort of performance would you expect from a machine which has to grow several billionfold during the course of manufacture—and which has to be completely and continuously rebuilt, molecule by molecule, every few weeks? This is what happens to all of us, all the time; you are not the man you were last year, in the most literal sense of the expression.

Most of the energy and effort required to run the body goes into its perpetual tearing down and rebuilding—a cycle completed every few weeks. New York City, which is a very much simpler structure than a man, takes hundreds of times longer to remake itself. When one tries to picture the body's myriads of building contractors and utility companies all furiously at work, tearing up arteries and nerves and even bones, it is astonishing that there is any energy left over for the business of thinking.

Now I am perfectly well aware that many of the "limitations" and "defects" just mentioned are nothing of the sort, looked at from another point of view. Living creatures, because of their very nature, can evolve from simple to complex organisms. They may well be the only path by which intelligence can be attained, for it is a little difficult to see how a lifeless planet can progress directly from metal ores and mineral deposits to electronic computers by its own unaided efforts.

Though intelligence can arise only from life, it may then discard it. Perhaps at a later stage, as the mystics have suggested, it may also discard matter; but this leads us in realms of speculations which an unimaginative person like myself would prefer to avoid.

One often-stressed advantage of living creatures is that they are self-repairing and reproduce themselves with ease—indeed, with enthusiasm. This superiority over machines will be short-lived; the general principles underlying the construction of self-repairing and self-reproducing machines have already been worked out. There is, incidentally, something ironically appropriate in the fact that A. M. Turing, the brilliant mathematician who pioneered in this field and first indicated how thinking machines might be built, apparently committed suicide a few years after publishing his results.

The greatest single stimulus to the evolution of mechanical— as opposed to organic—intelligence is the challenge of space. Only a vanishingly small fraction of the universe is directly accessible to mankind, in the sense that we can live there without elaborate protection or mechanical aids. If we generously assume that humanity's potential *Lebensraum* extends from sea level to a height of three miles, over the whole Earth, that gives us a total of some half billion cubic miles. At first sight this is an impressive figure, especially when you remember that the entire human race could be packaged into a one-mile cube. But it is absolutely nothing, when set against Space with a capital "S." Our present telescopes, which are certainly not the last word on the subject, sweep a volume at least a million million million million million million million million million million times greater.

Though such a number is, of course, utterly beyond conception, it can be given a vivid meaning. If we reduced the known universe to the size of the Earth, then the portion in which *we* can live without space suits and pressure cabins is about the size of a single atom.

It is true that, one day, we are going to explore and colonize many other atoms in this Earth-sized volume, but it will be at the cost of tremendous technical efforts, for most of our energies will be devoted to protecting our frail and sensitive bodies against the extremes of temperature, pressure, or gravity found in space and on other worlds. Within very wide limits, machines are indifferent to these extremes. Even more important, they can wait patiently through the years and the centuries that will be needed for travel to the far reaches of the universe.

Creatures of flesh and blood such as ourselves can explore space and win control over infinitesimal fractions of it. But only creatures of metal and plastic can ever really conquer it, as indeed they have already started to do. The tiny brains of our Pioneers and Mariners barely hint at the mechanical intelligence that will one day be launched at the stars.

It may well be that only in space, confronted with environments fiercer and more complex than any to be found upon this planet, will intelligence be able to reach its fullest stature. Like other qualities, intelligence is developed by struggle and conflict; in the ages to come, the dullards may remain on placid Earth, and real genius will flourish only in space—the realm of the machine, not of flesh and blood.

A striking parallel to this situation can already be found on our planet. Some millions of years ago, the most intelligent of the mammals withdrew from the battle of the dry land and returned to their ancestral home, the sea. They are still there, with brains larger and potentially more powerful than ours. But (as far as we know) they do not use them; the static environment of the sea makes little call upon intelligence. The porpoises and whales, which might have been our equals and perhaps our superiors had they remained on land, now race in simpleminded and innocent ecstasy beside the new sea monsters carrying a hundred megatons of death. Perhaps they, not we, made the right choice; but it is too late to join them now.

If you have followed me so far, the protoplasmic computer inside your skull should now be programmed to accept the idea —at least for the sake of argument—that machines can be both more intelligent and more versatile than men, and may well be so in the very near future. So it is time to face the question: Where does that leave man?

I suspect that this is not a question of very great importance —except, of course, to man. Perhaps the Neanderthalers made similar plaintive noises, around 100,000 B.C., when H. sapiens appeared on the scene, with his ugly vertical forehead and ridiculous protruding chin. Any Paleolithic philosopher who gave his colleagues the right answer would probably have ended up in the cooking pot; I am prepared to take that risk.

The short-term answer may indeed be cheerful rather than depressing. There may be a brief golden age when men will glory in the power and range of their new partners. Barring war, this age lies directly ahead of us. As Dr. Simon Ramo put it recently: "The extension of the human intellect by electronics will become our greatest occupation within a decade." That is undoubtedly true, if we bear in mind that at a somewhat later date the word "extension" may be replaced by "extinction."

One of the ways in which thinking machines will be able to help us is by taking over the humbler tasks of life, leaving the human brain free to concentrate on higher things. (Not, of course, that this is any guarantee that it will do so.) For a few generations, perhaps, every man will go through life with an electronic companion, which may be no bigger than today's transistor radios. It will "grow up" with him from infancy, learning his habits, his business affairs, taking over all the minor chores like routine correspondence and income-tax returns and engagements. On occasion it could even take its master's place, keeping appointments he preferred to miss, and then reporting back in as much detail as he desired. It could substitute for him over the telephone so completely that no one would be able to tell whether man or machine was speaking; a century from now, Turing's "game" may be an integral part of our social lives, with complications and possibilities which I leave to the imagination.

You may remember that delightful robot, Robbie, from the movie *Forbidden Planet*. (One of the three or four movies so far made that anyone interested in science fiction can point to without blushing; the fact that the plot was Shakespeare's doubtless helped.) I submit, in all seriousness, that most of Robbie's abilities—together with those of a better known character, Jeeves—will one day be incorporated in a kind of electronic companion-secretary-valet. It will be much smaller and neater than the walking jukeboxes or mechanized suits of armor which Hollywood presents, with typical lack of imagination, when it wants to portray a robot. And it will be extremely talented, with quick-release connectors allowing it to be coupled to an unlimited variety of sense organs and limbs. It would, in fact, be a kind of general purpose, disembodied intelligence that could attach itself to whatever tools were needed for any particular occasion. One day it might be using microphones or electric typewriters or TV cameras; on another, automobiles or airplanes—or the bodies of men and animals.

And this is, perhaps, the moment to deal with a conception which many people find even more horrifying than the idea that machines will replace or supersede us. It is the idea that they may combine with us.

I do not know who first thought of this; probably the physicist J. D. Bernal, who in 1929 published an extraordinary book of scientific predictions called *The World, the Flesh and the Devil*. In this slim volume recently reprinted by the Indiana University Press, Bernal decided that the numerous limitations of the human body could be overcome only by the use of mechanical attachments or substitutes—until, eventually, all that might be left of man's original organic body would be the brain.

This idea is already far more plausible than when Bernal advanced it, for in the last few decades we have seen the development of mechanical hearts, kidneys, lungs, and other organs, and the wiring of electronic devices directly into the human nervous system.

Olaf Stapledon developed this theme in his wonderful history of the future, *Last and First Men*, imagining an age of immortal "giant brains," many yards across, living in beehive-shaped cells, sustained by pumps and chemical plants. Though completely immobile, their sense organs could be wherever they wished, so their center of awareness—or consciousness, if you like—could be anywhere on Earth or in the space above it. This is an important point which we—who carry our brains around in the same fragile structure as our eyes, ears, and other sense organs, often with disastrous results—may easily fail to appreciate. Given perfected telecommunications, a fixed brain is no handicap, but rather the reverse. Your present brain, totally imprisoned behind its walls of bone, communicates with the outer world and receives its impressions of it over the telephone wires of the central nervous system—wires varying in length from a fraction of an inch to several feet. *You would never know the difference if those "wires" were actually hundreds or thousands of miles long, or included mobile radio links, and your brain never moved at all.*

In a crude way—yet one that may accurately foreshadow the future—we have already extended our visual and tactile senses away from our bodies. The men who now work with radio isotopes, handling them with remotely controlled mechanical fingers and observing them by television, have achieved a partial separation between brain and sense organs. They are in one place; their minds effectively in another.

Recently the word "Cyborg" (cybernetic organism) has been coined to describe the machine-animal of the type we have been discussing. Doctors Manfred Clynes and Nathan Kline of Rockland State Hospital, Orangeburg, New York, who invented the name, define a Cyborg in these stirring words: "an exogenously extended organizational complex functioning as a homeostatic system." To translate, this means a body which has machines hitched to it, or built into it, to take over or modify some of its functions.

I suppose one could call a man in an iron lung a Cyborg, but the concept has far wider implications than this. One day we may be able to enter into temporary unions with any sufficiently sophisticated machines, thus being able not merely to control but to *become* a spaceship or a submarine or a TV network. This would give far more than purely intellectual satisfaction; the thrill that can be obtained from driving a racing car or flying an airplane may be only a pale ghost of the excitement our great-grandchildren may know, when the individual human consciousness is free to roam at will from machine to machine, through all the reaches of sea and sky and space.

But how long will this partnership last? Can the synthesis of man and machine ever be stable, or will the purely organic component become such a hindrance that it has to be discarded? If this eventually happens—and I have given good reasons for thinking that it must—we have nothing to regret, and certainly nothing to fear.

The popular idea, fostered by comic strips and the cheaper forms of science fiction, that intelligent machines must be malevolent entities hostile to man, is so absurd that it is hardly worth wasting energy to refute it. I am almost tempted to argue that only *un*intelligent machines can be malevolent; anyone who has tried to start a balky outboard will probably agree. Those who picture machines as active enemies are merely projecting their own aggressive instincts, inherited from the jungle, into a world where such things do not exist. The higher the intelligence, the greater the degree of cooperativeness. If there is ever a war between men and machines, it is easy to guess who will start it.

Yet however friendly and helpful the machines of the future may be, most people will feel that it is a rather bleak prospect for humanity if it ends up as a pampered specimen in some biological museum—even if that museum is the whole planet Earth. This, however, is an attitude I find impossible to share.

No individual exists forever; why should we expect our species to be immortal? Man, said Nietzsche, is a rope stretched between the animal and the superhuman—a rope across the abyss. That will be a noble purpose to have served.

IV

Computers and the
Intelligence Argument

Introduction to Section IV

"It is desirable to guard against the possibility of exaggerated ideas that might arise as to the powers of the Analytical Engine. In considering any new subject, there is frequently a tendency, first to *overrate* what we find to be already interesting or remarkable; and, secondly, by a sort of natural reaction, to *undervalue* the true state of the case, when we do discover that our notions have surpassed those that were really tenable.

"The Analytical Engine has no pretensions whatever to *originate* anything. It can do whatever we *know how to order it* to perform. It can *follow* analysis; but it has no power of *anticipating* any analytical relations or truths. Its province is to assist us in making *available* what we are already acquainted with."

Such was the comment of Ada Augusta, Countess of Lovelace, daughter of Byron, and a foremost interpreter of the work of Charles Babbage. A century later the controversy to which these words are directed is still very much with us. Many of today's experts in automation would agree wholeheartedly with Lady Lovelace that machines cannot—and never will be able to—achieve any task they are not programmed to carry out. Others believe that the computer has the potential, for better or worse, of rivaling and even surpassing human intelligence. The simple question "Can computers think?" is guaranteed to raise the temperature at any meeting of electronic engineers or philosophers.

There is, of course, plenty of evidence to support both sides in the controversy—those who argue that we will ultimately face the danger of being taken over by machines and those who

412

assert that computers will never really amount to much in terms of intelligence. On the one hand, computers can perform tasks totally beyond the capacities of man, such as guiding space flights to the moon (although it is worth mentioning that when the Apollo 13 moon craft met with disaster in April, 1970, the emergency return orbit suggested by astronaut John Swigert moments after the ship exploded turned out to be exactly the one calculated by NASA's computers minutes later), and can also carry out certain tasks in remarkably human fashion—M.I.T., for example, has a computer program that can perform a convincing psychiatric interview. On the other hand, computers have not lived up to the more optimistic forecasts of the early fifties. As yet no computer is in a position to make important management decisions, nor has any program emerged which can guarantee a machine victory over even an average chess player.

The crux of the controversy concerns the true meaning of the terms intelligence and thinking, in both the human and machine contexts. Thus, the first two articles of this section are devoted to exploring these definitions. Probably the most lucid exposition of the problem and its possible solution is that proposed by the late British mathematician Allan Turing. Turing argued that one way of determining whether or not computers are intelligent in human terms would be to discover whether or not it is possible to distinguish between a computer and a person simply by communicating with them, thus removing all the obvious sensory inputs which tell us whether we are communicating with a man or a machine. "We do not wish to penalize the machine for its inability to shine in beauty competitions," wrote Turing, "nor to penalize a man for losing in a race against an aeroplane. The conditions of our game make these disabilities irrelevant." To date, no computers exist that cannot be distinguished from humans in this fashion, but the possibility remains.

Another vital aspect of the problem of computer intelligence involves the question of originality in machines. On the one hand is the argument that machines can do only what they are programmed to do, and no more. On the other hand is the contention that computers can go far beyond their programmers' intentions, eventually becoming so intelligent that they may threaten to take over the world. Ulric Neisser's article advances a middle-of-the-road approach; machines can possess intelligence, he suggests, but not the specifically human form that involves motivation, emotion and an ability to consider a wide range of goals simultaneously. And in the final article of the section, Norbert Wiener speculates on the possibilities of cooperation betwen man and machine.

But whether machines think like man or in their own unemotional fashion, the question of their ability to rule those who once regarded them as servants is likely to remain, and the words of Samuel Butler are as pertinent today as when they were written a century ago. "There is no security against the ultimate development of mechanical consciousness in the face of machines possessing little consciousness now," he observed in the first version of *Erewhon*. "Reflect upon the extraordinary advance which machines have made during the last few hundred years, and note how slowly the animal and vegetable kingdoms are advancing. The more highly organized machines are creatures not so much of yesterday, as of the last five minutes, so to speak, in comparison with past time.

"Do not let me be misunderstood as living in fear of any actually existing machine; there is probably no known machine which is more than a prototype of future mechanical life. . . . What I fear is the extraordinary rapidity with which they are becoming something very different to what they are at present."

The Many Faces
of Intelligence

Donald G. Fink

Difficult as it may be to define what we mean by intelligence in man, it is even more so when we turn to artificial intelligence. Most of the definitions which use comparisons with human attributes are nebulous, to say the least. Here Donald Fink, a long-time technical journalist and officer of the Institute of Electrical and Electronic Engineers, argues that the basic criterion of machine intelligence is the ability to learn, as shown by the capabilities of organizing data and adapting to changes in the environment.

"Artificial Intelligence: (a) The ability of machines to organize information into meaningful patterns; ability to recognize, store, recall, and manipulate such patterns in playing games, solving problems, answering questions, etc., and in controlling the actions of other mechanisms; (b) the ability of a machine to adapt to its environment, particularly to respond to patterns of stimulation not explicitly foreseen in its design; (c) the observed performance of such machines, as measured by comparison with, or in competition against, human intelligence." We judge a man's intelligence by his words and deeds. The core of the argument for artificial intelligence lies in the fact that computer systems can be observed, by *their* words and deeds, to behave in similar ways. A machine can learn. It can respond (when programmed with sufficient sophistication) to a new situation. It can solve problems. It can direct conduct (as in

415

oil refineries and space explorations; all astronauts are guided in the first, critical miles of take-off by computers that observe and correct the trajectory of the space vehicle). It can even answer certain questions from standard intelligence tests. In these matters, the observed behavior of computers and men differ not in *kind,* but in *degree.*

Those who argue against the idea of artificial intelligence do not deny the validity of these observations of similar behavior. But they insist that the similarity is confined to the end results of problem solving; they question whether the methods of mind and machine can be compared at all. There is, they insist, a world of difference between the conscious striving of man's intellect and the blind mechanistic manipulation of symbols in a computer program. They point out that man must make the computer program and interpret the results. They agree that computers can be intellectual tools of great aid to the human mind. But that they have any standing as intelligent beings in themselves—that they can compete with the human mind on an equal footing—no. Even the apparently contrary evidence of the 7094 computer defeating champion Nealey is dismissed as not significant, because it took a very brilliant (and very patient) man to think out the program for checker-playing.

Dr. Samuel himself, while admitting that his program can consistently defeat his own mind in that game, insists that his computer could never out-think him in planning the grand strategy of the program itself. He feels that the programmer must always, inevitably, work with abstractions of greater power than those he puts into his program.

Certainly this qualification is true of his work, and of the work of every other contemporary master programmer. For each new routine mastered by a computer, however elaborate and powerful, a still more elaborate and powerful routine has been developed, and used, in the mind of man. Many, perhaps most, computer philosophers agree with Dr. Samuel that this must always be so.

But not all computer scientists agree. Several of the "positivists" point out that Dr. Samuel's own work has proved the superiority of a machine in the particular job it was programmed to do; and they ask why a computer cannot write its own program, using its own higher abstractions. Is there an intellectual revolution in the making? We can shed light on this question if we observe that it matters little that the programmer is (perhaps must be) ahead of his machine, so long as the machine is ahead of its user. The automobile is the creature of its designers in Detroit, but the housewife needs to know nothing about its design. She can use it to achieve feats of locomotion unattainable without it. That is an achievement of the Industrial Revolution.

In the same sense, checkers champion Nealey could use the 7094 computer to defeat human opponents whom he could not defeat himself (however unsportsmanlike this would be). In another sense, when Newell and Simon's logic theory program (to prove simple theorems of symbolic logic) was able, in fifty-two tries, to find even one proof shorter and more elegant than those given in the classic treatise *Principia Mathematica,* it scored a victory of competitive intelligence. Since brevity and elegance are points on which the tournaments of mathematics are scored, this isolated instance is a notable straw in the wind. These examples, and there are others, are the early achievements of the intellectual revolution.

Real versus Apparent Intelligence

Before we can define artificial intelligence, we must accept the fact that any workable definition will be written in terms of the machine's observed performance. Superficial observation in this field of inquiry, as in most others, can be highly misleading. So we must devise definitive tests that will help to distinguish between "real" intelligence and the "mere appearance" of intelligence.

Take, for example, the often-quoted definition: "Artificial intelligence: Behavior by machine that, if exhibited by a human, would be called intelligent." Without further qualification, this simple and attractive definition can lead to much confusion. If we did not know how the high-fidelity phonograph works we might think it intelligent because it exhibits a highly intelligent form of human behavior, the ability to speak meaningfully. But the phonograph, as we happen to know, merely reproduces the unalterable pattern of speech waveforms embedded in the grooves of its record. It is not designed to make any contribution whatever to the form or the content of its recorded message. Quite to the contrary, it is designed to avoid any such contribution; that is, to be as faithful as possible in reproducing its input data without change.

Such rote recitation, however "human" in form, can hardly qualify as intelligence. But if a phonograph existed that did make a significant contribution to its message (for example, if it was observed translating prose into poetry), we might feel that it deserved the approbation "creatively intelligent." Similarly, if we observed a machine translating Russian into English, we might be tempted to attribute "intelligence" to it. But we might be wrong, at least in certain respects that we shall consider later.

How, then, can we test a machine's intelligence? One approach is to provide some unanticipated variation in its input data, carefully contrived to reveal whether the machine can adapt, that is, whether it can *learn from its experience*. We take this italicized phrase from Webster's definition of natural intelligence and use it in constructing our definition of artificial intelligence.

We must, of course, be explicit about what we mean by "learn from experience" as applied to a machine. In learning, we human beings recognize and remember, through repeated exposure, patterns in our environment. We assign meanings to these patterns and organize them into new ones, having more comprehensive implications, by noting similarities and differences, accepting logical relations, rejecting illogical ones. In the end, by relying on logical organization and reorganization of generalized information patterns, we build a body of stored knowledge which we use in reasoning and acting.

Machine learning, however different in the detailed methods employed, is the same. A machine that possesses the ability to recognize, store, recall, and manipulate patterns of information and to organize and reorganize these patterns into new, more comprehensive, or more meaningful patterns is *by definition* a machine that learns from its environment.

The first key to testing for machine intelligence, then, is to test for ability to organize information. The phonograph will fail this test. It merely repeats information. Our program to compute π will fail it. All the organization is provided in the program; the 225 computer did not alter the program within itself. It was not *programmed* to learn.

Many computer programs, particularly those designed for playing games and solving problems, will pass the learning test. One of the surest clues appears when the machine is able to deal with patterns of input information (such as moves in checkers, instructions to prove theorems or to recognize pictures) which the programmer did not explicitly foresee. The machine with this ability must adapt its program to the specific patterns applied to it, within the more general framework of the problem area for which it is programmed. It must be able not only to organize data within itself but also to adapt to changes in its environment.

Computing Machinery and Intelligence

Allan M. Turing

Here is a detailed treatment of the question that lies at the very center of research into artificial intelligence: can machines think? The author, a brilliant British mathematician who met a tragic death at the age of forty-two, considers the multitude of objections that have been raised against the idea that machines can indulge in thought. In process, he destroys a number of preconceived ideas about human thought processes, and asks probing questions about what we humans are really doing when we exhibit our "intelligence."

1. The Imitation Game

I propose to consider the question, "Can machines think?" This should begin with definitions of the meaning of the terms "machine" and "think." Instead of attempting such a definition I shall replace the question by another, which is closely related to it and is expressed in relatively unambiguous words.

The new form of the problem can be described in terms of a game which we call the "imitation game." It is played with three people, a man (A), a woman (B), and an interrogator (C) who may be of either sex. The interrogator stays in a room apart from the other two. The object of the game for the interrogator is to determine which of the other two is the man and which is the woman. He knows them by labels X and Y, and at the end of the game he says either "X is A and Y is B" or "X is B and Y is A." The interrogator is allowed to put questions to A and B thus:

C: Will X please tell me the length of his or her hair?

Now suppose X is actually A, then A must answer. It is A's object in the game to try and cause C to make the wrong identification. His answer might therefore be:

"My hair is shingled, and the longest strands are about nine inches long."

In order that tones of voice may not help the interrogator the answers should be written, or better still, typewritten. The ideal arrangement is to have a teleprinter communicating between the two rooms. Alternatively the question and answers can be repeated by an intermediary. The object of the game for the third player (B) is to help the interrogator. The best strategy for her is probably to give truthful answers. She can add such things as "I am the woman, don't listen to him!" to her answers, but it will avail nothing as the man can make similar remarks.

We now ask the question, "What will happen when a machine takes the part of A in this game?" Will the interrogator decide wrongly as often when the game is played like this as he does when the game is played between a man and a woman? These questions replace our original, "Can machines think?"

2. Critique of the New Problem

The new problem has the advantage of drawing a fairly sharp line between the physical and the intellectual capacities of a man. No engineer or chemist claims to be able to produce a material which is indistinguishable from the human skin. It is possible that at some time this might be done, but even supposing this invention available we should feel there was little point in trying to make a "thinking machine" more human by dressing it up in such artificial flesh. The form in which we have set the problem reflects this fact in the condition which prevents the interrogator from seeing or touching the other competitors, or hearing their voices. Some other advantages of the proposed criterion may be shown up by specimen questions and answers. Thus:

Q: Please write me a sonnet on the subject of the Forth Bridge.
A: Count me out on this one. I never could write poetry.
Q: Add 34957 to 70764.
A: (Pause about 30 seconds and then give as answer) 105721.
Q: Do you play chess?
A: Yes.
Q: I have K at my K1, and no other pieces. You have only K at K6 and R at R1. It is your move. What do you play?
A: (After a pause of 15 seconds) R-R8 mate.

The question and answer method seems to be suitable for introducing almost any one of the fields of human endeavor that we wish to include. We do not wish to penalise the machine for its inability to shine in beauty competitions, nor to penalise a man for losing in a race against an aeroplane. The conditions of our game make these disabilities irrelevant. The "witnesses" can brag, if they consider it advisable, as much as they please about their charms, strength or heroism, but the interrogator cannot demand practical demonstrations.

The game may perhaps be criticised on the ground that the

odds are weighted too heavily against the machine. If the man were to try and pretend to be the machine he would clearly make a very poor showing. He would be given away at once by slowness and inaccuracy in arithmetic. May not machines carry out something which ought to be described as thinking but which is very different from what a man does? This objection is a very strong one, but at least we can say that if, nevertheless, a machine can be constructed to play the imitation game satisfactorily, we need not be troubled by this objection.

It might be urged that when playing the "imitation game" the best strategy for the machine may possibly be something other than imitation of the behaviour of a man. This may be, but I think it is unlikely that there is any great effect of this kind. In any case there is no intention to investigate here the theory of the game, and it will be assumed that the best strategy is to try to provide answers that would naturally be given by a man.

3. The Machines Concerned in the Game

The question which we put in § 1 will not be quite definite until we have specified what we mean by the word "machine." It is natural that we should wish to permit every kind of engineering technique to be used in our machines. We also wish to allow the possibility that an engineer or team of engineers may construct a machine which works, but whose manner of operation cannot be satisfactorily described by its constructors because they have applied a method which is largely experimental. This prompts us to abandon the requirement that every kind of technique should be permitted. We are the more ready to do so in view of the fact that the present interest in "thinking machines" has been aroused by a particular kind of machine, usually called an "electronic computer" or "digital computer." Following this suggestion we only permit digital computers to take part in our game.

This restriction appears at first sight to be a very drastic one. I shall attempt to show that it is not so in reality. It may also be said that this identification of machines with digital computers, like our criterion for "thinking," will only be unsatisfactory if (contrary to my belief), it turns out that digital computers are unable to give a good showing in the game.

There are already a number of digital computers in working order, and it may be asked, "Why not try the experiment straight away? It would be easy to satisfy the conditions of the game. A number of interrogators could be used, and statistics compiled to show how often the right identification was given." The short answer is that we are not asking whether all digital computers would do well in the game nor whether the computers at present available would do well, but whether there are imaginable computers which would do well. But this is only the short answer. We shall see this question in a different light later.

4. Digital Computers

The idea behind digital computers may be explained by saying that these machines are intended to carry out any operations which could be done by a human computer. The human computer is supposed to be following fixed rules; he has no authority to deviate from them in any detail. We may suppose that these rules are supplied in a book, which is altered whenever he is put on to a new job. He has also an unlimited supply of paper on which he does his calculations. He may also do his multiplications and additions on a "desk machine," but this is not important.

The idea of a digital computer is an old one. Charles Babbage, Lucasian Professor of Mathematics at Cambridge from 1828 to 1839, planned such a machine, called the Analytical Engine, but it was never completed. Although Babbage had all the essential ideas, his machine was not at that time such a very attractive prospect. The speed which would have been available would be definitely faster than a human computer but something like 100 times slower than the Manchester machine, itself one of the slower of the modern machines. The storage was to be purely mechanical, using wheels and cards.

The fact that Babbage's Analytical Engine was to be entirely mechanical will help us to rid ourselves of a superstition.

Importance is often attached to the fact that modern digital computers are electrical, and that the nervous system also is electrical. Since Babbage's machine was not electrical, and since all digital computers are in a sense equivalent, we see that this use of electricity cannot be of theoretical importance. Of course electricity usually comes in where fast signalling is concerned, so that it is not surprising that we find it in both these connections. In the nervous system chemical phenomena are at least as important as electrical. In certain computers the storage system is mainly acoustic. The feature of using electricity is thus seen to be only a very superficial similarity. If we wish to find such similarities we should look rather for mathematical analogies of function.

5. Contrary Views on the Main Question

We may now consider the ground to have been cleared and we are ready to proceed to the debate on our question, "Can machines think?" and on a variant of it: "Are there imaginable digital computers which would do well in the imitation game?" If we wish we can make this superficially more general and ask "Are there discrete-state machines which would do well?" We cannot altogether abandon the original form of the problem, for opinions will differ as to the appropriateness of the substitution and we must at least listen to what has to be said in this connexion.

It will simplify matters for the reader if I explain first my own beliefs in the matter. Consider first the more accurate form of the question. I believe that in about fifty years' time it will be possible to programme computers, with a storage capacity of about 10^9, to make them play the imitation game so well that an average interrogator will not have more than 70 per cent chance of making the right identification after five minutes of questioning. The original question, "Can machines think?" I believe to be too meaningless to deserve discussion. Nevertheless I believe that at the end of the century the use of words and general educated opinion will have altered so much that one will be able to speak of machines thinking without expecting to be contradicted. I believe further that no useful purpose is served by concealing these beliefs. The popular view that scientists proceed inexorably from well-established fact to well-established fact, never being influenced by any improved conjecture, is quite mistaken. Provided it is made clear which are proved facts and which are conjectures, no harm can result. Conjectures are of great importance since they suggest useful lines of research.

I now proceed to consider opinions opposed to my own.

(1) The Theological Objection

Thinking is a function of man's immortal soul. God has given an immortal soul to every man and woman, but not to any other animal or to machines. Hence no animal or machine can think.[1]

I am unable to accept any part of this, but will attempt to reply in theological terms. I should find the argument more convincing if animals were classed with men, for there is a greater difference, to my mind, between the typical animate and the inanimate than there is between man and the other animals. The arbitrary character of the orthodox view becomes clearer if we consider how it might appear to a member of some other religious community. How do Christians regard the Moslem view that women have no souls? But let us leave this point aside and return to the main argument. It appears to me that the argument quoted above implies a serious restriction of the omnipotence of the Almighty. In attempting to construct such machines we should not be irreverently usurping His power of creating souls, any more than we are in the procreation of children: rather we are, in either case, instruments of His will providing mansions for the souls that He creates.

However, this is mere speculation. I am not very impressed with theological arguments whatever they may be used to sup-

---

[1] Possibly this view is heretical. St. Thomas Aquinas [*Summa Theologica,* quoted by Bertrand Russell (1945, p. 458)] states that God cannot make a man to have no soul. But this may not be a real restriction on His powers, but only a result of the fact that men's souls are immortal, and therefore indestructible.

port. Such arguments have often been found unsatisfactory in the past. In the time of Galileo it was argued that the texts, "And the sun stood still . . . and hasted not to go down about a whole day" (Joshua x. 13) and "He laid the foundations of the earth, that it should not move at any time" (Psalm cv. 5) were an adequate refutation of the Copernican theory. With our present knowledge such an argument appears futile. When that knowledge was not available it made a quite different impression.

(2) The "Heads in the Sand" Objection

"The consequences of machines thinking would be too dreadful. Let us hope and believe that they cannot do so."

This argument is seldom expressed quite so openly as in the form above. But it affects most of us who think about it at all. We like to believe that Man is in some subtle way superior to the rest of creation. It is best if he can be shown to be *necessarily* superior, for then there is no danger of him losing his commanding position. The popularity of the theological argument is clearly connected with this feeling. It is likely to be quite strong in intellectual people, since they value the power of thinking more highly than others, and are more inclined to base their belief in the superiority of Man on this power.

I do not think that this argument is sufficiently substantial to require refutation. Consolation would be more appropriate: perhaps this should be sought in the transmigration of souls.

(3) The Mathematical Objection

There are a number of results of mathematical logic which can be used to show that there are limitations to the powers of discrete-state machines. The best known of these results is known as Gödel's theorem (1931) and shows that in any sufficiently powerful logical system statements can be formulated which can neither be proved nor disproved within the system, unless possibly the system itself is inconsistent. There are other, in some respects similar, results due to Church (1936), Kleene (1935), Rosser, and Turing (1937). The latter result is the most convenient to consider, since it refers directly to machines, whereas the others can only be used in a comparatively indirect argument. The result in question refers to a type of machine which is essentially a digital computer with an infinite capacity. It states that there are certain things that such a machine cannot do. If it is rigged up to give answers to questions as in the imitation game, there will be some questions to which it will either give a wrong answer, or fail to give an answer at all however much time is allowed for a reply. There may, of course, be many such questions, and questions which cannot be answered by one machine may be satisfactorily answered by another. We are of course supposing for the present that the questions are of the kind to which an answer "Yes" or "No" is appropriate, rather than questions such as "What do you think of Picasso?" The questions that we know the machines must fail on are of this type, "Consider the machine specified as follows. . . . Will this machine ever answer 'Yes' to any question?" The dots are to be replaced by a description of some machine in a standard form. When the machine described bears a certain comparatively simple relation to the machine which is under interrogation, it can be shown that the answer is either wrong or not forthcoming. This is the mathematical result: it is argued that it proves a disability of machines to which the human intellect is not subject.

The short answer to this argument is that although it is established that there are limitations to the powers of any particular machine, it has only been stated, without any sort of proof, that no such limitations apply to the human intellect.

(4) The Argument from Consciousness

This argument is very well expressed in Professor Jefferson's Lister Oration for 1949, from which I quote. "Not until a machine can write a sonnet or compose a concerto because of thoughts and emotions felt, and not by the chance fall of symbols, could we agree that machine equals brain—that is, not only write it but know that it had written it. No mechanism could feel (and not merely artificially signal, an easy contrivance) pleasure at its successes, grief when its valves fuse, be warmed by flattery, be made miserable by its mistakes, be charmed by sex, be angry or depressed when it cannot get what it wants."

This argument appears to be a denial of the validity of our test. According to the most extreme form of this view the only way by which one could be sure that a machine thinks is to *be* the machine and to feel oneself thinking. One could then describe these feelings to the world, but of course no one would be justified in taking any notice. Likewise according to this view the only way to know that a *man* thinks is to be that particular man. It is in fact the solipsist point of view. It may be the most logical view to hold but it makes communication of ideas difficult. A is liable to believe "A thinks but B does not" whilst B believes "B thinks but A does not." Instead of arguing continually over this point it is usual to have the polite convention that everyone thinks.

In short, then, I think that most who support the argument from consciousness could be persuaded to abandon it rather than be forced into the solipsist position. They will then probably be willing to accept our test.

I do not wish to give the impression that I think there is no mystery about consciousness. There is, for instance, something of a paradox connected with any attempt to localise it. But I do not think these mysteries necessarily need to be solved before we can answer the question with which we are concerned in this paper.

(5) Arguments from Various Disabilities

These arguments take the form, "I grant you that you can make machines do all the things you have mentioned but you will never be able to make one to do X." Numerous features X are suggested in this connexion. I offer a selection:

Be kind, resourceful, beautiful, friendly, have initiative, have a sense of humor, tell right from wrong, make mistakes, fall in love, enjoy strawberries and cream, make some one fall in love with it, learn from experience, use words properly, be the subject of its own thought, have as much diversity of behaviour as a man, do something really new.

No support is usually offered for these statements. I believe they are mostly founded on the principle of scientific induction. A man has seen thousands of machines in his lifetime. From what he sees of them he draws a number of general conclusions. They are ugly, each is designed for a very limited purpose, when required for a minutely different purpose they are useless, the variety of behaviour of any one of them is very small, etc., etc. Naturally he concludes that these are necessary properties of machines in general.

There are, however, special remarks to be made about many of the disabilities that have been mentioned. The inability to enjoy strawberries and cream may have struck the reader as frivolous. Possibly a machine might be made to enjoy this delicious dish, but any attempt to make one do so would be idiotic. What is important about this disability is that it contributes to some of the other disabilities, *e.g.,* to the difficulty of the same kind of friendliness occurring between man and machine as between white man and white man, or between black man and black man.

The claim that "machines cannot make mistakes" seems a curious one. One is tempted to retort, "Are they any the worse for that?" But let us adopt a more sympathetic attitude, and try to see what is really meant. I think this criticism can be explained in terms of the imitation game. It is claimed that the interrogator could distinguish the machine from the man simply by setting them a number of problems in arithmetic. The machine would be unmasked because of its deadly accuracy. The reply to this is simple. The machine (programmed for playing the game) would not attempt to give the *right* answers to the arithmetic problems. It would deliberately introduce mistakes in a manner calculated to confuse the interrogator. A mechanical fault would probably show itself through an unsuitable decision as to what sort of a mistake to make in the arithmetic. Even this interpretation of the criticism is not sufficiently sympathetic. But we cannot afford the space to go into it much further. It seems to me that this criticism depends on a confusion between two kinds of mistake. We may call them "errors of functioning" and "errors of conclusion." Errors of functioning are due to some mechanical or electrical fault which causes the machine to behave otherwise than it was designed to do. In philosophical discussions one likes to ignore the possibility of such errors; one is therefore discussing "abstract machines." These abstract machines are mathematical fictions rather than physical objects. By definition they are incapable of errors of functioning. In this sense we can truly say that "machines can never make mistakes." Errors of conclusion can only arise when some meaning is attached to the output signals from the machine. The machine might, for instance, type out mathematical equations, or sentences in English. When a false proposition is typed we say that the machine has committed an error of conclusion. There is clearly no reason at all for saying that a machine cannot make this kind of mistake. It might do nothing but type out repeatedly "0 = 1." To take a less perverse example, it might have some method for drawing conclusions by scientific induction. We must expect such a method to lead occasionally to erroneous results.

The claim that a machine cannot be the subject of its own thought can of course only be answered if it can be shown that the machine has *some* thought with *some* subject matter. Nevertheless, "the subject matter of a machine's operations" does seem to mean something, at least to the people who deal with it. If, for instance, the machine was trying to find a solution of the equation $x^2 - 40x - 11 = 0$ one would be tempted to describe this equation as part of the machine's subject matter at that moment. In this sort of sense a machine undoubtedly can be its own subject matter. It may be used to help in making up its own programmes, or to predict the effect of alterations in its own structure. By observing the results of its own behaviour it can modify its own programmes so as to achieve some purpose more effectively. These are possibilities of the near future, rather than Utopian dreams.

The criticisms that we are considering here are often disguised forms of the argument from consciousness. Usually if one maintains that a machine can do one of these things, and describes the kind of method that the machine could use, one will not make much of an impression. It is thought that the method (whatever it may be, for it must be mechanical) is really rather base.

(6) Lady Lovelace's Objection

Our most detailed information of Babbage's Analytical Engine comes from a memoir by Lady Lovelace (1842). In it she states, "The Analytical Engine has no pretensions to *originate* anything. It can do *whatever we know how to order it* to perform" (her italics). This statement is quoted by Hartree (1949) who adds: "This does not imply that it may not be possible to construct electronic equipment which will 'think for itself,' or in which, in biological terms, one could set up a conditioned reflex, which would serve as a basis for 'learning.' Whether this is possible in principle or not is a stimulating and exciting question, suggested by some of these recent developments. But it did not seem that the machines constructed or projected at the time had this property."

A variant of Lady Lovelace's objections states that a machine can "never do anything really new."

The view that machines cannot give rise to surprises is due, I believe, to a fallacy to which philosophers and mathematicians are particularly subject. This is the assumption that as soon as a fact is presented to a mind all consequences of that fact spring into the mind simultaneously with it. It is a very useful assumption under many circumstances, but one too easily forgets that it is false. A natural consequence of doing so is that one then assumes that there is no virtue in the mere working out of consequences from data and general principles.

(7) Argument from Continuity in the Nervous System

The nervous system is certainly not a discrete-state machine. A small error in the information about the size of a nervous impulse impinging on a neuron, may make a large difference to the size of the outgoing impulse. It may be argued that, this being so, one cannot expect to be able to mimic the behaviour of the nervous system with a discrete-state system.

It is true that a discrete-state machine must be different from a continuous machine. But if we adhere to the conditions of the imitation game, the interrogator will not be able to take any advantage of this difference. The situation can be made clearer if we consider some other simpler continuous machine. A differential analyser will do very well. (A differential analyser is a certain kind of machine not of the discrete-state type used for some kinds of calculation.) Some of these provide their answers in a typed form, and so are suitable for taking part in the game. It would not be possible for a digital computer to predict exactly what answers the differential analyser would give to a problem, but it would be quite capable of giving the right sort of answer.

(8) The Argument from Informality of Behavior

It is not possible to produce a set of rules purporting to describe what a man should do in every conceivable set of circumstances. One might for instance have a rule that one is to stop when one sees a red traffic light, and to go if one sees a green one, but what if by some fault both appear together? One may perhaps decide that it is safest to stop. But some further difficulty may well arise from this decision later. To attempt to provide rules of conduct to cover every eventuality, even those arising from traffic lights, appears to be impossible. With all this I agree.

From this it is argued that we cannot be machines. I shall try to reproduce the argument, but I fear I shall hardly do it justice. It seems to run something like this. "If each man had a definite set of rules of conduct by which he regulated his life he would be no better than a machine. But there are no such rules, so men cannot be machines." The undistributed middle is glaring. I do not think the argument is ever put quite like this, but I believe this is the argument used nevertheless. There may however be a certain confusion between "rules of conduct" and "laws of behaviour" to cloud the issue. By "rules of conduct" I mean precepts such as "Stop if you see red lights," on which one can act, and of which one can be conscious. By "laws of behaviour" I mean laws of nature as applied to a man's body such as "if you pinch him he will squeak." If we substitute "laws of behaviour which regulate his life" for "laws of conduct by which he regulates his life" in the argument quoted the undistributed middle is no longer insuperable. For we believe that it is not only true that being regulated by laws of behaviour implies being some sort of machine (though not necessarily a discrete-state machine), but that conversely being such a machine implies being regulated by such laws. However, we cannot so easily convince ourselves of the absence of complete laws of behaviour as of complete rules of conduct. The only way we know of for finding such laws is scientific observation, and we certainly know of no circumstances under which we could say, "We have searched enough. There are no such laws."

6. Learning Machines

The reader will have anticipated that I have no very convincing arguments of a positive nature to support my views. If I had I should not have taken such pains to point out the fallacies in contrary views. Such evidence as I have I shall now give.

Let us return for a moment to Lady Lovelace's objection, which stated that the machine can only do what we tell it to do. One could say that a man can "inject" an idea into the machine, and that it will respond to a certain extent and then drop into quiescence, like a piano string struck by a hammer. Another simile would be an atomic pile of less than critical size: an injected idea is to correspond to a neutron entering the pile from without. Each such neutron will cause a certain disturbance which eventually dies away. If, however, the size of the pile is sufficiently increased, the disturbance caused by such an incoming neutron will very likely go on and on increasing until the whole pile is destroyed. Is there a corresponding phenomenon for minds, and is there one for machines? There does seem to be one for the human mind. The majority of them seem to be "subcritical," *i.e.,* to correspond in this analogy to piles of subcritical size. An idea presented to such a mind will on average give rise to less than one idea in reply. A smallish proportion are supercritical. An idea presented to such a mind that may give rise to a whole "theory" consisting of secondary, tertiary and more remote ideas. Animals' minds seem to be very definitely subcritical. Adhering to this analogy we ask, "Can a machine be made to be supercritical?"

The "skin-of-an-onion" analogy is also helpful. In considering the functions of the mind or the brain we find certain operations which we can explain in purely mechanical terms. This we say does not correspond to the real mind: it is a sort of skin which we must strip off if we are to find the real mind. But then in what remains we find a further skin to be stripped off, and so on. Proceeding in this way do we ever come to the "real" mind, or do we eventually come to the skin which has nothing in it? In the latter case the whole mind is mechanical. (It would not be a discrete-state machine however. We have discussed this.)

These last two paragraphs do not claim to be convincing arguments. They should rather be described as "recitations tending to produce belief."

In the process of trying to imitate an adult human mind we are bound to think a good deal about the process which has brought it to the state that it is in. We may notice three components.

    (*a*) The initial state of the mind, say at birth,
    (*b*) The education to which it has been subjected,
    (*c*) Other experience, not to be described as education, to which it has been subjected.

Instead of trying to produce a programme to simulate the adult mind, why not rather try to produce one which simulates the child's? If this were then subjected to an appropriate course of education one would obtain the adult brain.

We have thus divided our problem into two parts. The child programme and the education process. These two remain very closely connected. We cannot expect to find a good child machine at the first attempt. One must experiment with teaching one such machine and see how well it learns. One can then try another and see if it is better or worse. There is an obvious connection between this process and evolution, by the identifications

    Structure of the child machine = hereditary material
    Changes of the child machine = mutations
                Natural selection = judgment of the experimenter

One may hope, however, that this process will be more expeditious than evolution. The survival of the fittest is a slow method for measuring advantages. The experimenter, by the exercise of intelligence, should be able to speed it up. Equally important is the fact that he is not restricted to random mutations. If he can trace a cause for some weakness he can probably think of the kind of mutation which will improve it.

We normally associate punishments and rewards with the teaching process. Some simple child machines can be constructed or programmed on this sort of principle. The machine has to be so constructed that events which shortly preceded the occurrence of a punishment signal are unlikely to be repeated, whereas a reward signal increased the probability of repetition of the events which led up to it.

The use of punishments and rewards can at best be a part of the teaching process. Roughly speaking, if the teacher has no other means of communicating to the pupil, the amount of information which can reach him does not exceed the total number of rewards and punishments applied. It is necessary therefore to have some other "unemotional" channels of communication. If these are available it is possible to teach a machine by punishments and rewards to obey orders given in some language, *e.g.,* a symbolic language. These orders are to be transmitted through the "unemotional" channels. The use of this language will diminish greatly the number of punishments and rewards required.

Opinions may vary as to the complexity which is suitable in the child machine. One might try to make it as simple as possible consistently with the general principles. Alternatively one might have a complete system of logical inference "built in." In the latter case the store would be largely occupied with definitions and propositions. The propositions would have various kinds of status, *e.g.,* well-established facts, conjectures, mathematically proved theorems, statements given by an authority, expressions having the logical form of proposition but not belief-value. Certain propositions may be described as "imperatives." The machine should be so constructed that as soon as an imperative is classed as "well established" the appropriate action automatically takes place. To illustrate this, suppose the teacher says to the machine, "Do your homework now." This may cause "Teacher says 'Do your homework now'" to be included amongst the well-established facts. Another such fact might be, "Everything that teacher says is true." Combining these may eventually lead to the imperative, "Do your homework now," being included amongst the well-established facts, and this, by the construction of the machine, will mean that the homework actually gets started, but the effect is very satisfactory. The process of inference used by the machine need not be such as would satisfy the most exacting logicians. There might for instance be no hierarchy of types. But this need not mean that type fallacies will occur, any more than we are bound to fall over unfenced cliffs. Suitable imperatives (expressed *within* the systems, not forming part of the rules *of* the system) such as "Do not use a class unless it is a subclass of one which has been mentioned by teacher" can have a similar effect to "Do not go too near the edge."

The imperatives that can be obeyed by a machine that has no limbs are bound to be of a rather intellectual character, as in the example (doing homework) given above. Important amongst such imperatives will be ones which regulate the order in which the rules of the logical system concerned are to be applied.[2] For at each stage when one is using a logical system, there is a very large number of alternative steps, any of which one is permitted to apply, so far as obedience to the rules of the logical system is concerned. These choices make the difference between a brilliant and a footling reasoner, not the difference between a sound and a fallacious one. Propositions leading to imperatives of this kind might be "When Socrates is mentioned, use the syllogism in Barbara" or "If one method has been proved to be quicker than another, do not use the slower method." Some of these may be "given by authority," but others may be produced by the machine itself, *e.g.,* by scientific induction.

The idea of a learning machine may appear paradoxical to some readers. How can the rules of operation of the machine change? They should describe completely how the machine will

[2] Or rather "programmed in" for our child machine will be programmed in a digital computer. But the logical system will not have to be learnt.

react whatever its history might be, whatever changes it might undergo. The rules are thus quite time-invariant. This is quite true. The explanation of the paradox is that the rules which get changed in the learning process are a rather less pretentious kind, claiming only an ephemeral validity. The reader may draw a parallel with the Constitution of the United States.

An important feature of a learning machine is that its teacher will often be very largely ignorant of quite what is going on inside, although he may still be able to some extent to predict his pupil's behaviour. This should apply most strongly to the later education of a machine arising from a child machine of well-tried design (or programme). This is in clear contrast with normal procedure when using a machine to do computations: one's object is then to have a clear mental picture of the state of the machine at each moment in the computation. This object can only be achieved with a struggle. The view that "the machine can only do what we know how to order it to do," appears strange in face of this. Most of the programmes which we can put into the machine will result in its doing something that we cannot make sense of at all, or which we regard as completely random behaviour. Intelligent behaviour presumably consists in a departure from the completely disciplined behaviour involved in computation, but a rather slight one, which does give rise to random behaviour, or to pointless repetitive loops. Another important result of preparing our machine for its part in the imitation game by a process of teaching and learning is that "human fallibility" is likely to be omitted in a rather natural way, *i.e.,* without special "coaching." Processes that are learnt do not produce a hundred per cent certainty of result; if they did they could not be unlearnt.

We may hope that machines will eventually compete with men in all purely intellectual fields. But which are the best ones to start with? Even this is a difficult decision. Many people think that a very abstract activity, like the playing of chess, would be best. It can also be maintained that it is best to provide the machine with the best sense organs that money can buy, and then teach it to understand and speak English. This process could follow the normal teaching of a child. Things would be pointed out and named, etc. Again I do not know what the right answer is, but I think both approaches should be tried.

We can only see a short distance ahead, but we can see plenty there that needs to be done.

The Imitation of Man by Machine

(The view that machines will think as man does reveals misunderstanding of the nature of human thought.)

Ulric Neisser

The source of much of the argument on whether or not machines can think is the tendency to regard thought and intelligence as purely human attributes. Controversy rages over whether or not machines can actually think in the same way people do. Here, Ulric Neisser, a professor of psychology at Cornell, steers a middle course through the controversy. Computers can possess intelligence, argues Neisser, but not human-type intelligence. The machines lack motivation, emotion and the ability to direct their thought toward a multitude of goals at the same time, all characteristics of human thought.

Popular opinion about "artificial intelligence" has passed through two phases. A generation ago, very few people believed that any machine could ever think as a man does. Now, however, it is widely held that this goal will be reached quite soon, perhaps in our lifetimes. It is my thesis that the second of these attitudes is nearly as unsophisticated as the first. Yesterday's skepticism was based on ignorance of the capacities of machines; today's confidence reflects a misunderstanding of the nature of thought.

There is no longer any doubt that computing machines can be programmed to behave in impressively intelligent ways. Marill does not exaggerate in saying, "At present, we have, or are currently developing, machines that prove theorems, play games with sufficient skill to beat their inventors, recognize spoken words, translate text from one language to another, speak, read, write music, and learn to improve their own performance when given training." Nevertheless, I will argue that the procedures which bring about these results differ substantially from the processes which underlie the same (or other) activities in human beings. The grounds for this assertion are quite different from the "classical" reasons for skepticism about thinking machines, but the latter should be considered first. This amounts to reviewing the similarities between men and computers before stressing the differences.

First of all, it was formerly maintained that the actions of a mechanism will never be purposive or self-derived, whereas human behavior can be understood only in terms of goals and motives. Two counterexamples will be enough to show that this argument has become untenable. In the realm of action, it is difficult not to be impressed with the "homing" missile, which pursues its target tenaciously through every evasive action until it achieves its destructive goal. On the intellectual level, the "Logic Theorist" of Newell, Simon, and Shaw is just as persistent: determined to prove a theorem, it tries one logical strategy after another until the proof is found or until its resources are exhausted. If anything, the argument from purpose cuts the other way: machines are evidently *more* purposive than most human beings, most of the time. This apparently excessive persistence reflects one of the fundamental differences to be elaborated later—one that could, however, be superficially eliminated by disconnecting the goal-setting part of the program at random intervals.

Secondly, machines were once believed to be incapable of learning from experience. We now know that machine learning is not only possible but essential in the performance of many tasks that might once have been thought not to require it. Simple problems of pattern recognition, such as the identification of hand-printed capital letters, have been solved only by programs which discover the critical characteristics of the stimuli for themselves. The success of Samuels' checker-playing program is based on its capacity to store and use experience from previous games; no program without the ability to learn has been nearly as successful. This argument, too, is more interesting when viewed the other way. In a sense, computers learn more readily than people do: you can teach checkers to a 3-year-old computer, but not to a 3-year-old child. The reason will appear later; it is evidently not just that the computer is the more intelligent of the two.

Finally, it has often been asserted that machines can produce nothing novel, spontaneous, or creative—that they can "only do what they have been programmed to do." This is perhaps the most widely held of the negative beliefs, yet it is the first to be relinquished by anyone who actually tries to write programs for a digital computer. Long before a programmer succeeds in getting the machine to learn anything, or to behave purposefully, he repeatedly encounters its capacity to act in astonishing, unpredicted, and (usually) frustrating ways. For example, he may change a few steps in a familiar program involving thousands of instructions and find that the output printer produces reams of unintelligible gibberish. Careful diagnostic procedures are needed to discover that one comma was omitted in a single instruction. As a result the computer interpreted two small adjacent numbers as a single large number, executed the wrong instruction in the program, and continued blithely on from a point where it was never expected to be.

Such an event may seem trivial, both because the reason for the unpredicted outcome can be discovered in retrospect and because the effect was maladaptive rather than useful. But neither of these are necessary properties of unpredicted computer output. Existing programs have found original proofs for theorems, made unexpected moves in games, and the like. The belief that a machine can do nothing qualitatively novel is based on a false dichotomy between quality and quantity. What has become a truism in physics also applies to information processes: large changes in the magnitude of phenomena always imply major changes in the "laws" through which these phenomena can be understood. The result of 200,000 elementary symbolic operations cannot be readily predicted from knowledge of the elements and the program. The sheer *amount* of processing which a computer does can lead to results to which the adjective *novel* may honestly be applied. Indeed, complexity is the basis for emergent qualities wherever they are found in nature.

Some Observable Differences

It appears, then, that computers can learn, and can exhibit original and purposive behavior. What can they not do? At first reckoning, their intellectual defects seem trivial and nearly irrelevant. Nevertheless, a list of the inadequacies of present-day artificial intelligence is worth making for its suggestive value. Two or three of the inadequacies have already been mentioned. When a program is purposive, it is too purposive. People get bored; they drop one task and pick up another or they may just quit work for a while. Not so the computer program; it continues indomitably. In some circumstances the program may be more effective than a man, but it is not acting as a man would. Nor is such singlemindedness always an advantage: the computer is very likely to waste its time on trivialities and to solve problems which are of no importance. Its outlook is a narrow one: with Popeye, it says, "I am what I am," and it lets the rest of the world go hang while it plays chess or translates Russian relentlessly. The root of the difference seems to be more a matter of motivation than of intellect. Programs have goals, but they do not acquire or use their goals as a man would.

Computers are more docile than men. They erase easily: an instruction or two can wipe out anything ever learned, whether pernicious or useful. The decision to acquire new knowledge or to destroy old memories is a deliberate one. Usually it must be taken by the programmer, though in principle the program could decide for itself. Human memory seems much less flexible. A man rarely has single-minded control over what he will learn and forget; often he has no control at all. Thus, he lives willy-nilly in an accumulating context of experiences which he cannot

limit even if he would. The result is both stupidity and seren-
dipity: if he is inefficient, he also can become wise in unexpected
ways. Youth is not doomed to ignorance even though it would
like to be, and no one can entirely avoid growing up. A program or a programmer, in contrast, can easily prevent any
change that appears superficially undesirable.

By the same token, any apparently desirable change in a program can be carried out, at least if the necessary techniques are
known. There is no need to embed it in an orderly sequence of
growth, no resistance from an organism that has other things to
do first. In this respect artificial intelligence is conformist, and
precociously so. Again this is a problem of motivation, but it
is a developmental question as well. We would be rightly worried about a child who played chess before he could talk; he
would seem "inhuman."

Growth is a process of self-contradiction, but computer programs are never at cross-purposes with themselves. They do
not get tangled up in conflicting motives, though they may
oscillate between alternative courses of action. Thus, they are
good at problem solving but they never solve problem B while
working on A.

Artificial intelligence seems to lack not only breadth but
depth. Computers do not dream, any more than they play. We
are far from certain what dreams are good for, but we know what
they indicate: a great deal of information processing goes on far
beneath the surface of man's purposive behavior, in ways and
for reasons that are only very indirectly reflected in his overt
activity. The adaptive significance of play is much clearer. In
playing, children (and adults) practice modes of thought and
action that they do not yet need. Free of any directing immediate necessity, skills can develop into autonomous units that can
later serve a variety of ends.

Taken one at a time, these differences between natural and
artificial intelligence are not impressive. All together, they give
rise to the suspicion that the cognitive activities of machines
and men are still substantially different. In stressing the differences, my purpose is not to disparage current work in artificial
intelligence. The research that has been done and is being done
has important practical implications; it is also providing us with

valuable models for some kinds of human thinking. Its incompleteness is emphasized here for two reasons. For *psychologists*, I wish to stress that contemporary computer models are oversimplified in the same sense that early stimulus-response psychology and early psychoanalytic theory were oversimplified. It may be well to regard "artificial intelligence" with the same mixture of hopefulness and suspicion that was appropriate to those earlier efforts. For *programmers*, I make a prediction. As computers are used for increasingly "human" activities, either directly (as in simulation) or indirectly (as in situations where the criteria of performance are psychological and social), new and difficult problems will arise. The focus of difficulty will no longer be in pattern recognition, learning, and memory but in an area which has no better name than "motivation." In support of these assertions, I describe, in the remainder of this article, three fundamental and interrelated characteristics of human thought that are conspicuously absent from existing or contemplated computer programs.

1) Human thinking always takes place in, and contributes to, a cumulative process of growth and development.

2) Human thinking begins in an intimate association with emotions and feelings which is never entirely lost.

3) Almost all human activity, including thinking, serves not one but a multiplicity of motives at the same time.

Cognitive Development

The notion of "development" involves more than the obvious fact that a newborn baby has a great deal to learn. The intricacies of adult behavior cannot be acquired in just any order, to suit the convenience of the environment. Certain attitudes and skills must precede others. In part this is a matter of simple prerequisite learning: one must know how the pieces move before one can invent winning chess combinations. Moreover, the cumulation of learning is interwoven at every point with inborn maturational sequences. It may or may not be true that one must walk before he can run, but it is clear that neither skill can be taught to a 6-months-old baby. Therefore, no baby of that age can have the adequate conceptions of space and localization that genuinely do depend on experience. By the time a child has the opportunity to discover other rooms and other worlds, he already has a year's worth of structure with which to assimilate them. He will necessarily interpret his own explorations in terms of experience that he already has: of losing love or gaining it, of encountering potential disaster, joy, or indifference. These preconceptions must affect the kind of explorations he makes, as well as the results of his ventures; and these consequences in turn help to shape the conceptual schemes with which the next developmental problem is met. A child who could move about from the very beginning would grow into an adult complexly different from any of us.

In Piaget's useful terminology, human development consists of two reciprocal phrases: "assimilation" and "accommodation." The first is the transformation and recoding of the stimulus world which is performed by the child's cognitive equipment of the moment. Computers also assimilate in this sense; for example, they reduce photographs to bit-patterns through specialized input devices. Accommodation is harder to imitate. It refers to change in the cognitive apparatus itself, as a result of the attempt to assimilate novel material.

In a loose way, accommodation may be equated to learning, and it is evident that computers can learn (for example, by optimizing probability-weights or other internal parameters). But the most important accommodations in human development are changes in the structure of the processing itself. The child's visual and physical exploration of space does not result merely in the assignment of specific quantitative values to an innate spatial schema. On the contrary, the weight of the evidence suggests that such fundamental concepts as objective permanence, three-dimensionality, and tangibility must themselves be formed by development. And we do not yet have any realistic hope of programming this type of growth into an artificially intelligent system.

It is instructive to consider game playing from this point of view, because it has been a focus of interest for both programmers and developmental psychologists. Young children cannot be taught to play such games as checkers and chess because they cannot be reconciled to the restrictions imposed by the rules. Having grasped the idea that he should try to capture pieces, a young child proceeds to do so with any "move" and any piece of his own that comes to hand. He will avoid the loss of his own piece by every possible maneuver, including removing it from the board and putting it in his mouth. If the piece is taken nevertheless, the child may have a tantrum and stop playing. According to Piaget there is an interesting later stage in which the schoolchild thinks of the rules as sacrosanct and eternal; it takes an adult to admit that what was arbitrarily established may be arbitrarily altered. Such a history must leave its mark on a human chess player, in the form of a hierarchical organization of purposes as well as strategies. Nothing comparable exists for the computer program, which works steadily toward its fixed goal of legal victory. There is no obvious reason to doubt that a specialized program may some day play chess as well as a man or better, but the intellectual processes of the two are likely to remain fundamentally different.

Emotional Basis of Cognitive Activity

The activity of a newborn baby is very largely organized around the satisfaction of needs. While there are intervals dominated by visual or tactile exploration, major events in the baby's life are hunger and sucking, irritability and sleep, pain and relief, and the like. This suggests that stimulus information is assimilated largely with reference to its need-satisfying and need-frustrating properties. The first accommodations to such basic features of the world as time, distance, and causality are interwoven with strongly emotional experiences. Moreover, the fluctuations of the child's internal states do not have any very obvious relation to the logic of his environment, so that months and years are needed before his thinking and his actions become well attuned to the world around him. To put it another way: the pleasure principle yields to the reality principle only slowly.

Many psychologists, such as Robert White, have recently stressed the opposite point: that activity directed toward mastering reality is present from the very beginning. They are surely right, but even the beginning of competence and esthetic pleasure depend heavily on internal structures. What the baby explores, and how he reacts to it, is not determined only by realistically important features of the environment but by the schemata with which that environment is assimilated.

Needs and emotions do not merely set the stage for cognitive activity and then retire. They continue to operate throughout the course of development. Moreover, they do not remain constant but undergo growth and change of their own, with substantial effects on intellectual activities. Some emotional growth, such as the gradual differentiation of specific fear from general anxiety, is the result of interaction with the environment. Other changes, like those of puberty, seem to be relatively autonomous. It would be rash indeed to believe that events so important to the individual's life play no role in his thinking. One fundamental way in which they exert their influence is discussed in the next section. In addition, it is worth noting that one of the most common and frequently discussed modes of learning—that of reward and punishment—operates through an open involvement of strong and historically complicated emotions.

To think like a man, a computer program would need to be similarly endowed with powerful internal states. We must imagine these states, which have both short- and long-term dynamics of their own, to be in almost complete control of information processing at first. Later their influence must become more subtle, until their final role is a complex resultant of the way in which preset internal patterns have interacted with the flow of experience. Perhaps such programs can be written, but they have not been, nor do they appear to be just around the corner.

Multiplicity of Motives

Human actions characteristically serve many purposes at once. Any activity whatever could serve as an example, but it will be instructive to consider chess playing again. Typically, a computer which has been programmed to play chess has one overriding goal—to win—and establishes subordinate goals (capturing pieces, controlling open files, and the like) when they may be useful to that end. Human chess players do this also, but for them winning is itself only one goal among many, to which it is not always related in a simply subordinate way.

For instance, a chess player may also seek the esthetic pleasure which comes from an unexpected and elegant combination. This desire has surely been responsible for the achievement of many spectacular victories in the history of chess; the search for such a combination is also responsible for an uncountable number of defeats. It is likely, too, that most players seek the experience of success, either for the internal satisfactions or for the public acclaim which it brings, or for both of these reasons. The avoidance of the inner or outer humiliation which defeat brings must also play a frequent role. None of these motives is fully interchangeable with any other. Each has its own attendant retinue of potential substitute satisfactions, reactions to frustration, and interactions with the concrete reality of the game. However, it is very possible for all of them to exist in the same chess player at the same time.

Chess can serve other purposes as well, which are certainly not without their effect on the actual sequence of moves. It is a social occasion, and serves as a vehicle or a relationship to another person. As such, chess can be an instrument of friendship, but it is double-edged because each friend is trying to defeat the other. Thus, the game becomes an outlet for aggression, in which one may aim for destruction of his opponent in an entirely nonphysical (and so nonpunishable) way. It is not only the opponent who may be symbolically destroyed. Reuben Fine, who is both grand master and psychoanalyst, has argued that the presence of a "king" and a "queen" on the board may give chess a deeply symbolic value, so that very primitive fantasy goals can become relevant to the progress of the game.

Apart from consideratons of winning and losing, playing chess may reflect many other human motives. One man may adopt what he considers to be a "daring" style of play because he wants to think of himself as a bold person; another may play conservatively for analogous reasons. Both men may be *playing* because (that is, partly because) chess is only a *game*—an activity in which they can succeed and be respected without growing up or competing in what they regard as more adult, and thus more frightening, realms. Some people probably play chess because it is at least something to do and a means of avoiding the anxiety-laden or self-destructive thoughts they might otherwise have. Others, of both sexes, may play because they somehow think of chess as a masculine rather than a feminine activity and playing it makes them more certain of their own sex identity. And so on; the list is endless.

Every sort of human behavior and thought is open to this type of analysis. No person works on a mathematical problem as contemporary computer programs do: simply to solve it. No person writes a scientific paper merely to communicate technical information, nor does anyone read such a paper merely to be better informed. The overt and conscious motives are important but they never operate in isolation. In the early days of psychoanalysis it was fashionable to devalue the obvious motives in favor of the unconscious ones, and to assume that cognitive activity was "nothing but" a way to placate instinctual demands. This tendency is happily no longer common; "rational" activities are unquestionably important in their own right to the person who engages in them. But we must be careful not to let the availability of computer models seduce us into the 19th-century view of a man as a transparently single-minded and logical creature.

Elsewhere I have discussed the multiplicity of thought, suggesting that much in human thinking is better conceptualized as "parallel" than as "sequential" in nature. The manifold of motives that I am describing here goes beyond that assumption, although it certainly presupposes a capacity for parallel processing. The motivational complexity of thought is more easily seen as depth than as breadth. It is what makes people interesting, and it is also what gives them the capacity for being bored. It is what the "shallow" characters of poor fiction lack, and it is the source of the inventive spontaneity of real people. People succeed in using experience with one problem in solving another because, after all, they want to solve both; and both solutions are only parts of an intricate system of needs and goals. Miller, Galanter, and Pribram have emphasized the hierarchical structure that human intentions often exhibit. Such a multiplicity of motives is not a supplementary heuristic that can be readily incorporated into a problem-solving program to increase its effectiveness. In man, it is a necessary consequence of the way his intellectual activity has grown in relation to his needs and his feelings.

The future of artificial intelligence is a bright one. The intellectual achievements of computer programs are almost certain to increase. We can look forward with confidence to a time when many complex and difficult tasks will be better performed by machines than they now are by men, and to the solution of problems which men could never attempt. Moreover, our understanding of human thinking may well be furthered by a better understanding of those aspects of intelligence which the programs display. This process has already begun: many psychologists, myself included, are indebted to computer technology for a wealth of new ideas which seem to be helpful in understanding man. But two systems are not necessarily identical, or even very similar, because they have some properties in common.

The deep difference between the thinking of men and machines has been intuitively recognized by those who fear that machines may somehow come to regulate our society. If machines really thought as men do, there would be no more reason to fear them than to fear men. But computer intelligence is indeed "inhuman": it does not grow, has no emotional basis, and is shallowly motivated. These defects do not matter in technical applications, where the criteria of successful problem solving are relatively simple. They become extremely important if the computer is used to make social decisions, for there our criteria of adequacy are as subtle and as multiply motivated as human thinking itself.

The very concept of "artificial intelligence" suggests that man's intelligence is a faculty independent of the rest of human life. Happily, it is not.

God & Golem, Inc.

Norbert Wiener

One of the most consistent voices calling for caution in our development of the computer was that of Norbert Wiener, the father of cybernetics. One manifestation of his concern was *God & Golem, Inc.,* in which he discussed the relation of cybernetics and religion. This chapter from the book offers a relatively optimistic view of the future—a look at the possibilities for cooperation between men and machines.

One of the great future problems which we must face is that of the relation between man and the machine, of the functions which should properly be assigned to these two agencies. On the surface, the machine has certain clear advantages. It is faster in its action and more uniform, or at least it can be made to have these properties if it is well designed. A digital computing machine can accomplish in a day a body of work that would take the full efforts of a team of men for a year, and it will accomplish this work with a minimum of blots and blunders.

On the other hand, the human being has certain nonnegligible advantages. Apart from the fact that any sensible man would consider the purposes of man as paramount in the relations between man and the machine, the machine is far less complicated than man and has far less scope in the variety of its actions. If we consider the neuron of the gray matter of the brain as of the order $1/1,000,000$ of a cubic millimeter, and the smallest transistor obtainable at present as of the order of a cubic millimeter, we shall not have judged the situation too unfavorably from the point of view of the advantage of the neuron in

450

the matter of smaller bulk. If the white matter of the brain is considered equivalent to the wiring of a computer circuit, and if we take each neuron as the functional equivalent of a transistor, the computer equivalent to a brain should occupy a sphere of something like thirty feet in diameter. Actually, it would be impossible to construct a computer with anything like the relative closeness of the texture of the brain, and any computer with powers comparable with the brain would have to occupy a fair-sized office building, if not a skyscraper. It is hard to believe that, as compared with existing computing machines, the brain does not have some advantages corresponding to its enormous operational size, which is incomparably greater than what we might expect of its physical size.

Chief among these advantages would seem to be the ability of the brain to handle vague ideas, as yet imperfectly defined. In dealing with these, mechanical computers, or at least the mechanical computers of the present day, are very nearly incapable of programming themselves. Yet in poems, in novels, in paintings, the brain seems to find itself able to work very well with material that any computer would have to reject as formless.

Render unto man the things which are man's and unto the computer the things which are the computer's. This would seem the intelligent policy to adopt when we employ men and computers together in common undertakings. It is a policy as far removed from that of the gadget worshiper as it is from the man who sees only blasphemy and the degradation of man in the use of any mechanical adjuvants whatever to thoughts. What we now need is an independent study of systems involving both human and mechanical elements. This system should not be prejudiced either by a mechanical or antimechanical bias. I think that such a study is already under way and that it will promise a much better comprehension of automatization.

One place where we can and do use such mixed systems is in the design of prostheses, of devices that replace limbs or damaged sense organs. A wooden leg is a mechanical replacement for a lost leg of flesh and blood, and a man with a wooden leg represents a system composed both of mechanical and human parts.

Perhaps the classical peg leg is not interesting, as it replaces the lost limb only in the most elementary way, nor is the limb-shaped wooden leg much more interesting. However, there is some work being done on artificial limbs in Russia, in the United States, and elsewhere by a group to which I belong. This work is much more interesting in principle and really makes use of cybernetical ideas.

Let us suppose that a man has lost a hand at the wrist. He has lost a few muscles that serve chiefly to spread the fingers and to bring them together again, but the greater part of the muscles that normally move the hand and the fingers are still intact in the stump of the forearm. When they are contracted, they move no hand and fingers, but they do produce certain electrical effects known as action potentials. These can be picked up by appropriate electrodes and can be amplified and combined by transistor circuits. They can be made to control the motions of an artificial hand through electric motors, which derive their power through appropriate electric batteries or accumulators, but the signals controlling them are sent through transistor circuits. The central nervous part of the control apparatus is generally almost intact and should be used.

Such artificial hands have already been made in Russia, and they have even permitted some hand amputees to go back to effective work. This result is facilitated by the circumstance that the same nervous signal which was effective in producing a muscular contraction before the amputation will still be effective in controlling the motor moving the artificial hand. Thus the learning of the use of these hands is made much easier and more natural.

However, as such, an artificial hand cannot feel, and the hand is as much an organ of touch as of motion. But wait, why can an artificial hand not feel? It is easy to put pressure gauges into the artificial fingers, and these can communicate electric impulses to a suitable circuit. This can in its term activate devices acting on the living skin, say, the skin of the stump. For example, these devices may be vibrators. Thereby we can produce a vicarious sensation of touch, and we may learn to use this to replace the missing natural tactile sensation. Moreover, there are still sensory kinesthetic elements in the mutilated muscles, and these can be turned to good account.

Thus there is a new engineering of prostheses possible, and it will involve the construction of systems of a mixed nature, involving both human and mechanical parts. However, this type of engineering need not be confined to the replacement of parts that we have lost. There is a prosthesis of parts which we do not have and which we never have had. The dolphin propels itself through the water by its flukes, and avoids obstacles by listening for the reflections of sounds which it itself emits. What is the propeller of a ship but an artificial pair of flukes, or the depth-sounding apparatus but a vicarious sound-detecting and sound-emitting apparatus like that of the dolphin? The wings and jet engines of an airplane replace the wings of the eagle, and the radar its eyes, while the nervous system that combines them is eked out by the automatic pilot and other such navigation devices.

Thus human-mechanical systems have a large practical field in which they are useful, but in some situations they are indispensable. We have already seen that learning machines must act according to some norm of good performance. In the case of game-playing machines, where the permissible moves are arbitrarily established in advance, and the object of the game is to win by a series of permissible rules according to a strict convention that determines winning or losing, this norm creates no problem. However, there are many activities that we should like to improve by learning processes in which the success of the activity is itself to be judged by a criterion involving human beings, and in which the problem of the reduction of this criterion to formal rules is far from easy.

A field in which there is a great demand for automatization, and a great possible demand for learning automatization, is that of mechanical translation. In view of the present metastable state of international tension, the United States and Russia are filled with an equal and opposite necessity for each to find out what the other is thinking and saying. Since there is a limited number of competent human translators on both sides, each side is exploring the possibilities of mechanical translation. This has been achieved after a fashion, but neither the literary qualities nor the intelligibility of the products of these translations has been sufficient to excite any great enthusiasm on either part.

None of the mechanical devices for translation has proved itself deserving of trust when momentous issues depend on the accuracy of the translation.

Perhaps the most promising way of mechanizing translation is through a learning machine. For such a machine to function, we must have a firm criterion of a good translation. This will involve one of two things: either a complete set of objectively applicable rules determining when a translation is good, or some agency that is capable of applying a criterion of good performance apart from such rules.

The normal criterion of good translation is intelligibility. The people who read the language into which the translation is made must obtain the same impression of the text as that obtained from the original by people understanding the language of the original. If this criterion may be a little difficult to apply, we can give one that is necessary if not sufficient. Let us suppose that we have *two* independent translating machines, say, one from English into Danish and the other from Danish into English. When a text in English has been translated into Danish by the first machine, let the second translate it back into English. Then the final translation must be recognizably equivalent to the original, by a person acquainted with English.

It is conceivable that a set of formal rules be given for such a translation so definite that they can be entrusted to a machine, and so perfect that it will be sufficient for a translation to accord with these rules to be satisfactory as to the criterion which we have given. I do not believe that linguistic science is so far advanced as to make a set of rules of this sort practicable, nor that there is any prospect of its being so advanced in the predictable future. Short of this state of affairs, a translating machine will have a chance of error. If any important consideration of action or policy is to be determined by the use of a translation machine, a small error or even a small chance of error may have disproportionally large and serious consequences.

It seems to me that the best hope of a reasonably satisfactory mechanical translation is to replace a pure mechanism, at least at first, by a mechanicohuman system, involving as critic an expert human translator, to teach it by exercises as a schoolteacher instructs human pupils. Perhaps at some later stage the memory of the machine may have absorbed enough human instruction to dispense with later human participation, except perhaps for a refresher course now and then. In this way, the machine would develop linguistic maturity.

Such a scheme would not eliminate the need for a translation office to have attached to it an expert linguist whose ability and judgment could be trusted. It would, or at least it might, enable him to handle a considerably larger body of translation than he could without mechanical assistance. This, in my mind, is the best that we can hope of mechanical translation.

Up to this point we have discussed the need of a critic sensitive to human values, such as, for example, in a translating system where all but the critic is mechanical. However, if the human element is to come in as the critic, it is quite reasonable to introduce the human element in other stages, too. In a translation machine it is by no means essential that the mechanical element of the machine give us a single complete translation. It can give us a large number of alternative translations for individual sentences that lie within the grammatical and lexicographical rules and leave to the critic the highly responsible task of censorship and selection of the mechanical translation that best fits the sense. There is no need whatever why the use of the machine in translation should leave the formation of a complete closed translation to the machine even in the sense that this translation is to be improved by a criticism as a whole. Criticism may begin at a much earlier stage.

What I have said about translating machines will apply with equal or even greater force to machines that are to perform medical diagnoses. Such machines are very much in vogue in plans for the medicine of the future. They may help pick out elements that the doctor will use in diagnosis, but there is no need whatever for them to complete the diagnosis without the doctor. Such a closed, permanent policy in a medical machine is sooner or later likely to produce much ill health and many deaths.

A related problem requiring the joint consideration of mechanical and human elements is the operational problem of invention, which has been discussed with me by Dr. Gordon Raisbeck of Arthur D. Little, Inc. Operationally, we must consider an invention not only with regard to what we can invent but also as to how the invention can be used and will be used in a human context. The second part of the problem is often more difficult than the first and has a less closed methodology. Thus we are confronted with a problem of development which is essentially a learning problem, not purely in the mechanical system but in the mechanical system conjoined with society. This is definitely a case requiring a consideration of the problem of the best joint use of machine and man.

A similar problem and also a very pressing one is that of the use and development of military devices in conjunction with the evolution of tactics and strategy. Here, too, the operational problem cannot be separated from the automatization problem.

Not only is the problem of adapting the machine to the present conditions by the proper use of the intelligence of the translator or the doctor or the inventor one that must be faced now, but it is one that must be faced again and again. The growing state of the arts and sciences means that we cannot be content to assume the all-wisdom of any single epoch. This is perhaps most clearly true in social controls and the organization of the learning systems of politics. In a period of relative stability, if not in the philosophy of life, then in the actual circumstances that we have produced in the world about us, we can safely ignore new dangers such as have arisen in the present generation in connection with the population explosion, the atomic bomb, the presence of a widely extended medicine, and so on. Nevertheless, in the course of time we must reconsider our old civilization, and a new and revised one will need to take these phenomena into account. Homeostasis, whether for the individual or the race, is something of which the very basis must sooner or later be reconsidered. This means, for example, as I have said in an article for the *Voprosy Filosofii* in Moscow, that although science is an important contribution to the homeostasis of the community, it is a contribution the basis of which must be assessed anew every generation or so. Here let me remark that both the Eastern and Western homeostasis of the present day is being made with the intention of fixing permanently the concepts of a period now long past. Marx lived in the middle of the first industrial revolution, and we are now well into the second one. Adam Smith belongs to a still earlier and more obsolete phase of the first industrial revolution. Permanent homeostasis of society cannot be made on a rigid assumption of a complete permanence of Marxianism, nor can it be made on a similar assumption concerning a standardized concept of free enterprise and the profit motive. It is not the form of rigidity that is particularly deadly so much as rigidity itself, whatever the form.

It seemed to me important to say something in that article which would emphasize the homeostatic function of science and would at the same time protest against the rigidity of the social application of science both in Russia and elsewhere. When I sent this article to *Voprosy Filosofii,* I anticipated that there would be a strong reaction to my attitude toward rigidity; in fact, my article was accompanied by a considerably longer article pointing out the defects of my position from a strictly Marxist standpoint. I have no doubt that if my original paper had been first published over here, I would have had a similar and almost equal reaction from the standpoint of our own prejudices, which if not as rigidly and formally expressed are very strong. The thesis which I wish to maintain is neither pro nor anticommunist but antirigidity. Therefore, I am expressing my ideas here in a form that is not too closely connected with an evaluation of the difference between the dangers lying in these parallel but opposed rigidities. The moral I have wished to stress is that the difficulties of establishing a really homeostatic regulation of society are not to be overcome by replacing one set pattern which is not subject to continual reconsideration by an equal and opposed set pattern of the same sort.

But there are other learning machines besides the translation machine and the checker-playing machine. Some of these may be programmed in a completely mechanical way, and others, like the translation machine, need the intervention of a human expert as arbiter. It seems to me that the uses for the latter sort greatly exceed those for the former sort. Moreover, remember that in the game of atomic warfare, there are no experts.

About The Editor:

John Diebold is an internationally acknowledged leader in the fields of management and technology. As president and founder of The Diebold Group, Inc., management consultants, he has established many of the concepts which are today accepted as basic in management and in the application of technology in business and government. He is a director and trustee of a number of public and private-sector institutions. Three volumes of his papers and speeches have been published.